SOUL UNSUNG

Popular Music History
Series Editor: Alyn Shipton, journalist, broadcaster and lecturer in music
at the Royal Academy of Music, London, and at City University, London.

This series publishes books that challenge established orthodoxies in popular
music studies, examine the formation and dissolution of canons, interrogate
histories of genres, focus on previously neglected forms, or engage in archae-
ologies of popular music.

Published

Being Prez: The Life and Music of Lester Young
Dave Gelly

Chasin' the Bird: The Life and Legacy of Charlie Parker
Brian Priestley

Handful of Keys: Conversations with Thirty Jazz Pianists
Alyn Shipton

Jazz Visions: Lennie Tristano and His Legacy
Peter Ind

The Last Miles: The Music of Miles Davis, 1980–1991
George Cole

Lee Morgan: His Life, Music and Culture
Tom Perchard

Lionel Richie: Hello
Sharon Davis

Out of the Long Dark: The Life of Ian Carr
Alyn Shipton

Soul Unsung: Reflections on the Band in Black Popular Music
Kevin Le Gendre

Soul Unsung

Reflections on the Band in Black Popular Music

Kevin Le Gendre

Published by Equinox Publishing Ltd.

UK: Unit S3, Kelham House, 3 Lancaster Street, Sheffield, South Yorkshire S3 8AF
USA: ISD, 70 Enterprise Drive, Bristol, CT 06010

www.equinoxpub.com

First published 2012

ISBN: 978-1-84553-543-8   (hardback)

British Library Cataloguing-in-Publication Data

A catalogue record for this book is available from the British Library.

Library of Congress Cataloging-in-Publication Data

Le Gendre, Kevin.
   Soul unsung : reflections on the band in black popular music / Kevin Le Gendre.
      p. cm. -- (Popular music history)
   Includes bibliographical references and index.
   ISBN 978-1-84553-543-8 (hardback)
   1. Soul music--History and criticism. I. Title.
   ML3537.L4 2012
   781.64409--dc23
                        2012020302

Printed and bound in the UK by MPG Books Group.

For brother Curtis

Contents

1 Introduction: behind the groove

Here are some names. Chances are they may mean something to you: Aretha, Otis, Marvin, Stevie, Sam, Ray. If we want to be modern as well as classic in our references, the names Luther or perhaps Erykah could well lend even more grace to that list. The common denominator between these iconic IDs in soul music is that they are all esteemed singers, artists whose standing is such that there is no need to cite a family name – just as, in jazz, there is no need to supplement Miles with Davis and no need to say that his trumpet stood for his voice.

Yet Stevie is also a player of instruments, several at that. And indeed, musicians – bassists, drummers, guitarists, keyboardists and horn players – have been an integral part of the genre right from soul's 'pre-history' as rhythm and blues in the early 1960s, to the extent that without their ingenuity many of the canon's great songs would simply not be the gems they are. 'Behind every great singer is a great band' may sound like a disposable cliché, but it holds an imperishable truth.

Soul Unsung is concerned first and foremost with these musicians and the instruments that have marked soul music with the gamut of sounds the genre has produced over five decades. This is not a book about singers. This is a book about players.

A number of good biographies have already been written about several of the music's defining vocalists, the most notable perhaps being David Ritz's *Divided Soul*, which offers great insight into the dramatically conflicted man who was Marvin Gaye as well as the work of a vocalist who advanced pop by skilfully dramatising dilemma, joy and pain in song.

All the rich biographical and sociological data that enriched Ritz's text are of great value, but that kind of detail is not on the agenda here. The mission statement is specifically to explore the form and content of a bass line, drum beat or guitar figure and to shed light on the technical excellence, the lateral thinking and enormous depth of imagination their respective creators have consistently brought to the table.

There is little doubt that soul, with its heady emotional electrification, its sense of thudding in the chest or the tingle and glow that may snake around your entire body, can be achieved overwhelmingly by nothing less than the deployment of the human voice. That does not mean, though, that the 'cry' of an instrument is incapable of soul. It is the combination of these two agents of sound that has often proved outstanding.

During the 'rare groove' revival, when 1970s soul was rewound to refresh '80s soul, alto saxophonist Maceo Parker's 'Cross The Tracks' was as, or if anything more, popular than 'The Payback', the anthem by his boss James Brown. That was because the whole engine of the Parker track was ecstatically fuel-injected by its leader's horn.

But Brown himself had already testified to the brilliance of his deadliest henchman and sideman. Right in the middle of Parker's searing improvisation on 1968's 'Cold Sweat', the Godfather of Soul is heard flying into raptures over the reed's piercing sound, hollering 'so much soul!' as if he'd learned that the most blessed hosanna in the Bible was cast in crotchets and quavers rather than letters and commas. The saxophone was the Word. The horn made the walls come tumbling down.

Parker would go on to make instrumental music throughout his career, as did several of his colleagues in Brown's band, and to prove that he did not need the Godfather to excel – even though their partnership yielded one of the greatest bounties heard in recent popular music.

Because soul music has, over the course of its history, given birth to many compelling personalities who have penned fine lyrics of enormous socio-cultural and political substance, the tendency to overlook the contribution of the accompanying musicians, or to summarise them fleetingly by reference to the tightness of the band or the strength of the backbeat, has been marked. This in turn may have contributed to a more general undervaluation of many highly gifted musicians.

To a large extent, observations on the tightness of the band have almost become a dismissive reflex, if not a default position to be adopted before addressing the serious business of the brilliance of the singer or the intellectual or emotional gravitas of the song. However, that point of view – that soul music is first and foremost heart and not head, raw, gut emotion rather than musical training and long years of study – may also have contributed to a lack of focus on a song's arrangement, as if this were just a form of sonic sauce that was sprinkled on the lyrical ribs.

Furthermore, the invisibility of accompanists, by dint of the lack of credits on a huge number of recordings made between the 1960s and '80s, also largely reinforced the notion that the rhythm or horn section was behind the singer, both in an hierarchical and an artistic sense.

Hence the decision by Motown to credit its house band, the fabled Funk Brothers, on record sleeves in the 1970s was a major political breakthrough that went some way towards restoring the balance between the singer and the player. It ended the invisibility of musicians who, legend has it, had been kept deliberately standing in the shadows to avoid being poached by any number of opportunistic rivals.

Today the name of James Jamerson, the behemoth of the bass guitar whose immense talent provided a major foundation for the label, is more recognised than was the case several years ago. But there are still a large number of Jamerson's peers who are languishing in obscurity.

To shine a spotlight on *all* the great musicians who have dotted the history of soul would require not one but several books. Legends like the Funk Brothers or other 'house' bands like the Bar-Kays (Stax) or MFSB (Philadelphia International) are not my main focus because I want to move beyond their specific legacies, rich as they are. The point of this text is not just to list the sum total of 'forgotten foot soldiers' but rather to tell the story of the use of a particular instrument in the band. To do this as effectively as possible, I have sought to identify principal changes in thinking over time and to point out the interesting, if not subversive, approaches to instruments such as the bass guitar, guitar or keyboards.

Imagination is the rocket fuel in the vehicle of technique. The ability to think beyond what is actually deemed conventional, acceptable or even logical could be among a musician's greatest assets. Scanning the history of black popular music, one finds numerous examples of players making an instrument do something it wasn't supposed to do, by dint of an astute quirk or a flight of conceptual fancy. As countless artists have stated over time, it's about reaching for what isn't there, rather than what is.

An appetiser: Professor Longhair was one of the great pioneers of 1940s New Orleans rhythm and blues, a purveyor of danceable, bustling songs, often implying a son or calypso beat. He is not generally regarded as a technical innovator or a man who extended the sonic range of pop. Longhair was a pianist who *just* played grooves, so received wisdom holds. Yet he drew a unique timbre from the keyboard on tunes like 'Walk Your Blues Away', and this was because Longhair not only pounded the piano with great force and accuracy but also modified it, prepared it, turned it into percussion by attaching a drumhead to the underside of the body and hammering it with his foot. Longhair was not taught to do that.

A microphone would sit between his legs. Longhair was adapting the relatively basic technological means available to him to create sounds that he wanted to hear, thereby showing that a determined and free-thinking player would flout convention if it suited his artistic needs. In this case, this could have led to a cable being a minor health hazard. Ahmet Ertegun, a key composer and arranger for Atlantic Records, one of the defining labels in the history of black music, saw Longhair perform in New Orleans in 1949 and wanted to sign him, but failed to do so. As history would show, Ertegun found worthy replacements elsewhere, the embarrassment of riches exemplified by names like Ray Charles and Aretha Franklin.

Saxophonist King Curtis Ousley was also an essential part of the Atlantic set-up, in so far as he produced and arranged a large number of the label's sessions. Curtis became an industrious, highly creative member of Atlantic's backroom staff, who helmed a number of superlative horn and rhythm sections during the label's glory years in the late 1960s. The biggest hit he chalked up under his own name, 1967's 'Memphis Soul Stew', remains one of the great instrumentals in the whole history of black pop. Perhaps more importantly, though, it stands at the crossroads of jazz, funk and rock, making the point that soul music has enjoyed a far-reaching relationship with several of the other key genres in pop.

My text is not intended to provide a definitive history of how soul music has evolved through the decades, but rather to chart different developments from different points of view. So before telling the story of the bass, guitar, drums, keyboards and horns in soul, I shall consider the existence of several 'continuums' – soul–jazz, soul–funk and soul–rock – in an attempt to show that the boundaries between these different forms have been extensively crossed and that a common denominator, namely blues and, to a degree, Latin music, has maintained their interaction. Soul music is rich precisely because it has not evolved in a vacuum. In the course of my research of the use of instruments in soul, it became abundantly clear to me that musicians were using rhyme ad poetry decades before the advent of hip hop, and very often in instrumental songs. Many good players were also able proto-rappers.

As well as focusing on the creativity displayed by instrumentalists in soul, I shall also examine the role played by the spoken word in the genre over the years. Oral culture and the whole tradition of 'testifying' have been extremely pervasive in soul music, cropping up time and time again in a wide range of fine instrumental and vocal songs.

The latter stages of the text move away from an explicit analysis of sounds – the anatomy of a band, if you will – and consider soul as international music. This is of prime importance, given that the genre's exponents in Europe and particularly Britain, as well as in Africa and the Caribbean, have produced fascinating work since the mid-1960s.

To bring matters up to date, 'fusions' of soul and newer black popular music – hip hop, house and techno – also come under scrutiny. Although all these recent sub-genres can be traced in some way or other back to rhythm and blues, funk and disco, they are, for the most part, forms in which machines, samples and sequencing are prevalent.

That said, it is a truism that soul has been electronic music, or at least relevant to it, over four decades. This view may not be common currency because soul doesn't fit the image of electronica, which, for the most part, is a genre in which state-of-the-art synthesizers are not readily associated with the rudiments of rhythm and blues.

But the fact is that there'd be no A Guy Called Gerald without men like Jam & Lewis. The former's productions in the late 1980s were certainly inspired, if not shaped, by the latter's work for a wider range of artists like the considerably successful SOS Band in the early '80s.

In any case, house and broken beat are also part of the soul canon because some of their most creative practitioners, artists such as Blaze, Masters At Work and I. G. Culture, have stood wholeheartedly on the foundations of Earth, Wind & Fire and Quincy Jones. They have also engaged with anything from ragga to techno and hip hop, all the while incorporating strident Afro-Latin rhythms into their work – something that again strengthens these artists' historical roots. Their adventurous futurism is not at all incompatible with 'core values'.

Soul music thus remains something complex, disparate and multifarious. What is perhaps needed is an ecumenical appraisal of where the music is at today, a willingness to consider I. G. Culture or M. Nahadr – putative avant-gardists – alongside the overtly classicist Nicole Willis or Sharon Jones. Yet these names are rarely mentioned in the same breath. It's much easier to say that contemporary soul has been reduced to a fey Motown or Stax retread with far fewer record sales.

It just ain't that simple. The music continues to spring many surprises because the thoughts and feelings behind it, borne of the African diaspora, slavery and civil rights, are anything but one-dimensional. If soul the music has proved fertile artistically, then soul the aesthetic, the worldview, is also too rich for an Instamatic push-button definition.

What soul is, how soul is, where soul is, why soul is and who soul is are questions well worth asking precisely because – if we really want to reach below the surface of the subject – they are liable to prompt investigations involving anything from people to pictures, food to colloquialisms, and voices from yesterday to today. We might need to start south of the border before we can move on up north.

2 What is this thing called soul?

Security is strong and tight but polite.
(Flyer for a West Indian dance in East London, 2008)

A water brother

Mexican writer Laura Esquivel tasted sweet success all over the Hispanic world with her novel *Como Agua Para Chocolate* in 1989. More than a decade later, after the book, a highly imaginative, mystical love story, had been successfully adapted to the big screen, Chicago rapper Common used the English translation of the title to name his fourth album.

The sleeve of *Like Water For Chocolate* features a monochrome picture of an African American mother and daughter in front of a 'Colored Only' drinking fountain *circa* 1955, an image that taps full-bloodedly into the iconography of Civil Rights.[1] This was a time when the idea of a black US president would have been met with derision if not outright scorn, long before Barack Obama proved that nation-rallying hope could crystallise in a person of colour, a mere mortal oft seen as something else.

Clad in crisply starched white dresses, the mother and daughter are strikingly elegant, suggesting they are *en route* to a wedding or important family function, rather than just ambling through town on a Sunday afternoon stroll. Then again, pictures from that era stand out for the kempt nature of their subjects, an elegance comparable to that of sharp-suited West Indian migrants disembarking in England in 1948.

When I asked him why he used that particular image on the sleeve of his album, a work recorded four decades after the scene in question, Common replied: 'I always thought that picture had some soul.'[2]

Granted. But why? 'That's just what it says to me. It's *just* got a lot of soul.' And with that the conversation stuttered on, as if the statement had a self-evidence needing no further illumination. All of which prompts the obvious enquiry: what *exactly* does soul mean, and why would it be the most appropriate term to use in this context?

Soul is one of the most intriguing words in the English language. Its meanings are multiple but some of its definitions are ambiguous, if not contentious. Its range of nuances is sufficiently wide to accommodate ideas that are spiritual as well as material, artistic as well as culinary.

If one man can look at an image of a mother and daughter and pronounce that it has soul, then another might well ask not just what this is but how it is acquired in the first place. In this respect, a loose parallel can be drawn with a word such as style. Beyond references to panache in appearance or fashion flair, style is invariably dissociated from dress sense when earnest attempts are made to get to grips with its essence. If you had a pound for every time a fashionista – *faux* or real – said it's not just what your garms are but how you wear them and, better still, you either have style or you don't, then you'd probably have enough money to dress like a lord. But you might not necessarily have style, as any number of vulgar socialites, with minds as shallow as their pockets are deep, will duly attest. Style has something to do with stance and attitude, and those elements, like love, don't easily reduce to a rationale.

Is there something similar at play with soul? Is it something that you either have or don't have? Is it created by the hand that fate deals you or the way you play the game of life? Is it something that can be passed on or handed down? Can it be learned, studied, bottled, sold? Is it a state of being or a state of mind? As much a feeling as a meaning? Something constant or subject to change? If Cole Porter asked 'What is this thing called love?', I might enquire 'What is this thing called soul?'

According to the third edition of the *Oxford English Dictionary* (2010), the word has a range of definitions: 1. 'Spiritual or immaterial part of a human being or animal, regarded as immortal; a person's moral or emotional nature or sense of identity.' 2. 'Emotional or intellectual energy or intensity, especially as revealed in a work of art of artistic performance.' 3. 'The essence or embodiment of a specified quality.'

Also listed are soul food, 'Food traditionally associated with black people of the Southern US', and soul music, 'A kind of music incorporating elements of rhythm & blues and gospel music, popularised by American black people and characterised by an emphasis on vocals and impassioned, improvisatory delivery, it is associated with performers such as Marvin Gaye, Aretha Franklin, James Brown and Otis Redding'.

What emerges from the first three definitions listed above is a sense of something profound; something that is right at the centre of our being; something that is not at all light, frivolous or shallow. Soul is deep.

And then, right in the middle of the metaphysics, there is music and food. More precisely, a form of black music whose prime constituents are blues and gospel. We have a specific racial and cultural framework, so we know there is a meaning in soul that pertains to a particular community and the culture it has produced over time, although one could take issue with some of the details. Should some musicians, such as the organist Bobby Sparks or the guitarist Jef Lee Johnson, be squeezed into the pantheon of singers? Should 'American black people' be called African Americans?

Soul music and soul food are tangible manifestations of black culture, but soul has an association with blackness that reaches beyond tunes and chitlins. With that in mind, perhaps the most important thing to do is to establish a historical framework for soul as a phenomenon that relates to people of colour; namely, to determine when the noun first came into regular usage, and why it was coined in the first place.

Exactly how far back in the history of the black community the word soul reaches is hard to pinpoint, perhaps because the term appears to be very deep-rooted and elemental. One can draw a loose parallel with words such as blues and funk, which also seem so old, so folk-like.

To all intents and purposes, soul became more widespread and was heard more often at a time when African Americans were referred to as Negroes: during the 1950s, as the Civil Rights Movement, the struggle for blacks to obtain full equality in American society, gathered momentum.

'Soul jazz' emerged as a popular sub-genre of jazz, one with marked gospel resonances, around the middle of the decade. To play soulfully was to engage others, to create some sense of warmth or celebration. And to have soul, as a personal characteristic, possibly implied a similar form of life enhancement or rallying energy amidst a daily sack o' woe.

For African Americans, one of the defining events of the decade was the Supreme Court's ruling in the *Brown vs Board of Education of Topeka* (1954) case that segregation in public schools was unconstitutional. This judgment effectively made more real the possibility of equal rights and the knowledge that, in the face of outright discrimination in as crucial a battleground as the classroom, blacks would at least have concrete legal redress at their disposal. They were granted new possibilities.

Which is not the same as a certainty, or a guarantee, of new status or stake in society. An inescapable truth about *Brown vs the Board of Education* was that it did not mean an end to segregation in the areas of public life that no race could possibly hope to avoid – washrooms, buses, restaurants and lunch counters, places where blacks were visible – although in the eyes of diehard bigots they were invisible.

Taken in 1956 by the pioneering black photographer Gordon Parks in Alabama, the picture of the black mother and daughter at the 'Colored Only' fountain that journeyed to Common's 2000 album *Like Water For Chocolate* shows, through the clarity of its composition, struggle inexorably passing from one generation to the next, pushing both a parent and child onto the front line of second-class citizenship.

This is an action shot. Parks has caught the mother at the precise moment she lowers her head to the jet of water, so that her arched back creates a meaningful, if not haunting, association of the subject with a far-reaching historical tableau: the slave stooping to work in a field.

The servitude of one era thus shadows the segregation of another. From the bend for cotton to the bend for water; the dipped posture, the lowering of the head, becomes a signifier for the black condition.

It is hard not to be moved by this portrait. Perhaps to understand soul is to look at it and feel something, be it sadness, shame, fear or pride.

Perhaps to understand soul is to know something of the history behind the thoughts, emotions and actions of those captured next to the water.

Happy clappin'

Some of the key entries in the soul-music canon that overtly celebrated the genre itself were made when the 'Movement' was at its height; Arthur Conley's 'Sweet Soul Music', for example, was recorded in 1967, a year before the assassination of Martin Luther King. This suggests the 's' word, whether it refers explicitly to art or politics, song or struggle, conveys something of a spirit of positive thinking, if not idealism, among people of colour seeking to redefine themselves. The word soul appears largely to frame the transition from the Negro to the Black.

Whoever was the first person to use the 's' word may have felt there was finally a brighter day on the horizon for blacks and that the Good Lord himself, the Supreme Being floating above Supreme Courts, had something to do with it. Soul is as much a religious as a metaphysical term, and given the prominence of religion in black America since the days of slavery, it is entirely possible that the new meaning of soul really emanated from the pulpit and pews of the black church, a place that was known to 'rock' when the spirit took over fervent congregations.

A Southern black Baptist church is even more rocking because, for many, the roots of soul – what passes as 'deep soul' – are in the South.[3]

Perhaps the sense of intensity that often defines the experience not just of singing but of listening to sermons in a black church – the highly participatory relationship of the faithful, the call and response between preacher and flock, the spontaneous vocal accompaniment – is a crucial component of soul. That level of heightened emotion, the ecstatic nature of gospel music, passed directly into rhythm and blues. So it makes perfect sense to call it soul.

This is a genre of music that often moves its constituents to tears. But soul is also joy. It has a rousing energy, under the impulse of gospel, which is perhaps best conveyed by the term 'soul clappin''. This refers to the double-time percussion created by the vigorous slap of palm on palm that kick-starts 'spirituals' or secular songs. Soul clappin' really makes the most sense when an entire congregation in a church hall or an audience in a nightclub gamely partakes of it. Everybody has to keep time together, though. Rhythm then becomes a joyous, unifying force.

While the existence of terms such as soul music and soul clappin' reflects the pervasive influence of the church in the life of black America, the coining of the expression 'soul food' enriches the substance of the 's' word, since diet is as fundamental an aspect of any community as art is. It's not so much that you are what you eat; more that you eat whatever the limits of your resources and personal circumstances allow in the first place. When soul became conjoined with other nouns like food, brother, sister, walk, or handshake, it was clear that the term was generic and embodied a notion of what Negroes were or did. Soul was a black thing.

Or, at least, soul had something to do with how black people lived. Several of the key tropes prevalent during the 'Movement', such as My People and Soul People,[4] thus became practically interchangeable.

More to the point, soul might well have encapsulated a sense of blacks achieving solidarity, certainly at the height of the civil rights struggle, because there was a common enemy in the American establishment and mainstream society that actively resisted the enfranchisement of the black population.

As well as unity, soul was fortitude, a mental strength to draw on, a sort of anchor that would hold steady in times of stormy weather or keep spirits up if you had to get low down for a drinking fountain.

Soul appeared to be a fundamental form of grace under pressure.

This was made explicit by jazz organist Freddie Roach on his 1967 album *My People (Soul People)*. The poem below features on the back of the sleeve. The front features Freddie Roach. He is a black man in a cage.

> My people have so much soul,
> A system of mind control,
> That lets them be high
> When they are down,
> Just see how they laugh and play,
> In spite of the dues they pay,
> In spite of the history they know.[5]

The year before Freddie Roach recorded *My People (Soul People)*, Stokely Carmichael, leader of the Student Nonviolent Coordinating Committee, a key dynamo in the Civil Rights Movement, used the term 'Black Power' in a speech in Jackson, Mississippi. He subsequently issued a stark warning to those who stood in the way of the liberation of people of colour: "Move over, or we're going to move on over you".[6] His linguistic gymnastics were memorable.

To the alarm of some of Carmichael's fellow activists, it has to be said. There is, nonetheless, an at least partial intersection of soul and Black Power, in so far as both symbolise progress for people of colour, although the exact means of liberation was, and still is, a nation-sized imponderable. With deep-rooted prejudices based on skin tone, a range of class conflicts, and acute frictions between the urban and rural Negro, absolute consensus within the black community could only be the heaviest of loads.

Else you wouldn't be in here

Cross soul with Black Power and what do you get? Black Soul and Soul Power. The first is, in light of the discussion thus far, tautological, whereas the second offers much more food for thought, not least because it is the title of one of the great pieces of popular music recorded in the last four decades. And you know who wrote it …

Does the name James Brown or the title Soul Brother No.1 pop into your head first? If it is the latter, do you think of this as a positivist expression that represents fulfilment, the conclusion of a journey that began in the inauspicious circumstances of destitution in a shack in Barnwell, South Carolina and ended in triumph on international stages?

Brown was the archetype of the Negro with everything against him: broke, uneducated and *country*, a son of the South, which was the place many blacks wanted to flee in order to avail themselves of greater opportunities in the North. Indeed, the large-scale migration to Chicago, New York and Philadelphia from 1910 onwards irrevocably changed the face of mainstream and black America.

Having started out with the odds stacked heavily against him, Brown – who endured incarceration as well as extreme poverty in the early stages of his life – turned his fortunes around through a combination of great natural talent, a Trojan work ethic and the intelligence to model his own dynamite performances on the explosive moves of black preachers.

Interestingly, although Brown finds complete self-realisation in this anthem, the manifesto of 'Soul Power', he does not do so strictly from the viewpoint of his own navel. What is striking about the piece is its duality of self and community, the dexterity with which Brown makes himself the centre of the universe – 'I'm still on the case and my rap is strong' – yet brings an emphatically collective outlook, the interests of the wider group, to bear on his text, turning what could well have been 'What *I* need is Soul power' into 'What *we* need is Soul Power.'[7] It is a superlative intellectual and lyrical pirouette, a great thrust of mind power. Soul thus stands as a rousing personal muse and a cogent binding force, an agent of social cohesion in the wider black community.

'Soul Power' was an emblematic statement as well as a song, but of no less importance is the fact that it came from the same individual who, between 1968 and 1974, penned other politically charged compositions such as 'Mind Power' and 'Say It Loud – I'm Black And I'm Proud.' All these pieces are really essential complements to 'Soul Power.'

Few matched Brown for strength of character. He was a man of extraordinary drive and determination, which is possibly why his own take on soul, its meaning as Brown sees it, is more compelling than that of other claimants. There is a marked difference in psychological and emotional depth between 'Soul Power' and several other contemporaneous pieces. What Brown's whole persona and spirit conveyed was the sense that his soul power was drawn from deep within, and could inspire and uplift others, particularly those of his own race who could relate directly to the indignity of shining shoes or picking cotton.

There was thus humanity, democracy and individuality at play. Brown was a self-made man, and if his soul power connected with black power, even though each dynamic has its own distinct nuance, his steadfastly personal worldview was not subsumed by the political will of anybody other than his bad self. He refused to lose but would not allow 'nobody to give him nothing' for free. He would surely overcome, but others would have to come over to his world. He did not always spell out where it was.

Hence Brown, in a wonderfully nonchalant but terribly meaningful line on another hit, 'Get on the Good Foot', evokes a place where 'soulful people know what it's all about' without explaining who the soulful people are, or indeed what it's all about.[8] Better still is a fine song by Bobby Byrd, the singer and organist who was the accompanying voice on 'Soul Power', that offers the response to Brown's call. If the title of the 1971 anthem 'I Know You Got Soul Or Else You Wouldn't Be In Here' isn't elliptical enough, then the key illumination of the text – 'because you got the feeling' – is emphatic in its vagueness. There is no specific context outlined here, no place that is safe for the race, no unequivocal identification of black people, even though the song establishes a clear sense of communal energy. This is soul as code. Those who know can relate. And those who do not simply won't make it through the door.

'I Know You Got Soul' is a thrillingly energised, rhythmically muscular piece of music. But above all it features a striking vocal from Bobby Byrd, who delivers the lines with an intriguing blend of authority and indolence, because *he* knows what he means and he knows that *you* know what he means, and the dialogue really has to end there. It is a natural finish.

And maybe that is a key aspect of soul: its implicit as well as explicit nature, the fact that it may be as meaningful when unsaid as said.

Being soulful, therefore, can be a different thing from singing or playing soulful. And if one really is soulful, then maybe one doesn't need to define it: certainly not in any terms that may be laid down by others.

The feeling of soul, a sense of both life and life enhancement, may come from that precise moment when you put down your thing, and then realise it has achieved some kind of osmosis with my *thang*, without a single word having to be exchanged between you and I and I and you.

To this idea of the spontaneity of soul one might add the notion of the 'natural'. In material terms, back in the 1960s and '70s 'natural' was embodied by the decision of blacks to break away from aesthetic norms imposed on them by mainstream white society. The most visible and psychologically loaded of these norms was processed hair, something that maintained the notion of straight hair as acceptable or 'good' hair.

The emergence of the Afro was thus part of the general soul dynamic, as a direct manifestation of black self-acceptance and refusal to justify or explain oneself to a nonplussed outside world.[9]

Perhaps what is more significant is that some did not feel the need to slap names on everything that was part of the natural way of being. Over the years, I've met many older black Americans who have made it clear in no uncertain terms that they did not call their diet 'soul food' because there was no *need* to. Both they and the communities they came from knew what chitlins and hog maws were, and were aware that they ended up on kitchen tables because many black people had no choice. What they ate was what they could afford. Soul food is not just black folks' food. It is poor black folks' food. Or, at least, it was, back in the day.

Labelling is a thorny issue at the best of times, and in the case of an ethnic minority that has endured the dehumanisation of slavery, the trauma of seg-regation and a violent struggle for constitutional rights, the question of how to refer to oneself and one's culture – something deemed worthless by the mainstream – is not at all easily answered.

While there is no doubt that soul embodied a notion of blackness and of the positivity therein, it was also contentious, or at least contestable by the very people it was applied to, because they recognised that there was a pos-sibility it would turn to cliché and commodity.

Every song with soul in its title wasn't automatically rich artistically or soulful, meaning liable to move you, to raise your spirit in the way the best gospel music could. But its chances of shifting units might have increased as soul acquired some notable cultural capital. It became a buzzword. The music industry loves nothing better than a buzz.

For blacks to say they had soul was a necessary part of their self-empowerment during the struggle for civil rights, but there was a real danger that the term could become a simplistic, if not reductive, definition.

It's like style. There's no need to yadda yadda yadda about it if you know you have it in the first place. Else you wouldn't be in here.

Yours and mine

Then again, if you are at ease with your own identity, you can indulge in all man-ner of irony, parody and goofball bizarrerie around a notion such as soul, espe-cially if you feel that it may fall short of your own personal *Weltanschauung*. Maybe soul is a blessed blackness and heightened humanity, the recognition that life experience can have specific and universal currency. Humour is the first worldwide traveller's cheque.

So in the lyrics that George Clinton wrote for his band Funkadelic's 1970 piece 'What Is Soul?', there is a juvenile playfulness and subversion that enables Clinton to deflate any excessive pomp that may be attached to the 's' word. Possibly this is because he wants power on his own terms, possibly because he is an irrepressible independent thinker, and possibly because he is his own king who can't resist playing the fool.

Soul does not automatically have to equate with all things deep. There is frivolity as well as profundity in Clinton's aesthetic, and that is the main reason why he is a key addition to the concept of soul. Clinton presents a more comprehensive definition of humanity, complete with imperfections, quirks, narcotics and unusual breakfast menus. His cheek is shameless: 'Soul is a ham hock in your cornflakes./Soul is the ring around your bathtub./Soul is a joint rolled in toilet paper.'[10] These lyrics are inventively layered. Black America derails white America by sabotaging its breakfast cereal with a soul food staple. And yet Nigger and Whitey are united in issues of hygiene and recreation, or the real need to improvise when options are limited. Drugs are often smoked in secret places. How can you not get all puffy in a loo roll?

Clinton stokes merry confusion here. He is resolutely of and beyond blackness, and as such moots the possibility of soul as something fluid, dynamic and liable to change from one mind, or one era, to the next.

With the Civil Rights Movement ebbing in the 1980s, black America did undergo substantial upheaval, touching both new highs and lows. On the one hand, inroads were made into the entertainment mainstream via the phenomenal success of television stars such as Bill Cosby and Oprah Winfrey. On the other hand, record numbers of young black males were sent to languish in jails as drugs and police brutality performed a deadly pincer movement on many communities dumped in the projects.

Stating that materialism and individualism took hold of the black community is questionable since they were always present, as were the same flaws that afflicted mainstream society. But perhaps the balance between individualism and collectivism, the juggling of the impulse to ensure 'I get mine' and 'we get ours' tipped to the former.

It's James Brown's successor singing 'What *I* need is soul power', not 'What *we* need is soul power', even though his rap may still be strong.

Given the tremendous change that occurred in the lives of the constituents, or should we say diverse manifestations, of soul, the people who had lived through the shifts in thinking mapped by the replacement of Negro by black and of black by African American, it was entirely pertinent that critics like Nelson George and Greg Tate should evoke post-soul culture and the New Black Aesthetic in attempts to confront this change and find new methods of discourse to document it.[11] The 'feeling' related by Bobby Byrd or James Brown was unmistakably more ambiguous than at any time during the 1970s.

If the word 'soul' were only tied to music and food, then it wouldn't be such a problematic notion. But it is not. Ray Charles said that soul was 'the way black folk sing when they leave themselves alone'.[12] Today that needs qualification; namely, what kind of black folks are we talking about, and where does one locate their solitude?

So rapid has been the pace of change both in the various cultures created by African Americans and the world in general that it is entirely possible the depth of division that used to exist between a country and a city 'Negro' could be found within certain pockets of either one of these environments. Whether communities have remained truly localised or have been subsumed into a globalised economy and culture is also important.

So how much soul an individual has may matter less than whether they have a smart phone, Internet access and a blessed flock of 'friends' with whom they may or may not have broken bread, let alone lifted their voices during an almighty rocking rendition of 'We Shall Overcome'.

If W. E. B. Du Bois, author of *The Souls Of Black Folk*, the seminal 1903 treatise on race in America, undertook to show 'the strange meaning of being black here in the dawning of the Twentieth Century',[13] then one might contemplate the strange meaning of being a human being – white, black or white and black – here at the dawning of the twenty-first.

The very word black is thus vying for space with notions of cyber-modernity, of fluctuating economies and identities. Soul as a *terrain d'entente*,[14] a Utopian, unifying agent of blackness, is almost unfeasible because the psychological, cultural, political and socioeconomic fault lines within the black community are firmly entrenched. Soul as a worldview that binds *every* kind of person of colour is well nigh impossible, given their heterogeneity and the increasingly puzzling nature of the relationships between race, class, faith, gender and nationality.

The reality of disparate black mentalities, rather than a sole black outlook, militates against any kind of simplistic, monolithic soul community. A new black aesthetic must signify new black *aesthetics*.

If soul was once a black thing, what is a black thing now? Or rather, how many ways of being black can one imagine, and accept?

Can we imagine and accept that some black people would rather listen to classical music than R&B? Can we imagine and accept that some black people find the music of P. J. Harvey, Radiohead or Kate Bush as, if not *more*, soulful than the music of R. Kelly, Usher or Luther?

All the things black people relate to is a subject that still needs to be embraced, let alone properly understood, so that if a person of colour said yes to all the above, fewer eyebrows would be raised.

Whether or not the difference between the foibles, whims and unpredictability of one race and those of another are that marked, insurmountable or interesting, is also a moot point. The common ground, the common fears, the common phobias are real in themselves.

They show up in pop culture. A white man from the north of England says 'Nowt so queer as folk'. A black man from Jamaica says 'People funny, boy'.

For all that, complexity and paradox have always been an absolutely integral part of the Negro experience in America. Dubois' concept of 'double consciousness' – the notion that descendants of slaves have to develop two ways of behaving in order to negotiate the partition of black and white America – announces that only beguiling, if not resolutely contradictory, forces could be bumping and grinding away in the mind of individuals defined by their otherness.

Maybe the real story of American race relations is that marginalisation is chameleonesque, constantly shifting tone and context as the country's sociopolitical history evolves. So if a black man is in the White House, one applauds what seemed impossible in the soul era, all the while noting that there are still not enough game-changing non-white faces in media, fashion and film: pervasive, influential industries that greatly govern how people see themselves and others. So much of America's self-esteem is based on the identification and termination of an enemy – be it within or without – that it is not surprising the other, the black, the brown, the red, the un-American, is a threat to a homeland tied to the need for security and the compulsion for power.

Patti don't go pop

Trusty *Oxford English Dictionary* in hand, we remind ourselves that soul is a type of black music. But if we wanted to be more precise, we would say that it is a type of black popular music. And if we wanted to be even more precise, we could say that it is a type of black popular music that has largely been displaced in the hearts and minds of modern-day youth by hip hop, a genre that hugely pervades global mainstream culture. Aretha Franklin may have sung at Obama's inauguration, but there might not have been a party without Jay-Z's big-up of his candidacy.

Hip hop is rooted in rhyme and soul in song. Hip hop is often far removed from soul in terms of its imagery, mythology and general aesthetics, to the extent that one might feel it safe to assume that the 's' word really has no place in the vocabulary of hip hop's practitioners.

Of all the manifestations of a post-soul world, then, hip hop was surely the most striking and arguably the most vibrant, because it offered such a plurality of impulses: from the most angry and nihilistic to the most lighthearted and slapstick; from guys who would scare you senseless to guys who would have you rolling on the floor with laughter. Certainly in hip hop's early years, rappers were fresh, stupid and stupid fresh.

How all these juvenile antics of homeboys with baseball caps and murder raps might square with the image of a besuited singer with lyrics that, for the most part, dealt with romancing and dancing, was not at all obvious. Hip hop appeared to be such a departure from soul music.

And yet what is interesting is that the word 'soul', apparently so anchored in a past where people said 'Right on', was not entirely absent from a present where people said 'Aw right'. The 's' word did not find itself entirely kicked to the kerb by rappers who were born after the heyday of Aretha, Otis and the JBs.

After all, what is the name of one of the finest exponents of hip hop, a group that has stayed together for many years, as was the case with many of the greatest combos of 1970s black pop? De La Thugs? No. De La Rhymes? No. De La Beats? No. Or rather, non. De La Soul. Mais, oui, homeboy.

Kelvin Mercer, David Jude Jolicoeur and Vincent Mason, three teenagers from Long Island, New York, chose to rechristen themselves Posdnous, Trugoy and Maseo and to form a band in the mid-1980s, almost two decades after Arthur Conley recorded 'Sweet Soul Music'. They constructed a name for this band by taking, or perhaps resurrecting, an iconic term in black culture and then applying it to a French grammatical structure. As far as names go, De La Soul was real *de la beauté*.

Soul is so closely identified with the 1960s and '70s that it is perhaps surprising to see the word crop up in the name of a key exponent of a revolutionary genre of music from the 1980s, a time that marked a significant shift in the form and content of black popular music. Nonetheless, the fact that Posdnous, Trugoy and Maseo became De La Soul highlights the timelessness of core ideas in black popular culture.

In any case, there is an emotional and intellectual depth to the group's best work that places it in the lineage of excellent lyric writers.

Three Feet High And Rising, the band's 1989 debut, appeared to represent the light to the dark of the uncompromisingly militant stance adopted by Public Enemy or KRS-One and Boogie Down Productions at the time.

De La Soul were altogether more playful, pun-heavy and, in their dress sense as well as lyrical sensibilities, leaned towards a peacenik, vaguely hippie point of view, embodied by the proclamation that they were the harbingers of 'the Daisy Age'.

Yet all this colourful optimism did not mask a psychological and emotional complexity and a social conscience that would lead to pieces such as the anti-drugs anthem 'Say No Go'. What De La Soul made clear on their debut and its follow-up, 1991's provocatively titled *De La Soul Is Dead*, was that they were cerebral as well as jovial and that, as much as they were African American kids wholly in the now, they were not entirely disconnected from some of the trials and tribulations endured by their forebears. Whether they were calling what they did soul was not as important as what they were thinking.

Nineteen ninety-three's *Buhloone Mindstate* is De La Soul's finest album to date. It is a highly embroidered, densely packed album in which references, from the most ancillary and implicit of details to the loudest, explicit assertion, tell us something of black culture and history in the broadest sense. It can be blink-and-miss-it subtle, like the line over the o's in Buhloone representing the tape deck of a boom box, one of the great ciphers of early hip hop.

Or it can be overtly and unapologetically political, such as the subject of 'Patti Dooke': the ongoing struggle of the black artist in a music industry set against a background of shameless corporate cynicism.

Halfway through the piece, the voice of a character cast clearly in the role of an exploitative record company executive or manager declares quite brazenly: 'We decided to change the cover a little bit because we see the big picture ... negroes *and* white folks are buying this album'.[15]

'Patti Dooke' deals with the age-old syndrome of 'crossing over': in other words, how black artists attempt to escape the ghetto of black pop music and to reach the mainstream, a process involving compromise, if not a painful moral dilemma over how much whitewash may have to be applied to a song or the packaging in which it is sold.

An album sleeve may have to change if it's too black and too strong. De La Soul broach the issue with a boldness that is very much in keeping with the straight talking at the heart of hip hop. Yet in an intriguing development towards the end of the piece, they announce casually that they are 'Down with the old school ... legitimate .... Soul!'[16]

It is a highly meaningful statement, one that shows how a leitmotiv of the past, a word pregnant with history such as 'soul', could still burst into the present and, more to the point, carry real substance because of the discursive framework in which the language is deployed.

Whether by accident or design, De La Soul have put their finger on one of the realities of the soul generation of the 1970s: the fact that the 's' word served as a partial explanation of Negroes to white people, or at least a word that gave a wider swathe of mainstream America something to grab hold of if it engaged with the minority.

Rappers are not supposed to pull punches, though, and De La Soul sign off with a wickedly confrontational assault on the phenomenon of white artists appropriating black music, a recognition that the blues and rhythm and blues that preceded soul music were repeatedly plundered by those on the right side of the racial divide: 'How many ever crossed over to *us*? I never seen five niggers on Elvis Presley's album cover!'[17]

Although possibly not a prime MP3 selection for fans of the King of Rock and Roll, 'Patti Dooke' is a happy as well as an angry song. The backing track is a sunny-sounding funky jazz beat, over which De La Soul chant 'It might blow up ... but it won't go pop!' with the smiley brio of munchkins easing on down the Yellow Brick Road. If they do make it big, it won't be for having planted a *baiser* on the wizard's bumper.

'It might blow up ... but it won't go pop!' is brilliant in the way the phrase taps directly into a key metaphor used by the hip hop generation – to blow up, as in achieve massive overnight success, like a credit bubble in the world of high finance – and yokes it to the age-old term for selling out – to go pop. Inflation thus makes merry with deflation. Opposites are juxtaposed. The net result is that 'Patti Dooke' displays sharp intellectual and verbal dexterity. It shows how to handle a serious subject with humour and dialectical rigour, how to define the present while recognising that the struggles of the past ain't over and out.

Casket blues

Artists such as De La Soul and other rappers took lyric-writing to a very high level of achievement in the 1980s and '90s. But they were building on a solid foundation, mainly because they drew extensively on the African American vernacular and love of wordplay that can be traced all the way back to the earliest blues singers and comedians.

Education was one of the key areas of segregation in America. The very idea that blacks were worthy of being taught language and literature on the same terms as whites was something that was actively resisted by many in the mainstream. The notion that blacks could make a real and worthwhile contribution to the world of letters, that they could become writers or orators, was considered something fanciful.

And yet what is remarkable is how much skill African American culture brought to the manipulation of words, how subversive some of the descriptions and metaphors could be. Astute, wily means of expressing either enthusiasm or cynicism were widespread. One of the best examples is the way blues guitarists talked about pianos. They did not do anything as transparent as call a piano a piano. Or even a keyboard. They were morbid; and deathly funny. They chose to say of a piano: 'Ain't nothing but a guitar in a coffin'.

This is the blues as an idea that knows no shame, a thought that doesn't do apologies, an opinion that has no fear of offence as debate or insult as charm. This language is vital. The words are rich in irony and imaginative piquancy. The image does not want for either provocation or conviction.

Part of the power of the blues is that it is an ever-changing constant, a sense of past, present and future in shifting dialogue, so that if one man muses on when the blues will leave, he indirectly invites another to muse on when the blues first came and when they will be back.

If these folks are musicians, then each blues will sound different when they look to express that sense of existentialism. For they are individuals amid a binding, unstintingly democratic experience, presenting the human condition as something defeating yet inspiring. By admitting you are down to the world, you entertain the possibility of the world lifting you up. Yet if sorrow makes you worn and weary, your words can't be hollow or dry.

This is why the language of the blues, typified by the impish description of keyboard as coffin, is continually inventive. It has to be. If a man experiences the same feelings again and again and again, especially a beaten-down man whose destiny is controlled by another, he may counteract this crushing inevitability through the spring of creativity. The immediate form of that creativity is his thinking, talking, singing.

Playing pianos, guitars, drums or horns is also an essential part of this dynamic. But one thing that becomes apparent, when one really pays attention to the titles of iconic tracks in instrumental jazz, soul or blues, is that the richness of language mirrors the power of the music.

I can think of no finer example than 'Better Git It In Your Soul' by double bassist, bandleader and composer Charles Mingus. Recorded in 1959, the track is a roof-raising piece of gospel/blues/jazz that brings the intense heat of the black church to bear on ambitious horn arrangements, while the sheer exuberance and joy of the music is brilliantly encapsulated in the words the composer uses in his title.

Consider how unapologetically rough and ready yet rousing this language is. Mingus didn't say 'Blessed Are The Righteous' but he implied the need for righteousness by way of a figure of speech that has a wholly earthly undertone, a shuffle from the pulpit to the street corner.

From the omission of the subject 'You' to the preference for the colloquial verb 'Git' over the formal 'Get' and the choice of the ambiguous pronoun 'It', Mingus digs right into the deep bedrock of the blues vernacular to create a sacred motto that has reverberated down through the ages in many profane contexts. Spirituality is bound up with sexuality.

'Git It' has a shameless urgency and forthright immediacy whose strong carnal undercurrent has flowed into countless pieces of black pop in which the desire, the need to git it, or to git some, refers to urges of a physical rather than spiritual nature. From Mingus springs first James Brown and then Snoop Dogg. They all sound so different. But there is a bond in words.

Language is thus a leveller, a kind of common denominator between blues, soul and hip hop. All three genres have been marked by similar linguistic verve over the years, primarily through their anchor in black popular culture. Hence, if the *Oxford English Dictionary* definition of the word 'soul' lists soul music and soul food as important variants, then one might supplement these entries with soul speak or soul talk. But it would perhaps be more appropriate to call it Black Talk.[18]

This ingenuity is thrillingly demonstrated by 'the dozens', that enduring African American tradition of trading insults, because the simplicity of the form is offset by the complexity of the content and the skill of the performance. Disrespecting somebody's mama is easy but doing it with ingenuity, so as to draw laughter rather than anger, is not.

Causing offence is not the object of the exercise. Pushing the verbal imagination to the limit is at the top of the agenda, and that impulse can be found in many other uses of black quotidian speech, where language under the volcano, language inside the volcano, language from *out* of the volcano, language as eruption, is a life-enhancing core value.

Sometimes immense soulfulness can be generated by deploying words that are not specifically 'black'. Shouting about collard greens, 'the dap' or 'nappy' hair will only increase communication between 'brothers' if the terms are underscored by a degree of emotional honesty or spontaneity. But what may appear to be less colourful or recondite language can strike right to the heart of black culture. Hence an expression such as 'Ain't that the truth?' is soulful. The rhetoric has to be swung like that, though. 'Isn't that the truth?' is as dry as a bone. It is bad meaning bad and not bad meaning good.

'All of you' does not have the same emotional and musical charge as 'Y'all'. There is a relish, a kind of vivid aroma that arises from the elision of 'You' and 'all'. It captures something of the African American's drive and energy, and it generally enriches the tonality of the English language.

There is as much soul and political power in a spontaneous 'Y'all' as there is in an Aretha record blaring top whack at a women's march.

Small words, simple prepositions such as 'on', 'down' and 'up', have become resoundingly effective in black popular culture over time. A blues lyric is richer in its suggestiveness and erotic intent if the language is moulded as 'Come On In My Kitchen' instead of 'Come Into My Kitchen'. There would be far less soul in 'Move On Up' without that precious 'On'.

Other words have a richness that belies their prosaic character. At some point in the 1990s, terms such as 'bounce', 'flavour' and 'flow' were invested with new meanings, connotations or resonances that directly reflected the way hip hop, as a new form of African American expression, was decisively setting the cultural agenda – just as a word like 'cat' became enormously emblematic of the Jazz Age of the 1920s.

Black talk thus has enormous vitality. What the African American experience has continually done over the years is bring imagination to language, to the extent that words can be dynamic rather than static entities, with the possibility of changing either form or meaning.

'Brother' is indelibly associated with blackness but it is also a riff to improvise on, a theme inviting variation that may bring additional emotion. 'Brother' becomes deeply soulful when it turns into 'brotherman', in the same way that in the Jamaican vernacular 'yoot' gains a flourish, a cultural plenitude, when it grows into 'yootman'.

If you know something of the Black Americas as well as Black America, then you will recognise that your brother could be your brotherman, your brotherman could be your bredrin and your bredrin could be your brahmin. These remixes all have great meaning. There are many types of brother.

Peeps and passports

Hence this phenomenon is not exclusively African American. Oral culture in the Caribbean – and Ireland, too, for that matter – has a similar dynamism, as markedly different as the histories of these territories are. In real terms, that means black talk reveals itself as evolutionary and relentlessly inventive. And it is often these things in the most informal of situations.

Back in 2008, for example, on the same day you could pick up three flyers advertising various dances in West Indian clubs around London.[19] The first one stated that, in response to the capital's tragic rise in gun crime, 'security is strong and tight'; the second that 'security is strong and tight but polite'; and the third that 'security is tight like outta airport'. That's soul, straight up. It is freedom of expression – and three improvisations on a blues chord.

That is language as music, or at least, language as a foretaste of music.

Consider, for a moment, the psychological and emotional depth in the last remix of that initial line: 'Tight like outta airport'. It holds great universal resonance for many blacks, precisely because of the racial politics of airports, spaces that act as an acid test for colour-coded power.

Airports have sharp detectors for 'the other', 'the alien'. JFK, Heathrow and Roissy can all be places of two-tier transit, and they become a haunted *terre commune* for Africans, African Americans, West Indians and Black Britons and British and American Asians, despite the tangible cultural differences that frequently exist between the many peoples within these peoples.

The airport is often a barometer for the changing level of threat encoded in an ethnic minority. It is a button of sociopolitical sensitivity. And it is pushed. You know the *real* meaning of 'tight like outta airport'. You relate. You feel it. Or else you wouldn't have been *in there*.

This is also why the ultimate soul man may be a writer, poet, comic, a virtuoso of the verb, a purveyor of story and rhyme, a champion of working-class colloquialism and off-the-cuff aphorism. Mind you, the killer couplet recited by O. J. Simpson's sharper-than-thou black lawyer, Johnny Cochrane – 'If the gloves don't fit/you must acquit' – shows that same oral dynamism is part of the weaponry of a highly educated courthouse gladiator. So it was really hip hop that saved squire O.J.'s ass, at least the first time.

Speed of change in language is such an integral part of Afro-Diasporan culture. To use 'diggin' it' today, when 'feelin' it' is so heavily equated with the dominant hip hop vocabulary, would be virtually unthinkable. The challenge for any putative black artist or community leader is to find images, metaphors or similes that will capture the imagination and uphold this longstanding tradition of oral invention, a particularly difficult task if one is running for the highest office in the land.

Sociology of any description tends to inaccuracy because its primary data are people, and people are hard to decipher because they are dynamic not static entities. Even more so ethnic minorities who, as second-class citizens in America and Europe, have needed to become extremely versatile, if not inventive, at developing systems of coded language and wily behavioural conceits simply in order to survive.

Any attempts at defining soul can only really be generalised because of the ingenuity of the society that frames soul. Although one can point to concrete manifestations of its spirit, such as music, dress or attitude, soul can assume far-reaching psychological ramifications. This was reinforced in no uncertain terms by the New Orleans jazz trumpeter Abram Wilson, when he described a gifted younger musician who had an exceptionally big sound for his age: 'There's this little boy pointing his horn to the sky ... he had more soul, more maturity than anybody I had heard'.[20]

That conjunction of soul and maturity struck me as a beautiful and profound notion: soul as a kind of life force that sustains a junior on the road to senior status; soul as a spirit to bolster a youth who has to grow up fast, possibly in the face of hostile forces, which is a situation countless African Americans have endured over time.

Like the best thoughts, Wilson's wisdom has roots that run deep into cultural history. What was Muddy Waters, one of the greatest of blues conjurors, after all? He was not a boyish man. He was a mannish boy.

Soul could mean unity, the warmth of community, the safety of togetherness. Soul could mean positivity. Soul could mean heroism, freedom, food, art, dance, music, a zest, ripeness or 'swing' in the use of language, the shameless irreverence that imagines a kickstand on your mama's peg leg, a chinstrap on her Afro and a fish in her glass eye. Soul could mean that the disenfranchised somehow look like kings and queens among the enfranchised. Soul could mean surviving beautifully, making art from the ashes as well as the fire. Soul could mean singing a song for the unsung. Soul could march in like the truth and be stranger than fiction. Perhaps when this puckish genie drifts among all kinds of blacks, in the same way that a 'stupse', a sharp suck-teeth, may pass the lips both of an estate hoodrat and corporate slicker, soul is a kind of democracy.

These moments are not certainties of black unity, though. They are possibilities. Change is the only enduring constant here. The generation gap within the black community is as wide as in any other. When I see young black Britons – whose West Indian grandparents, like my own West Indian parents, endured concerted hostility upon arrival in the 'mother country' – tell Poles or Turks or, more sadly, Britons of Polish or Turkish descent, to get back where they came from, I wince at the cruel irony and fear for soul as a kind of joyfully communal glue in the year 2010.

Yet they have a right to the same ignorance and small-mindedness that have afflicted whites for years, and in a strange way they are reinforcing the point that black folks are just as plain ordinary, as fallible, as anyone else. Hence there's no reason to consign these kids to oblivion, or to tell them what the form of their culture is. If they choose to discriminate, we have to educate. If they choose to oppress, we have to redress. We can only explain what their real, multifaceted history is, and hope they subsequently uncover a truly liberating humanity on their own terms.

We can only remember that sometimes the mainstream makes no distinction between them and us, in the worst cases of blanket racism.

We can only remember that us and them often speak a very different language, even though we have similar physical characteristics, and that our perception of a thing called soul is certainly bound to differ.

Besides, trying to be soul is precisely what being soul is not. It cannot be programmed. It's difficult to explain because there should be no need to define something apparently so natural as to be insignificant – which is why Bobby Byrd's contention that he knows 'you got soul or else you wouldn't be in here' says, with much beauty, everything and nothing.

It doesn't say that you are black or white, man or woman, dope or rope-adope. It doesn't say what you might be thinking or feeling.

However, if you know what brother B has got, chances are you'll get it. And if you know what you've got, then chances are you'll really get it.

3 Aged in soul

To truly deal with the evolution of our music on to the future, it is imperative that we define our musical past. (Quincy Jones)

Red Cross Rent Party

On 5 November 2008, the day after Barack Obama was declared America's first black president, Al Green played London's Royal Albert Hall. Or rather, a reverend came to preach. An absorbingly theatrical two hours were punctuated by soliloquies, moments of reflection and introspection, anecdotes, memories and, every so often, a quip that hovered quite tantalisingly on the border of great humour and corniness.

Green talked a lot. By the end of his performance, during which he was clad in a sharply cut black tuxedo, his speaking voice had become as familiar as his singing voice, making it as clear as Green's brilliant smile that story and song formed a whole, with a strong communicative dynamic running evenly across the two. His monologues were lengthy and detailed, recalling the 'raps' delivered by Isaac Hayes in his 1970s classics. Of Obama's triumph, Reverend Al – who found the Lord in the middle of the aforementioned decade after intoning countless love songs – opined that it was 'just as God had planned it'.[1]

Flirtation was still an integral part of Green's character, and the stream of women, their faces as hotly flushed as those of many watching Barack on big screens during the prelude to the gig, rushing to the front of the stage for a rose and an embrace, made it clear that his charm had not faded over time.

For all Green's luminous charisma on classics like 'Let's Stay Together', though, the Albert Hall gig came alive in the moments when, first, the singer's voice blended with those of his three female backing singers, so that they soared like a church choir; second, when the band's rhythm section and horns potently entwined; and, third, when all the above conspired to lay down as one.

The two key components of the gig – the vocals, their sense of grandeur and abandon borne of subjugation and service to the Holy Spirit; and the band, its form and content and its handling of pulse, texture and timbral colour enhancing the singers and standing as a rich voiceless voice in its own right – are the elements underpinning all the best soul music.

Their synergy has marked the beauty of soul over the years. Just mentioning the grand names registered in the pantheon during that time makes it abundantly clear. When considering performances by Al Green in 2008 or Erykah Badu in 1998, via Luther Vandross in 1988, Stevie Wonder in 1978 and Aretha Franklin in 1968, one invariably hails the brilliance of the human voice: a jewel of sound, its dazzle caught in nothing more than a half note, that stirs intense emotion in the unseen, inexplicable place known as the soul.

One should also, though, hail the ingenuity of the accompanying musicians for their skill in framing the voice without masking it, underwriting its rhythm and harmony to create an audio rainbow, and sometimes a spectrum of hues that shimmer without a voice. So one might highlight the gleam of Charles Hodges's Hammond organ alongside the diamanté glint of Green's voice and, by extension, James Poyser's keyboards for Badu, Marcus Miller's bass guitar for Vandross, Gregory Phillinganes's synthesizers for Wonder and King Curtis's saxophone for Franklin. Soul music is a palace of vocal regents guarded by great chevalier players.

Discussion of instrumental prowess in the genre is important, even though soul music can be extremely well made without a band. It has been. Listening to gospel choirs as they hit a natural high – the blessed moment when, for all believers, the spirit takes over – one is rarely left wanting the beat of a drum, the push of a bass or the heraldic line of a trumpet. And if there is one instant that can be particularly dramatic when soul features both a singer and a band, it is precisely when the band drops out.

But things can go the other way just as easily. Without the many musicians asserting themselves either as accompanists of great skill or as highly expressive soloists, a major part of the history of the music would have been left impoverished. The thought of Aretha Franklin's two verses on 'Respect' not being followed, relieved, completed and enhanced by King Curtis's saxophone solo, the narrative arc of his statement remarkable for its creative plenitude in the space of just eight bars, is a far from edifying prospect.

And if there is one instant that can be particularly dramatic when soul features both a band and a singer, it is precisely when the singer drops out.

Reaching right back in time to the forebears of these artists, one is struck by their guile and resourcefulness, their ability to create in far from favourable conditions, and the enduring complexity of the relationships that arose between the use of voices and instruments, the skill with which an instrument could be fashioned from discarded objects or animal carcasses, springing to life through the well of the imagination.

Prior to emancipation in 1863, a time of field hollers and work songs, slaves are without pianos or horns, both of which are proscribed. So they hammer a beat on the beasts of the field or the human body, as witnessed in songs like the hambone, where the knees and hands are deployed as percussion. It is music by any means necessary.

From this none-too-advantaged point of departure, the river of sound in which the African American voice bathes flows into several tributaries – namely, blues, ragtime and, later, jazz – where black musicians gain access to a wide range of European instruments. Meanwhile, Negro Spirituals – the sound of the black church, with its unique combination of European-derived hymn forms and harmonies with African vocal nuances – eventually evolve into gospel, a genre as effective when a choir performs with musicians as it is when the choir members, sometimes numbering fifty, sing *a cappella* and lift their voices as high as all God's chillun imagine the heavens to be.

Casting an eye over African American music in the first three decades of the twentieth century, one is struck by the array of expression that material-ised in many specific lexicons, be it the bracing, shuffling drive of the stride piano in New York, or the wail of clarinets and the blast of the trumpets in New Orleans, or the dry, grainy finger-picking of guitars in the Mississippi, or the harsh 'shout' of a singer in Chicago.

The distinctions between all these sounds are clear. The greatest divide is between the solo performer and the group or orchestra. Were one looking for a pair of icons to encapsulate this divide, then obvious candidates would be Leadbelly, the guitarist-singer from Louisiana, and Duke Ellington, the pianist-composer-bandleader from Washington. The former greatly shaped folk, country and blues, using nothing more than his voice and a twelve-string guitar, while the latter made his mark on the big-band swing era at the head of a twelve-piece orchestra, replete with brass and reeds, that occasionally expanded and also included a guest singer.

Standing very much at opposite ends of a sonic spectrum – the former was making minimalist music and the latter maximalist orchestral works – Leadbelly and Ellington are nonetheless bound by an essential understand-ing that the blues is not just a musical form but a sociological and emotional lexicon that enables them to capture something of the realities of black life. What this means is that Leadbelly sings of 'Red Cross Store Blues' while Ellington writes a musical arrangement for 'Rent Party Blues'. Leadbelly sings of 'Leaving Blues' and Ellington writes a musical arrangement for 'Farewell Blues'.

Leadbelly communicates with great immediacy; Ellington conveys myriad subtleties.

Thematically there is a connection between the last two pieces, but soni-cally they are worlds apart, not least because the former is a vocal piece and the latter an instrumental.

A pop–art divide is also clear. Leadbelly lowers the tone for the black bourgeoisie with his rough-hewn vignettes. Ellington, although capable of producing hot and hard-swinging music, raises the tone with his ambitious symphonic intricacies. Indeed, he was actively promoted as a serious artist, 'creator of a new vogue of music', whose work was worthy of a place in the grandest of concert halls.

Part of the vitality and originality of Ellington's orchestral music flowed not just from the rhythmic and harmonic skill of the various sections of his bands, but from the vocal quality of horn players such as Bubber Miley and Johnny Hodges. On the other side of the fence, many jazz singers modelled their work on horn players, so the relationship between the vocal and the instrumental was a complex, interactive one.[2] The evolution of this duality, particularly with the later input of spoken word and rhythmic chanting that would crystallise as 'rap', is paramount in black music.

The aforementioned Ellington and Leadbelly pieces were recorded between 1929 and 1940, during which time the record labels Victor, Columbia and Okeh purveyed 'Race Music', a term designating the music of black America, the 'other America'. Okeh had in fact launched its 'Colored catalog' several years earlier in 1921, and other companies jumped on the bandwagon, realising there was big money to be made in selling music to blacks: even in pre-Civil Rights America, profit was a post-racial reality.

Sacred and profane texts were aligned in Race Music, and the cover of a Victor Records catalogue from 1929 depicts a full-lipped black singer-guitarist in song, eyes closed, head thrown back expressively, the caption gathering together 'vocal blues, religious, spirituals, red-hot dance tunes, sermons and novelties'.

Huddled under this umbrella of Race Music, these sub-genres were perceived above all as risqué entertainment. And although religious differed greatly from red-hot dance tunes, new forms would arise from a mash-up of the two, the mingling of blues and gospel lyrics. A mouthful it may be, but a 'red-hot religious blues' was something that came to pass, and duly marked a significant advance in popular music.

Skinny dip

Determining the precise conditions in which a new genre of music is born is very difficult, given the generally complex nature of most societies in which musicians emerge. Certainly in the case of black America in the 1930s, with its great population shifts from south to north, its growing class divisions, its intricate caste system, its range of opinions on how to combat continued oppression by the mainstream, that was inevitable. Black voices, rather than a black voice.

And perhaps black voices within a black voice, musically speaking. Blues is a vague term after all, and it is worth remembering that some of the characteristics generally attributed to swing and red-hot dance tunes existed, perhaps to lesser degrees, within the blues. There were walking bass lines and improvisations that, while less harmonically advanced than in swing and dance tunes, were not lacking in invention.

Generally working with simpler song structures and fewer instruments than jazz musicians, blues players – certainly those who have made their mark on the form – nonetheless showed ingenuity in bringing nuance to their work, such as sliding a bottle on guitar strings to bend pitches, just as a horn player might do with a mute. Other techniques were also impressive. For example, Leadbelly deftly used his thumb to play pronounced walking lines on his twelve-string guitar while he strummed chords with his fingers. One of his predecessors was Papa Charlie Jackson, known to his fellow players as a 'musicianer' due to his ability with a six-string hybrid guitar-banjo. Furthermore, many blues singer-guitarists routinely featured a second guitarist or a harmonica player, either soloing freely behind them or finishing their vocal lines with a short but often pithy and well-constructed improvisation.

Rooted though he was in the secular world, Leadbelly occasionally sang church tunes like 'Swing Low, Sweet Chariot'. Other musicians straddled the sacred–profane divide. That Thomas A. Dorsey, a highly influential composer from the black church, played the blues with Ma Rainey in the 1920s before working with Mahalia Jackson, the gospel diva who paved the way for Aretha Franklin, in the '30s is also significant.

To the cynics, Dorsey didn't turn his back on the devil's music for the blessed hymn of the Good Lord on account of any spiritual conversion, but rather for the more earthly, indeed material, reason that he was able to fatten his wallet more easily in gospel.

Then again, Dorsey claimed that he found religion and as a result did not ever go back to the sinful ways of the blues once he had seen the light.

In any case, the existence of common denominators, in the shape of a musician or a musical technique, between the different lexicons gathered under the moniker of Race Music rendered some kind of dialogue, if not cross-pollination, highly likely.

Powerful white impresarios such as John Hammond still exerted control over high-profile 'happenings' in black music and it was he, known first and foremost as the man who 'discovered' Billie Holiday, who used the connections and influence artists did not have to stage the 'From Spirituals To Swing' concert at Carnegie Hall in 1938. This gala saw jazz stars Count Basie and Benny Goodman grace the same bill as blues giants 'Big' Bill Broonzy and 'Big' Joe Turner as well as gospel favourites Golden Gate Quartet and Mitchell's Christian Singers. Translate that into today's language and you roughly have Herbie Hancock, R. Kelly and Kirk Franklin in one space.

In the same year, there was what might be termed a defection from the sacred to the secular camp that met with shock and disbelief, mooting the possibility of a new form if gospel singers were to transfer their impassioned, highly dramatic vocal technique to a context in which praise of the Lord were replaced with a desire for pleasure of a sentimental or even carnal nature. If that could be done while the musicians were swinging, the result would indeed be 'red-hot religious dance tunes'.

Guitars were less prevalent in black church music at the time, because they were associated with the hobo, the lowlife and the blues man. Yet the likes of

Blind Willie Johnson accompanied himself on said instrument on over thirty recordings of gospel music during the late 1920s. There were others who followed, such as Sister Rosetta Tharpe.

Playing the guitar from the age of six, Tharpe accompanied her mother Katie Bell Nubin on the tent revival circuit in the Southeastern United States before they settled in Chicago. Tharpe won over audiences with a sterling version of 'Jesus On The Mainline' and a number of other well-known church songs – even though, unbeknown to her devoted fan base, she often played the blues at home and also liked uptempo swing jazz bands.

She eventually acted on that interest and appeared with Cab Calloway's orchestra at New York's Cotton Club, the venue where Duke Ellington had largely made his name. Shortly afterwards, Tharpe reprised Thomas Dorsey's 'Hide Me In Thy Bosom' as 'Rock Me', turning the song's submission to the will of God into a yearning of an altogether more primal kind, a pirouette that was performed much to the dismay of 'betrayed' churchgoers.

Beyond the scandal of crossing the sacred–secular divide, Tharpe was hugely important because of the breadth of her music. A jazz orchestra led by Lucky Millinder backed her on the above recording and Tharpe went on to lead her own trio consisting of double bass, piano and herself on guitar, recording the even more scandalous 'I Want A Tall Skinny Papa' in 1942 before enjoying a hit gospel record when she joined forces with her mother on the righteous 'Ninety Nine And A Half Won't Do' in 1949.

Tharpe encapsulates the dexterity of the black artist in relation to the sacred and the profane, in so far as she was constantly shuttling between jazz/blues and gospel music.

Her career would not hit those heights again and her recording activities wound down considerably in the subsequent decade, even though Tharpe continued to tour, coming to Britain in the 1950s and '60s to play with the Chris Barber band. Her success would effectively provide a glimpse of the future, a time when artists might bring sacred and secular music together, perhaps in a closer, more tightly entwined way.

A woman and a mannish boy

To a large extent, Tharpe's case exemplifies the traffic and mutability of black music at the dawn of the 1950s. The fact that a sacred melody written by a gospel composer such as Dorsey, who had a direct engagement with the blues, could then be reprised, re-versioned or 'remixed' as a secular song – not about love but sex – and set to an arrangement with distinct jazz leanings says a lot about the remarkable fluidity of the form.

Blues chord changes and the fundamental verse/chorus structure, sometimes with a middle eight bar break and sometimes without, was a foundation built on in increasingly diverse ways. The movement of horn and piano players from swing jazz big bands to smaller groups, playing both instrumental and vocal music with solos, contributed to a gradual change in black popular music. Acquiring faster tempos and more swing, thanks to the above input, the blues became rhythm and blues.

Like the Race Music tag it replaced, this was above all a general term. The real point here is that, although 1950s R&B had a rhythmic and timbral identity different from '30s and '40s blues, it retained a range of approaches and regional variations.

New Orleans alone, with its marching brass-band traditions, its Mardi Gras drummers, its Dixieland combos, and its long line of piano 'professors' with their 'galloping' left-hand rhythm figures, produced a wealth of artists whose music could have anything from a specific Afro-Latin influence – the sly, sensual whirl of Professor Longhair – to frenetic, authoritative shouters like Chubby Newsome or Erline 'Rock 'n' Roll' Harris.

The various brands, types, strains of R&B – jump, bar, boogie, shout – all attested to an enormous verve and plurality in black popular music. Its evolution was multilateral rather than linear, with musicians borrowing basic riffs from each other, adapting melodies and rhythms, or altering them through major changes of instrumentation.

Tunes in which the theme was played by a raucous tenor or alto saxophone in front of a hard-swinging band, possibly augmented by more horns, stood in stark contrast to the much smoother sound of the polished, teen-friendly doo-wop groups, the gilt-edged romantic vocal ensembles specialising in creamy four- or five-part harmony that could be traced back to the tradition of gospel groups singing in barbershops.

How many ways can a song be sung? How effective is a saxophone as a lead voice? How many types of arrangement can be devised to accompany it? Whether these questions were being asked consciously is not really the point here. What matters is that basic, formative musical data – chord progressions, approaches to the pulse, horn figures, piano and guitar licks – were being developed and deployed to make rhythm and blues a vibrant pop music with an energy that was missing among mainstream crooners. First and foremost, it was billed as 'music with a beat'. The beat changes. The beat goes on.

R&B was always likely to be interesting because it was vocal and instrumental music, and the tension between these two approaches to song – the blend of the concrete, explicit meaning of the former and the more abstract, implicit feeling of the latter – could only challenge as well as comfort listeners. Dancing to a hard-rocking saxophonist and listening to a tender love ballad engages different senses. Any music with the means to affect both the body and the mind has potential for complexity.

Hearing a very skilled saxophonist such as Louis Jordan intersperse pithy, spicy lyrics with artfully mapped horn breaks, in which reeds and brass would be latticed as in the heyday of big bands, reflected the capacity for precise, detailed arrangements that opened up new pathways in pop during the 1940s and '50s.

On the one hand, Jordan's music clearly presaged to some extent the rock and roll of Chuck Berry. On the other, it surely informed the soul of Ray Charles, for listening to Jordan's 1945 piece 'Caldonia' and Charles's 1954 'I've Got A Woman' reveals a clear continuity both rhythmically and tonally.

Above all, what is easily discernible in the two pieces is a common perspective and education, a tight grip on jazz rudiments, by way of the extremely fleet-footed swing, the incisive construction of the horn arrangements and the split-second precision with which the musicians chart their course through the chord changes. These are by no means difficult, but every single dip, lean and swerve of the harmony is made to count – a skill not to be dismissed.

Marked as the musical continuity is, the vocal performances are very different. Charles's voice is burning hot whereas Jordan's is bubbling, cute, the tone cheeky. There is such an urgency and a sense of compelling emotional release in the way Charles talks of the woman who 'gives me money when I'm in need' that it's clear his artistry at this point in time is being guided wholeheartedly by the ways of gospel.

And it is perhaps the fact that Charles is so vividly inhabited by the eruptive, ecstatic and overpowering spirit of a black church singer, against the backdrop of a secular music drawn from blues, jazz and popular song, that heralds the birth of soul.

Crucially, this stands in the lineage of Sister Rosetta Tharpe's 'Rock Me', in so far as it has the same sense of heat. But there is something more urbane and worldly in Charles's persona, suggesting that when gospel dynamics are brought to the world of R&B, they can achieve more than a profane praise song or a red-hot religious dance tune. Tellingly, Charles conjoined spiritual language with earthly concerns a year later when he recorded 'Hallelujah! I Love Her So', even more scandalous because it posits the idea that the pursuit of the opposite sex can actually be conducted in the name of the Lord.

Hence for the most part soul is not so much reinvention as evolution of R&B, a recasting of some of the many elements that had existed under the banner of Race Music, so that blues, gospel, pop and jazz collided to delineate a new form.

Many artists contributed to this crystallisation. To the name of Ray Charles one might also add those of Charles Brown, who indeed exerted a major influence on Charles, as well as Sam Cooke, Nina Simone and James Brown. All of them, in different ways, shuttled between several fields of black music in order to define a certain individuality in their aesthetic that would lay something of a foundation for others in the embryonic soul genre.

Certainly in its early history, around the late 1950s, soul was a different name for R&B, and that was perhaps necessary since the word itself, as explained in the previous chapter, gained credence within the black community in America. It is interesting that some exponents of the 'old genre', such as

Irma Thomas, were indifferent to the new nomenclature because they foresaw the probability of clichés and bandwagons.

Regardless of whether certain musicians felt uncomfortable with the 's' word, it gained ground as a marketable term for black popular music as the 1960s dawned. It is worth noting that Motown, a definitive label in the genre that emerged in 1959, while promoting its product mainly as 'the sound of Young America', also used the word 'Soul' on the inner sleeves of its albums.

Technology, in any case, would play a part in bringing modernity to black popular music. It altered the sound. As the 1960s wore on, more R&B musicians 'plugged in',[3] availing themselves of the bass guitar and Fender Rhodes electric piano as well as the Hammond organ. By the end of the decade, the majority of soul artists had a tonality in their work that was louder, harder and heavier than in the acoustic R&B that had complemented vocals with the softer double bass and acoustic piano.

Which is why many of the great blues artists found in urban areas such as Chicago, the likes of Muddy Waters being the obvious example, were important in the development of soul. They announced these elements of loudness, hardness and heaviness in some of their fierce electric guitar-driven songs, of which 1955's 'Mannish Boy' was a paradigm. These artists conveyed, through the unapologetic attack of their six-string riffs, the muscularity that would be heard in funk, the rhythmically aggressive strand of soul whose progenitor was James Brown.

The differences in sound, improvements in the engineering and mixing of records, the influx of new percussion instruments, and a wider range of electronics and keyboards, all contributed to a flourishing creativity in soul music throughout the 1970s, during which time the music acquired many templates. It could be intensely polyrhythmic or orchestral and densely layered bordering on the symphonic.

Maybe the richness of the idiom was defined above all by the fact that some of its exponents rightly considered as prime movers managed to develop a songbook that was overwhelmingly individual, its marks of distinction very easy to identify. Hence the music of James Brown differed greatly from that of Stevie Wonder.

Soul, as R&B before it, thus became another umbrella term, one that covered a wide range both of sounds and approaches to rhythm and tempo. Yet blues and gospel harmony remained consistently at its core, providing something of a skeleton to be fleshed out according to the imagination of the given practitioner. And perhaps the real story of soul is not so much how new it has been able to sound but how many new riffs can be spun from its pentatonic scales and chord changes, how threads have emerged because many progressive artists debuted in one era and evolved in another.

Wonder, George Clinton, Sly & The Family Stone, Curtis Mayfield and Marvin Gaye all adopted vastly different approaches to arranging their songs, but all of them, at some point in their idiosyncratic aesthetics, referenced classic harmony vocal techniques – particularly Clinton and Gaye, who cut their teeth in doo-wop ensembles (The Parliaments and The Moonglows respectively) in the days of R&B.

Because the blues has fed into jazz, funk and rock, and remains one of the roots of soul, it is thus logical that relationships have developed between these genres, that a soul–jazz continuum, a soul–funk continuum and a soul–rock continuum now exist – lineages in which one hears different configurations of the mass of chords, riffs, grooves and beats that have accumulated during the grand history of black music.

In the forthcoming chapters these continuums will be discussed in more detail, to frame as effectively as possible our understanding of the evolution of soul.

The profound historical sign of black music

Changes in instrumentation, rhythmic accents and tempo, the effect of speeding up or slowing down the basic engine of 'the beat' – that primary distinction between black and white pop – brought myriad sub-genres to soul. Disco, go-go and boogie reflected the great verve with which the 4/4 pulse that had largely underpinned blues licks for decades could acquire a semblance of newness through the way time was managed. This made it clear that something as apparently anachronistic as the speedy soul-clappin' traditions of the Baptist church could still prove relevant to a musician with some vision.

Genres of music are not just shaped by access to historical information, though. There is also technology and instrumentation to consider, elements that were decisive in helping R&B to morph into soul during the 1960s and contributed to a further shift in the music during the '80s. That was when drum machines, synthesizers and sequencers became more prominent, as many of the large bands from the '70s scaled down due to economic constraints, shedding the horn sections and string orchestras that had imparted textural sheen to their music. Now the keyboards brought a different kind of gloss to the table.

Soul becoming more electronic was not an abrupt change: the music had leant heavily towards that palette anyway, certainly in the hands of artists such as Wonder and Clinton. What was more important was how the music might be affected in the early 1980s by the new genre of hip hop: or, more to the point, the new culture of hip hop that stood both inside and outside the blues aesthetic.

Inside in the sense that hip hop was predicated on storytelling, spoken-word traditions and rhythmic speech that could be traced right back to the 'the Jubah-this Jubah-that Jubah skin the alley cat' chants of plantation workers, via the combative couplets of Muhammad Ali and the derisory detonations of 'the dozens'. Outside in the sense that hip hop undermined a sacrosanct core of black music: band, instruments, players.

Now came the confusing idea that music could be made by people who were not musicians, but who imagined how they wanted to hear music and pursued their vision by technological means. This was something completely in step with the notion of virtual reality that gained marked credence in the coming age of cyber communications.

By replacing a rhythm section, horns and strings with drum machines or turntables, the new generation of African American artists deviated from a norm that had held sway for decades. The paradigm shift was seismic, the net result being that several 'traditional' musicians, listeners and journalists denounced this evolution as a regression. Some would later relent, loosely mirroring initial perceptions of jazz.

Radical as it may have been, hip hop was, on the one hand, also a curious case of history repeating itself. The obvious thing to note about its practitioners was that they were not the first to make music from objects not usually regarded as instruments. The turntable can be used to create a 'break' that serves as the rhythmic base for a song, but it is also a percussion device broadly reminiscent of the washboard, a household item that was used by blacks who were looking for the perfect beat back in the 1890s.

Rather ingeniously, DJs also developed sophisticated scratch techniques on the decks, encompassing a range of different sound types. One of the most striking was a volley of high-pitched cuts that suggested human laughter. And, by the most charmingly intriguing of twists, musical history: jazz trumpeters did the same thing decades before.

Furthermore, listening to a beatboxer purse his lips or slap his chest to mimic instruments, you can also hear a distant echo both of a doo-wop singer bringing to life the bass through the back of his throat and of cane workers, denied the use of respectable axes like pianos and violins, beating their bodies and improvising vocally to create the intricate rhythms that would accompany a variety of song and dance.

In days of old, blacks were seen as non-musicians. Hip hop empowered non-musicians. Playing guitars wasn't the point. Creatively manipulating audio, from any source, was. Hip hop revitalised moribund mainstream pop in the process.

Furthermore, there was a shift in the conception of how an artist might present himself. If nobody imagined that kids who couldn't play a C major scale would make music, then nobody foresaw a performer calling himself Old Dirty Bastard, which is something that raw, X-rated African American comedians had implied but not dared adopt as a moniker.

Ultimately, hip hop was a scrambling of history, a juxtaposition of ancient and modern rather than an outright attack by the latter on the former. And certainly in the larger-than-life personalities of its exponents one could see direct manifestations of the self-empowering bravado that was among the essentials of the blues. Muddy Waters knew he would be the greatest man alive from the age of five. Big Daddy Kane was the only man who would ever be left when all the others were all done and cold busted for theft.

Several great singers, notably Luther Vandross, Anita Baker and Jeffrey Osborne,[4] continued to make excellent soul music as hip hop grew in both commercial and cultural significance. But it became clear by the end of the 1980s that soul music might become more interesting if it succeeded in capturing some of hip hop's funky molten energy: the rebel stance, the thing that connected James B to Chuck D.

In any case, the dawn of the 1990s would see hip hop, a samples-led genre, became the new black popular music while soul, an instrument-led form, was increasingly perceived as classic black popular music. Meanwhile the term 'R&B' was revived, somewhat confusingly, to designate music leaning towards hip hop and pop, in so far as instrument-led dynamics and blues harmony were by no means a prerequisite.

Guessing how this range of sounds might crystallise into something new is one of the best games a listener can play. One thing that has continued to enrich black music is its post-modernism, the tantalising, often beguiling way in which the past – fragments of it, adjustments, remixes – keeps coming back at the present. Prince, so steeped in pyschedelic soul, P-Funk, blues and rock and roll, was an obvious case in point. Yet there were others, less mercurial perhaps than Prince, who also counted.

Black church music, it seemed improbable to think, couldn't come remotely close to the power of something like hip hop or rock and roll, the attitude and mythology that superseded it. Yet lo and behold, it turned out that a thirty-seven-piece gospel choir duly formed an alliance with a six-piece rhythm section, a four-piece horn section and producers with state-of-the art kit to create sounds that were pure volcanic action.

Sounds of Blackness, hailing from Prince's home state of Minnesota, were that group. More to the point, they were a grand political statement. On their 1991 debut, *The Evolution Of Gospel*, the group stood, their pseudo-military garb making them officers to Public Enemy's troopers, on an ecumenical platform that embraced 'every member of the African-American family of music: African melodies, field hollers and work songs, spirituals, blues, ragtime, jazz, gospel, rhythm & blues, rock & roll and rap'.[5]

It was a bold formalisation of any debate grappling with issues of education and culture, heritage and roots. Quincy Jones, one of the great pillars of modern black music, the man who played with and wrote for Dizzy Gillespie in the 1950s, scored for Ray Charles in the '60s, and produced Michael Jackson and many others in the '70s and '80s, reinforced the group's position in his sleeve notes for the album:

> To truly deal with the evolution of our music on to the future, it is imperative that we define our musical past. The music you hear

from the Sounds of Blackness recognizes the profound historical sign of black music, and then proceeds to keep the 'goodfoot' on a true righteous path.[6]

All of which draws a parallel with jazz, a genre that has always had an elaborate relationship with its past, using it as a source both of reference and renewal. Issues of form and content, structure and sound, whether a group should be electric or acoustic, have marked the genre for many years, as its exponents have mused on what is the most effective means of presentation for their ideas, and how the history of the music can be encoded in tandem with integrating these concepts.

Inevitably, there are actions and reactions. Artists accept or reject the points of view of their peers and predecessors, leading to a wide range of creative possibilities gathered under the vague but resonant banner of jazz. With its multiple and often conflicted strands of historical development, the music possesses a wealth of cumulative knowledge.

Soul has also seen reaction to action, and amalgamations of both the action and the reaction, while it has grappled with questions of feel, warmth and texture. Hence the emergence of the so-called 'Nu Classic' or 'neo soul' artists in the mid-1990s.[7] The reversion to playing instruments, rather than applying the beats-based methodology of hip hop or post-hip hop R&B, in the work of these artists, occurred primarily because the latter formats were perceived as an increasingly synthetic and frigid setting for the exploration of strong emotions. That is something of a problematic notion, when one considers that Stevie Wonder has made startlingly emotive music using nothing more than keyboards. Then again, he is a virtuoso player rather than a programmer or a DJ.

Exactly what constitutes the most effective format for soul music remains an unanswered question. For while the band, the players with their potential for improvisatory flourishes that maintain the genre's connection with jazz, remain essential, it is interesting that some of the most creative artists to have emerged over the last two decades, be they Me'Shell NdegéOcello, Bilal Oliver or Erykah Badu, have all engaged with hip hop's state-of-the-art production techniques, sequencing and programming to greater or lesser degrees. Songwriter and beatmaker need not be incompatible.

Melody and rhythm, the putative fortes of the former and latter respectively, sometimes prove to be incompatible entities in pop. Yet this needn't be the case. It doesn't have to be an either/or situation, and perhaps soul stands as a genre that has excelled in its exploration of each element in turn, and in their conjunction. This means a listener can find deep fulfilment in mouthing the theme of 'A Change Is Gonna Come', not wanting for a drum track; or in tapping out on a table the bass line of 'Sex Machine', not wanting for a lead vocal to glide through a verse, chorus, interlude or bridge.

Something utterly magical comes out of the intersection of these paragons. It is that moment when a well-marshalled backbeat and a smart melody coalesce amid all the crackling electricity of gospel. It lies deep in the crash of the pianist and the burn of the vocalist, so that several senses are affected at once: the heavy, percussive bass pushing the listener down while the emotionally charged singing provides a spiritual elevation. It is the beauty of a song that can also be a beast of a groove.

Drums, bass, guitar, keys, horns, strings and voice can achieve all this marvellously. Great art can be created through the union of a soul singer and a jazz band, for the standard of playing in black pop, from Ray to Aretha to Stevie, has always been high. That's one of the reasons why they are icons: precisely because they were doing more than just pouring out emotion, and often they recruited the best improvisers to support them. Recent collaborations between soul artists like the singer Erykah Badu and jazz musicians such as the trumpeter Roy Hargrove are the latest strand of this long-standing lineage.

4 The soul–jazz continuum

There were a lot of jazz gigs before we did our soul thing.

(Maurice White, Earth, Wind & Fire)

River Jordan

There are several historical precedents for soul singers using jazz soloists in their groups. Some of these soloists were freelancers – often established leaders in their own right – while others were fully paid-up band members gigging on the road as well as clocking up studio time with the artist in question.

Working back in time, some examples just of saxophonists who have performed this role might include Joshua Redman for Me'Shell NdegéOcello in the 1990s; Michael Brecker for Cameo in the '80s; and 'Pee Wee' Ellis and Maceo Parker for James Brown in the '70s and '60s.

Parker's solos were a particularly important feature of Brown's music. They had a stinging, pungent attack that maintained the surge of excitement generated by the leader's voice. They were also extremely precise in rhythmic construction, forging a continuum between vocal and instrumental expression.

Brown recorded lengthier tracks that were not simply a vehicle for his own vocal, but rather showed it was one of a range of elements in his band that might grab the spotlight. What is striking about an anthem such as 'Mother Popcorn' is its organisation as a joint showcase for singer and saxophonist. Parker *becomes* the lead voice for thirty-two bars at the halfway mark, and then for sixteen bars in the coda.

Moments such as these were echoes of another era. Funk percolated at the base of the music but both the solo reed statements and the weighty, high-impact horn section, its unison lines dispensed in cut-and-thrust patterns against the pulse of the music, bore a faint residue of the 1930s big bands – a movement that had mostly bottomed out by the time that a young James Brown rose to the top.

Ray Charles kept the model alive to a certain extent. His body of work between the late 1940s and early '60s saw him use anything from trios to twelve-piece bands to the eighteen-piece orchestra of Count Basie, who along with Duke Ellington was a towering icon of the swing era.

Genius + Soul = Jazz, the 1959 album that Charles cut with the Basie band under the direction of a young Quincy Jones, seemed to symbolise in grand fashion the position of its author at the confluence of two key streams of black music, one pop and one art. For the most part, though, the album was also an emphatic reminder of how much power could be generated by a battery of brass and reeds whose exponents were able to harmonise effectively their individual tones.

These musicians played great riffs. Short stabs or bursts of colour, lasting sometimes no more than three or four chords, and giving way to a lengthier twenty-four- or thirty-two-bar solo from a saxophonist or trumpeter over a steady, taut walking bass, enabled Basie to fill floors as his 'jump blues' became a dominant form of dance music in the pre-war years.

Listening to Basie's work today, with the sharp, regular swing of its solid 4/4 time, it is clear that big bands provided something of a foundation, or at least a form of instruction, for much of the rhythm and blues that would evolve in later years – not least because the keening, caressing regularity of the pulse and the thrust of the ensemble voice are organising principles of sound that are enormously communicative.

Swing was catchy; rhythm and blues held on to that characteristic.

Some of the brisk high tempos that had been prevalent in swing also started to permeate the generally slower pace of the blues. It created a form of rhythm and blues that also benefited from the presence of several players from the old big bands, who had found work either backing popular singers or manning small combos that pumped out dancefloor-friendly tunes while retaining their improvisatory content.

Having experienced big-band players in R&B groups meant that the straighter swing beat was well handled and that tonal flourishes entered the music: the brilliant cameo solos around the singer had the sharp precision of orchestral section playing, the focus and economy of the phrases a virtue not to be taken lightly.

By the middle of the 1940s, though, swing was stultifying into overly for-mulaic music and the orchestras were becoming prohibitively expensive. The big bands started to scale down. In their place came a new form of small-group jazz dubbed bebop, which was much more fragmented rhythmically and hugely demanding of soloists, due to its slalom course of chords and gen-erally lengthy, serpentine melodies, themselves like miniature suites. Above all, the new genre revelled in daring displays of improvisation, often on blues harmony. Its prime movers, Dizzy Gillespie and Charlie Parker, audaciously whipped up interest in rapid, gymnastic solos, the phrasing taking off on har-monic tangents that upped the thrill factor.

Hence the focus shifted for the listener. The comfort of a theme was replaced by the discomfort, the danger, the daring of a soloist without con-cessions – for Parker was essentially asserting his right to be complicated, just as at least one hip hop emcee would do years later.

An appropriate adjective to capture what jazz represents to the layperson is probably complex or enigmatic. The African Americans at the root of the music let loose a probing, inquisitive nature that often favours opacity over transparency, trickster manoeuvres over easily discernible strategies, even though links to popular culture, be it a Broadway tune or a rock anthem, have often been maintained.

Over time, the most remarkable exponents of jazz have distinguished themselves by their desire to retain an uncompromising individuality, to research and explore a wide range of composing and improvising methods, to create sounds and forms that convey newness, audacity, adventure. Jazz is challenge, risk, gamble. It is supposed to test player and listener. It is supposed to unsettle what passes as a certainty.

Eventually, this led to the most recognizable, and perhaps the most comforting, form of structure there is – theme, melody, tune, or at least traditionally identifiable combinations thereof – being blown away by the tempest known as the New Thing or avant-garde, the school of jazz that brewed in the mid-1960s and made space for the ideal of spontaneous improvisation, one of the ultimate double-or-quits wagers in modern music. It can produce results ranging from the rapturous and engrossing to the tedious and alienating.

Beyond any notion of complexity, jazz is a question that begs another question as soon as an answer is put forward. The question is, or at least should be, as much a why as a what or a how (to play, that is), and this restively inquisitive dynamic has fostered the music's mutation from 1950s bebop to '60s free to '70s fusion to the dot-dash post-modernism that has prevailed for the past thirty years.

By contrast, R&B's overriding mission statement is not so much why but will the crowd move – and if they deign to, will they twist, watusi, funky chicken, bump, robot or run the running man all the way down.

Response, or rather immediacy of response, is all. Listeners can be moved to depths of sadness or heights of joy by jazz but the music does not always have a direct effect on them as recreational beings, meaning it may not soundtrack aspects of their social intercourse, especially now that the jitterbugging days of the swing era lie in the distant past. Jazz is not, for the most part, functional.

It mostly happens in venues for listening, not dancing. It still has the power to touch listeners, particularly by way of inspired solos, but its identity has largely acquired a distinct earnestness of tone, a solemnity. Even if jazz musicians write and play love songs, chances are they will not introduce them to an audience using tropes such as 'This one is for the ladies' or 'This is a slow jam for the lovers in the house'. Whether it is entertainment, art, entertaining art or artful entertainment, R&B usually creates a context for a key human activity, and that is invariably the vital push of dancing or the revitalising pull of romancing. R&B is, for the most part, functional.

Tellingly, after R&B evolved into soul during the late 1960s, it became a convention for soul albums, particularly in the '70s and '80s, to create a clear divide between dancing and romancing. So one side would comprise up-tempo party tunes and the other down-tempo love songs, to the effect that a couple could chart their progress from club to bedroom by way of the first and second halves of a recording.

R&B, a largely vocal genre, once had some of the *savoir-faire* of jazz, a largely instrumental genre, without necessarily sharing its *raison d'être*. It had dancers and lovers to satisfy, rather than being creative for creativity's sake. Then again, black music has remained fascinating precisely because sophistication and crudity, folk and art, the figurative and the abstract, the serious and the frivolous, the functional and the non-functional, have not been mutually exclusive components. Winning a pop audience does not always mean playing 'em cheap creatively. Proof positive are the bluesmen who play a *lot* of guitar and sing, rather than singing and playing a scratch of guitar.

Most obviously B. B. King springs to mind. But prior to the man who cut loose so sharply on the bebop warhorse 'Blue 'n Boogie', years before he sang the meltingly soulful blues 'The Thrill Is Gone', others blurred the art-entertainment boundary and also bridged the serious-humorous gap that now largely distances jazz from R&B.

Louis Jordan was an alto saxophonist who learnt the ways of section playing in Chick Webb's Orchestra during the 1940s before he started his own highly successful band, the Tympani Five. It went on to enjoy huge popularity playing a shuffle-based blues, whose robust, at times raucous, swing beat strode boldly in the vanguard of R&B.

Cookin' hits such as 'Saturday Night Fish Fry' or 'Choo Choo Choo Boogie' never lost faith in nailed-down blues changes, a formula from which Jordan rarely deviated. But these tunes did not lack for panache in their arrangements, the fine brush strokes coming by way of an astute deployment of reeds and brass that betrayed the leader's formative years as a big-band member – an experience whose relative rarity today is bemoaned by senior jazz musicians, who believe their successors may suffer from experiential impoverishment as a result.

'Caldonia', one of Jordan's biggest hits – cut in 1945, the year that Charlie Parker launched into the outrageous, whirlwind runs of 'Koko' – featured a twenty-four-bar instrumental break after the first verse that significantly galvanised the whole piece through a concise, pithy interplay of solo and unison saxophones. The impact was accentuated by a vocalised trumpet growling in counterpoint. The music laughs and smiles but it is also played seriously, and skilfully.

In that inspired, controlled riot of horns one hears a precursor of instrumental sax-led rock and roll and R&B – think Joe Houston or King Curtis – and also the rolling, tumbling rhythmic propulsion that would inform both James Brown and Ray Charles.

Fully deserving of his genius status, Charles was more than a gifted vocalist and multi-instrumentalist. He was also a sterling representative of an era in which blues, R&B, jazz and pop could all intermingle and successfully cohere in the repertoire of an artist who understood how to tell a story in song, how to stir emotions by way of superior musical craftsmanship.

Many other vocalists had a similar stylistic range: a cursory list would include the likes of Dinah Washington, Pearl Bailey, Joe Williams and Lou Rawls.

Then there was a certain Aretha Franklin. The preacher's gifted daughter was born to be the Queen of Soul. But before she acceded so majestically to that throne, Franklin recorded a fair amount of jazz.

Say what in seventy-two bars

Many are the older African American musicians who have told me over the years that the majority of jazz musicians learned their craft playing jazz and paid their bills playing R&B, soul and, to a certain extent, pop.

Be that as it may, it's important to understand that there was a partial intersection in the repertoire used in these genres. The great American song-book of Kern, Porter, Hammerstein and others, which provided such staple source material for jazz artists, was also adopted by several key R&B singers. So standing in contrast to the raunchy blues of Johnny 'Guitar' Watson's 'Motorhead Baby' was his effete rendition of 'April In Paris'. In contrast to the gilded gospel-soul of Sam Cooke's 'A Change Is Gonna Come' stood his harmonically ornate take on 'Willow Weep For Me'. And in contrast to the raucous R&B of The Isley Brothers' 'Staggerlee' stood their sensitive interpretation of 'How Deep Is The Ocean'.

All the aforementioned pieces were recorded between the mid-1950s and early '60s and they reflect a certain overlap, a connectedness between many forms of black music that would recede over time as jazz became largely defined as highbrow art and R&B as popular entertainment. Yet a key component of the former – improvisation – was not entirely excised from the latter, and certainly artists like The Isley Brothers, a hugely successful act for Motown, still threw down horn or guitar solos in their songs. What is also important is that they and several other R&B bands sought to widen their rhythmic palette through the occasional use of Latin beats – just as had been the case in jazz, with its input from Cuban and Brazilian musicians, for many decades. The Isleys' 1964 hit 'That Lady' is a soul bossa nova.[1] Replace the lead vocal with a saxophone and extend the horn break, and 'Who's That Lady' would soon become a jazz bossa nova.

If R&B was still engaging with jazz, embracing one of its essential principles by bringing as many nuances as possible to the basic canvas of a song, then jazz actively engaged with R&B and with one of its formative elements, black church music, embracing its earthy rhythm and its ability to tap visceral emotion with clear song form.

Fittingly, this particular school was dubbed 'soul jazz'. It brought strong gospel melodies and pounding backbeats to the fore, largely simplifying the challenging harmony and rhythms of bebop and making the innovations of Dizzy Gillespie and Charlie Parker more palatable. Many jazz musicians would adopt the style and the likes of Horace Silver, Julian 'Cannonball' Adderley and Lee Morgan, all of whom showed Latin characteristics in their work, emerged as substantial commercial forces. Several of their hit singles, such as Morgan's groovy 1964 finger-snapper 'The Sidewinder', found favour with both pop audiences and R&B musicians, some of whom, such as Louis Jordan, had exerted an influence on players like Adderley.

Practitioners of black popular music who had lived through the big-band swing era, who had witnessed players from these orchestras' horn sections bringing their artistry to small-group R&B, who had seen bebop and soul jazz come to prominence and Latin rhythms ignite in a number of contexts, thus had a mass of data at their disposal as they went about developing new songbooks.

Two of the musicians who were instrumental in spearheading the transition from R&B to soul, namely Ray Charles and James Brown, had that wealth of knowledge.

They had both had hands-on experience of working in a big-band setting where the precise blending of instruments and layering of tonalities, as well as hair-trigger timing, were crucial. And they naturally favoured attention to detail, showing a desire to retain improvisation even if the material in question was predominantly riff- or groove-based. Furthermore, Charles and Brown would engage directly with jazz, particularly soul jazz, rather than just admiring the music from afar. They recorded songs by Silver, Adderley and Morgan.

All of that experience was fundamental to their own innovations, and certainly on a piece such as Charles's 1961 hit 'What'd I Say' one can hear a meshing of many different forms. Gospel may fire his screams but there is a clear soul-jazz flavour in the rhythmic foundation, while the rolling piano figure is heavily Cuban-slanted. So essentially the song straddles borders: it is really Latin jazz R&B.

Grabbing equal attention in the piece is the percussive drive of the drummer's ride cymbal, which occasionally superimposes 6/8 or 12/8 metres on the underlying 4/4 and acts as a reminder that some of the swing-based R&B of the mid-1950s and early '60s acquired an African-Caribbean feel because of these bustling polyrhythms.

Were one looking for a visual symbol of the continuum, the strong complicity between soul and jazz, then nothing would be more powerful than the sight of Charles hugging an alto saxophone or of Brown hunched over an electric organ, both taking up a stance as players, not singers.

Considerable swathes of the history of black popular music, certainly throughout the late 1960s and early '70s, grow from this premise: the co-existence and alternation of the vocalist and soloist in one being, the very real possibility that a great songwriter or groove merchant could also front a band with a large, well-drilled horn section playing arrangements that were not stripped of intricacy.

Singing and instrumental solos were thus integrated into the same piece. On a seven-inch single format, where Part 1 was assigned to the A side and Part 2 to the B side, musicians often had the chance to 'stretch out' either before or after the vocal erupted. One might note here that the full-length version of 'What'd I Say' features Charles soloing heatedly on electric piano for no fewer than seventy-two bars before he lets the mike catch his first breath.

Mind games

Arguably the clearest outgrowth of that moment is Stevie Wonder's 'Fingertips', the 1963 Afro-Cuban cooker (all parts 1 and 2 of it) in which the precocious '12 year-old genius'[2] proved he could play the harmonica with as much grit as Little Walter in the 1950s. Wonder's subsequent ascension to an artistic colossus who made grand concept albums, and whose songs involved harmonic and structural flourishes of great ambition, was made all the more impressive by the fact that sometimes his brilliance was so smartly condensed and concentrated.

Many a Wondrous song presents a sumptuous banquet of art in the introduction before it nourishes pop ears by way of a killer chorus.

Hence the four-bar prelude of 'Too High' has twenty-two delicately wafting notes, set in a hypnotic downward spiral, that any jazz musician would be proud to have composed. And the eight-bar overture of 'Sir Duke' has fifty-seven aggressively dancing notes, set in dizzying upward flights, that any other jazz musician would be proud to have improvised.

That progressive soloists such as Herbie Hancock, Roy Ayers and Lonnie Liston Smith drew from Wonder as well as from James Brown and Sly & the Family Stone, reflected a cross-pollination in black music that saw soul and jazz intermingle on some kind of loose centre-ground, where the former enriched its harmony through the latter and the latter its rhythm and sonic scope through the former.

Apart from Wonder, the likes of Marvin Gaye, Gil Scott-Heron, Don Blackman, Leroy Hutson and Donny Hathaway also possessed strong jazz sensibilities. These singer-songwriters often produced material with a certain harmonic and orchestral sophistication, betraying a desire to embellish melody. They were advocates for advanced arrangements.

Several 1970s soul bands had similar values. As well as rhythm sections, many of these groups had horn sections that presented opportunities to bring rich, rainbow-like timbres to their compositions.

Keen as they were to write catchy songs, these acts were not willing to compromise on the rococo flourishes in their performance.

Certainly Earth, Wind & Fire evinced a desire to make elaborate, expressive music that might reflect something of the extensive, highly diverse formative experiences of drummer/vocalist Maurice White, the group's founder. As a teenager, White played with R&B organ combo Booker T. & The MGs and with rock and roll hero Chuck Berry before joining jazz pianist Ramsey Lewis's group and working with many other improvising musicians based in Chicago during the mid-1960s.

Adept as they were at writing great melodies, Earth, Wind & Fire, who enjoyed a lengthy run of hits between the mid-1970s and the early '80s with classic albums like *That's The Way Of The World* and *All 'N All*, did not limit themselves musically. So the latter album featured pieces such as 'Runnin'' and 'Magic Mind', both of which were overtly danceable tunes set in shifting, undulating structures. Availing themselves of sometimes as many as four horns, in addition to a rhythm section in which Afro-Latin percussion was prominent, Earth, Wind & Fire had a full, dense, very layered ensemble voice into which White often wove unconventional chords that reflected his formative years. 'There were a lot of jazz gigs before we did our soul thing, and that gave us a base, you know, a strong foundation' he told me in 2004. 'That's why some of the tunes just came out the way they did.'[3]

'Magic Mind' is a piece that absolutely does not deny White's training, education and culture. It covers the various poles of his immense experience as a player by way of an arrangement that changes rhythmic identity, tempo and levels of harmonic intricacy with all the skill of a film director mapping out a series of related yet distinctly different scenes that tell a bigger story.

Here's a rough synopsis. Scene A: two bars of blues guitar licks + two-bar bebop mini-fanfare. Scene B: twenty-four bars of high-tempo funk (verse and chorus). Scene C: eight bars of high-tempo funk (verse). Scene D: two-bar bebop mini-fanfare. Scene E: twelve bars of high-tempo funk. Scene F: ten bars of mid-tempo swing *à la* big band. Scene G: thirty-two bars of high-tempo funk (verse and chorus and double-time horns). Scene H: unaccompanied eight-bar bebop fanfare as false ending. Scene I: fourteen-bar funk vamp as real ending. Scene J: final eight bars of this section have overdubbed bass solo that fades to black. All the while, as the brass, reeds and rhythm section slash away with quasi-gladiatorial energy, doo-wop falsetto vocals soar like a choir announcing a titanic clash in the fantasy arena evoked by the highly theatrical nature of the piece.

Devastatingly funky as it is, and 'Magic Mind' can tear the roof off any house party, the song could not have been written without a grasp of bebop, simply because the horns are too intricate and the whole structure too interlude-heavy. Moreover, the use of relatively unconventional ten-bar counts reflects a jazzer's desire to break with four-, eight- and twelve-measure orthodoxy.

Clearly there is a composer, in the sense of sound as novel, interacting with a songwriter, in the sense of sound as short story, in the conceptual space circumscribed by Maurice White and the other members of Earth, Wind & Fire.

'Magic Mind' is one example of the two elements in union – dare one say, a balanced form of 'fusion.'

Soul-funk of this kind, prevalent at the beginning of the 1970s, was bound to have a certain jazz resonance because many of its exponents were either singers who deployed orchestras of highly skilled musicians or eight- to ten-piece bands with the technical resources – namely, brass, reeds and rhythm sections – that maintained a link to the evolutionary staging posts of James Brown, Ray Charles, Count Basie, Louis Jordan and Lee Morgan. Some of these classic funk groups could actually be termed *small big bands*.

They did not play swing as Basie had in the 1930s, but these '70s soul-funk groups nonetheless provided an echo, a distillation of that vocabulary, particularly in their deployment of saxophones and trumpets, which often played phrases with the fast, zippy, darting character of arrangements used by the Count and the Duke.

Led by ensembles like War, Mandrill, Pleasure and Kool & the Gang, many soul groups with singers recorded at least one or two instrumental funk tracks per album, giving a pianist or sax player the chance to blow. This reflected the depth of jazz culture in black pop. Players still studied John Coltrane. Kool dedicated a solemn song to him and reprised a piece by one his disciples, Charles Lloyd.

Jazz musicians, particularly horn players, also performed on many sessions with both soul groups and singers. The pay cheque was very welcome for artists whose audiences and record sales had been shrinking since rock music became big business in the mid-1960s.

Playing soul for the sake of financial security did not mean that musicians approached the task in a perfunctory fashion, and in some cases the experience had a major emotional and cultural resonance since the musicians had actually played blues or R&B before 'graduating' to jazz. A few highly rated horn players also became members of soul outfits after they had held down jazz gigs. For example, saxophonist George Adams, once a Charles Mingus sideman, joined The Fatback Band (later known as Fatback).

Essentially, jazz can be viewed as the ultimate basic training for any musician: a tough, stringent and demanding induction because the music, with its focus on the outer limits of harmony or the exploration of rarely used metric pathways, is notoriously difficult to play. All this means that if a musician can succeed in mastering a basic standards book, then the less chordally advanced content prevalent in soul and funk becomes easier to negotiate, even though this form of pop has specific conceptual demands that not every improviser can fulfil. Not every jazz musician plays soulful, bluesy or funky – in some cases because the musician regards these forms as inferior or can't hear the valid idiosyncrasies they have acquired.

Whether or not equal in standing, these genres were never entirely separate in purely structural terms. Any musician of a mind to investigate fully the history of a few talismanic pieces of soul will learn that some of their tastiest constituents – the physically charged pulsations of the bass, the curling pentatonic guitar and keyboard lines, the stabbing horn fanfares – can be traced back to the journeys hitherto undertaken by improvisers. A key example of this continuum is the way in which a fragment – dare one say a hook – from the horn score of Miles Davis's 'So What' was recast smartly as the prime sax riff that greatly bolstered James Brown's 'Cold Sweat'.

Jazz has tantalising relationships with time, space, and size, weight and density of information; pop less so. These variables are in fact largely invariables. A decision such as writing a tune over three minutes, allocating pride of place to instrumental rather than vocal parts, and overloading the verse-chorus backbone with too much creative data, can become a major source of contention.

So much pop is about editing. So much jazz is about extending information or at least concentrating a large amount of it in a small space. Hence the jazz artist's resolution to take liberties with time, and to let a track's life cycle unfold over anything from 2–10 minutes to an hour, is part of an essentially liberating dynamic.

Significantly, soul and funk in the 1970s broke out of the same straitjacket of time constraints as jazz did in the '50s and '60s. Songs stretched to longer than five minutes and many albums had only three tracks per side. A piece could thus have a prelude, interlude and coda. Where R&B was tunes, soul became compositions, or more intricately composed tunes. Many soul albums included 'reprises' in which the musicians waxed two takes of the same song, loosely reconnecting with a jazz aesthetic that had already set great store by revisiting, re-appraising and reinterpreting a previously made statement. The trend also broadly presaged hip hop, in so far as the reprise was a less technology-driven form of the modern remix.

Since that time, soul and jazz have generally moved further apart due to greater music-industry partitioning and the dissolution of an essential form of glue between them: the small big band, with horns that could impart elements drawn from the swing and bebop vocabularies. It must be noted, though, that the likes of Quincy Jones, the monumental jazz producer-arranger-thinker whose history reaches right back to Count Basie and Ray Charles, exerted a sizeable influence on mainstream pop culture throughout the 1980s. Jones's input can be found in the work of anyone from The Brothers Johnson to Michael Jackson. All of this meant there was a torchbearer, a man who embodied a great welter of jazz history, applying his verve to commercially very successful black music.

Furthermore, it could be argued that the very reason why soul hit such a creative peak in the 1970s was because it retained a strong connection to jazz, all the while embracing funk, rock, Latin music and an array of electronics. Certainly when one listens to all those fancy chords that Willie Mitchell slipped under Al Green's voice, or to the complex arrangements of Quincy Jones or Stevie Wonder, the jazz sensibility is strong. In the right hands, the art strand of black music embellishes the pop strand without reducing its communicative nature or tipping it into opacity. History says that soul might well have become poorer had it departed too much from jazz.

Both genres have grown from the common seedbed of the blues, and although soul is more readily concerned with melody, or at least catchy hooks, an integral part of its canon is music that has a fair amount of complexity 'under' or around the main theme, as exemplified by Wonder's songs, many of which are by no means easy to play.

This musicianship also flows from soul's roots in R&B that had been partially shaped by big-band music. The defining features of that music are the arrangements and the intelligent use of rhythm and horn sections, two elements that afford considerable creative possibilities. Seventies soul, whether presented as a three- or a ten-minute piece, was often big-band orchestral music, certainly when strings were added, and handling all these sections required skills and imagination. That is why the magical art of *arranging* endured in soul, and why many of its arrangers had a grasp of jazz rudiments, as can be heard in the structural finesse of the 'blaxploitation' soundtracks that were recorded by Marvin Gaye, James Brown and Earth, Wind & Fire.

Watch and learn

Few figures in soul can equal the brilliance at musical construction of a Jones or Wonder. But the fact remains that these artists have been an enormous influence on some three generations of singers. And if the incumbents really do their homework and earnestly study their deep artistic provenance, they may create something of an echo of Charles and Ellington in one or two post-Stevie creations.

Musicians need to know who has influenced their influences if they are to understand, absorb and hopefully transcend those influences.

Even though there was a less explicit trace of Sir Duke's ornate tapestries, jazz still permeated black pop in the 1980s. In some of the decade's electronics-based funk that might be dismissed by some as simply post-disco or dance music, there are often very intricate rhythm patterns and occasional lava-flow solos that say much about the musicians' determination not to rein in their expressive capacities. There is also training to consider. One is startled by the venomous keyboard flurry that graces D-Train's 'You're The One For Me'. And then one checks the CV of the man behind it, Hubert Eaves, and learns that he played jazz with a handful of Miles Davis's key band members in the previous decade, chief among them the exceedingly gifted guitarist-arranger Reggie Lucas.

This is not an isolated case. Because of the divisions that opened up between soul and jazz in the music industry, and the fact that these genres were marketed to different audiences, it is perhaps hard to imagine an exponent of soul having once had a close connection with jazz. But that was true of several artists, some of whom enjoyed major success.

Perhaps the most striking example is Randy Crawford. She came to epitomise an easy-on-the-ear, radio-friendly brand of soul in the 1980s, taking the charts by storm with singles like 'You Might Need Somebody' and 'One Day I'll Fly Away'. Yet there was artistry in these radio-friendly numbers and it relates to Crawford's background.

The guest vocals she provided for jazz-fusion ensemble The Crusaders on their big-selling single 'Street Life' in 1979 showed that Crawford could use her beautifully limpid voice with enormous precision. But she had already worked with improvising musicians before that.

In 1975 Crawford appeared on the legendary alto saxophonist Cannonball Adderley's ambitious oratorio *Big Man*. Cynics might argue that the journey from *Big Man* to 'One Day I'll Fly Away' represents Crawford's move towards less challenging circumstances, a desire to forsake struggle on the fringes for the comfort of a less creative mainstream: selling out, in other words.

That's too harsh a judgment. Crawford's later music had integrity, not to mention a flickering soulfulness, and it served as a reminder that soul music is indeed a form of popular music, in which melody and tightly focused, smartly constructed arrangements are at a premium.

And improvisation may be a key element of jazz, but it is not the only principle jazz practitioners hold dear. Melody and tightly focused, smartly constructed arrangements also have their place in this music. The big question facing any jazz musician is how all these different impulses will be negotiated within the musician's own aesthetic.

All this means that an open-minded and sharp-eared jazz musician might well view soul not as an inferior, lesser genre but as an idiom in which creativity can be expressed, and whereby a truly daring artist might subvert as well as uphold formal convention.

Soul is essentially songs but songform can be stretched.

Hence we come to 'Cannonball' Adderley's old boss, Miles Davis, who ascribed star status to one of the icons of 1980s soul and pop. Prince, according to the trumpeter, was a new Duke Ellington and that in itself is a significant indication of how art and populism might cohere beyond expectations. It is a reminder that Davis, one of the ultimate jazz artists, could write riffs as well as symphonies and that Prince, one of the ultimate pop artists, was capable of disguising a symphony as a series of riffs, as was the case with Parliament and Funkadelic. Moreover, as a conjure man with a mojo that worked, Prince would sell the whole thing as hot sex on a platter.

Which is why 'Alphabet Street' has to last longer than three minutes. Why it has to cajole us with a beautiful melody and then kill it. Why it has to combust into a mini-riot of sound that would warrant terms such as 'avant-garde' were the artist not so, erm, big. Why it has to include several key changes. Why it has to play with dynamics. Why it has to dangle the promise of its impish loverman starring in his own XXX flick, only to concede limply: 'Tonight ... I would like to ... *watch*'.

Nobody sees that lick coming. The whole song is nothing other than great modern art music mischievously masquerading as pop. And nothing could be more jazz in a way, because encoded in those five minutes of methodical madness is the 'thought of surprise' as well as 'the sound of surprise'. As with Earth, Wind & Fire's 'Magic Mind', the relationship between song and arrangement is being questioned and toyed with.

'Alphabet Street' is a landmark piece of work because it draws together lyrical as well as musical strands of black-music history.

Often, and rightly so, it is asserted that Prince owes a debt of gratitude to Little Richard for his otherworldly flamboyance. But his lyrical ingenuity, wordplay and lateral thinking also flow from a wellspring even more deeply rooted in black-music history, one that would include the likes of Cab Calloway, Dizzy Gillespie or Louis Jordan. Jordan's innuendo and metaphorical take on carnal relations were part of a blues vernacular that was not alien to jazz. His talk of enjoying 'plenty of meat in his stew'[4] simmered with a sexiness that presaged Prince's deviant delectations.

First and foremost an instrumental music, jazz is often assessed according to the deft technique of its pianists or horn players – fair enough, given their colossal feats over the years. Yet wily writers of words and linguistic acrobats are also a part of the wider jazz aesthetic that is common to soul and funk. So beyond any musical connections, *characters* like Prince and Louis Jordan should be seen in the same light as Dizzy Gillespie and George Clinton, because of their ability to wring dynamic new images and neologisms from the English language. Dizzy uncorks be-bop, George breaks out P-funk. One coughs up 'Ool ya koo', the other shouts out 'Yippie yo yippie yeh'.[5] One draws a wry smile with 'Salt peanuts, salt peanuts!', the other tickles a fresh fancy with 'Do fries go with that shake?'[6]

Make your brown eyes green?

To a large extent, the soul–jazz continuum actually operates on a number of different levels. On the one hand, there are soul musicians who specifically look to stretch the structural base of what they do through advanced harmony and improvisation, perhaps calling on input from jazz musicians to achieve that goal. On the other hand, there are jazz musicians – and they may belong to the avant-garde, bebop or fusion schools – whose work, in spite of its chordal or metric complexity, sometimes reflects a direct engagement with black pop, the music these artists may have played and danced to as callow youths before they moved on to the world of improvisation.

Even more interesting is the existence of several artists who will not or cannot stop the two forms from interacting. This is because they have a firm grip on the deep-rooted history of black music, in which the relationship between soul and jazz was present in the first place. So just playing the blues is very much a springboard for music that may have marked funk ramifications as well as soul and jazz possibilities.

Artists who understand this can be very different in character. It is not just the prerogative of socially conscious warriors and mavericks like Wonder or Prince. It also applies to players who are interested in challenging themselves and audiences by pushing expressivity to its limits, as well as affecting those audiences emotionally.

Tempting as it may be to ascribe the first quality to jazz and the second to soul, this cerebral–emotional dichotomy would be a crude interpretation. There can be immense feeling in avant-garde music and great artistry in pop. It is perhaps a question of the way complexity and simplicity are calibrated within each idiom. A figure such as Marcus Miller, for example, has shown since the mid-1970s that he has a firm grasp on the history and vocabulary of jazz and soul, and an almost innate feeling for bridge-building between art and pop culture. As a virtuoso bass guitarist and songwriter, Miller's achievements are manifold. But nothing is more significant than his role producing a substantial body of work for Luther Vandross and Miles Davis. And although the former is soul and the latter jazz, the two are linked by the beauty of their aesthetics and the skill with which these aesthetics were deployed under Miller's stewardship.

All the above underlines, moreover, that exactly where one genre ends and the other begins is by no means crystal clear. Close inspection of Vandross's cultured, eye-of-the-needle phrasing on 1985's 'The Night I Fell In Love' flags up the jazz sensibility that Marvin Gaye drew from Nat 'King' Cole. And it is not unreasonable to call much of Davis's 1989 *chef d'oeuvre Tutu* sophisticated funk.[7] Since then several jazz artists have not shied away from recording soul material, and if an iconic figure such as Davis's ex-sideman Keith Jarrett reprises Randy Crawford's 'One Day I'll Fly Away', then few will take issue with his decision. Yet there can still be snobbery directed at one jazz musician by another if it is felt that he is playing too 'simple'.

That might mean using a backbeat. Or using vocals. Or playing a song with a joyous chorus. For an artist such as guitarist-singer George Benson, there is little doubt that his great success in the pop market has made it more difficult for him to return to jazz. Some of Benson's recent work has been underwhelming, to say the least. Yet his discography contains many soul songs – for example, the gorgeous 'Star Of The Story' from 1980 monster-seller *Give Me The Night* – shaped by a harmonic beauty that should not be dismissed because these songs managed to crash the charts.

Benson also chose his collaborators well. He never sounded better pitched between virtuosity and accessibility than when he was produced by the man who understood just how those two impulses might be harnessed to the optimal effect: Quincy Jones.

Such matters became largely inconsequential when hip hop emerged as the dominant black popular music in the late 1980s, because the idiom was less tied to the notion of musicianship or arrangements and more to a beguiling mixture of sonic and lyrical effervescence.

More often than not, that meant a substantial rhythmic propulsion both in the stream of the backing track and the river of rhymes. That explains why 'flow' is such a crucial leitmotiv in hip hop. But the magic of the idiom also lies in the way sounds or sound effects often jump dramatically out of the agitated confluence of words and music.

The band, an essential common denominator between soul and jazz in the 1960s and '70s, was thus redundant. With the player replaced by the producer and samples, there was no longer any call for 'chops'.

Knowing how to invert chords or how to improvise on them with a sax or trumpet became a less valued skill in a genre where key signatures and tempo changes were not the guiding principle.

If pop is largely about editing, then hip hop is extreme editing: boiling down and distilling recorded material to its very essence, to the two bars of a long organ or guitar lick that hits the listener hardest, and then ensuring the sense of body rock is not lost when the old riff is recast as a new beat. As for the text, the lengthy soliloquy of a rapper, almost a saxophone solo in vocal form, often peaks with a couplet that fires off a wickedly humorous put-down, passes wry comment on current events, or hammers home a bold sociological or political truth that transcends the confines of individuality.

For example, this line by Phife, of A Tribe Called Quest – 'I'm just a short brother, dark skin face/Weigh a buck fifty, 36 waist'[8] – is notable because the confessional impulse has a candour totally inconceivable for a 1980s soul star like Luther Vandross, who for most of his career struggled valiantly with the bathroom scales. Admitting as much to journalists he trusted was acceptable, but writing a song that acknowledged he had a less than gym-fit physique, and then *not* apologising for the fact – that was well nigh impossible.

Hip hop snared this sort of inhibition and funky-drummed it into exhibition.

Hip hop refused to apologise for things other than its body weight.

Hip hop took the minus of fatness and made it the plus of phatness.

Harmonically elaborate genres like soul, and certainly jazz, did not communicate with audiences with such brazen immediacy. And they offered nothing comparable in terms of lyrical richness or rhythmic aggression.

For any music to be embraced by listeners, it has to represent something emotionally. So if jazz was seeping out of black pop by the late 1980s, one should ask what it meant to the hip hop generation. Phife clarified not what the genre was but *how* it was perceived by himself and his peers on 1991's 'Jazz (We've Got)': 'I love jazz but that doesn't mean that I'm timid'.[9] It is a highly symbolic and meaningful statement. Jazz, regardless of the challenging playing of some of its exponents, had come to embody timidity or, dare one say it, politeness while hip hop was mostly about brashness, punkness, *roughneck rudeness*. So the genres were poles apart psychically. Paradoxically, though, they were also entwined because Quest and other hip hop acts were drawing heavily on jazz samples, mostly culled from the soulful 1960s and '70s Blue Note catalogue, just as British DJs were dusting off old James Brown tunes during the 'rare groove' revival that also fed into rap. Hence the sounds rather than the structures of soul and jazz could be found in hip hop. Although hip hop was harder than jazz, the former still recognised that the latter was a great resource. Jazz had many sounds that hip hop could usefully deploy or, rather, recondition and recontextualise.

For the most part, the late 1980s was a time of mesmerising flux in black pop, precisely because musical history became such a fluid, malleable entity and the traditional means of creating sounds, namely through instruments and bands, were suddenly called into question.

But black pop always had its non-conformists and conformists. And given the heady nature of a time in which African American youth could elect to say fuck the police and use the crackle and hiss of vinyl to replace a blues chord, it was perhaps inevitable that somebody, somewhere would say 'no go' to the dominant *modus operandi* and dare to use a blues chord in place of the crackle and hiss of vinyl. Or indeed use a blues chord *with* the crackle and hiss of vinyl.

On the one hand, British artists like Young Disciples, The Brand New Heavies and Omar did just that, bringing to life the kind of tasty riffs heard in samples and also displaying a degree of harmonic ambition through their horn arrangements, guitar and keyboard solos. On the other hand, American bassist-vocalist Me'Shell NdegéOcello was a revelation because she offered the brashness of hip hop, could play soul and funk, but was also interested in the detail of jazz.

Plantation Lullabies, her 1993 debut, proved to be one of the key releases of the decade, precisely because it brought improvisation and accomplished playing – by way of pianist Geri Allen, saxophonist Joshua Redman and drummer Gene Lake among others – to songs that flouted the jazz timidity evoked by Phife two years earlier.

The work was forthright, angry, groovy, horny, tender, danceable, political, too black and too strong. NdegéOcello asserted her right to be complicated, as more than one jazzer had done in the days when aspects of their lifestyle were worthy of parental advisory status.

NdegéOcello was both kicking with and against hip hop, embracing modernism and retroism in line with her interest in contemporary cultural norms and her allegiance to a deep-rooted tradition of playing in black music. In the three years or so that followed her debut, several other artists – Maxwell, Adrianna Evans, D'Angelo: the so-called 'neo soul' wave – would follow. And although all these artists engaged with hip hop to greater or lesser degrees, they made reference to a 1970s soul template whose finesse served as a clear

Vocalist Omar shows that soul got jazz (photo courtesy Jean Marmeisse).

reminder that their predecessors – Wonder, Earth, Wind & Fire and others – were highly jazz-informed.

The real value of a piece like D'Angelo's 'Brown Sugar', the singer's quite gorgeous 1995 breakout hit, was that, for all its low, thick drum sounds that hit the breakbeat generation square in the chest, it also had an airy, walking bass line that came from the era before speakers tested the chassis of a jeep. 'Brown Sugar' had swing.

What that also meant was that the piece operated in a broad historical context. It resonated with lovers of modern hip hoppers A Tribe Called Quest – not surprising given that their producer, Ali-Shaheed Muhammad, was the song's co-writer – and it appealed to fans of classic soul artists like Al Green or Stevie Wonder. 'Brown Sugar' skilfully brought traditions together.

An artist who went on to make that explicit was the brilliant New Orleans vocalist Ledisi. In the early millennium she recorded 'Sugar/Brown Sugar', a piece that cleverly segued saxophonist Stanley Turrentine's 'Sugar' into D'Angelo's 'Brown Sugar', thereby showing how relevant hip hop-edged soul was to jazz. It was a perfect fit. One piece, written in 1971, flowed into the other, penned in 1996.

That historical collage was not just a superficial bout of showboating. The reason it has value is because Ledisi continues to represent all the above strands of black music in her work. In real terms, this means that in concert Ledisi will follow a funk tune with an *a cappella* rendition of Thelonious Monk. She will do scat solos. She will improvise. She will take risks.

It's hugely important that younger audiences in particular see Ledisi.

What you hear at her gigs is the beauty of song, as in verse–chorus structures that are very well written, and then passages of improvisation, where the singer might urge her keyboard player to let rip. This reveals some of the complex harmony distilled in the songs. Different strands of black music thus make an organic whole.

Roughly speaking, this is the art-house and populist ends of the blues in conjunction. And if you were looking for the soul–jazz continuum in shorthand, it could be found in just such a concert. There is comfort and danger, or rather certainty and possibility: the idea that an artist might communicate with great immediacy, by way of melody or 'hooks', and then develop a piece or a whole performance so that it becomes more challenging. That might involve intricate arrangements and great musicianship.

You could also say that, in the case of an artist like Ledisi, there is a blend of the functional and the non-functional in the whole *raison d'être* of the music. What that means is that some songs, like 'Joy', are really for people who want to dance and romance, while others, like Thelonious Monk's 'Straight, No Chaser', are for those who want to listen hard. Then again, these models are not at all incompatible. There is plenty to listen to in 'Joy'. And Monk is not entirely un-danceable.

Exactly how soul and jazz interact in a post-hip hop as opposed to a pre-hip hop world continues to be an intriguing question. The advent of several improvisers – think Roy Hargrove, Chris Dave and Robert Glasper – who have built bridges between all these genres is exciting, as is the work of singers like the influential Erykah Badu.

Bursting onto the soul scene in 1997 with her debut *Baduizm*, the Texan vocalist declared herself part of hip hop culture, was raucously funky, and also had a clear jazz sensibility. That marked the highpoints of her 2000 album *Mama's Gun*, which stands as her finest to date.

Crucially, Badu had developed a strong working relationship with the aforesaid Hargrove, as well as with players straddling soul, funk and hip hop, such as keyboardist James Poyser, bassist Pino Palladino and drummer Ahmir ?uestlove Thompson.[10] She effectively drew an arc from sample-led songs to composed pieces in which the quality of these musicians was at a premium.

The album concluded with 'Green Eyes', a dramatic ten-minute jazz ballad whose course was mapped by a charming stride piano prelude, several changes of key and tempo. The piece is actually more of a suite than a song, certainly a radio-friendly number, and it remains one of Badu's best vocal performances.

Her phrasing and tone tantalisingly alternate between the tough and the tender, the plurality of her blues expression firmly intact, the historical references as much Chakha Khan as Billie Holiday.

5 The soul–funk continuum

From beginning to end, 365 days of the year
I want your same ole love.

(Anita Baker)

Drop your drawers.

(Lester Young)

There are ladies present

One of Billie Holiday's close collaborators, tenor saxophonist Lester Young, the jazz statesman dubbed Prez to her Lady Day, emerged from Count Basie's big band to become an innovator on his instrument in the 1940s.

There was a sonic complicity between Holiday and Young. Both suggested something liquid and vaporous in their phrasing, a swooning quality that imbued much of their work with great emotional richness, vividly reflecting the ebb and flow of human life, and especially the deep complexity of affairs of the heart.

Young the character was also fascinating, for his habit of attributing nicknames to his peers and for generally showing pithy, outlandish verve with language. Often he would twist vocabulary away from its habitual paths: legend has it that Young was one of the first 'cats' to call money 'bread'.

The tenor saxophonist's interest in colloquialisms provides a useful insight into what meanings exactly could be ascribed to a word like 'funky' – a term used in the African American community to denote strong odours, possibly from a lack of personal hygiene or from insufficient ventilation in a given space. Out-takes of the session Young recorded in 1952 with the Oscar Peterson Trio feature an exchange between Young and producer Norman Granz that is both funny and revealing.[1]

After a second false start of 'It Takes Two To Tango', a rare gem in Young's discography in that it features him singing, Granz, an engineer or some assistant in the control booth asks the saxophonist to get ready for another take, and to make his entrance after a 'little funky intro'. Instantly Young reprimands him, his dry tone almost that of a schoolmaster chiding a pupil for a particularly reckless infringement of decorum: 'There's some ladies out here. You said some funky introduction, there's ladies out here'.

Proceedings take a surreal turn, though. As soon as Young settles down and starts singing on the take, he proceeds to crank an X-rated lyrical handle, telling his paramour to 'drop your drawers' – cheekily and mischievously rather than commandingly or threateningly, it has to be said. Nonetheless, the whole dynamic of the piece is set by a carnal rather than a sentimental agenda. The irony is immense: for here is Young, after chastising his producer for mouthing the profanity 'funky', acting as arch skirt-chaser of funky mind and presumably funky body. That moment graphically illustrates an important element in the history of funk as a concept in African American mores, regardless of whether the term is applied to music or not: namely, that it conveys offence, a threat to polite society or respectable sensibilities. The semantic link between jazz and funk is that both were once bad words. Both were not good.

Psychologically and emotionally, the F word has a core feeling. On many occasions the adjective 'old' is conjoined with 'funk' to emphasise the descent into some kind of dysfunctional state, be the object in question a 'funky old piano' or a 'funky old grandpa'. The implication is that the less than tip-top working order or physical diminution imparts some peculiarity, an endearing, disorientating or disquieting sensation.

Young's reaction to the use of the F word reflects this understanding. His sensitivity to it may well have been wrought by admonitions he himself had received. It is possible Young knew that his predecessors had also transgressed, and none more so than early-twentieth-century jazz pianist Jelly Roll Morton, whose 'I Thought I Heard Buddy Bolden Say', referencing the music's mythical progenitor, was originally entitled 'Funky Butt'.

Epithets such as nasty, freaky, greasy or gritty are frequently offered to clarify what funk might mean, what the sensory impact of its notes might be. And the modulation of funk to *fonk*, thing to *thang* or nasty to *nastay* is not insignificant, as the change in orthography induces a theatrical expressivity full of sharp, mannish-boy ribaldry.

'Nastay' suggests that a musical note is ripe, rotund, fat and full. If it really flows from funk, then it has honesty, shamelessness and dirtiness. Nastay is a body unclothed, a gesture unplanned, a smell untreated.

Funk affects; negatively, perhaps. A funky old piano may well have suspect tuning. A funky riff may not be a sophisticated one. A funky riff may not even be the musically correct one. After attempting to nail a particularly difficult rhythm during a gig at Charlie Wright's bar in London in 2007, the gifted jazz bassist Victor Bailey said he didn't quite have the line down, that a few notes were out, but what he was doing was nonetheless 'still fonky, right?' Many heads bobbed in assent.

On Lester Young's 'It Takes Two To Tango', that vexed 'little funky intro' is a series of blues riffs played by the pianist Oscar Peterson. Essentially there is little attempt to stretch the harmony constructed on five chords, and the prelude is not excessively ornate. But the notes are trilled with sufficient force to create warmth, if not a sense of heat.

Blues, in terms of the player's touch, the attack, the emphasis on certain intervals, is the agent of funk here. This is totally in keeping with the hard bop and soul jazz sub-genres mentioned in the previous chapter, where the bluesiness of the playing is a fundamental characteristic of the music. Certainly in the case of a pianist like Horace Silver, who entitled a piece 'Opus De Funk' in 1953, the sense of heat that can be found in Peterson's work with Young often crackles into a raging fire, such is the intensity of Silver's playing.

Twelve-bar blues forms such as on the aforementioned piece had been used in both R&B and jazz for years previously, and throughout the 1950s many artists in both genres achieved a marked 'funkiness' not dissimilar to what is described above. Although marked by differences in harmonic complexity, both genres employed a swing pulse – Louis Jordan exemplified that perfectly as a kind of bridgehead between the two – and the steadiness of the walking bass, usually changing chords every few bars, gave pianists, horn players or singers clear signposts to accent a phrase so that, just as a skilled cook would tease the juice from a well-chewed bone, they could wring out the most bluesiness possible – which in turn could mean funkiness.

Gospel music, characterised by its crisp, tambourine-led backbeat and joyous, rousing melodies, also exerted a decisive influence on soul jazz, particularly on exponents like Bobby Timmons, who emerged – as Silver did – as a member of Art Blakey's Jazz Messengers, and penned several irresistibly catchy hits such as 'Moanin'' and 'Dat Dere'. The fact that many described these 'sanctified' Baptist-flavoured songs as 'funky' reflected the sacred–profane duality at the heart of black pop.

Charting the transition of the kind of upbeat blues that could be dubbed 'funky', in the sense of churchy or bluesy, into a music that could be heard as funk, in the sense of a distinct, new kind of funky, is by no means an exact science, given that many artists in black pop were experimenting fruitfully with rhythm at this point in the 1950s.

Generally speaking, it is fair to say that a reduction of swing in the pulse and a focus on a heavier backbeat, whereby more abrupt, sharp eighth notes were played on the snare and bass drum rather than the lighter, flowing triplets on the ride cymbal, facilitated this evolution.

Swing, though, is an imprecise, mysterious concept. Technically speaking, it describes a sensation of steadiness, emphasis and perceived incremental shift in the beat, a kind of lean or sway. And some funky drumming *does* have that quality. It's just that the slip-slide is on the drilling snare and kick rather than in the fluttering, ching-a-ling cymbals.

New bags and honky tonks

Suggestions, forewarnings, prototype elements of funk can be heard in a number of different contexts in the run-up to the 1960s. The electric Chicago blues of Sonny Boy Williamson, Willie Dixon and Muddy Waters, with its pronounced heavy guitar chords – not so much crashing down to earth as scraping right along the floor, such is their density and gravitational pull – was instructive in terms of the sound of the instruments, by dint of new amplification, gaining a thickness matching that of the voice. And maybe that was a major step forward: the heaviness, loudness and downward thrust of the music reinforcing the loudness and downward thrust of the singer.

Essential as the advent of electric blues was as an appetiser for funk, let's not forget that there were still a few big bands in operation. And the fact that one of the biggest names in black pop, Ray Charles, kept faith in an orchestra was important: it meant there was a source of volume distinct from the guitar – the power of horns. One thing about an orchestra with sections – say, five saxophones, four trombones and five trumpets – is that it is capable of generating enormous sonic bulk, the unison lines of reeds and brass injecting great adrenalin shots into the music.

Any singer who has experienced performing with a big band may raise their funkiness quotient through direct exposure to that kind of power. It is telling that superlative bluesy jazz singers, notably Joe Williams and Dinah Washington, had that very experience. It may also be worth mentioning that a formative period spent performing in a gospel choir also provides some kind of grounding in funk power, because of the sheer ecstatic thrill of that setting. Lyrically, nothing is further removed from the profanity of funk, but a church ensemble can match a big band for raw, uncut energy.

What does not pass as funky, what doesn't feel funky, is invariably music with some undercurrent of restraint or perhaps politeness, as in an R&B sub-genre such as doo-wop, which puts its emphasis on the smoothness of the vocal harmonising and the often measured, at times subdued, nature of the rhythm section. Contrast doo-wop with gospel and it really sounds as if the latter has a kind of urgency, a spontaneous energy taking it over, whereas the former is airy and mellow, happy to whisper sweet nothings rather than holler hallelujahs.

Unfunky music may provoke more internal than external reactions.

Gospel is about the spirit, but it also rouses the body and maybe that is an essence of funk: a pressing compulsion to do something, to *move* in some way. Clap your hands. Shake your thing. Shake your *thang*.

In any case, a range of models of 1950s black music – gospel choir, big band, electric blues, soul jazz – were all funky to varying degrees. What was needed to bring about a true crystallisation of funk was a figure who could draw all the strands together. As a singer who modelled his first bands largely on that of Ray Charles and who paid close attention to black music of all kinds, James Brown was ideally placed to fill this role.

Creating a new form in any art is not just about vision and some inkling of the unknown, unseen or unheard. It is about profound insight into what is known, seen and heard: namely, a research of history and precedents. One of Brown's most revealing declarations was that he 'dug' jazz pianists like Horace Silver because of their 'drive'.[2] They gave a foretaste of the dynamism he would develop.

Hence a range of funky vibrations surrounds Brown and other musicians in the mid-1960s who are living through a significant change in R&B. The music acquires a full electric rhythm section, with bass guitar and guitar, that alters its punch and bodyweight, enabling it to become what is known today as soul. A lot of Stax, Chess and Motown recordings from the period are funky without necessarily being funk. Or rather, they sound funkier than the acoustic strains of the R&B that preceded them. And in the stark, tough backbeat of the songs of Otis Redding and Muddy Waters, there is a febrile, physical quality that suggests the possibility of funk materialising as an idiom apart.

Many figures from New Orleans, Chicago, Memphis and Detroit were heading towards a similar goal of developing funk as an independent genre. So to contend that there was a single inventor of the music would be overly simplistic. Nevertheless, James Brown was the artist who managed to strike the most potent balance between a great percussive drive at the base of his rhythm section – something prevalent in New Orleans music – and the vehement, hefty thrust that characterised big-band jazz. The approach became a style of its own.

When funk materialises in Brown's aesthetic, it does so by moving gradually from the liquidity of swing to the solidity of a backbeat – the feted science of the 'One', which invested the first beat of the bar with all the authoritative drama of a judge's gavel. And the difference is clear in two pieces recorded in the same year, 1965: 'I Got You (I Feel Good)' and 'Papa's Got A Brand New Bag'.

The structure is similar in both cases: a barrage of short, interlocking riffs spread across horns, guitar, bass and drums. But in the second piece the accents are markedly more clipped and staccato, almost like tonal electric shocks, and the jolt and jerk of the rhythm section, bolstered by a louder, choppier bass drum, impart a hardness absent in the first cut. Liquid gives way to solid. The bottom end of the music is both weighty and mobile.

Minimalism of a kind is at play here. The attack of the horns is in fleet two- or four-chord motifs or an elongated trill at the verse endings. But the horns do not unwind into more verbose phrases, as would be the case in a well-arranged big band, so the notes pop off like champagne corks to create stuttering agitation and a network of colliding sounds with the virtue of being busy and energising without sounding overly elaborate.

Different degrees of funkiness can be discerned across the two tracks. 'Brand New Bag' is brawnier, edgier, whereas 'I Got You' has more of an airy, caressing quality, with the horns suspended in *deedle eedle eedle ee* figures that waft blithely around the central drums-bass axis. The whole piece has a notably more lithe, swaying feel that implies much less aggression and explosiveness.

Funk is essentially crystallising here from a confluence of different types of black music – swing jazz, R&B, gospel, blues – and it's clear on the basis of these songs that Brown wants to make the beat heavier than it was on his previous work through the band's snarling attack. He is crafting tightly focused rhythmic contrasts, teasing with the horns and then hammering with the bass and drums, which fling forward when they zero in on the 'one'. Which means it's great to shake a tail feather to. It's hard not to want to dance. The cut 'n' thrust motifs are shots in the arm.

Another source of inspiration in this respect may have been organist Bill Doggett's 1956 hits 'Honky Tonk' and 'Hold It',[3] precisely because they had a similar quality of short, synchromesh riffs skilfully woven so that, in the latter case, the tenor sax and guitar performed an effective, joyous call and response. The catchiness is devilishly hard to resist.

Under Brown's stewardship, funk evolved in earnest into a sub-genre that was distinct from, though obviously related to, the funky blues of Horace Silver *et al*. Brown's use of more repetition, syncopated drums and knotted, overlapping riffs brought a sustained, unifying thrust to the whole ensemble, so drums, bass, guitar and horns often played stabbing, spiral-like blues figures that pumped like expertly synchronised pistons in an advanced polyrhythmic engine. Instruments became more percussive and pummelling. Melody was not entirely discarded but it became less legato and floating and more presto and speech-like. Rhythm reigned.

'Brand New Bag' is about a rebirth of the beat, a reboot of the groove.

And yet for all the ownership of funk Brown can claim, sure of his status as a father figure of the genre, he does not escape the blues: politically; ideologically; musically. That is to say, the piece that should be his funkiest, the meaningfully titled 'Just Plain Funk', is actually a blues – a rhythmically twisted one, in which the horns slip-slide around the beat quite anarchically, as if they thought they were mannish enough to go head to head with Muddy Waters and his mojo. This is the blues as a protean force – an ages-old energy that brings forth a brand new bag.

Your funky ass will lead

By the late 1960s, R&B had become soul, and funk a distinct strand of soul. Every soul artist, and certainly the ones cognisant of the genre's blues and jazz foundations, had the potential to be funky. So the overarching theme of black popular music in the '70s is the alternation and blending of soul and funk, the birth of soulful funk and funky soul.

Hence there were distinct poles, contrasts in the emotional-physical connotations of each idiom. Soul was the soft centre to the hardcore of funk; one was romantic sigh while the other was orgasmic yelp, the sense of sound and feeling bursting forth, as Prince explained concisely on 'Pop Life': 'Life it ain't 2 funky unless it's got that pop … dig it?'

Many of the artists who reached iconic status, be they James Brown, Stevie Wonder or Aretha Franklin, entwined these idioms or shuttled between them.

There is no better demonstration of this than Franklin's ability to produce a song as wistfully soulful as 'Day Dreaming' and one as desperately, raggedly funky as 'Rock Steady'.

If, as seems largely to hold true, soul is love and funk is sex, then rhythm & blues, as mother of both, will become more interesting in any context where romance and carnal relations engage in a *corps à corps*. We're talking the impact of body and mojo on heart and mind.

This is one of the great triumphs of Parliament and Funkadelic, the two groups with overlapping personnel that would produce works of astounding invention throughout the 1970s. There is an enormous, at times overwhelming, lust – if not downright horniness – expressed in the bulk of the recordings these groups have made since their genesis in the late '60s. Yet the lust is woven into a rich fabric of political thinking, outré comedy, alternative belief systems, self-made mythology, extreme invention in both language and visual art, and the kind of tenderness with which a newborn is cradled. As a song like 'Into You' makes crystal clear, George Clinton has both a penchant and an aptitude for a love song, a whisper-and-sigh romanticism delivered with sufficient conviction to remind us that his first artistic incarnation in a barbershop vocal harmony group is not just an anodyne CV entry.

Like James Brown, New Jersey-born Clinton, the overlord of the two ensembles, came from R&B. Clinton formed his doo-wop ensemble, The Parliaments, in 1956, moving to Detroit and signing to Motown without actually releasing any material. These origins are not insignificant, as they meant Clinton's formative culture was set in vocal harmonising as a means of creating dynamics in music. And that experience has never left him; it's just that it has bathed in an ocean of novel sounds.

The influence on Clinton of innovators from rock, funk and jazz – namely, Jimi Hendrix, James Brown and Sun Ra – was clear enough, but another essential component of his musical vocabulary was gospel, in all its joyous richness. Clinton's vocals were always highly layered and choral. He recast The Parliaments as Parliament in 1970 and also formed Funkadelic from a growing aggregation of players. Throughout the decade, these two units produced not so much music as musical theatre, in which high-camp characters, otherworldly settings and oddball plots were *de rigueur*. Humour, humanity, sexuality and scatology abounded.

Clinton's unique qualities are aptly summarised by one of the most provocative, epigrammatic statements in modern pop, Funkadelic's *Free Your Mind And Your Ass Will Follow*.[4] It is basically a remix of a manifesto for well-being that is so old, nobody really knows who envisioned it first: the synergy of a healthy body and a healthy mind, the alliance of liberty of thought and lack of shame of the self, right down to the funky butt. This is a foundation of the blues, yet the verve with which the formula is reconfigured, the daring focus on matters psychic and sexual, gives the idea a whole new lease of life. The conjunction of 'mind' and 'ass' reprises and extends the mischievous sexuality encoded in Lester Young's referral to the F word in 1952.

Musically, the album *Free Your Mind* is also a striking example of the interplay and the push and pull of soul and funk as sub-genres that are fluid enough to flow in and out of each other. They are like shades on a canvas, revealing along the way a common future – what might happen when a simple structural decision is taken, namely, to replace horns with guitars – and a common past – what the result might be if instruments are absent, as in a church. Things start as rock and end as gospel.

From *Free Your Mind*'s opening title track to the closing piece, 'Eulogy And Light', there is a relentless shifting and shuffling of rhythmic and textural emphasis, from starkly grounded backbeats to floating tempos, the pulse gaseous and hazy, as cloudy as Young's voice and tenor saxophone. Before that final piece, which is nothing more than the band camping up a preacher's sermon amid a barren sonic landscape in which drums, bass, keys and guitar have been vanquished by voices running backwards, ecstatic bits of a church service in mind-scrambling flashback, Funkadelic do a wholly significant thing: they play a blues.

Right in the middle of a maelstrom of sonic experimentation, a tapestry of noise in which voices and electro-chorales clash with tubular bells humming in hyperactivity, the group lays down a straight-up honky-tonk guitar riff on 'Some More' while a church organ smoulders away in the background. What is important here is that 'Some More' stands directly on the shoulders of James Brown's 'Just Plain Funk', both musically and politically. So the roots of funk in blues, the underpinning of the former by the latter, the debt of the child to the mother, are writ large for whomever dares to dance, be they free of psyche and at one with their posterior.

How the blues might be covered, embellished or subverted, not so much by new genres such as soul or funk as by new sounds, has been one of the great puzzles in the ingenious evolution of black pop over the last four decades. To a certain extent one could say that the formula of the blues – its chords, its vivid emotional narrative by way of movement between pitches – is so strong that it doesn't need reinvention so much as an exponent with a distinct life experience or perhaps a novel sonic context: new tones from new instruments or a previously unheard backdrop of sound that could make the thirds, fifths and sevenths on the piano, bass or guitar affect us somewhat differently.

Clinton's marriages of the musical and the extra-musical do just that. They are extra-musical in so far as the lava flow of electronics and cartoon voices that suggest cinema, supernature and outer space is not always strictly conceived in a key or meter but enriches the core timbres of the rhythm section and strengthens its property of escapism. Funk thus transcends the physicality of a beat to become a sonic fantasia.

Sly & The Family Stone did similar things between the late 1960s and mid-'70s. Their body of work, the highlight of which is *There's A Riot Goin' On*, features miniature squalls of sound, fleeting splurges of quite ghostly reverberations that come in and out of the songs at various junctures. Sometimes the impression is of the static or hiss you might hear when turning the dial to tune in the radio. In Sly & The Family Stone there is humour and danger in more or less equal measure.

As with Clinton, Stone was a producer as well as a musician. The whole point about the great beauty of the timbres he fashioned with his group is that they were expertly arranged around the central backbone of the blues harmony in which, by and large, Stone kept steadfast faith. Some of the songs – a case in point being 1967's 'Trip To Your Heart' – skilfully brought extra-musicality into collision with this musicality, so that six bars of what sounded like elephant shrieks were somehow so perfectly lodged within the overall song structure that they appeared coherent, compatible with the prevailing funkiness.

To a certain extent Stone the songwriter, the man who in his formative days penned doo-wop hits like Bobby Freeman's 'The Swim' and who also reprised the odd Otis Redding and Herbie Hancock tune, was battling Stone the sonic buccaneer. That is why the music not only took remarkable twists and turns but stayed tightly focused. Tellingly, the bulk of Stone tracks are just over three minutes long but they often feel longer, the goal being to squeeze maximum detail into minimal space.

Understanding why Stone's take on the blues was idiosyncratic means appreciating his ability for lateral thinking, which is a prerequisite for any originality. When he worked as a DJ for San Francisco's Radio KSOL, Stone often did on-air commercials, the norm being to sell the merchandise with a heartily delivered, snappy and, above all, funky rhyme.

One day a new product came in, a laxative called Ex-Lax. Instead of voicing a proclamation for emancipation from constipation, Stone decided *not* to get busy on the studio microphone and instead took the unprecedented step of filling the airwaves with nothing but sound-effects –namely, the discomforting cascade of a flushing toilet. What counts here is funkiness of the mind, the intent, the vision. As with Lester Young's audacious demand that a lady 'drop her drawers', Stone's thinking betrays a cheeky juvenility, a freshness and zaniness that relates to and underpins funk's playful deviation from decorum.

Funk may just be a collision of sexuality and parody, love-making and joke-making, the recognition that physical union is both life-enhancing and rib-tickling in its potential for dysfunction – there being as many, if not more, things that can go wrong as they can go right when the up for the down stroke is positioned as primo black erotica. That may be why sometimes a small man, a 'horny pony' at that, one who imagines himself as a 'Big Dipper', is wont to declare to she who sizzles in the greatest of expectation: 'Tonight … I would like to … watch'.[5]

Baker Street

Between them, Brown, Clinton and Stone – and all they influenced – took soul-funk to very high levels of creativity in the first half of the 1970s. By the middle of the decade, though, a new sub-genre known as disco had brought a decidedly new flavour to black popular music. For the most part it had higher tempos, a generally smoother tonal canvas and a hissing sensation in the pulse of the rhythm section, created through the use of insistent, highly metronomic eighth notes on an open hi-hat.

Disco would eventually become synonymous with both hedonism and a commercial, largely formulaic dance music, characterised by inane lyrics and arrangements lacking in guile or imagination – an accusation that could justifiably be levelled at studio projects in which producer, session musicians and a makeweight singer ploughed through material with no semblance of the essential chemistry found in a real band.

However, condemning the genre wholesale is dangerous. Disco was a vague term for many kinds of rhythmic and structural approach, chief among them a distinctly African-Caribbean pulse that drew on calypso. Another approach leaned heavily towards gospel. Both of these specificities yielded music that, in the case of releases on the TSOP or Salsoul labels, reached a fever-pitch intensity by no means far removed from the work of James Brown.

Soulful and funky disco, exemplified most effectively by a group such as Chic, did not sever its links to the Godfather's aesthetic at all, but rather brought a wide range of textures into play. It is perhaps fair to say that this new music gained a touch more gloss in its production, all the while (as in the aforementioned case) holding on to some grit rhythmically.

By the beginning of the 1980s, disco had more or less run its course and the sound of soul was changing markedly. Horns and strings were less widespread and the prevalence of synthesizers and drum machines made some funk harder and some stiffer, the experimentation with new keyboards creating a whole range of sonic extremes that rendered the genre both postmodern and highly relevant to electronic music.

Generally speaking, the big names of the decade – namely, Luther Vandross and Anita Baker – are held up as examples of the moment when soul became slick if not overly varnished. But for all their delicacy and effete romanticism, these artists didn't entirely relinquish a blues-funk dynamic, not least because Vandross had the extraordinary bass guitar of Marcus Miller as his rhythmic backbone.

As for Baker, jazz was a key component of her aesthetic. The subtlety of her phrasing and harmonic finesse suggested an affinity for the likes of Phyllis Hyman and Johnny Hartman, particularly on Baker's debut, *The Songstress*. But there was a forcefulness and edginess in her voice, a hint of defiance in the darker depths of her tone, that was daringly masculine at times and contrasted sharply with the wispier flutter in her mid- and high range. Baker would deploy all these hues, so that her soulfulness acquired a sharp, often saturnine twist of funk.

Moderate shifts in arrangements would echo and heighten this effect. An obvious example is the quite beautiful song 'Same Ole Love', from Baker's monster-seller *Rapture*,[6] a key entry in the canon of 1980s soul. The piece is essentially a mid-tempo ballad, a meditation steeped in nostalgia and long-ing, in which the rhythm section plays a static beat on the verses, allowing keyboard colours to drift into the lead voice and swirl languorously around 'flashbacks of the times we've had'.

Then the chorus kicks in and all the soul in the verse instantly bulks up into funk, teaching us that the idiom is not just about hardness but *hardening* of sound, the flexing of rhythmic muscle. The change is bold, direct and potent. Musically, the means by which it is engineered are relatively simple. The snare drum is thickened by a crisp hand clap on the downbeat and the bass guitar-ist slaps rather than fingers the strings, so that more tension instantly snakes through the notes, as if the whole rhythm were a large fist clenching up with intent to do damage.

These shifts in the physical-emotional contours of the piece are expertly handled. The band lays heavier on the beat in the chorus, increasing its weight and impact, but without essentially derailing the delicate carriage of the song. Thus a funkiness comes into soul, shakes it up, beefs it up and builds it up, before seamlessly gliding back down to the more poised decorum that defined the preceding verse.

Sitting in artful balance with this sudden surge is Baker's voice. She conveys more urgency, declaring: 'From beginning to end, 365 days of the year, I want your same ole love'. What is interesting is that the abandon and plenitude of this statement is cogently rendered by Baker's delivery without recourse to histrionics. And yet there is absolutely no less funkiness as a result, the want and the desire for Baker's fêted paramour crystallising with as much convic-tion as when others talk of funk as something that they need and absolutely must have. As far removed as 'Same Ole Love' is from the sound of James Brown, Parliament-Funkadelic and Sly Stone, it is nonetheless a very impor-tant kin – a somewhat distant cousin, perhaps, but a member of the extended family and one not to be disinherited rashly.

To understand fully the soul–funk continuum as a function of the richness and flexibility of the blues, then it is crucial that performances such as this, with their more muted inflections, are included in the same analysis as the wilder, more raucous outpourings. Otherwise we are basically reducing these idioms to quite crude stereotypes.

Tempting as it is to cast funk exclusively in the role of the rugged and rough rider of black pop, the idiom has sufficient depth to be able to accom-modate a refined, if not smooth, signature without becoming anodyne or sedate. Baker may not threaten but she doesn't bore.

Images are an issue here. Baker does not conform to an overriding archetype of funk: the more profane and licentious being who is liable to express 'nastiness' as opposed to goodness. For the most part, Baker could justifiably be equated with the latter, such is the poise, elegance and quintessential dignity of her music and appearance.

One imagines funk in hot pants and thigh-length boots – and we're talking about the unfair as well as the fair sex in this instance – rather than evening gowns, a diamanté brooch or a tuxedo, accoutrements overwhelmingly perceived as belonging to cabaret. Yet even clothed in such 'safe' attire, there is something dangerously hot about the voice of Gladys Knight, especially when she is body-slamming the songs of Sly Stone[7] or Teddy Pendergrass, that gives them the funk in spades. Baker actually has that too, albeit with a vast spectrum of subtleties.

Look at her emotional substance too. Or, more to the point, feel it. Desire is a major component of *Rapture*. A demand like 'From beginning to end, 365 days of the year, I want your same ole love' does not stem from someone holding back pressing emotional or physical yearnings. She calls it her same *ole* love, recognising the charm of imperfection, which is also what a roadhouse musician does when he speaks of his funky *ole* pianna.

Baker's song is not the 'sex machine' *à la* Brown but sex processed by *another* machine, or at least freighted by a different vessel. All of this means that a soul artist does not necessarily have to look, talk or act funky as defined by another. They can be funky in their own way.

Our understanding of what is funky should not be restricted by the prevalent iconography of what passes for funky. The world counts legions of Sly sycophants and Clinton clones who have both the glide in their stride and the dip in their hip but amount to nowt but true fakery, simply because they are not honest enough to admit they can't live without their same ole love for anything less than a calendar year.

Muddy melons

Funky she may have fleetingly been, but Anita Baker did not carry the funk into the 1990s and beyond. Nor did James Brown. Nor George Clinton, for that matter. For the most part soul didn't. But hip hop did.

A major theme of black pop is its ongoing increase in sonic hardness - the evolutionary curve being that country blues hardened into urban blues, acoustic blues into electric blues, R&B into soul and soul into funk. And finally, funk hardened into hip hop.

Or rather, hip hop brought back funk in a much harder, tougher form.

Hip hop became a kind of aural concrete from the mid-1980s onwards. Whether it was the fuzzy low register grind of a turntable scratch, or the metallic crunch of drum machines, or the comical but affecting bass in beatboxing, the new black pop seeping out of the streets of New York had a cold-crush force and conspicuous density missing elsewhere.

Democracy of sounds rules in hip hop. Tones that are apparently non-musical can become musical, the echo of a voice can be more important than the voice itself, a distorted keyboard can be more resonant than a clearly articulated chord. For the most part, these sounds gain power because their oddness reinforces the sense of dysfunction and aggression common to some of the great exponents of funk.

Funk had reduced the harmony of jazz-informed soul sometimes to just one chord. And now hip hop took things further, thinking not in terms of a key or tonal centre but exploring the rhythmic organisation of any sound, be it a mechanised siren or a man-made scream. Crucially, rhythm was constant: like a machine that would not stop, the indestructible Terminator-like groove that rocked you again and again, then again and again, and again and again, the beat that simply went on and on, and on and on.

The sample in hip hop deleted human error. A sound that could be drawn from any source, the loop would spin round with the tenacity of a robot programmed to spit profanities and smack down all before it. The loop was a snatch of the past recast into the beat of the present. The loop was a formidable, iterative force. It was a metronome that, unlike the Pope or the papes, proved infallible.

An obvious form of continuity between hip hop and funk was that the older music had been directly suggestive of sequenced beats. Relentless repetition, particularly in the music of James Brown, was at a premium. Most of Brown's songs did not formally conclude but faded out, creating the impression that they would go on forever. The dance was endless.

As the Godfather claimed, he was 'Doin' it to death', which was absolutist on all fronts, be they time or space. Funk was doin' it all night and taking over the floor. Hip hop wanted to rock the whole house.

Even more important was a link back to another tradition. If black folks talking in rhyme over records evokes one thing, it is the classic radio shows hosted by legendary announcers such as the Ace from Space. The best hip hop albums sound like black broadcasts tailored to a more rigid, less improvised format, so that the musical accompaniment becomes essentially one huge drumbeat against which the opinionator proceeds to pummel and pound.

Furthermore, this drumbeat can be wrought from disparate sources. It can be a snippet of guitar bolted to a slice of synthesizer, or a rhythmic vocal phrase that melds James Brown shouting 'Talkin' loud ...' in one key with Bob Marley chanting 'Sayin' something' in another. As such, the 'mix', the art of sonic patchwork, sometimes takes call and response to daring extremes. The call can come from funk in America and the response from reggae in Jamaica. The globe is spun for the perfect beat.

If hip hop is a listening party, then it will raise the roof when there is the possibility of rogue sounds gatecrashing from any time or space. Last night a DJ saved your life, and not just with a song but with any bit of any song, or several bits of several songs, cut up with puckish abandon.

Disc jockeys or their cousins, stand-up comics, often blended humour and danger in their persona, and those forces also framed funk, whose conceptual base had dysfunction and drive. To a large extent, hip hop accentuated the duality. Among the ultimate exponents of the genre were Public Enemy, whose two frontmen, Chuck D and Flava Flav, were such potent embodiments of those two strands.

If Flava was James's smile, Chuck was Mr Brown's scream. There was a blend of juvenility and virility, a conflation of high jinks with high stakes, a summary of rap as a vehicle for both comedy and horror narratives.

Early 1980s hip hop reconnected with classic funk explicitly by sampling James Brown and many of those he inspired. Then the sound, the audio architecture, started to shift as a wider range of noise, static and sound-effects assumed the role of energising rhythmic devices.

Everything seemed to be going lower – mostly the bass frequencies and kick drums, sampled from old records. They were taking up more space in the mix, to the extent that the decibel metre on the majority of hip hop releases, and especially on many of those issued from the early 1990s onwards, lurched straight into the red. On an old turntable that needed a penny to keep the arm straight, they made the distressed needle shake and shimmy on the vinyl out of the sheer force of the low tones.

Hardness, weight and density of pitch. What had been one of the distinguishing features of James Brown's music, taken on occasion to thrilling heights by the use of as many as three drummers on stage, was now pushed further down the line towards audio violence, so that the listener didn't just lend an ear to hip hop tunes but had it assaulted. Eric B & Rakim's call to 'Let The Rhythm Hit 'Em' was essentially making explicit and more intense what James Brown had expressed a few decades before, when he turned to his alto saxophonist Maceo Parker on 'Cold Sweat' and yelled 'Let 'em have it. Put it on 'em. Blow your horn!' with all the snarling menace of a mob boss instructing a henchman to lead-belly a rival.

Beat as battle-weapon was a principle that bridged the underlying intent of the old funk (i.e. funk) and the new funk of hip hop. Exponential increases in magnitude of feeling were reflected above all in the ongoing evolution of the African American vernacular. The 1970s had 'bad tunes'. The '90s had 'ill beats'.

The rediscovery of old sounds alone did not a musical revolution make, though. The funk–hip hop continuum was a vital development in black popular music because rhythm was not confined to the bottom of a tune, as had always been the case with R&B and its derivatives, regardless of the percussive way in which those vocalists attacked melody.

Over the rhythmic foundation of a song, the rapper – the singer's replacement – sprayed rhythm instead of melody. This is why hip hop, mostly a rhythmic form in which percussion suffuses the organisational structure of the music, marks a disjuncture with soul, which is predominantly a song form. With explosive, eruptive vocal rhythm piled on top of instrumental rhythm, be it bass, drums or other noise shaped into a pulse, there was a graphic sense of funk taking over a piece: rising from the bottom, heading upwards to where melody held sway and kicking it into touch, something Brown had long implied with his vocals.

Hip hop is so heavily rooted in reference. The allusions are local, national, universal, historical and cultural, and they're flying at you at the speed of thought. So just as you grab one idea, another one turns your head and sets off associations. For example, if Malik B of The Roots says 'you can even ask Anita about the Rapture',[8] then you may think about how the need for the same ole love is relentless: 'From beginning to end, 365 days of the year'. But you have to know who Anita is in the first place. You have to register Ms Baker. You have to feel the spirit in her tunes.

And you also have to ask yourself how you feel about hearing a young African American cast himself in the role of the doyenne of British crime fiction, Agatha Christie, use the word 'sissy' as if he's trading insults in a playground, then call himself an ex-offender who's ready for the next contender, although he grips mics rather than Remington typewriters. You have sixteen brisk bars in which to catch these flights of fancy.

Be that as it may, some hip hop lyrics are undeniably bland. But what can save a couplet as trite as 'her dress was yellow/she said hello' is the richness of the voice that delivers it. Apart from writing quotable rhymes, one of the greatest feats a rapper can pull off is taking a telephone directory and making it a talking book by way of intonation.

Rhythmatising the mundane requires vocal trickery. Hip hop is a vocal art. It is a performance art. It is a vocal performance art.

Heretical as the idea may seem, hip hop can still be madly exciting if one somehow (impossibly) ignores the meaning of the words and focuses solely on their movement, their rise, fall, dip and curve, as if they were actually a foreign language – which, given the substantial complexity of the vernacular in some verses, can appear to be the case. The rhythmic whirl is often akin to the vocalised, wah-wah wail of guitars or the jagged thrust of clavinets, two key instruments deployed in funk.

Hip hop words frequently have the grind and growl prevalent in funk.

Fire, I would contend, is funk. Aggression is funk. Hardness is funk. How fast is funk, though? Generally speaking, one thinks of speed, pace of some kind, vigour, as befits the notions of attack and punch, the aim of 'letting the rhythm hit em', as Eric B & Rakim would put it. And certainly in the 1960s and '70s the bulk of songs that featured funk in the title were the brisk, pacy dance numbers, while the soul tunes tended to be the slumber-down songs.

Stop to consider, though, 'People Get Up And Drive Your Funky Soul'.

Featured on the soundtrack to the 1973 blaxploitation flick *Slaughter's Big Rip Off*, it is one of James Brown's funkiest grooves. But that isn't as significant as a simple fact: 'Drive Your Funky Soul' is a medium *slow* song. It is unhurried.

The drummer and bassist here are very relaxed in their touch and handling of the beat. Rather than running, they're strolling, even walking with the tempo. They give an invaluable lesson: rhythm is not necessarily speed. It is the command of an arc of notes to create a regularity of motion that may prompt hypnosis. Slowness can advantage funkiness because it enables the attack of the beat, particularly the lower frequencies of the kick drum and bass guitar, to exert their full impact on the body. One hears a similar science at work in hip hop's leisurely pieces, where the low end acquires the bruising weight of a medicine ball. If funk punishes at high tempos, then it can positively *hurt* when thrown down at low tempos.

Slowness can be very suggestive of thickness, heaviness, weightiness.

Rhythm can 'hit 'em', to quote Eric B & Rakim again, with more of a dramatic sensation – particularly in the dark, bass register – when it decelerates, because the increased space between the notes creates more anticipation which, in turn, induces a stronger reaction when these notes burst into life.

Curiously, several good if not great funk bands have, when performing live, totally compromised their funkiness by deciding to play their songs much faster than on record. But excess of tempo doesn't always further the cause of funk. Some of the bands in soul and hip hop that made their mark on black pop in the 1990s – for example, The Brand New Heavies and The Roots – really understood this. Their grasp of contrasts, pacing and drama through variations in speed enabled them to make the point in concert that the 'good groove' isn't always about the hell or the leather.

Soul and funk that skilfully embraced hip hop, strapping a sub-sonic saddle onto their trusty rhythmic steed, realised that, with extra weight in the low end, they didn't need to have the legs running at 150 beats per minute to knock down whomever may have stood up on the dance floor. Music made by artists such as Me'Shell NdegéOcello, D'Angelo, Maxwell and Erykah Badu around the mid-1990s was often at its most affectingly funky when it was leisurely muscular rather than busy muscular.[9]

Adrianna Evans, a vastly underrated soul singer with jazz inclinations, displayed a similar quality on her eponymous 1997 debut. It remains one of the best soul albums of recent history. Produced by Dred Scott, a hip hop artist interested in very detailed arrangements and the careful conjunction of instrumental performance and programming, *Adrianna Evans* had rap's 'head-nod factor' down pat: its backbeat had an almost bulldozer sluggishness. But it also crafted peaks and troughs in tempo throughout the set.

In concert at London's Jazz Café that year, Evans demonstrated amply that she too had realised how effective such manoeuvres could be, leading a band with a tight, flexible rhythm section. The highlight of the gig was a fine sequence in which she moved from a tense, mid-paced piece, 'Reality', to a rendition of Herbie Hancock's 'Watermelon Man', a great piece of Latin-flavoured 1960s soul jazz.

But the band changed its beat, abruptly breaking to half time and making the pulse float in a hazy, lazy, slurred slow motion. The bass guitarist elongated some of his notes to a flabby wobble as the kick drum gained a touch more roundness. The effect on the music – the black-iron crash of the downbeat, its accentuated dread plunge – was absolutely devastating.

This was a reversal of the adage that speed kills. Here, terror was lack of tempo and the very palpable sense that the musicians, with fewer notes in a bar to negotiate, were practically digging rather than playing each phrase, making the whole sound heavier. A juggernaut, they seemed to imply, might actually feel more frightening at 10 mph than 60 mph.

All the funk that had been bubbling in the higher tempo erupted in the lower one, the heavier groove prompting members of the audience to push hips downward, the erotic charge in the air crackling more perceptibly than it had done at any point in the evening. Some of their wilder screams recalled the 'old' blues records of Muddy Waters.

6 The soul–rock continuum

I'm riding in your car,
I turn on the radio.
You're pulling me close,
I just say no.
I say I don't like it,
But you know I'm a liar.

(The Pointer Sisters, 'Fire', composer Bruce Springsteen)

Oh my Dixon days

Listening to Muddy Waters's 'Mannish Boy' next to Chuck Berry's 'Johnny B. Goode' is like listening to a mace that drags along the floor next to a rapier that slices through curtains. Where the combination of guitar and voice on the former is about tone subject to gravity, the combination of guitar and voice on the latter is about tone creating its own cheeky levity, flying around in flurries of fast, percolating licks while the same keys hammered on the piano mimic a ringing bell.

The first case is blues, trudging and dredging on the beat with little concern for punctuality. The second is rock and roll, whirling and whizzing to tease time into catching up with it. The two are kindred. After all, the first gives the second something to speed up, something to energise and inebriate. And the second gives the first something to slow down, so as to create the comedown needed after every high.

Berry's record came out in 1958, just three years after Waters's. By this time blues, rhythm and blues and rock and roll had all shown themselves to be branches of the same tree, shaking with varying degrees of emphasis and reckless abandon. This great mutability of the blues, its potential to pull on a new skin while remaining as hot-blooded as ever, is such that the gap between these genres could constantly widen or narrow, yet idioms born after them – such as soul and rock – would inevitably retain some connectedness. After all, they have common antecedents, none more so than Waters and Berry, Ray Charles and Louis Jordan.

Although tempo was a key distinction between old blues and new rock and roll, there was also a question of theatricality and emotional pitch. The latter, certainly in the hands of Berry, Bo Diddley and Little Richard, assumed a hot, frenzied and, at times, hysterical overtone. A great bolt of electricity snakes through Richard's 'Tutti Frutti', above all in the way the 'a-wop-bop-a-loo-bop' neologisms fizzle with fantastical delight.

The whole delivery, and Richard's dramatic character, from his firehouse screams right down to the flurry of torrid hand and shoulder movements, his fervent head rolls and freak-show eyes, have a quality that starts in the church and escapes, like an unchained spirit, time and time again in the history of black pop: delirium. It's there in today's hip hop and yesterday's rhythm and blues, a kind of explosiveness in vocal or instrumental sounds that suggests something is heating and bubbling away within the pressure cooker of the performance.

Regardless of any musical richness that might be attributed to it, rock and roll had important cultural and psychological ramifications. The expression originates from the African American vernacular, referring to love-making, and the use of an image of motion is a particularly sharp-witted way of evoking lusty behavior without resorting to crudity. It's timeless. Then it was rock and roll; now it's bump and grind.

In any case, the sheer exuberance, if not urgency, with which the great New Orleans R&B vocalist Roy Brown performed 'Good Rockin' Tonight' in 1947, where he can hardly restrain his joy at the prospect of seeing his nature rise long after the sun has gone down, emphasises in no uncertain terms the erotic charge held in the language.

The sexual connotations of rockin' are part of a wider dynamic of risqué, offensive language that would include funk. As I explained in the previous chapter, the term came to encompass anything from lack of hygiene to dysfunction, particularly in the case of the adjective 'funky'.

Performers such as Brown basically made the point that black popular music could have an electrifying and arousing quality in its intent and execution, for the lyric of 'Good Rockin' Tonight' is matched by a very ballsy delivery. There is immense power in black pop as a vehicle for a primal human impulse such as sex – a surefire way to capture the imagination of legions of baying hormonal teenagers.

A form of music that encapsulates sex can only gain in substance if it is performed by an artist who encapsulates sex. And that is where Little Richard came into his own, for in addition to the high-camp theatre and hysteria, the delirium of his persona, there was boundless eroticism.

With that in mind, it is fair to say that rock and roll is as much about theatre as it is about music. The idea of a musical performance that hinged as much on visual excitement as on listening pleasure obviously made the genre highly relevant to both the television age and the mass communications that would gain ground in the 1950s. Thanks to his stage presence, Little Richard – born Richard Wayne Penniman in Macon, Georgia – was also known as 'The Human Atom Bomb', 'Warhawk' and 'The Brown Bomber'. All this suggests a fantastical adventure series or a boxing ring spectacle, something that has to be seen as well as heard.

Rock and roll is sight and sound as a punch. It's not a soft, subtle caress.

Between them Richard, Chuck Berry and Bo Diddley reveal the great potential of the blues to shift into other forms by way of nuance and incremental adjustments in a basic structural formula. The result was anything from a dark, disturbing tangent into proto-pyschedelia to a raw, unadulterated and babyish heavy metal or a burgeoning Latin-rock, often involving an injection of timbral ruggedness amid a danceable sensuality. Diddley's tendency to mangle sounds, to play highly abrasive, dissonant guitar chords and juxtapose them with a sashaying maracas beat, gave his work huge scope, wheeling it seamlessly from blues to R&B to rumba. Yet at its core was an unerring faith in the blues riff that showed how much mileage there was in the basic guitar-vocal engine. Taking a pentatonic scale and creating a seemingly limitless variety of short, darting motifs upon which a song could be built; laying down a couple of chords and setting them up as a tonal centre around which a melody might be woven – that is an enviable skill.

Willie Dixon had it in spades. Double bassist, producer and leader of the Chess Records house band, Dixon is a remarkable figure in black pop in so far as his powers as a tunesmith had flexibility while retaining a sense of self. Astoundingly, between 1955 and 1965 he wrote Little Walter's 'My Babe', Muddy Waters's 'Mannish Boy', Howlin' Wolf's 'Spoonful', Bo Diddley's 'You Can't Judge A Book By Its Cover', Etta James's 'I Just Want To Make Love To You' and Koko Taylor's 'Wang Dang Doodle'.

The marked differences in the personalities of all of the above goes some way to explaining why this body of work is so pluralistic. Yet were one to take the singers away, the richness of the writing and arrangements would still stand up, such is the structural strength of each piece. This is no better illustrated than by the parallels between 'Mannish Boy', a slice of proto-funk disguised as a slip-sliding stomp, and 'I Just Want To Make Love To You', a song that swings so sweetly it could pass as jazz. One grates a guitar, the other pounds a piano. The central riff is similar.

Markedly different in timbre, not to mention vocal character, these two pieces –sprung from the mind of the same composer – reveal R&B as the seedbed of two major growths to come in popular music: the Waters flower announcing a bare, hard-scraped rock, the James flower pointing to a more lush, delicately handled soul.

Dixon is mainly associated with Chicago through his remarkable input into the city's Chess label, a historic imprint that charted the passage of blues to rhythm and blues, rock and roll and soul through the aforementioned iconic hits and many others. But originally Dixon was a Southerner, born in Vicksburg, Mississippi in 1915. There he caught African American music in a state of great ferment, listening to the blind pianist Little Brother

Montgomery before making his debut as a bass vocalist in a local gospel quartet called the Union Jubilee Singers.

Since the days of the Great Migration, Chicago had been a hotbed of musical creativity, nurturing the Jazz Age in the days of Louis Armstrong, King Oliver and Jelly Roll Morton, and then, after World War II, receiving a power surge of energy from the influx of rural blacks whose big voices found big sounds in the electric guitars wailing and whining round them. It was this new sound that Dixon came to embody.

His genius lay in his decisive infusion of gospel into R&B, keeping its power understated yet intact in 'My Babe', the piece Dixon wrote for Little Walter. The fact that it is built on a Negro spiritual, *This Train*, is meaningful because it shows how much sass and sexiness there could be in church melodies. That wired, body-electric quality could strengthen the blues as a creative force with a shape-shifting, mutative potential. This is absolutely crucial in the bigger story of modern black pop. Dixon's work, or rather the wide range of his work, makes the point that the music was waiting to change. Whether the result was R&B, rock and roll, soul or funk is not as important as the richness of the modifications wrought by Ray Charles, Sam Cooke, Chuck Berry, James Brown and Dixon himself in the mid-1950s.

Rainy Waterloo

Regardless of the fact that all the above genres are traceable to the blues, that they have shared common musical ground, they also had differences – and, more to the point, they came to be perceived differently within the record industry. On the one hand, it is correct to say that rhythm and blues and rock and roll are really one and the same thing. On the other hand, it is inaccurate because the latter genre was thus named to open up that music to a mass market beyond the niche of 'race records' – principally white consumers.

The phenomenon of a black rhythm and blues record becoming a white rock and roll record was epitomised by Bill Haley & The Comets' reprise of Big Joe Turner's 1951 single 'Shake, Rattle & Roll' in 1953. The commercial success that would ensue if a black voice were matched with a white face crystallised in Elvis Presley, whose status as the king of rock and roll presumably made Little Richard the emperor.

Rhythm and blues was an umbrella term for a number of styles and inevitably rock and roll, as its cash-cow doppelgänger, also embraced a range of specificities that reflected urban as well as rural origins, although rock and roll became defined first and foremost as metropolitan pop.

Charlie Gillett's *The Sound Of The City* lists five styles of rock and roll: country boogie showbands, singers, New Orleans combos, Rocking Chicago blues and vocal groups. Gillett also outlines the enormous impact all these sub-genres would have in the subsequent decade:

Between them, these styles provided the basis for all the major producers and artists of the sixties, obviously the Four Seasons, the Beach Boys, and the Motown groups in the States, and the Beatles and the Rolling Stones in Britain, and less obviously, Bob Dylan and Sly Stone.[1]

In England, UK Rock was largely distinguished from US rock and roll courtesy of groups like the Yardbirds, Cream and The Who, as well as the Stones from the middle of the 1960s. The wild aggression of their music, the higher volume and the novel references all enriched the pop canon. This new transatlantic dimension was interesting. The Stones took their cue from Muddy Waters but the movement of black pop between the New World and the Old produced different signposts and sensibilities. An imitator rarely matches an original but an original imitator may discover something worthwhile if he or she knows the power of the source. In the case of the blues, part of this is celebration of the local, the sense that one point of view can illuminate the whole world. Hence British rock finds its feet when Tobacco Road leads to Abbey Road and A Rainy Night In Georgia turns into a Waterloo Sunset.

White Britons doing black American music in Britain was one thing, but what if the lines were further blurred? What if there were somebody from over there who came here? What if the original came to the imitator and the two of them somehow put their heads together?

Rock is too small a word for Jimi Hendrix, just as, to a large extent, soul is too small for Stevie Wonder. These genres are essentially approximations, rough pointers rather than wholly accurate identifiers. Too much stylistic and conceptual ground is covered in the *oeuvre* of both artists for just four little letters to encompass the full scale of their work.

Hendrix is really what happens when rock and roll and R&B – embodied by someone who had first-hand experience of these genres on the frontline, playing the storied 'chitlin circuit' in the South with the likes of Curtis Knight, The Isley Brothers and Little Richard – becomes rock but doesn't stop probing the pre-history of the music, as well as exploring not so much a future genre as a future sound. All the pictures of Hendrix in rumination behind the mixing desk of a studio are as meaningful as the ones of him with guitar raised and eyes closed, as if the instrument had cast a spell on him.

The material the Seattle-born artist cut between his arrival in London in 1967, his rebirth there amid the likes of Cream and The Who, and his death three years later, has that same creative restlessness written all over it.

Power is a key word to describe Hendrix's aesthetic, in so far as the incendiary nature of his guitar playing, the gargantuan, theatrical surge of the sounds as well as the unapologetic, fright-night volume at which they burst into life, reflects an obvious desire to hit the audience in the same way a gospel holler or funk backbeat would.

Most ingeniously, Hendrix was able to make sounds play with our perception of borders, of where and when a song might originate.

'Voodoo Chile' sounds like an older-than-old blues that is country in its indolence, its insistence on taking its time, and urban in its petulance, its insistence on changing your time and elbowing its big 'n' bashy noise into your consciousness with more force than the machine-led disruption liable to be heard in a city's cacophony at any given moment. Geographically, it is an astute piece of music for the way it seamlessly entwines these apparently opposite forms of scenery. This kind of push and pull, of citified country and countrified city resonances, is one of its most appealing traits in Hendrix's work.

To a large extent, whether Hendrix's music is rock or soul, white or black, under-souled or over-funked is less interesting than whether he appears to be an ancient country Negro or a future urban African American – or perhaps both. In the changing form of his music and his own persona lies an intensely enigmatic and protean spirit. Hendrix was using sound as a tool that enabled him to move backwards and forwards in time.

It's often in the fine details: 1968's 'Crosstown Traffic' is 1980s heavy metal in its brutal, macho power chords but the six bars of snakish kazoo scat that open the piece are a jokey distillation of '30s swing motifs.

Because of his grounding in blues and R&B, and his understanding of the input big band music had into the genesis of his work, Hendrix showed a marked jazz sensibility in some of his music. There is an intricacy of construction in many of his songs, above all in the ripping 'Tax Free', that would present a challenge for most improvisers.

Essentially, Hendrix demonstrated that the blues is a flexible conceptual tool, a kind of musical modelling clay that can bend and stretch into jazz, soul, funk, rock or odd shapes in between. That's where Hendrix really scored highly. His roots in the blues are too deep for him to deny them, but his imagination, his fascination with sound and narrative richness, are far too great for him to be hemmed in by them.

When Bobby met Jimi

'He had a real quiet way about him. Jimi was an oddball in this gang of soul musicians and he knew it. He said to me, "The whites don't want me cos they feel I'm imitating them and the blacks don't want me because they say I am a misfit. I'm between a rock and a hard place."' So says Bobby Womack, one of the greatest of soul men, in his effortlessly entertaining and informative 2006 autobiography, *Midnight Mover*.[2]

At the time of that quote, roughly 1964, both men were sharing a tour bus doing the chitlin circuit. Womack was playing with the gospel-soul outfit The Valentinos and Hendrix with the R&B vocalist Gorgeous George Odell. If

Womack is to be believed, there was a real friendship, if not a bond, between the two men that was partly forged by them both being left-handed guitarists and loving nothing better than trading licks backstage in between the nightly sets they performed.

Hendrix's feeling of alienation is one of the neatest summaries of the warped psychology that pervaded both the music industry and society in the mid-1960s. If he was concerned about rejection because he was seen as imitating whites, then the obvious response is, who were *they* imitating in the first place. And when is a black not a misfit in a world that has led African American sanitation workers to plead the case for his civil rights by taking action as drastic as parading down the street – braving violence, it should be noted – with a placard stating the tautology 'I Am A Man'? What else is there to demand when one is constantly called a boy?

A rock and a hard place indeed. Hendrix's great success – very substantial record sales, huge stadium gigs, adulation from the rock press – could not mask the enormous complications caused by issues of race both in the American record industry and society in general as the late 1960s drew to a close amid tumult and polarisation.

If the misgivings that Hendrix expressed to Womack several years before were partially attenuated by what he achieved, then they were not entirely resolved by the end of his life. So much so that 'Belly Button Window''s sunny but chillingly nonchalant intimation of mortality – 'And I'm wondering if they want me around' – assumes considerable pathos.

Without doubt, the odds were stacked heavily against a figure such as Hendrix from the outset. If rock and roll was appropriated by white artists, then rock as a derivative of rock and roll, played by a black artist with an authentic blues sensibility, could only occupy a wholly problematic position on the music-industry exchange.

Hendrix's first group, The Experience, was largely perceived as British and was not actively marketed to a black audience by his record company. Yet a more interesting question than how Hendrix's music should be described is where it should be placed – or, more precisely, what artists should be heard before and after it? Play Sonny Boy Williamson before 'Voodoo Chile' and Bo Diddley after, and words such as 'rock', or the idea of black rock, make much more sense than they do when 'Voodoo Chile' bridges the songs of James Brown and Aretha Franklin. Play Diddley before 'Voodoo Chile' and follow it with Curtis Mayfield's *Live At The Bitter End*, where the guitar-led instrumentation has a stark, flinty resonance that is evidently rock in character. You can immediately hear how relevant Jimi Hendrix is to a stripped-down, red-raw brand of funky soul music.

Yet something that is abundantly clear from any cursory trawl through the defining exponents of soul music in the 1970s – add Stevie Wonder and George Clinton to Mayfield – is how sonically expansive, how voraciously baroque its central line of evolution was. Electronics and synthesizers were shaping the idiom as much as, if not more than, rhythm sections and horns. The amazing Technicolor vistas of Wonder, in particular, made the three-piece guitar set-up, the standard rock template, look increasingly monochrome. So to a great degree one can understand why soul fans would not so much have rejected as not felt the need to gravitate towards rock, given what was on offer. Rock may have been louder than soul but it lacked its starburst textural rainbow.

Ironically, the three-piece guitar-led template was what Hendrix was also trying to escape towards the end of his life, precisely because he realised it had limitations. And it's obvious he was interested in extending the vocabulary of the guitar towards that of a synthesizer. The work Hendrix recorded with horns (the seductively jazzy 'South Saturn Delta') and the planned session with Miles Davis are a tantalising taste of what might have been. That Hendrix died before he had a chance to record with Davis was one of two great missed opportunities in modern music, be it black or white. That he died before having a chance to record with Stevie Wonder was the other.

Given the pivotal position Hendrix occupied as a bridge between several different forms derived from the blues, it is tempting to suggest that the soul–rock continuum, or the likelihood that soul artists might have rock sensibilities and *vice versa*, diminished with his passing.

That did not happen. In fact, several significant figures in soul music, the most notable being Sly & The Family Stone, Parliament-Funkadelic, The Bar-Kays[3] and The Isley Brothers, all carried forward a kind of proxy Jimi–Stevie union in much of their work, with intriguing thickets of sound constructed from carefully focused, entwined figures played on guitars, keyboards and horns.

Whether citing Hendrix, Cream, Led Zeppelin or Iron Maiden, most definitions of rock music highlight either the prevalence of high volume or a strong, brawny beat, and it is reasonable to assume that these characteristics are significant.

However, they are not exclusive to rock music. There are many genres that are loud and use crashing drum sounds. But in terms of examining the soul–rock continuum, it should be noted that a strong or 'tough' beat, within the context of electric instruments, applies to another sub-genre of black popular music, and that is funk.

So within the soul–rock continuum one can point more specifically to the funk–rock continuum. The prevalence of the backbeat – the beefy smack on the bass drum and snare, so that the primary rhythm underpinning a song feels as if it rests on a solid, granite-like platform – is a binding ingredient in a great many funk and rock combos.

Both constituencies pride themselves on music best described as hard or *heavy*.

From a technical point of view, rock often lacks the agility and dancing quality of funk, primarily because rock has more of a square than a circular quality in its rhythmic construction. There's less slip-sliding around the beat and there are fewer accents off the pulse. Rock bass usually has less of a pumping, scalar quality than in funk, and rock guitar often opts for thick chords rather than funk's thinner, busy single notes.

Yet rock and funk often land on some sort of common ground when they are played at low tempo. This is primarily because the time feel of the music – certainly in terms of the kick drum in the rhythm section as well as the guitar, keyboard or horn section – becomes more dramatic and menacing, almost akin to a blast or a thrust, due to the greater sustain applied to the notes. Think of the many rock songs that clearly take their cue from the grindingly decelerated, fraught groove of Jimi Hendrix's 'Foxy Lady' and the large number of funk tunes closely modelled on the hard, heaving, slow drag of Sly & The Family Stone's 'Thank You For Talking To Me Africa'. Both are punishers. Both hammer the ear.

There is a strong kinship in these pieces and those grown from them.

It's all about a bullying quality in the music, an intent to bump and bustle the listener. So when a funker shouts 'Let's rock, y'all!', there is the same thrill-as-threat as when a rocker screams 'We will rock you!'

Besides, rock as a *raison d'être* is absolutely crucial in black music, and it has taken on many ramifications over time. It is the way a whole congregation 'rocks' in the fervour of a gospel song. It is the way a blues man moans 'Rock Me, baby! Roll all over me!' on a Saturday night, his mind full of entirely different thoughts from those he hears when he shakes in his church pew on a Sunday morning. It is the way a jazzman is 'rockin' in rhythm' as his band cuts loose. It is the way the backing singers in a soul band call 'Rock!' and then respond with 'Freak!' It is the way a rapper hails a 'Chief Rocka' in eulogistic rhymes.

Rock, as in sensation and effect, is not owned by rock the genre. Rock, as in fire and power, is in the genres of gospel, blues, jazz, soul, funk and hip hop.

Motor love

There is more to the soul–rock continuum than this kinship between rock and funk, something arguably best encapsulated by a musician such as Jimi Hendrix. Binding all the above is the vocabulary of the blues. The chords, rhythmic patterns, vocal mannerisms and subject matter of rock's founding fathers like Muddy Waters or Chuck Berry radiated out into the world of pop music beyond the time and space of their birth.

This information not only shaped rhythm and blues and rock and roll, it became part of the vocabulary of a vast swathe of modern songwriters and performers. If we cast our minds back to Charlie Gillett's *The Sound Of The City*, we can recall Gillett asserting that this core vocabulary was irrepressibly pervasive and would subsequently affect 'Motown groups in the States, and the Beatles and the Rolling Stones in Britain, and less obviously, Bob Dylan and Sly Stone'.

Active during the late 1950s and '60s, these artists nonetheless had a major impact on subsequent generations. It thus follows that the major figures in popular music during the '70s and beyond might well have reflected this influence, either explicitly or implicitly. Hence soul artists could logically have rock resonances, or at least feel some kind of affinity for rock, because they could hear in its drama and narrative structure a residue of rock and roll and, by extension, the blues.

Conversely, rock artists could incorporate at least the echoes of soul if they knew something of the far-reaching history of the music, and how a figure such as Hendrix had been decisively influenced by the likes of blues man Elmore James as well as, to a certain extent, Bob Dylan.

Inevitably, there were also artists who brought together the two strands organically in their work. In the 1970s and '80s this vein was represented by the very successful Hall & Oates, a Philadelphian duo who wrote beautiful songs such as 'Sara Smile', and the less successful but equally interesting Garland Jeffreys, a Brooklyn-based singer-songwriter who artfully stirred laconic reggae offbeats into his rock-soul cocktail on intriguing albums such as *Ghost Writer*.

Beyond the existence of artists such as these, the real depth of the soul–rock continuum is best expressed in a single work, a composition that stands as something of a bridge between the two genres and owes its existence and excellence to artists on both sides of the river.

A good example would be 'Fire'. Penned in 1978, it is a highly accomplished piece of soul music. The song was first recorded by the little known rockabilly singer Robert Gordon before it was performed, with much greater commercial success, by the Pointer Sisters, a brilliant four-piece vocal group from San Francisco whose members, Ruth, Anita, Bonnie and June, made up an exciting and very agile harmony ensemble. They could skilfully handle the heavy, gutbucket, funky New Orleans soul of Allen Toussaint's 'Yes We Can Can' as well as the fizzing, hyperactive bebop of Dizzy Gillespie's 'Salt Peanuts'.

'Fire', recorded when the Pointer Sisters had scaled down to a trio following Bonnie's departure, was an altogether more soothing and romantic proposition, a love story set to a gentle slow-to-mid tempo in which a crackly, finger-picked blues guitar created a terse but resonant central motif. The song had an artfully teasing first verse:

> I'm riding in your car,
> I turn on the radio.
> You're pulling me close,
> I just say no.
> I say I don't like it,
> But you know I'm a liar.
> Cause when we kiss,
> Ooo ... fire.[4]

The scenario strikes right at the heart of rock and roll mythology: girl and boy in a tantalising no-means-yes seduction, who, crucially, play out their love game in a car, the setting that gave so much mileage to Chuck Berry and countless others. The radio is on, obviously. What could be on the airwaves? Anybody, one imagines, from Little Stevie Wonder to the Rolling Stones, the artists who made The Sound Of The City. For the words and music of 'Fire' embody a rich fabric of American pop stitched from the entwined threads of rhythm and blues and rock and roll.

Rhythmically and melodically, the piece is really a Stax Records tribute.

Yet 'Fire' was written by neither Isaac Hayes nor David Porter, two of the label's greatest tunesmiths, as one might well expect. Nor by their Motown counterpart Smokey Robinson. Its author is Bruce Springsteen. That is important because Springsteen has been one of the defining figures in rock over the past five decades. Although he is an emblem of the white, working-class hero from New Jersey, whom many hailed as the successor to both Presley and Dylan on the release of his 1973 debut *Greetings From Asbury Park, N.J.*, Springsteen nonetheless proved on 'Fire' that the blues is an integral part of his composer's arsenal and can become an identifiable element of his creative output at any given moment. The blues can provide an expressive framework for any writer with imagination, regardless of their race or subject matter.

One would be hard pressed to say that Springsteen has a soul voice. But the point is that he draws on the soul-music tradition in his aesthetic, as proved by a range of songs other than 'Fire', most notably, 'You Can Look (But You Better Not Touch)', 'Hungry Heart' and 'I'm On Fire'. Were it played at slow tempo and laced with vocal harmonies, the last of these would make a passable doo-wop tune.

Springsteen's *oeuvre* underlines that whenever rock tends to the blues, it has the potential to be soulful, just as soul has the potential to be rocky whenever it tends to the blues, and particularly if a strident electric guitar is the predominant timbre in a song's arrangement.

Throughout the 1970s and '80s, American popular music yielded many great songs by artists who continued to negotiate the rhythm and blues–rock and roll duality. Whether a piece was classified as soul or rock really depended on the vocal quality, the gospel quotient of whoever was pouring his or her broken heart out over a car radio. Without that experience, the sound of the city is really inconceivable.

Part of the power of the blues lies in the newness its raw materials, its melodic motifs and rhythmic strategies, can acquire when an artist constructs a song from them, either stamping a personal vocal imprint on the performance or enriching the arrangement with sounds that defy cliché, such as the cry of an unusual instrument.

So Springsteen's 1982 hit 'Born In The USA', one of the most emblematic songs of the decade for its artful double edge of patriotism and protest, sounds like a fresh piece of rock, partly because the central high-pitched keyboard riff is highly reminiscent of a bagpipe. But underneath it all is urban R&B. The song is really a blues.

Had Little Richard written that piece, with a zippy piano replacing the guitar to suit his more frenetic, hot-wired vocal delivery, then that point would be abundantly clear. But whether Springsteen is associated first and foremost with black music or not, there are other examples of how a single song, or a riff, can span the genres of soul and rock music when it lands in the lap of two different artists.

So we turn back to the Pointer Sisters, a group Springsteen knows only too well. After enjoying success in the soul market during the 1970s with albums such as *Having A Party*, the Sisters hit the mainstream in the early '80s. Their sound became glossier and more pop-oriented, yet the material still wasn't entirely divorced from their origins in black music. One of their best songs from that period, 1982's 'I'm So Excited', was really a rocking shuffle blues. It was both an echo of the past and a glimpse of the near future. In 1983 Elton John dented the pop charts with 'I'm Still Standing', the best track he'd penned in several years. Play the song after 'I'm So Excited' and you can hear the structural kinship loud and clear. It's really a case of same song, different wig.

Both records are bound by starkly forceful, straight-on-the-beat stabs of piano, bass and drums, and the steady, relentless momentum of the whole rhythm section, the tense forward motion, is almost identical. Essentially, this is rhythm and blues flowing straight into rock and roll and *vice versa*, like two neighbouring sounds of the city.

Dream on, 'Shell

Together, 'I'm So Excited' and 'I'm Still Standing' encapsulate both the enduring impact of black pop on mainstream pop and how the guiding principles of soul music could produce interesting works outside soul music. Connected though they were, the two songs were nonetheless divided by the image of their respective performers. The sight of a middle-aged white man with eccentric eyewear did not symbolise soul any more than three black women with volcanic hair symbolised rock.

Elton John is a brilliant example of how rhythm and blues can be used as a point of departure to make great pop that retains a soulful, if not bluesy edge. His love of Stax and Motown has surfaced to greater or lesser degrees in the rich body of work he has created between the 1960s and present day. That in turn has influenced many artists in soul.

Exactly how one artist or one song might affect or shape another is an inexact science. The extent to which melodies, rhythms, bass lines and drumbeats can drift across genres, when they are consciously appropriated or when they are subconsciously internalised, is not easily determined. But if one accepts that rhythm and blues has laid an indelibly strong foundation for modern popular music, then it stands to reason that just about any artist can intentionally or unintentionally reference its raw materials. The interesting thing is when fragments of a song reappear, perhaps adulterated, in a different time and cultural space.

It doesn't take that much imagination to see that 1970s punk rock owes a huge debt to '50s electric blues. But more significant is the way that '60s R&B, sometimes leaning towards the smooth, doo-wop strain, can and does resurface in '70s punk. For example, what do you hear in Television's classic 'Prove It', for example? Not Muddy Waters's 'Mannish Boy'. Not Howlin' Wolf's 'Spoonful'. You hear Ben E. King's 'Stand By Me'.

Even though the instrumentation is very different – Television are all scratchy electric guitars, King gentle percussion and strings – the Latin feel of the rhythm and the similar harmony and bass line on the verse are clear enough. The great thing is that Television then shift those roots elsewhere in the chorus, basically showing how a riff or a few chords from one source can be used as a creative springboard that will take an artist with integrity to an unforeseen destination.

If there's something bluesy in the performance, it's Television's blues.

Race can be a particularly divisive concept in life, but in the music industry it can lead to sadly crass distortions. The binary notion that blacks do soul and whites rock leads to raised eyebrows when the colours and genres are mixed up. But because of their shared root in the blues, the possibility, if not likelihood, of black rock and white soul, or rather black soul that rocks and white rock that got soul, isn't much of a scandal, especially if the incumbents know their deep musical history.

Regardless of how much fans of rock, funk and soul might have enjoyed each other's respective musical repositories, the record industry still kept the partitions fairly impenetrable throughout the 1970s, long before the disrespectful, anarchic genre of hip hop came along and started sampling Led Zeppelin, then stood back and chuckled when a lot of black kids said they didn't know white boys could be *that* funky.

Culture, in any case, is a political battleground. Popular music is notoriously tribal because it is about youth, about pitting youth against adult, and youth against fellow youth. So that allegiance to a genre will always come to represent more than just taste in music.

Any society that has a macro-scale notion of *them and us* planted in the tragically, often mortally divisive ground known as race is more than likely to see that conflict played out in many micro scales, so an opposition of black and white people will echo powerfully in battle lines drawn up over what might pass as *their* music and *our* music.

America, having enshrined the separation of black and white through its segregation laws, has a long history of them and us: what they do and what we do, what is their way of life and our way of life, what they listen to and what corrupts us. The irony is that many whites sought the thrill of that corruption, even though many black artists struggled for the right to play in the most equitable way possible.

For proof of some progress in the right of a black musician to play white music (rock) derived from black music (blues), the obvious case study is Prince, one of the defining figures of 1980s pop who, like Michael Jackson and Madonna – the other sides of the megastar triangle in that decade – contrived to create something bigger than music.

Musically omnivorous, Prince seemed to have ducked his head in just about every river in American musical history, from blues and gospel to soul, jazz, funk and rock and rock and roll, so that from his most easily discernible role model of Little Richard, he branched out to reference Elton John and Bob Dylan, Curtis Mayfield and Jimi Hendrix.

In addition to Prince, the seminal African American groups Fishbone and Living Colour emerged in the mid-1980s,[5] the former blending dirty thrash-metal funk licks with sunny, brassy Jamaican ska offbeats, the latter playing a challenging, intricate hard rock with a great deal more intelligence, political commentary, irony and blues than was the norm in the genre. Furthermore, in Vernon Reid they had a brilliant guitar hero in the lineage of Hendrix with a solid grounding in jazz.

Yet despite the success of Living Colour, Prince and, by the end of the 1980s, Lenny Kravitz, the music industry and, just as importantly, the broadcast media functioned for the most part as a highly stratified, colour-coded marketplace, in which the notion of a black artist embracing rock as one branch of the tall tree of rhythm and blues was still highly problematic. Radio programmers, in particular, reasoned that the latest incarnations of soul and funk, primarily horn- or keyboard-led genres, really had to stay in one corner and guitar-led rock in another, regardless – and this is the really sad part – of the way these genres influenced each other. There would have been no Beatles without the blues, but Stevie Wonder's 'Village Ghetto Land' would not have sounded the way it did had he not heard 'Eleanor Rigby'.

Perhaps at the hub of this whole regrettable situation is a lingering ambiguity over what constitutes black music, where it begins and ends, and how its many forms might be located in a wide historical lineage.

How US rock and roll, UK rock and Jamaican ska are linked by the core vocabulary of rhythm and blues is considered too difficult a story to tell to a partitioned media and music industry, in which black music has singular rather than plural possibilities and where the sound of the present takes precedence over that of the past. The upshot is, if a black artist plays black music that presents black musical history in an interesting, lateral or cryptic way, and flouts expectations, he or she may subsequently be deemed unsuitable for black radio and audiences.

Such confusion largely mirrors feelings about black people: what they might be able to enjoy or at least intelligently critique, regardless of whether it might seem something they can *relate* to. But loud guitars and soft country voices are neither as scary as the big bad wolf nor as the spook who scats through the door. I mean, did anyone ever consider how much love Led Zeppelin got in *Jamaica*? Did anyone ever consider how much love Jim Reeves got all over the dear wee Windies?

Audiences, in both cases, prove much more open-minded and receptive to what might be deemed unfamiliar timbres than received wisdom would give them credit for. If you talk to Jamaicans about Zeppelin or Bajans about Reeves, especially older couples dancing at parties like the Oistins Friday Night Fish Fry, what they will tell you is that the former had attitude and the latter, sweetness.

They appreciated the artistry of both. They could strike a rude-boy pose with one just as easily as they could dance and romance with the other.

They did not need to hear a Caribbean voice to feel the emotion. They could empathise with both the machismo and the gentlemanly conduct.

With that in mind, it stands to reason that the more adventurous practitioners of black popular music, the ones who want to tune into any art or culture that falls outside the norms mainstream society ascribes to them, might not just express admiration for 'foreign' music but actually embrace some of its content. And that is where the soul–rock continuum really becomes most interesting.

The foundation of the not-for-profit organisation Black Rock Coalition in 1985, with the aim of taking up that discourse and challenging music-industry stereotyping, was thus a necessary philosophical and political initiative that arguably remains very relevant to this day. Essentially, BRC stood for freedom of artistic movement, and the right of black artists to go wherever they wanted creatively. This meant that one of the Coalition's members, the very gifted vocalist and songwriter Marc Anthony Thompson, aka Chocolate Genius Inc,[6] could make music that was not at all easy to pigeonhole, and that the vast range of formative elements at play might well be European as much as African American.

Then again, what artists like Thompson want to transcend is categorisation of any kind, and certainly being automatically perceived as a purveyor of soul music simply because he's black. That's a fair point.

'Race is a bankrupt source of discourse,' Thompson has stated.[7] Classification according to colour is still common currency, though.

Some will assume with alacrity that a black artist is doing black music, regardless of whether it comes from a tradition of black music.

Similarly, eyebrows are still raised, as I've noticed on many occasions, if a black consumer dares to express a dislike for R&B. Yet no such admonishment awaits a white consumer who doesn't consider rock to be *their* music. The former is subject to more limiting assumptions.

Be that as it may, Thompson and others point out that their struggles, and the way they can be misunderstood, pale into insignificance compared with the wholesale, often debilitating exploitation many of their forebears were subjected to. They are grateful for the opportunity to develop their art in half-way decent conditions.

And yet one can only imagine how maddening it must be for the likes of Chocolate Genius Inc to be lumped in with a neo-soul artist such as Erykah Badu, simply because a lazy magazine editor has decided they belong together – possibly because they might both pass as black eccentrics, even though, musically, they are essentially night and day.

Linked as they may be, soul, rock, and their forebear, the blues, have spe-cificities. And more to the point, artists with real strength of character go about developing their own kind of blues, soul or rock, and in the best case scenario it just becomes its own genre.

Rock, lest we forget, has a transatlantic history. The music was made from black America affecting white Britain and from white Britain bringing some-thing of its own to the table, while a black American made the story even more intriguing by forming a group with two white Britons.

Hendrix looms large in this narrative. His influence, for those interested in how idiosyncratic the journey of the blues can be, is unavoidable. But any artist wishing to maintain their restless originality, their spirit of experimen-tation, has to realise that Hendrix lent an ear to what was happening both within and outside what passed as his own culture.

All this means that his real successors are the artists who seek not only to build on the soul–rock continuum but also to investigate both soul and rock made *after* Otis Redding and Hendrix. This might well point towards the P-funk of George Clinton and William 'Bootsy' Collins, the punk of Siouxsie & The Banshees or the indie rock of The Smiths.

To a large extent, this is exactly why Me'Shell NdegéOcello is such a fasci-nating figure in contemporary music. She has come from a rhythm and blues tradition but has refused to be confined by it. She leaves home, so to speak, and her destinations are unpredictable.

Most obviously, NdegéOcello loves Jimi. Less obviously, she loves Morrissey.

That was far from evident on her 1993 debut, *Plantation Lullabies*, a record that announced NdegéOcello, a member of the Black Rock Coalition, as a funk bassist of exceptionally high standard and a singer-songwriter with provocative lyrics that broached anything from sexuality to religion, emo-tional turmoil to the iniquities of capitalism.

Although the Washington native's 1996 release, *Peace Beyond Passion*, stayed in a soul-funk vein, her third, 1999's *Bitter*, was a folk-rock album that revealed even greater depths to her way with a lyric.

NdegéOcello's label hated it. The title refers to the resultant struggle with the artist.

If there was a fear that she might be a covert black Joan Baez or Michelle Shocked, a lack of acceptance that non-white singers might feel either one of those artists was as relevant to their culture as Prince, and concern that something anomalous rather than wondrous might occur if those influences coalesced, then some would have been alarmed by NdegéOcello's 2008 set, *The World Has Made Me The Man Of My Dreams*. At times she comes on like a feisty black Anglo-Saxon.

NdegéOcello dared to break one of the unbreakable taboos: a black artist basing their vocal tone and delivery on those of a white Briton, when for decades the *sine qua non* of popular music cognisant of the R&B–rock and roll duality had predominantly been the converse.

The world has made NdegéOcello the Eastender of her dreams, and in return she has made the world a nightmare for inflexible cultural stereotypes.

What would Hendrix have thought? Furthermore, what do we think Hendrix *really* was? Vernon Reid: 'I think that with him it was just *one* fluid thing – his songs; his playing; his whole vibe. People tend to get fixated on his playing, but the thing about Hendrix is he created the *context* for his playing to exist. That's the *real* genius.'[8]

Something similar is at play with NdegéOcello. What has effectively emerged in the course her recording career is a personality, a strength of character that is strong enough to transcend specific sounds. Her lyrics and her rhythmic and melodic sensibilities form a whole that is greater than the sum of the parts. And the parts can change.

They can be the loud, brash guitars that define indie rock or the electronic afterglow of dub production techniques or the bulge of a funk bassline. And the whole point about *The World Has Made Me The Man Of My Dreams*, the beauty of it, is that the rock doesn't replace the soul but co-exists with it. Whether the result is or isn't black music seems to matter little to NdegéOcello, although where she belongs in the music industry, how she should be categorised, is problematic. Be that as it may, she is both upholding and challenging several traditions. She is consolidating and subverting the soul–rock continuum by daring to inflect her voice, one of the most emblematic instruments in black pop, towards tonalities that are not black. Or maybe it is much more appropriate to say that she doesn't sound American, because there are plenty plenty black Britons with broad cockney accents, mate.

Over the years, NdegéOcello's work has gone through many mutations, some of which, such as the instrumental jazz project *Dance Of The Infidel*, have further confounded expectations of her. Yet there is always a sense that she is allowing any number of passing artistic influences, be they black or white, highbrow or lowbrow, to permeate her songwriting, arranging and her whole relationship with the world of sound.

Having said that, NdegéOcello was in her element playing bass with Paris-based Vietnamese guitarist Nguyên Lê. The title of his 2002 set, *Purple*, might suggest a set of interpretations of the music of Prince. In fact, it is a wholly accomplished Jimi Hendrix covers album.

***

A slight return: in January 2010, the British government launched a recruitment drive for secondary school teachers. One of the adverts trumpeted the joy of physics classes as residing in the exploration of complex phenomena like 'electrostatics, wave harmonics … and Jimi Hendrix'. Not very rock and roll, perhaps, though one could argue that science and technology, disciplines that often provide a sneak preview of the future, were where Jimi 'Astro Man' Hendrix was really at.[9]

7 A recipe from Memphis

We sell so much of this, people wonder what we put in it.

(King Curtis, 'Memphis Soul Stew')

Hail the King

One of the 1960s R&B gigs Hendrix had on American shores before crossing the water to London was with saxophonist King Curtis, who didn't take
too long to fire the upstart guitarist for being too hot to handle, both in the
musical and sartorial sense. Loosely comparable to Hank Crawford and David
Newman, sidemen for Ray Charles, Curtis straddled soul, pop and jazz. And
he always sported sharp threads and sharper hair.

Throughout the 1960s, Curtis became increasingly active for Atlantic
Records, the label Crawford and Newman were signed to, and he played solos
on R&B singles, several of which became monster sellers.

Among Curtis's prime credits as a solo saxophonist are the irresistibly
catchy tunes 'Yakety Yak', 'Charlie Brown' and 'Along Came Jones' by the
big-selling doo-wop ensemble The Coasters, a silky vocal group hailing from
Los Angeles. In each case his improvisations are real models of economy, his
short, clenched phrases and steamy, roaring tone enabling Curtis to sustain if
not enhance the momentum of the featured singers.

Sax breaks are vehicles for both tonal and perceptual change in music.
When a horn solo takes over from a vocalist, a song starts growing in a different way because the data that it presents are no longer literal. Words, which
have a direct meaning, can engage the intellect as well as the emotions. It is
telling that even if they are delivered in a foreign language, many listeners
often still *imagine* the artist is saying *something*, whether or not there is any
real substance to the lyric.

With an instrumental passage there is more ambiguity, precisely because
no specific, incontrovertible meaning can be ascribed to the succession of
sounds produced. But that doesn't necessarily mean feeling will be impoverished as a result, and in the best-case scenario the piano, guitar or horn solo,
if played shrewdly, provides relief, contrast or symmetry against the human
voice. This combination can make the overall performance more complete.

True as it may be that soul is by and large a singer's medium, the role of the saxophone in the music's 'pre-history' of R&B should not be downplayed. As was discussed in Chapter 3, a far greater complicity between jazz and R&B in the 1950s than is presently the case contributed decisively to this role, while the growing cult of the saxophone soloist in jazz – think Charlie Parker, above all – surely played a part. In any case, the fact that two hugely influential figures in R&B, Louis Jordan and Ray Charles, were both alto saxophonists as well as singers ensured that the instrument retained a degree of visibility.[1]

Among the albums made by R&B vocalists in the 1950s that took voice–horn complicity to its peak was Ivory Joe Hunter's *Ivory Joe Hunter Sings*, a compilation of sixteen songs that showcased both the great Texan vocalist's fabulously cultured voice and the expert skills of a sadly uncredited band. Dotted throughout the collection are eight- and twelve-bar sax, piano and guitar solos that serve tight, sharp arrangements. The quality of these arrangements may reflect the fact that Hunter himself was a competent leader of small jazz combos that undertook several tours of the West Coast and the South prior to his success in the R&B market with singles such as 'I Almost Lost My Mind'.

'Don't Fall In Love With Me' is without doubt the most striking example of instrumental-vocal balance on the set, in so far as it features a very delicately rendered sixteen-bar saxophone solo intro that sets up a vividly melancholic mood before the entry of Hunter's voice. And given the easy tempo, the beat not at all dissimilar to that of Fats Domino's 'Blueberry Hill', the horn enjoys mucho time, just over fifty seconds, to tell its tale.

This is not at all inconsequential in a song that lasts but 2:45 minutes.

Listening to the tune today is a curious experience as it emphatically highlights the marked change between classic rhythm and blues and contemporary R&B: the presence of a solo musician was much more conspicuous. Voices were paramount but black pop was not absolutely voice-centric, and the way Hunter's record was marketed by the label King, notable for its success with James Brown among others, also shows how instrumentalists found their niche alongside singers. A strapline at the bottom of the cover that reads 'Other King long-playing albums you will enjoy' stands above small packshots of LPs by singer Little Willie John and saxophonists Earl Bostic and Eddie Davis.[2]

Both were as much jazz as R&B players, and they were definitely hot soloists. The success enjoyed by another saxophonist who was also a vocalist, Eddie 'Cleanhead' Vinson, strengthened the complicity of horn player and singer. His sweaty, hard-rocking 1950s hits such as 'Kidney Stew' featured extended improvisations, often running to twenty-four bars, in the middle of the arrangement that raised the excitement level to that of his sung verses – although there was also much to be admired in the way Vinson could pack an enormous punch into shorter solos taken in the introduction to a piece. The blowing and singing powerfully cohere.

Playing a good twelve- or eight-bar solo is an art. *Saying* something worthwhile in such a short space of time can be harder for an improviser than doing so in sixty-four bars. Players who, within this constraint, either seduced with melodic charm or dazzled with tonal exuberance didn't have to be the greatest of soloists, but they did have to play a great solo – quickly.

Born in Fort Worth, Texas in 1934, King Curtis Ousley could do that and more. He had serious jazz credentials, having toured as a teenager with Lionel Hampton and led a trio with soul-jazz pianist Horace Silver before relocating to New York in the mid-1950s, where his work shifted more towards rock and roll and R&B. Curtis's burgeoning career saw him head instrumental ensembles like the Royal Men, and he further raised his stock by becoming musical director for Aretha Franklin, newly crowned queen of soul. The saxophonist was thus paired with the best in '60s black pop.

In addition to his arranging duties, Curtis was a noted producer and talent scout, helming work by stars in waiting – most notably singer-songwriter Roberta Flack – and giving an early break to a jobbing pianist-vocalist who became something of a cult figure for soul adepts in the early 1970s: Donny Hathaway. One of Hathaway's most enduring tunes, the sashaying Latin groove of 'Valdez In The Country', was first recorded by Curtis under the title 'Patty Cake' in 1969.[3]

Despite these credits, Curtis is a figure whose contribution to the development of black music is often overlooked. He can be seen as an intersection between different genres and geographical scenes.

Having spent his formative years in Fort Worth, Curtis was conversant with the fabled 'Texas tenor' tradition. This was a strain of jazz saxophone epitomised by hard-blowing players like Arnett Cobb and Buddy Tate, whose gutsy, full-blooded music often appealed to R&B audiences.

But adept as he was at producing raw, sassy and straight-to-the-point-with-thrills bluesy licks, Curtis also proved to be an articulate improviser who could skilfully stretch out on lengthy solos in the company of the leading figures in jazz of the 1960s. To hear him eloquently interpret the standard 'Willow Weep For Me', backed by Miles Davis's sidemen, pianist Wynton Kelly and bassist Paul Chambers, is to hear a player not wanting for musical intelligence or subtlety.

Rock patented the guitar hero in the 1960s but R&B minted a certain brand of sax hero, either a leader of his own ensembles or a star soloist with vocalists. Curtis was essentially both, a worthy addition to the lineage of Sil Austin, Red Prysock and Big Jay McNeeley. Yet his output was so diverse that he is relevant to all the continuums – soul–jazz, soul–funk, soul–rock – thus far discussed in this book. Moreover, Curtis's ability to galvanise a song with his solos was legendary. His take on Led Zeppelin's 'Whole Lotta Love' is a whole lotta blues tightly squeezed into a whole lotta trickster riffing.[4] The hail of saxophone notes has a visceral strength that would make any man's man of a singer proud.

Today's special

On 4 July 1967, King Curtis, accompanied by an eleven-piece band that included a four-piece horn section as well as two guitarists, piano, organ, drums and bass, entered a Memphis studio and cut 'Memphis Soul Stew', a very sassy piece of instrumental Stax soul. It was set in the trusty twelve-bar blues form, with a jumpy, jittery melody stated on the leader's tenor sax, a very funky rhythmic undertow and, as befits the resources deployed, a big, bulbous, swelling sound that evoked 1950s R&B orchestras *à la* James Brown and Ray Charles.

Though greatly defined by the hard kick of the ensemble work, 'Memphis Soul Stew' is also a vocal track. It features a short spoken-word introduction from the leader, a technique Curtis also employed on several of his other pieces, such as 'Instant Groove' and 'This Is Soul'.

Curtis's text lasts exactly forty bars, just over a minute and a half. And it is an important structural device because it brings a raconteur's presence to bear on a popular song format and fits into a wider lineage of African American oral culture, in which poetic devices are prevalent and more often than not are sharpened with a twist of zestful humour.

With that in mind, it is important to see 'Memphis Soul Stew' as nothing other than a concise display of Curtis's rapping skills, in the sense of talking rather than setting couplets to a specific cadence – although, very tellingly, he did *rhyme*, his delivery nonchalant but resonant, on 'Cook Out', a track recorded just a month after 'Memphis Soul Stew'.

Hence Curtis made a modest contribution to the repository of different forms of black speech, from the scat singing to the DJs to the street-corner slang, the comedy skits and the rhythmic witticisms and self-glorifications epitomised by Muhammad Ali, that would all prefigure and feed into a future music formalised as hip hop.

That an artist known first and foremost for his prowess with the saxophone could take such a step says much about the pre-eminence of the word in African American culture – the love of language, storytelling, debating, teasing and 'testifying' on anything from affairs of the heart to matters sociological that also materialises more extensively in the lengthy 'raps' recorded by Curtis's jazz peer, the alto saxophonist Julian 'Cannonball' Adderley, on albums such as *Country Preacher* and *Music You All* in the late 1960s and early '70s.[5]

For all its dancer-friendly, floor-filling qualities, 'Memphis Soul Stew' is a message song, a politicised rather than political record. It is a manifesto. It is empowerment. It hails the virtues of Southern soul – long lionised as 'deep soul', the real essence of the genre – through the simple allegory of the recipe, the cooking lesson in which Ousley casts himself as a chef in a soul-food restaurant. So it begins: 'Today's special is Memphis Soul Stew. We sell so much of this, people wonder what we put in it. We gonna tell you right now.'[6]

Thereafter, Curtis calls for the ingredients in turn: 'Gimme a half a teacup of bass… Now I need a pound of fatback drums… four tablespoons of boiling Memphis guitar… a pinch of organ… a half a pint of horn.' Each line is a direction. Every member of the band steps up and plays the instrument in question, for no more than a few bars, before Curtis moves on to the next ingredient in the dish, so the introduction becomes an explanation-demonstration of how the soul song is put together, or rather how the musical soul food is cooked.

Gleefully, Curtis hollers 'This gon' taste alright!' during the monologue to reinforce the culinary imagery, creating a picture of himself dipping his finger into the dish and giving it a lick, as befits a seasoned chef charting the progress of his next *pièce de résistance*.

This is a celebration of Southern soul via music and cuisine. And the geography represents a certain cultural depth, a subtext of authenticity and lack of artifice, a basic implication that this is the real thing – a proper 'down-home' affair.

Over the years, Southern soul has become identified with a certain raw if not unrefined quality. At times this is overstated by critics, yet there is no doubt that a great expressive richness defines a Southern soul sound, be it the voice of Otis Redding or the organ of Booker T. Jones. It stems perhaps from a conception of time that is less frenetic or busy and a quotidian intensity, the sensual thickness of the heat away from the North. 'Memphis Soul Stew' expresses this pride in place.

This is how we eat down South, this is how we play our music, and this is how we put our thing together, with guitars nothing less than boiling.

What Curtis is effectively doing is giving the listener an insight into the anatomy of a band, the organs of a living, breathing group. The great beauty of the performance is that each instrument is allowed the luxury of standing in isolation, of taking the spotlight, enjoying a miniature showcase during which it has the chance to establish clearly the riches it contributes to the vocabulary of R&B.

Throughout the 1960s and '70s, this model of a bandleader (sometimes a singer as well as horn player) asking his or her backing musicians to supply an ingredient for the musical meal, or to give the listener just a taste of what they could do – an appetiser for the ear, so to speak – was heard time and time again. One of the best examples is 'Funky Cat' by the Miami singer James Knight. He introduces each instrument in his band, The Butlers, asking the player to be 'funky' or 'mellow'. And indeed the tension between the drive of the beat and its relaxed feel is what creates the magic of the song. Then Knight says, with much teasing of syllables for dramatic emphasis, 'This thing gon' be al…right!' It's an uncanny echo of the King Curtis song.

It's worth noting that Curtis's intro on 'Memphis Soul Stew' also had an impish cousin in a piece recorded just a year later in 1968.

The song is iconic: Sly & The Family Stone's 'Dance To The Music'. Think about the verse structure of this early hit from the hallowed exponent of psychedelic soul. A vocal line cries, 'All we need is a drummer for people who only need a beat', and then the band drops out to let the sticksman lick a groove for four bars. A vocal line cries, 'I'm gonna add a little guitar and make it easy to move your feet', and the band drops out to let the six strings lick a groove for five bars.[7] Other instruments, from bass to horns via organ, follow, and in each case are allowed to *demonstrate* their prowess. The vocal lines clarify the effect of each, the sequence culminating in 'all the squares go home', which means the tune is a step-by-step guide for hip dancers.

The piece is explanatory. The piece is didactic. The piece is referential.

Sly's songs and Curtis's songs can be placed in a wider tradition of show-business tunes that celebrate the instruments used in a band. Prime examples would include Cab Calloway's 1932 piece 'The Scat Song', Wingy Manone's 1937 track 'The Music Goes 'Round And Around' and Louis Armstrong and Bing Crosby's 1956 duet 'Now You Has Jazz'. The above are jaunty, jovial celebrations of the art of making music, but they also make simple technical references to the way sound is produced on brass – 'I push the first valve down'[8] – drums, or rather 'skins', and strings – 'Then, you take a bass/Man, now we're getting some place'.[9] The instrument is the star. The instrument is placed centre stage.

Curtis casts his star instruments in a culturally specific framework. He is making Southern black music. His band members impart a particular flavour to the performance, and his focus on each element, each ingredient in the stew of sounds makes the point that what might pass as a simple 'lick' – a drum beat or bass line – is of crucial importance.

All this constitutes a huge validation of players in what is predominantly a singer's genre, soul music. Or rather, 'Memphis Soul Stew' serves as a reminder of the band's pivotal position within the idiom, because the range of sounds highlighted and celebrated in the course of the piece are the same as those to be found in the work of Curtis's vocalist contemporaries. The song exposes what lies behind a vocalist.

That in itself is deeply rooted in rhythm and blues and blues, since these genres are both vocal and instrumental. They are defined by bands who can hold their own without a singer, as well as by singers who occasionally make a saxophone, guitar or piano the lead 'voice'.

Humour, or at least good cheer, pervades Curtis's narration. The words are delivered with the smile of a joker rather than the earnest gaze of a scholar. Nonetheless, there is a gravitas in Curtis's voice as he asks for 'those boiling Memphis guitars' because he is describing a premium form of musicianship. The technical exigencies needed to make Memphis soul soulful are expressed most vividly in the term 'fatback drums'. This describes a very specific *quality* of sound, a method of playing, a certain tonal richness, whose importance was endorsed by its use as the name of a key band in 1970s funk (The Fatback Band).

Conceptually, the spoken-word intro to 'Memphis Soul Stew' is not anodyne. The content is light-hearted metaphor but the resonance is strong due to the celebration of the act of playing, the spotlight on the tools with which the deed is done, the unabashed self-conscious nature of the whole undertaking. Here is music that is about making music. Here is music that is about all the means by which music is made.

Whether or not Curtis was the first musician to do this matters very little. What really counts is that we can relate the tropes he used on 'Memphis Soul Stew' to some of the most meaningful declarations, some of the defining figures of speech in black popular music, expressions that have come to link genres and generations alike.

So the needle hits the record in 1967 and a saxophonist, before blowing his horn, says: 'I need a pound of fatback drums'. A sample of a 1971 James Brown record rings out, chicken-winging between two turntables in 2007, and it is saying: 'Give the drummer some'. The historical context changes, but the statements of intent are kindred.

Blow it, brother, blow it!

Throughout the 1970s the echo of this demand, nothing less than an explicit call to recognise the vital role of the musician, was heard on dozens of soul and funk records where a bandleader or singer would summon an audience to 'Listen to the bassman',[10] or call on a reed or brass player to 'Blow your horn!', or quite simply 'Blow!'. This is a deeply rooted custom. Consider that the revered stride pianist Fats Waller, a pivotal figure in the early development of jazz, actually fired up his trumpeter Herman Autry with the supplication 'Blow it brother, blow it!', before taking a quite superbly expressive solo on the composition 'Fractious Fingering' way back in 1936.

This is only one of many examples. Waller can be heard spurring on Autry with the command 'Toot that thing' on other songs, and there are various encouragements directed at different band members at different times. Even further back in jazz history is the song 'Dippermouth Blues', recorded in 1923 by the legendary cornet player King Oliver, whose band members are heard shouting 'Play that thing!' on the piece.

Announcing a player or an instrument is also important because it brings a very direct and palpable element of drama to the music. By signalling the impending appearance of a musician, a leader momentarily revels in the role of Master of Ceremonies and performs the invaluable function of creating expectation in the minds of the audience, preparing it for an experience: the freeze-frame in which breath will be held for eight bars or more. All this is an element of ritual, workable theatre, and it is something of a perennial and pervasive force in black popular music.

Highpoints in this process were attained by James Brown. Perhaps more than any other bandleader, he could present his players as veritable bombs to be thrown at the audience, who would then explode with joy as the notes detonated around them. Many are the times Brown summoned his alto saxo-phonist Maceo Parker,[11] and on some cuts the billing the leader would give his sideman reached fever pitch: 'Show 'em how funky you are!'. Hence the musician himself became a delicious threat-cum-education, an on-the-spot encapsulation of an art.

During the 1980s this practice was mostly confined to the stage rather than the studio, primarily because there were fewer bands in operation and soloists were given far less room to express themselves. However, it is interesting to see how hip hop in the '90s, though radically different in form to '60s soul, none-theless has upheld similar aspects of the ritual as defined by the likes of Curtis and Brown. The most obvious example is the way rappers name their DJ, calling him on to the creative front line of a song so that he can display his skills, be it 'talking with his hands', 'taking me out with the fader', riding 'the ones and twos' or being 'the man on the scratches... like his hands are two hatchets'.[12]

Ceremony is such an integral part of black popular music. The need to announce, to preview and present, is a kind of permanent and immutable aspect of African American performance art that resurfaces again and again despite marked changes in the forms of expression developed by successive generations of artists.

The spoken-word intro of 'Memphis Soul Stew' has the effect of creating both expectation and excitement, almost as a cinema trailer does. It also high-lights specific skills, almost as a good sports commentator does.

There is an element both of showmanship and pedagogy in the text.

As a dramatic format, the cookery lesson is a perfect vehicle for this because it presents such obvious opportunities for metaphors of tastiness – even though in modern times, when the bulk of artists do not shift consider-able units of records, it is almost quaint to hear King Curtis talk of selling 'so much of this, people wonder what we put in it'.[13]

Yet more than two decades after that piece was recorded, in 1993 the highly imaginative and often esoteric New York-based hip hop crew Ultramagnetic MCs cut a song, 'Raise It Up', that saw them slap on their metaphorical chef's hats and busy themselves over the grill in the introduction to the song, calling out for one ingredient after another.

'Yo Don, gimme a little bit of that chicken, that smooth chicken... some of that gravy', says rapper Kool Keith to producer Godfather Don over the sam-ple of a molten electric piano chord and a flickering ride cymbal in the song's intro.[14] Keith then continues the kitchen action – 'I want them old hot jazz biscuits' – and the murkiest of bass lines dredges in, descending menacingly as another instruction is heard – 'And a little bit of that blues butter' – before the final, meaningful command is issued: 'Bring in that snare'. We are back to the fatback. The drums were deemed crucial in the 1960s. They remained so in the '90s.

This is nothing less than an adaptation of Ousley's formula for the era of samples, a new recipe that attaches importance to processed sound rather than the live and direct input of players. Ousley calls for bass, drums, guitar, organ and horn, while Keith summons elements found on an old record. Now the producer, armed with beats, is the whole band.

Yet Keith has understood that the impact of the mechanised loop will be heightened through metaphor, so he dramatises through the imagery of soul food, blues butter and hot jazz biscuits. Curtis was cooking grooves down in Memphis; Ultramags are mixing breaks up in New York.

There is a historical continuum here, or at least there are two expressive impulses bound by a similar deployment of imagination, a desire to do more than just perform a song as a stand-alone entity. In both cases there is a prelude, an opening fanfare that is practically a call to order before the performance starts in earnest. The old way is with instruments in real time. The new way is with the consciously manipulated sound of recorded instruments.

And yet a direct intersection of these two strands of the tradition surfaces in an ensemble such as The Roots. Based in Philadelphia, the group's core members, are drummer Ahmir Khalib '?uestlove' Thompson, rappers Tariq 'Black Thought' Trotter and Malik B, beatboxer Rahzel, bassist Leonard Hubbard and keyboard player Kamal. The Roots have been one of the most intriguing forces in black music since emerging in the early 1990s, their primary definition as hip hop artists embellished by their use of a non-hip hop format (a band) and an engagement with jazz, soul, funk and rock that has continually stretched their conceptual framework beyond rap.

Do You Want More?!!!??!, issued in 1994, is one of the strongest entries in The Roots' discography, an album that finds the band at its most jazz-heavy, with fine soloists like alto saxophonist Steve Coleman and vocalist Cassandra Wilson contributing to a repertoire that veers from the rhythmic effervescence of 'Datskat' to the melodic lamentation of 'Silent Treatment'. In between, there is much ingenuity in the way that terse, testy riffs and strange shots of noise, be they a chatterbox kazoo or echo chambers of sinister laughter, are blended into fizzing cocktails of backbeat-driven 4/4 funk, which occasionally bubble into the uncommon brew of sixteen bars of brisk walking swing.

Most striking of all is the way in which the different members of the band are placed in the spotlight. Throughout the album there are constant references to each player: fleeting announcements of his presence and explicit naming of his instrument. The colourful climax is the soundcheck in 'Essaywhuman?!!!??!', which does the rounds of the various elements in the group in an expressly theatrical way. The echo of King Curtis's spoken introduction to 'Memphis Soul Stew' clear.

It is virtually impossible to listen to *Do You Want More?!!!??!* and come away without knowing that Hub is on the bass and ?uestlove on the drums, such is the frequency with which their interventions are singled out by rapper Black Thought, who heartily calls their names.

Hence there is a translation, an application and, to a certain extent, an elaboration of the James Brown/King Curtis principle: 'Give the drummer some/I need a pound of fatback drums'. Pole though the rapper's position may be, it is decisively framed and enriched by the various members of the band, who are a touch less than front men but much more than an expendable and anonymous supporting cast.

Thankfully, The Roots have retained band culture at a time when the singer + producer template largely holds sway in black pop. Their interest in the art of playing – of really putting the smack down, as rappers like to warn – with the aid of instruments as well as mics was recently demonstrated by a totally banging take on 'Melting Pot',[15] one of the great wordless, funky soul tunes by King Curtis' Atlantic Records colleagues Booker T. & The MGs, a group that provided superb backing for many of the label's iconic vocal stars, chief among them Otis Redding.

Tracks like this are invaluable not just because they are part of a rich tradition of rhythm and blues, but because they make the point that dance music – pop music, if you will – does not necessarily have to be vocal-led. This was also underlined with excellence by Curtis's brilliant sax-playing peer Junior Walker.

'Memphis Soul Stew' really served the same purpose, and it made a sizeable commercial impact in 1967, a vintage year in which the frighteningly stiff competition from the singers' camp included masterworks such as Aretha Franklin's 'Do Right Woman Do Right Man', Laura Lee's 'Dirty Man' and Jimmy Ruffin's 'What Becomes Of The Brokenhearted?'

Tragically, King Curtis was murdered outside his apartment in New York just a few years after cutting 'Memphis Soul Stew', in 1971, when he was at his creative peak. It is a great shame that his name has largely been edited from the history of soul music, given the rich body of work he amassed in the space of just over a decade, not to mention the decisive contribution he made to the genre's iconic voices – of which Aretha Franklin is the most obvious example.

'Memphis Soul Stew' remains a seminal artistic statement.

There is something both innocent and worldly in the way the song draws out of the shadows the instruments that can be used to create the magic complementing a singer. This 'players' anthem' also provides a yardstick against which to measure developments in the use of bass, drums, guitars, organ and horns since Curtis issued his manifesto.

Indeed, we shall use this piece as a point of departure to consider what have been the most interesting and unconventional new approaches to the various components of the band, and how they have affected and enriched the sonic vocabulary of black popular music since 1967. With 'Memphis Soul Stew' as a guideline, we shall consider one instrument at a time, so as to relate the history of the music from several different viewpoints. And as King Curtis does at the start of his succulent Soul Food 'rap', we shall first shine a spotlight on the bass.

8 A half a teacup of bass

I remember telling my mom I'm on a commercial on TV, she saw it but she was like, 'I don't hear no bass'. So I thought, OK, next time I'm on one of those commercials, let me experiment with playing with a bright, slappy sound because it might sound good on those small TV speakers, and that became a thing.

(Marcus Miller)

Got it going on

To all intents and purposes, Tommy Cogbill, the bassist featured on 'Memphis Soul Stew', is something of a footnote in pop-music history. His work consisted mostly of sessions for noted Memphis R&B and pop producer Chips Moman, a dynamic self-starter known for assembling studio bands to accompany vocal groups like The Gentrys and The Box Tops.

How Cogbill came to work with Curtis is not documented, but it is known that the saxophonist used a very large pool of musicians from both New York and Memphis for his recordings for Atlantic, either as a solo artist or arranger-producer. It is likely that the bassist may have become part of the 'Southern' aggregation along with a vast slew of itinerant players, one of whom was a young guitarist-for-hire who would grow into a great soul singer with greater tales to tell: Bobby Womack.

Strictly speaking, Curtis's very first words on 'Memphis Soul Stew' lacked a certain accuracy. He called for a half a teacup of bass. In fact, what rang out in response to that demand were the notes, their depth marked by a mildly cottony quality, of Cogbill's bass *guitar*.

This was not a mundane detail. In 1967 the bass guitar was still a relatively new instrument, the first models having been manufactured by Fender in 1951. But it made a substantial impact on the whole character of the rhythm section because it could be plugged into an amplifier, attaining a sharper, more stinging resonance, a more acutely defined sense of treble and a greater weight in the notes, than the previously used double bass – which in many cases was recorded through an external microphone.

Replacing an old acoustic instrument with a new electric one was a hugely significant factor in the transition from R&B to soul. It was like a booty booster to the rhythm section, padding it out with the necessary strength to withstand the expansion of instruments underway at labels such as Stax, Atlantic and

Motown. There, horns, strings, electric guitars and keyboards were all bedding down in studios whose roofs were already being raised by the boombox voices of Otis, Aretha *et al*. Poorly engineered double bass would not have cut through the noise.

Cogbill's figure on 'Memphis Soul Stew' was built, as was the case with so many bass and guitar lines in blues and R&B, on a pentatonic scale where a string of notes was used to create a sense of forward-springing motion in the song. So even before the drums make an appearance a few bars into the arrangement, there is a decisive feeling of propulsion in the air. The bass, with its low, rotund pitches, has a sure-footed, dynamic thrust.

Dynamism of this kind was by no means new. One only has to listen to the array of heavenly riffs written by Willie Dixon, the masterful bassist and songwriter who was the cornerstone of Chess Records in the previous decade, to hear how deeply rooted Cogbill was in an age-old vocabulary. 'Mannish Boy', the 1955 anthem that Dixon penned for Muddy Waters, stands as an antecedent, a bass blueprint for 'Memphis Soul Stew' and countess other tunes because of the bracing ricochet effect of the line, which snaps back and forth between three tones on two strings (the A and the E), creating the effect of both solidity and mobility.

To a large extent, the whole story of the evolution of soul bass-playing, and certainly its combustion into funk, is defined by the injection of greater kinetic energy into that line and a more markedly aggressive stance. Boosted by the technological advance of the bass guitar, players brought a much more audible and penetrating motion to the low register, instead of being swamped by all around them.

Increases in volume, tempo and overall drive are not the only things that came to make the bass such a key element in the whole aesthetic of soul during the mid-1960s. The defining exponents of that era had a degree of invention and, most importantly, a way of stamping their personalities on a song, that could complement decisively the lead singer or horn player.

Without a doubt, this was the greatest achievement of the two session deities who made such an invaluable contribution to the Atlantic and Motown catalogues, Chuck Rainey and James Jamerson, respectively.[1] To all their not insubstantial qualities of tonal richness, wonderfully clear articulation of a phrase and flawless timekeeping, one has to add a priceless ability to embellish memorably the harmony of a song with short incisive 'fills', sometimes lasting no more than three beats, sometimes a bar of four. They were great expressionists in miniature.

Pick any King Curtis or Stevie Wonder song from the period on which either one of these men played, particularly the latter's 'For Once In My Life', and the added colour that the fleet, glancing improvisations on the bass bring to the overall sound canvas is remarkable. What is being created is a series of fizzing, very funky subdivisions and swirling extensions of the main bass line underpinning the composition.

Both Rainey, a baritone horn player in high school, and Jamerson, who was a fundamental part of the storied Funk Brothers house band at Motown, were able to create lines working from nothing more than a grid of chords that mapped out the direction of the song. It is clear there was a rich, although often concise, improvisatory dynamic at play that explains the respect granted to these men by many jazz musicians.

Expressing oneself behind a singer and veering from the script to benefi-cial effect, all the while holding down the groove of a song, is a particularly demanding skill. It's easy to overplay. Jamerson in particular was a kind of hybrid accompanist-soloist who at times functioned almost as a pianist does for a jazz singer. That is to say, he could complete and resolve a phrase by Wonder or Marvin Gaye to create a sense of one long harmonically rich line, undulating out of the voice *into* the bass guitar.

On 'What's Going On', Gaye's *chef d'oeuvre*, although the song features a sizeable band, the only solos other than Jamerson's are a few terse woodwind excursions. The bassist, by contrast, is extemporising quite liberally through-out the suite, roaming and meandering around both the rhythms and melo-dies, often punctuating his fills with rapidly executed chromatic phrases that enhance the smooth, rolling fluency of the score.

Generally speaking, as R&B morphed into soul–funk, bass lines had less of a walking, swing beat and more of a groove feel – in other words, less of an airborne, upward sensation and more of a grounded, downward pull, in line with the generally harder, heavier backbeats that were being caned by the drummers. But it's worth pointing out that James Jamerson had both qualities in his work. This may have been a result of his 'pre-history' as a double bassist who played a lot of jazz. It is not insignificant that in the mid-1970s Jamerson was still occasionally asked by Stevie Wonder to drag his old acoustic upright to the studio.

Sex on a stick

From Rainey, Jamerson, and other great session players like Jerry Jemmott, Bob Babbit and the lesser-known Louis Satterfield, who was once in the Chess house band with a young drummer named Maurice White (the two of them subsequently working together in Earth, Wind & Fire), there emerged a vocabulary of richly expressive rhythmic lines and fills on the bass guitar that brought great verve to 1960s soul music.

Many of the songs for which these bass figures were written adhered to a classic popular song structure, with a key change for the middle-eight sec-tion or occasionally a twelve-bar pattern. This was the case with 'Memphis Soul Stew', where new chords were used on the fifth and ninth bars before a return to the root note on the final bar of the pattern. The sequence forms a backbone of black popular music that has endured because it is marked by such a clear sense of staging posts, a movement from beginning to middle to end that lends the whole cycle a simple but devilishly effective narrative logic.

Although this structure has become one of the most identifiable in blues-based music, it is by no means the only one. Songs with uneven bar divisions and no changes that rely on a single chord account for a major chunk of this music's heritage, the marvellously wry, pithy tales of John Lee Hooker, Howlin' Wolf and Muddy Waters unfolding without recourse to any harmonic modulations.

Bass lines in the work of these artists were repeated figures, and if they were properly amplified or used a bass guitar, then they delivered a kind of unerring primal punch, since there was no respite from the figure's attack for measure upon measure upon measure.

More often than not, repeated bass lines of this kind would comprise five to seven notes and would unfold over just one bar, so that listeners felt a clear sense of centre and structural regularity in the music, and the low end was sharply defined by figures that were mostly concise and compact.

Changes-free models had coexisted with changes-led models during the days of R&B, and that carried over into soul. As soul morphed into funk, the onus was placed on the heaviness and traction of the music, its sense of greater vitality being a major part of its appeal to revelers. There was a quasi-physical contagion, something vividly expressed in the rhyme 'I got ants in my pants/and I wanna dance'.[2]

Benefiting from a more incisive note quality and a more forceful presence in the mix than its predecessor, the double bass, the bass guitar emerged as an obvious agent for this momentum. It prompted a decisive shift in thinking that led progressives to view the instrument not just as part of the harmonic and rhythmic DNA of a piece, but as a central dynamo, a percussive engine that could effectively power and push a song forward as much as a horn section had done in times past.

Using fewer chords and changes made a lot of sense, because it gave the bass guitar an opportunity to find a pivot in the music and to keep spinning one line over and over again, so that wave after wave of big chunky tones kept hitting the dancer-listener. When set, as they often were, in a figure comprising small intervals with jerky, staccato eighth notes or pinched sixteenths, these notes created a skipping sensation in the low register that was supplemented by a surge of decibels. Hence repetition, or rather a sense of rotation, was enhanced by the new sharpness and loudness. Funk was super-sized by the bass guitar.

James Brown's music offers the perfect example of this paradigm. His none too subtle 1968 sex sermon 'Lickin' Stick', whose bass figure was played by Tim Drummond of The Daps,[3] was a marvel of low-end hyperactivity. What stands out is the marked expansion of the line compared with 'Mannish Boy' or 'Memphis Soul Stew'. In those templates the bass figure occupied just one bar, whereas here it stretches over two.

With four extra beats at his disposal, the bass player – most likely under the influence of some of Rainey and Jamerson's work – plays an eighteen-note pattern that drills and pumps up and down with terrific urgency, the enormous thrust of the line largely accentuated by its use of a small number of pitches, a technique that is also prevalent in reggae.

The sheer pummelling agitation of the figure is stupendous, the dynamism a defining element of the song's arrangement. And what further boosts its impact is simply the use of repetition: the figure is held with brilliant metronomic steadiness for exactly seventy-six bars, the entire duration of a piece that clocks in at just under three minutes.

The bass on 'Mannish Boy' has grown bigger, faster legs. Stomping forth with a punishing, quite vicious relentlessness, the eternal, unstoppable rhythm of 'Lickin' Stick' is a barrage of artfully mapped, focused violence. All this increased, effervescent movement in the low register imparts a greater sense of physicality to the music, pushing thick, muscular notes around with zest. It also announces a future of lengthy, often counter-melodic bass lines, figures spread out over two whole measures, of which Fatback's 'Keep On Stepping' and Slave's 'Just A Touch Of Love' are just a few of the most noteworthy examples.

Holding down a repeated bass line for a large number of bars is not a skill to be underestimated. Some jazz musicians complain about having to do nothing more than stick to a one-chord groove throughout a piece. But others recognise that executing figures *ad infinitum* can be key to the essential tension of a song, and that knowing when to mark a slight pause to invest character into a changeless pattern, even if it is just a few notes unfolding in a single measure, is far easier said than played.

A trumpeter once told me that the mark of a great musician was his or her ability to find 'freedom within repetition' rather than without it. There may well be some of that philosophy, either consciously or subconsciously, at play among some of the best funk bassists, who must not only nail the downbeat without fail but also accent their lines adequately in the rest of the bar – usually around the 'three', with no loss of momentum at high tempo. Again, it's easier said than played.

Many of these musicians were able to distinguish themselves through the unwavering steadiness with which they could play the same figure for 48 or 120 or even 200 bars, as songs became longer. They did so with no loss of grip on the pulse, all the while unveiling the slightest of changes in intonation or attack. The glittering promise of a player like William 'Bootsy' Collins was announced in no uncertain terms by the commanding assurance with which he kept on top of the lengthy A section of James Brown's 'Sex Machine', before upping the ante with a faster, choppier figure in the song's sixteen-bar bridge.[4]

This makes an enormous impact when it hits because it follows such a sustained passage of high tension. A rhythmic coil is steadily and unflinchingly tightened, and then it unwinds. Collins's A-section figure, characterised by the same terse, clenched forward motion as 'Lickin' Stick', is superbly held for no fewer than fifty-four bars, so that the comforting beginning-middle-end narrative of a twelve-bar pattern is now replaced by a relentless, trance-like circularity that implies infinity. The bass becomes an inextinguishable throb. It *could* keep on keeping on forever.

Most parts of a pop song are conceived in multiples of four bars and one might have expected the A section of 'Sex Machine', long by most standards, to be thirty-two, forty-eight or sixty-four bars. But it lasted fifty-four, which suggests the change was not preset and Brown called it on the spot, because he felt that fifty-four, not forty-eight or fifty-two or fifty-six, was the duration that put the ants in his pants before it was time to slide his insect-invaded self into the B section. Tight as its execution was, the song had a simple but nonetheless meaningful element of improvisation in its central structure. Brown retains a degree of spontaneity in his creativity. So alert and responsive are his accompanists, they can follow his every whim. His heat of the moment decisions were down to his ego, and perhaps his love of jazz musicians like Jimmy Smith who were known to stoke a fire during unscripted solos.

'It wasn't a certain amount of bars. It was all feeling. We *never* knew what James was gonna do', Bootsy told me in 2011.

> That's what funk was. It wasn't pre-set up, nothing was written in stone. That would have been against his religion. Whatever he felt, he gave us, we followed. We just had to watch his body language and look for his hand signals. That was the fun; that was like the foreplay. Not knowing was better than knowing. It kept us on it, just always expecting something.[5]

Few instruments are featured in 'Sex Machine'. There are no horns, no strings or keyboards, aside from a few splashes of piano, no group of three or four backing singers – and had they been used, the bass guitar would still have made its presence felt. But in this largely denuded setting, the instrument reveals itself by way of Collins's steadfast drive to be a loud, statuesque, self-contained rhythm section.

Were one to make a comparison with another genre, it could be said that the bass in funk became roughly equivalent in impact to the guitar in rock. But where the six-string set great store by the blast and bluster of power chords, the four-string valued the alliance of extensive, often swivelling movement and great size of tone. The instrument became the mighty upholstery in the seat of a song, but without remaining a static entity. The emphasis on bouncing, lengthy scalar figures, repeated with composure, enshrined this new authority.

Along with his brother Phelps 'Catfish' Collins, Cincinatti-born Bootsy joined Brown in 1970. He made key contributions to the canon of funk bass in that decade and beyond. Bootsy's tonal richness and muscular attack were

Bassman Bootsy Collins feeling the funk with James Brown (photo courtesy David Redfern/Redferns/ Getty Images).

combined with excellent timekeeping, all of which reached new heights when he joined forces with George Clinton under the banner of Parliament-Funkadelic and also led his own Rubber Band. Although he was a lead vocalist, Collins frequently made the bass line the essential fulcrum of his song. Moreover, the markedly percussive character of his playing was possibly enhanced by his proven ability as a kit drummer.

Talking bass

Between the late 1960s and the early '70s, the percussive function of the bass guitar in soul-funk expanded. Tunes such as 'Lickin' Stick' and 'Sex Machine' made that abundantly clear. Were one to discard their harmony, which is already minimal, these bass lines would take on the quality of a marching-band snare or of the wood-block or shekere beats used to such lively effect in Afro-Cuban and African music.

That isn't to say that harmony wasn't still an important element for players like Collins, Chuck Rainey and, above all, James Jamerson. The ingenuity of so many of the figures they wrote and improvised displayed an extensive knowledge of chords, scales and modes. But what is increasingly felt in the bass lines of the aforementioned pieces, and in the whole funk aesthetic that took James Brown as a point of departure, is a mindset that envisions the bass guitar as an instrument which can effectively uphold and carry the rhythm with as much momentum as, if not more than, that generated by a drum kit.

Given this development and its pervasive nature, seen in an inordinate number of variations on the whole 'Lickin' Stick'–'Sex Machine' blueprint, the big question any player with a certain amount of strength of character, if not a degree of artistic ambition, had to ask themselves and, ideally, answer was how this lexicon could be effectively enriched – or rather, wholly challenged.

Many funk bassists, in light of the increased prominence they gained in the rhythm section, simply asserted a strong identity, developing a certain way of attacking the line, a distinctive tone and, above all, touch that would mark them out from their counterparts. Generally speaking, these bassists did not use the plectrum or pick favoured by many of their rock peers. This choice enabled them to exert more control over their sound, to have their finger literally on the string, so they could bring out more differentiated shades in both volume and timbre. As was argued earlier, this had a significant bearing on the increasingly common lengthy passages of repeated bass figures.

Essentially, the bass in funk was acquiring more prominence not just as a rhythmic device in the song's arrangement but as a central thematic hook, a kind of attention-grabbing motif or sturdy, low-slung vocal line that would be the element many listeners latched on to and sang, as much as they would a vocal chorus, guitar riff or horn break.

One also has to consider the way many funk bassists embraced technology and made creative use of devices such as the mutron, an electronic concoction of 'envelope filters' that modulated tone and, in the hands of Bootsy Collins, created a woozy, squelchy sound. It was both interesting and, fittingly for Collins's personal aesthetic, comical.

Another important point to bear in mind was that funk bass rose in stature because electric guitarists in many ensembles were not playing crashing power chords that would drown the bassist out, but were opting for wispy upper-register strikes or for fast, fleet, finger-picked lines with a thin sound. Hence at times a single bass note, bashed out by a particularly aggressive player, was like a bulky, sponge-like chord against the slender, needle-like pitches of the 'smaller' string players.

Michael Henderson came across that way at times. As a teenager he cut his teeth with Stevie Wonder and Aretha Franklin, touring and appearing on sessions with the singers before he caught the ear of Miles Davis. The trumpeter used him on albums such as *On The Corner*, arguably one of the funkiest of Davis's early strides into 'fusion' that reflected his desire to engage with the pop culture of Sly Stone's funk and Jimi Hendrix's rock, all the while retaining an idiosyncratic feel to the music that brought to mind a polyrhythmic African drum corps.

Although there was great swagger in the way Henderson played very fluid, chromatic lines, he also possessed a gritty, bluesy economy that saw him deliver short, clipped phrases – the final note curt if not abrupt, so that his lines sometimes acted as vivid exclamation marks. Occasionally, Henderson's tone was gargantuan. He conjured the illusion of a vine of thick, dark chords that stood in marked contrast to the wiry single-note guitar lines, lighter foliage wrapping around the wide trunk of the bass. And that made conceptual sense, as Davis's dense, charged music evoked a creeping, menacing undergrowth in a concrete jungle.

Equally interesting is the music Henderson made post-Davis, where his ability as a songwriter and singer is manifested in solo albums such as *In The Night Time* and *Goin' Places*. Both of these albums saw him apply the same tonal and rhythmic ingenuity to more conventional song forms – very different from *On The Corner*, where Henderson had to hold his own in a gluey thicket of layered riffs. That he could sound so relevant in both contexts said much about the strength of Henderson's artistry.[6]

One hugely important thing about Henderson was how good he sounded when he either played mid or slow tempo. To an extent, he was funkier doing this than he was on more up-tempo numbers. This was primarily due to Henderson's tonal richness, but also because there is an argument that says a groove can be more memorable when it decelerates rather than accelerates. In this context, the bass can reinforce funk's function as a devastatingly dramatic and physically affecting form of slow music.

Players other than Henderson made a similar point. The perception that black popular music is a dance genre, predicated solely on velocity and a certain frantic quality in both the rhythm and vocal performance, simply does the genre a disservice. It doesn't recognise the music's capacity to encompass a wide range of approaches.

Slow, heavy, funky bass is almost a sub-strand of this wider lexicon. From the likes of James Brown and Bootsy to the slew of acts they influenced, like War, Mandrill and Kool & The Gang, the use of a relaxed, almost mellow groove was an option taken up enthusiastically by funk practitioners.

Constant streams of notes in the low register could create a vast swell of energy. But the simple 'less is more' approach was entirely relevant to a player like Henderson because of the size of his sound. Larry Graham was another bass guitarist who had an even greater impact at low tempo. During the late 1960s, he enriched a certain minimalism and unhurried playing style with a novel bass tone. Arching his thumb, stiffening it like a small hammer, Graham would slap the strings, drawing from the bass a resonance with a decidedly metallic quality. This rattle and ring was a radical departure from the much smoother, rounder and infinitely less abrasive feel of a note brought to life through the prevalent fingering techniques.

As a member of Sly & The Family Stone, the pyschedelic funk-rock heroes who were a primary source of inspiration to Miles Davis, Graham – a tall, charismatic Texan who debuted in a hotel trio led by his mother Dell – made a huge contribution not just to the vocabulary of the bass guitar but to free-thinking instrumentalists overall. His imagination and resourcefulness essentially said: 'Sound by any means necessary'.

Slap bass was thus a kind of subversion. Although some double-bass players had used it in rockabilly and country blues during the 1950s and in jazz during the late '20s – epitomised by musicians such as Pops Foster, Welman Braud and Al Morgan – nobody had thought to transfer the technique to an electric bass guitar, where the priority was the cleanest possible articulation of the notes.

Graham made a virtue of ruggedness. His sound was channelled force. On 'Thank You For Talking To Me Africa', the closing piece on Stone's 1971 masterpiece *There's A Riot Goin' On*, Graham gave a peerless display of the slap technique over a charmingly languid, almost slouch-lazy tempo.

As was the case with Henderson, on whom his influence is clear, Graham makes relatively simple lines go a long way. The bulk of the phrases he plays are just two or three notes, which scratch and scrape away, often jumping suddenly and dramatically in volume.

This provides a decisive complement to Greg Errico's drum kit: at many junctures the bass becomes a ringing cowbell. Graham is buck-wild loud. At times he hits the bass so hard, the notes send tremors through the ensemble, ducking it in a stream of clicks, clangs, clucks and such strange sibilant noises that his timbre approaches that of the gravel-rough guitars jangling their way through indie rock.

Musicians like Graham raised aggression levels in the bass register. He became an embodiment of funk because the music was largely defined by explosiveness, and his notes seemed to erupt into life rather than break their way out of silence. The beauty of such playing lay precisely in its controlled power, a kind of focused punch that upped the ratio of rock in funk, especially when the eruptions were conflated with the hard crackle of high-pitched percussion like bongos, claves and timbales.

Sonically, Larry Graham brought another material into play. Whereas the double bass, when recorded adequately, pushed the vibration of the instrument's wood to the fore, the slap on the bass guitar emphasised the hard steel of the strings, so the textures were radically different. Once there was a hum; now there was a pop.

Hence a predominantly low-register instrument acquired a higher, sharper treble that had almost the stark, altissimo punch of a horn.

Techniques like the slap gave bass players a significantly wider range of options in terms of the gamut of timbres that could be deployed in their work. In that respect, there is a strong parallel with a jazz aesthetic, as the new sound stemmed from a desire to hear beyond what was the accepted lexicon of an instrument.

If music is a form of language, then the slap came to represent one of the most important rhetorical devices that can be employed to humanise and dramatise a series of statements from a given speaker: the exclamation. Sometimes the technique is most effective when used sparingly, contrasting with a passage of conventionally fretted notes. The slap brightens the low range after a less aggressively fingered phrase, pushing into the upper range like a sharp vocal scream. This was something another great bass guitarist understood.

The Miller's tale

Like Michael Henderson, Marcus Miller really raised his profile when he played with Miles Davis. But Miller had already revealed an incisive, slap-heavy style on stints with the keyboard player, Lonnie Liston Smith, who had also briefly played with Davis. Some of the bassist's work was very elaborate and melodic, reflecting the evolution of both funk and one of its offshoots, disco where the bottom end could be very busy and agitated, with a line often using several pacy octaves that lent a distinct bounce to a song.

Before making his debut as a solo artist in 1983 with the album *Suddenly*, Miller – who enjoyed a lengthy and successful creative partnership with singer Luther Vandross – also did numerous gigs in New York studios, recording commercials and incidental music with lots of synthesizers, strings or horns. So one of his concerns was making himself heard, especially if his elders were liable to catch his fire on the small screen.

'I remember telling my mom I'm on a commercial on TV, she saw it but she was like, "I don't hear no bass",' Miller explained in 2009, backstage at the Barbican, London, where he was performing *Tutu*, the *chef d'oeuvre* that he wrote and produced for Miles Davis in 1986. 'So I thought, OK, next time I'm on one of those commercials, let me experiment with playing with a bright, slappy sound because it might sound good on those small TV speakers, and that became a thing.

'All of a sudden the producer was like, "Ah, that sounds great!" They were always figuring out how to make the music sound full, and this was before TV had big speakers, so, yeah, it helped me to get my slap technique together and I got very good at being subtle and playing little intricate things.'

Flippant though this remark may be, it nonetheless says a lot about the motivation behind certain artistic choices. It also brings us back to the central question of volume and presence in the audio landscape, an issue Larry Graham possibly faced several years prior to Miller and dealt with precisely by inventing the slap.

To be heard is essential; to be noticed, more so. Miller, influenced by jazz-fusion trailblazers Jaco Pastorius and Stanley Clarke, as well as by funk pioneers Larry Graham and Louis Johnson, stood out because he had an extraordinary way of playing funky lines that curled and purred around the basic harmony of a piece, gathering enormous colour and character. And the bassist's popping sound generated notes that were so razor sharp and high in pitch, they evoked a warped, electrified harp – a mighty loud one.[7]

Pushing the bass more stridently into the treble register like this had an odd yet compelling effect. What had previously constituted the darker tones in the mix were now, by way of the slap, recast in a weird bright light. With the bass thus functioning as an adulterated four-string guitar, the obvious option for a rhythm section was to have a second bass line with a tone low enough to put some ballast under the new high low tone.

Overdubs were used on occasion to thus combine a conventionally fretted, often melodic figure with a slapped rhythmic one, so that a wider range of timbres, moving from the thick and bulky to the thin and wispy, amounted to a simple but highly interesting form of bass polyphony.

Many classic 1970s soul-funk combos experimented with this increased range of low-register colours. Closer examination of the work of The Isley Brothers, Earth Wind & Fire, Fatback and Bootsy's Rubber Band reveals a fascination with the use of different qualities and characters of bass in arrangements that flouted the convention of one bass line per song.

Black pop wanted bass options. It therefore developed 'polybass'.

A memorable example of this approach is 'Roll With The Punches', a riotous rumble of instrumental funk cut in 1978 by Patrice Rushen, the gifted jazz pianist best known for her 1982 vocal soul hit 'Forget Me Nots'. 'Roll With The Punches' has a wildly explosive slap bass, creating a quite high-pitched percussive barrage against which a felt-like fretted bass plays a pert, singing line. The low register is hence split into two distinct tonalities. More to the point, it evokes two sensations or instruments: one hears bass as bongos and bass as bugle.

Another polybass concept gradually emerged and became one of the most curious, distinctive and original sounds in soul music's low register during the latter half of the 1980s. This was the combination of lines played on a bass keyboard and a bass guitar. It produced a novel intermingling of synthetic, electronic tonalities and analogue electric vibrations.

Soul and funk embraced the keyboard bass developed by the likes of Moog precisely because it offered a rich gamut of note types.

Pitches could be pushed right down to a squelch, sometimes with heavy sustain taking them towards a drone. This added thickness of tone dovetailed perfectly with the general pursuit of more substantial bulk in a rhythm section bolstered by layers of percussion.

Although the keyboard bass actually replaced the bass guitar on many tracks, the two instruments were also used together, a manoeuvre that presented the low register as an area in which the hardness of the machine and the hotness of the player joined forces.

One might have expected the new technology to make the 'old' axe entirely obsolete. But the alliance of the two devices showed that artists were entirely capable of thinking outside the box, or at least of letting their experimental muse lead them to uncharted, unheard territory.

Usually, the bass keyboard played very low, sometimes approaching a sub-sonic, blob-like tone while the bass guitar occupied the middle or high range and either doubled the line or played shorter fragments from the original figure. The net result was a graduated shading of textures in a single designated area of the sound canvas.

Bringing more detail to this effect was the use of a synthesizer to play another bass line that could slide into the space between the low keyboard bass and the high bass guitar. Thus the listener's focus was now blurred between several changing manifestations of the bass.

Exactly who was the first artist to start using the technique is hard to pin down. But it became a feature in the work of Bootsy, Cameo and the Gap Band from the mid-1970s. During the following decade, the likes of producers Jimmy Jam & Terry Lewis and the artist Mtume, a very good percussionist and yet another Miles Davis alumnus, used the slap bass like a game show buzzer, pinging out a high, sharp note once every two or three bars, so that it sliced through the big balloon of the keyboard bass underneath. As one note swelled, the other popped.

Tightness, or tightening, is what slap bass conveyed most vividly. This is why it induced tension, whereas a low keyboard bass presented tone as something flaccid and globular. So there were two diametrically opposed sounds in conjunction: as one contracted, the other expanded.

Interestingly, all the aforementioned had extensive experience of playing in bands. They did not just hole up in studios and create a mad-professor sound lab with a stack of synthesizers. Minneapolis-born Jam & Lewis were contemporaries of Prince who spent their formative years in The Time, where they played funk taking its cue from George Clinton and Bootsy Collins. As producers, Jam & Lewis supplemented their playing experience and their command of drums, percussion and bass guitar with a range of state-of-the-art keyboards.

Hence the use of synthesizer bass and bass guitar on many of the hits they produced for The SOS Band, Cherelle and Change,[8] among others, was a case not of technology replacing the musician but of the musician embracing technology and creating a continuum between the era of the band and that of the stand-alone electronic producer.

Compositionally, not all of this output passes muster in the cold light of day. But the history of any genre tells us that artistic success is sometimes less important than conceptual daring. What really counts here is the imagination displayed in relation to an element of the rhythm section often given much less prominence in other forms of pop music. From an average song one can take away a strange and sampladelic bassline.

End games

Funk's flirtation with many tones in the low register, or its view of the low register as a prism through which several tones can emerge, has been one of the most intriguing chapters in the rich story of the bass in black pop.

It was also an indirect, vague development of polybass in jazz in the 1960s, as exemplified by groups led by John Coltrane that had two double bassists, one of whom might play 'arco', while the other fingered lines.

Soul in the 1980s, in any case, embraced the idea of the bass as a weighty, substantial force that would be as conspicuous as other elements in an arrangement, and grow further during passages where the keys and vocals dropped out. Bass became a tower of strength in a twelve-inch 'dub' mix.

Hip hop's influence in the 1990s brought a heavier, inky low end into play. The prevalence of subsonic lines, programmed and manipulated on state-of-the-art electronic equipment, generally pushed the frequencies further down – and the bass was always edging towards murky waters anyway. The mission was to find tonal variety lurking down in the depths.

Searches for a new sound, a new character in the low register have certainly led producers as well as musicians on some adventurous and unexpected pathways. One major recent chapter in the history of the bass in black pop has been the return of the acoustic bass, primarily through scouring of vintage vinyl for precious new samples.

Sometime in the early 1990s, hip hop producers started to use breaks – mostly single bars – featuring double-bass figures from classic jazz records cut back in the '50s and '60s. They realised that the particular character of the sound – the hum of wood, the enormous richness of tone – was something as 'large' as any kind of programmed sub-bass. And it had a more human quality. The double-bass samples used by the Beatnuts, Digable Planets, A Tribe Called Quest *et al.* extended and enhanced the tonal range of hip hop. They also led gradually to a change in the image of what was essentially tagged as an old 'axe', perhaps dogged by the perception that its primary function was to provide a gentle undertow for effete mid-tempo swing or lights-down-low ballads.

Double bass was now recast as a sound that was impressively deep, glowing with warmth and, above all – certainly on a cut like the Beatnuts' 'Props Over Here' – capable of quite pounding aggression. Hardness, the component that funk started to lose in the mid-1980s and that hip hop duly took up, was given a further twist by the resurrection of a sound belonging first and foremost to jazz in the '50s. This historical scrambling was as bizarre and nonsensical as it was mesmerising.

But that's where hip hop pays its greatest creative dividends. The genre's chronology mash-up enables it to derail expectations of what era a listener might end up in when stepping into rap's audio Tardis.

What was more significant was the way either producers or groups went beyond samples of the double bass and started to use the instrument proper in real-time recording. Kicking things off on the aptly titled 1991 album *The Low End Theory* was a collaboration between A Tribe Called Quest and Ron Carter, one of jazz's foremost double bassists, a player whose beautifully creamy, broad tone and exemplary timekeeping had made him an invaluable member of Miles Davis's second great Quintet, a much lionised ensemble in the late 1950s.

Of equal importance was the use of the double bass by Leonard Hubbard of The Roots on their superlative 1994 album *Do You Want More?!!!??!*, a set that, under the undeniable influence of the aforementioned Quest material, brought an astute, well-wrought coherence to its expert entwining of hip hop, jazz, funk and soul.

Gradually double bass started to crop up in soul music as well. The appearance of Carter on Erykah Badu's 1997 debut *Baduizm*, an album that was one of the key documents of the so-called 'neo soul' movement, was possibly as much a reflection of the singer's engagement with hip hop culture, and her discovery of the 'old instrument' through sampling, as it was of a desire to share the studio with a senior jazz musician who had made a number of historical recordings.

Hearing the tone of the double bass underneath a soul singer, even though the super-sized 'fiddle' may have owed its revival largely to hip hop, gave a new twist to the soul–jazz continuum discussed in Chapter 3. The exponents in question often came from jazz and had a more pronounced swing than the average bass guitarist.

Swing is exactly what Carter does in the coda to 'Drama', the Badu composition on which he appears. If one wanted to chart the life cycle of the piece according to genre, it could be said that its birth lies resolutely in jazz – given the combination of moist, almost aquatic keys and of Carter's trademark slides down the neck – before it slinks into hip hop-edged soul in adulthood. The piece ages gracefully, shifting back to jazz as the double bass ambles into a swish, fluid walking line on the fade-out.

Moments such as these had not been heard in soul since the mid-1960s, when the genre was still termed R&B. One only has to think of how distinctive the swing pulse is in the double bass used on Mary Wells's 'My Guy', and then compare it with any number of bass guitar-led funk cuts from the following decade, to see that the upright, the 'tall tree' in black pop can bring a very distinctive slant to a song's arrangement.

Certainly the note quality, the fullness, the felt-like character of the purr between pitches on a double bass made a marked difference to much post-hip hop soul, or rather post-Quest soul. For example, the appearance of the veteran British jazz bassist Gary Crosby on Omar Lye-Fook's 1994 piece 'Little Boy' brought a resonance to the music that would be very hard to replicate on a synth bass or a bass guitar.

Liberated from its predominant association with straight jazz, the double bass now stands as a viable option for the contemporary soul artist, especially one plugged into hip hop. The sight of The Roots's Leonard Hubbard cradling the instrument while sporting a hoodie and a battle-royal B-Boy attitude on the sleeve of *Do You Want More?!!!??!* no doubt helped to restore a street cred that was missing during the 1980s. The fact that Lye-Fook's current bass man Colin McNeish alternates neatly between the acoustic and the electric reflects the enrichment of the low register that has marked soul over the last decade.

Still, the bass guitar remains a very valuable component of the soul ensemble and its more progressive champions have continued to experiment with all manner of tones as well as techniques. That five- and six-string basses have been widely embraced by black music is an indication of that mission. There is practically a new sub-strand of 'mo' lo' vocabulary, developed by highly accomplished musicians like Britain's Anthony Tidd,[9] who has worked to startling effect right across the spectrum of jazz, hip hop, soul and funk.

In any case, any presumed orthodoxy on bass lines has been bent out of shape. Certainly a superior player like Marcus Miller proves just how rich the whole polybass approach can be when he weaves together bass rhythm *and* melody on his songs. An enthralling example is 1997's 'Rush Over', where Miller lays down a synth line that conjures up a woozy double bass and then plays a razor-sharp slap motif on top of it.

Singing on that piece is Me'Shell NdegéOcello. The Washington native has also emerged as one of the premier bass guitarists of her generation. What she has done is built on the great legacy of James Jamerson and his descendants – notably, Bernard Edwards of Chic and Paul Jackson, a key element in Herbie Hancock's '70s Headhunters ensemble – so that flashes of these musicians illuminate her discography, from 1994's *Plantation Lullabies* through to 2007's *The World Has Made Me The Man Of My Dreams*.

Blessed as she is with impressive harmonic knowledge, NdegéOcello has understood that the bass guitar can be an entirely flexible instrument, as potent when it is deployed percussively, sometimes in short, fleet lines, as it is when used melodically. The best example of the latter is the lengthy undulation in 'Andromeda And The Milky Way', an outstanding piece from 2005's *Comfort Woman*. Spread languorously over two bars, the twelve-note figure functions practically as a piano hook.

Sonically, the bass in soul, from the use of slap technique to the synth bass-bass guitar combination to the return of the double bass, has sprung many surprises. And it remains among the most talismanic of all sounds in the genre, its presence emphatic, graphic, corporeal.

Successive generations of players have fashioned a range of textures and idiosyncratic 'characters of sound' in the low register. That is not as common in other genres, although rhythm (or rather percussion) remains a primary function of the bass in black popular music.

Bass is the first ingredient called by King Curtis on 'Memphis Soul Stew' because it sets time so solidly and effectively functions as a drumbeat. Indeed, many great funk tunes would still convey rhythmic dynamism if the drums were edited out of the mix – not that kick, snare and cymbal don't warrant their propers.

9 A pound of fatback drums

> He had this board, made of some sort of plastic. He used it on a lot of sessions, and it would make all these weird noises; these sort of wobbling rhythms that he just added on to a whole lot of other things that he had.
>
> (Martha Reeves on Jack Ashford, Motown house band percussionist)

It's all about expression

Once bass guitarist Tommy Cogbill has set the pulse on 'Memphis Soul Stew', King Curtis asks for 'a pound of "fatback" drums', and instantly Gene Chrisman kicks in with a rolling, tumbling pattern on the kit. The bass drum is booming out dry, sturdy three-note thuds, decisively bringing body and bulk to the track, while the snare has a much lighter, whiplash quality, its five-note quiver achieving a quicksilver, springy reverberation.

'Fatback' was a word that came from soul food and it essentially designated a generous ridge of pork belly, or meat often found in what was known as 'hog cracklings'. Carried over to a musical setting, the term – widely applied to drumming – retained this sense of fullness, a kind of pulpy ripeness in the sound, as well as the idea that the approach to the beat itself would be both assertive and emphatic.

Rhythm and blues in the 1950s, the decade that preceded the recording of the King Curtis piece, had its share of fatback drummers, notably Earl Palmer, Fred Below or Odie Payne, who recorded with Chicago's Chess Records heavyweights Muddy Waters, Willie Dixon and Little Walter. Generally speaking, though, the drumming heard on the bulk of songs in black pop at the time had less of the effervescence that would became a major mark of distinction in the approach to the instrument from the mid-1960s onwards. There was still a certain swing feel in these drummers' work, a looseness in the pulse and an occasional marked accenting of the ride cymbal that was an overlay of jazz – an entirely logical state of affairs, given that many drummers worked across both genres.

Using 4/4 as a basic metre, the majority of R&B drummers concentrated on keeping their time steady, anchoring a song so that the singer, or horn player in the case of the instrumental ensembles, felt comfortable stating a melody or launching into a solo. The mission statement was often to keep the dancer busy on the floor rather than dazzle a seated critic closely scrutinising every note.

Nonetheless, in the work of Motown drummers Benny Benjamin, Richard 'Pistol' Allen and Uriel Jones – pivots of the label's fabled house band, the Funk Brothers – there was a brilliant stylistic flexibility, an understanding of both force and finesse. It endowed a song like the Four Tops's 'I Can't Help Myself (Sugar Pie Honey Bunch)' with a very physical, pumping, four-to-the-floor drill – a clear harbinger of the rock lexicon – while a piece like Marvin Gaye's 'How Sweet It Is To Be Loved By You' had a caressing, wafting swing that suited the romantic tenderness of the theme.

As the 1960s progressed, R&B drummers became more aggressively per-cussive with the kick and snare, detonating notes liberally within a bar, get-ting busy almost as a bongo or conga would in Latin music. So the kit often became a little volcano of activity within the band.

Greater syncopation also came into play. Although the technical definition of this key word in the history of black music is the accenting of a weak beat or of the space between beats, the main thing to understand is that it gives the music a sense of sliding while it presses forward, so ultimately there is a degree of movement *within* movement, a kind of sly hopscotch performed by musical notes already up and running.

When a drummer's accents do not just fall squarely on beats one, two, three and four of a bar in 4/4 time, but rather flit around those markers, then the musician can create a sense of bend or curve, a deviation away from unerringly straight rhythmic lines. These blips are interesting.

The heavy, heated syncopation of traditional marching bands in New Orleans, home of the great Earl Palmer, filtered through many players and lent more spring and bounce to the drum kit. This synched potently with the increasingly agitated, effervescent character of funk, a genre in which the busy, bumpy course of the beat, its trajectory and impact on the listener-dancer, the way it drops and hits, are paramount.

Looming large here is Idris Muhammad, a Crescent City native who has proved to be one of the most polyglot figures in black music. Having started his career in the mid-1950s shuttling between the rock and roll of Fats Domino and the R&B of Lloyd Price, Muhammad went on to work with soul-jazz alto saxophonist Lou Donaldson in the mid-1960s, a tenure that saw him unveil a polyrhythmic intricacy bubbling with funkiness.

In fact, Muhammad has consistently divided his time between soul and jazz since then, leaning perhaps more towards the latter through his work with strong improvisers such as Pharoah Sanders and Joe Lovano.

Playing funk, Muhammad drew a beautifully sharp crackle from his snare, which he often syncopated heavily.[1] But perhaps the most striking aspect of his approach to the kit was the way he could lead with the bass drum, often creating faintly melodic lines that bounced along with the same energetic flu-ency as the other musicians in the rhythm section.

New Orleans funky drummer Idris Muhammad (photo courtesy Clayton Call/Redferns/Getty Images).

So when Muhammad played with bassists, he had an ability to lock into their lines, to complement and reinforce their phrases. When this peaked, something like a mirror image was created between the two musicians: the sonic whole was greater than the sum of the parts.

This is exactly what happens on Muhammad's 1972 rendition of 'Express Yourself', a sweet but stingingly funky soul anthem by Charles Wright & the Watts 103rd Street Rhythm Band. About halfway through the piece Ron Carter, flexing on bass guitar rather than the double bass for which he was fêted, drops out for a few bars to leave Muhammad in isolation. Yet Carter still, beguilingly, maintains a kind of ghost presence during his absence. That's because the drummer, all the while keeping perfect time, copies the bass figure note for note. The harmony instrument is subsumed and recast in rhythm, allowing momentum to become a pervasive force in the song.

It is a seamless descent into the low end. Bass segues into bass drum.

The birth pangs of hip hop, black pop's future, can be heard in those fertile four bars. From the father of fatback gurgles forth the baby of boom-bap.

Cultural specifics count here: New Orleans, Muhammad's heartland, had produced a line of drummers liable to do just the same. The strategy can be traced back to Freddy Kohlman, Chester Jones or Ernest Elly.

Advanced understanding between drummer and bass player has been a major building block for rhythmic excellence in soul-funk. But the richness of character, the majesty of sound that distinguish some of the sticksmen who have helped to define the vocabulary of the instrument should certainly not be played down. As in jazz, the touch of the musician matters.

Something that might be considered a minor detail can, and did, become a thing of beauty: the rimshot. A modest flicker of a note. Nothing more than the sound of the stick tapped precisely on the metal casing at the side of the snare drum. Easy to do in theory but hard to manipulate with the rapier poise of an Al Jackson Jnr or a Howard Grimes, two of the iconic drummers essential to the sound wrought by producer Willie Mitchell for Al Green and Ann Peebles – singers who, aided by these and other fine musicians, made timeless soul in the early 1970s. There was also artistry in the simple hesitation or anticipation shown by these musicians and their peers. Occasionally, the sticks would be flicked fractionally behind or ahead of the second or the fourth beat in the bar, giving a shade of swing that lent extra nuance of feeling to a singer.

Finesse is perhaps not a word readily associated with the idea of the funky drummer that came to prominence at this time. It is appropriate, though: despite all their dynamism, the one thing that bound together the players discussed so far was a large degree of lightness of touch. There was a marked stealth in their handling of the drum kit.

All the great funky drummers contrived to let their sticks *fall* on the skin of the drum through a loose, decidedly supple wrist action, rather than crashing down on the kit. This underlined that the febrile, feverish quality of funk could come from tightly controlled strength and not brute force. James Brown's two revered drummers, John Jabo Starks and Clyde Stubblefield, are arguably the epitome of this approach. Listening to what they do on 'Papa Don't Take No Mess' and 'Funky Drummer', it is remarkable the way they caress the snare, massaging the kinetic energy rather than flinging it forward, so there is both a feathery, floating levity and a solid gravity in the pulse of the song. There is a distinct quality of swing, a flitting between beats on the snare, but the rhythm also grooves heavily because the bass drum is so active. The movement is simultaneously earthbound and airborne.

Given the huge impact these musicians have had on the popular music that came after them, hip hop (through the countless times their work has been sampled), it might be useful to gain an insight into their methodology from a member of the hip hop generation who has emerged as a premier modern drummer, slyly retaining something of Stubblefield's flicker while reflecting the curt punctuations that mark programming in the 'breakbeat' era: Ahmir ?uestlove Thompson.

In conversation with David Weiss of *Drum! Magazine* in October 2007, The Roots's sticksman made a telling observation about the way both the equipment and the handling thereof shape a drummer's groove:

It truly does matter which sticks you use. I found out that the lighter the sticks, the funkier the song. As a matter of fact, the lighter you play the funkier the song. Listen to the James Brown records and watch Stubblefield playing on some of the footage. Clyde's playing very light. He's not doing the John Bonham thing with all his might.[2]

Bass guitarists will also tell you that the greatest drummers, often freelancers flying from one session to the next, are the ones who pull off an almost hypnotic sleight of hand and 'play some real shit but *don't* get in the way'[3] – meaning the flourish can be as subtle as the use of a half or a whole note where one might expect an eighth.

Session drummers, then, contributing to a wealth of recordings by many singers, have become revered for their very distinctive musical characters. One could big up anybody from Americans James Gadson and Poogie Bell to Brits Richard Bailey and Frank Tontoh.[4]

Hi-Jack'd

Funky drumming, with its skip and sashay, its increased internal movement, brought a significant change to the pulse and feel of black pop in the 1960s. But there was another agent of rhythm that made a sizeable impact on the whole identity of the music.

It was not a different philosophy or approach to the use of snare, kick and toms. Rather, it was the expanded use of another instrument or, more precisely, a family of instruments: percussion. This very general term embraces anything from congas and bongos to timbales, wood blocks, bells and cabassa. But really there is never any telling exactly what a 'hand drummer' may chose to pack his or her side of the stage or studio with. The majority of these musicians are constantly varying or updating their basic set-up.

Percussionists had been heard in R&B since the mid-1940s, particularly on New Orleans recordings by Professor Longhair, where the use of maracas, wood blocks and congas was not unusual. Yet these 'little' instruments were not part of the 'standard' piano- or guitar-led rhythm section plus horns that accompanied the bulk of singers at that time.

One percussion instrument that had been a very prevalent feature both of R&B and the gospel-flavoured 'soul jazz' of the mid-1950s was the tambourine, a device that came directly from the black church. There it was used with great fervour not just by musicians but also by members of the congregation sufficiently inspired to let the 'spirit' move them.

Bearing that in mind, the tambourine is significant because it stands as a democratic instrument, something easy enough for anybody to play, whether they are musically schooled or not. It is an agent of solidarity.

Sonically, the tambourine was a very important addition to the drum kit, as it produced higher tonalities than the snare or tom but had a different texture from the much lighter cymbals. The loud, clunky clarion it provided gave the rhythm section a touch more density.

Interesting tones could also be created by using the tambourine not only as a hand drum to be slapped against the palm or wrist but as a supplement to the kit, by placing the tambourine over the snare or hi-hat. The effect of this was a greater brightness and a ringing, bell-like note that astutely counterbalanced dark chords from the piano or several horns.

Tambourines were an integral part of the whole Motown sound, often playing right on the beat to send a shudder across the drum kit. The prominence granted to the instrument in the mix, along with whiplash effects on the snare that were also at daringly high volume, brought an added range of nuances in timbre. These were extended by the gradual introduction of more percussion instruments over time.

Three years after its inception in 1960, the Funk Brothers, Motown's house band, was augmented by two percussionists, Jack Ashford and Eddie 'Bongo' Brown. Between them, they substantially enriched both the timbral and the rhythmic base of the catalogue, introducing in the best cases a series of different hand drums at different stages of a piece's arrangement – which is exactly why those apparently simple three-minute songs bear repeated listening. Percussion was detail.

There was more, though. Many Motown tracks are full of these indefinable juddering noises that are sometimes like the galloping rhythms of a cabassa. But they vibrate at too high a pitch for that, suggesting a custom-built instrument is being deployed to fashion these slipstreams of strange beats for the rest of the instruments to bathe in. Martha Reeves, lead singer of the Vandellas – responsible for one of the label's signature hits, 1964's 'Dancing In The Street' – told an interesting story about Ashford backstage at the Jazz Café in 2008. This was after a gig where, incidentally, Reeves had worked a tambourine so hard, she must have packed industrial-strength titanium in her hips. 'Jack had this kind of board, made of some sort of plastic', Reeves explained.[5] 'He used it on a lot of sessions, and it would make all these weird noises, these sort of wobbling rhythms that he just added on to a whole lot of other things that he had.'

That Reeves was talking about an instrument with no name, an invented sound device, is not without significance. Ashford's creation of 'unidentified noise' is actually the goal of the progressive end of modern music, which sets great store by sonic novelty, particularly in the world of electronica. Alternatively, Ashford can be placed in a lineage of improvising musicians, like Rahsaan Roland Kirk, who used anything from discarded tuned metal to hose pipes to fashion their own instruments. And perhaps the connection between these musicians is not usually made because the former is pigeonholed as soul and the latter as jazz, so they remain segregated on different sides of the divide between pop and art music.

Kirk made an instrument from bamboo sticks. Ashford once saw fit to use a sheet from a hotel bedroom as part of his percussion arsenal.

Ashford was in the vanguard. He took the lead on the use of hand drums but eventually the percussionist became a standard member of the soul-funk ensemble. This addition, this alteration in the DNA of the band, constituted one of the major changes in the sound and character of black popular music between the 1960s, the decade in which Otis Redding had Al Jackson Jnr's snare pushing down into the valley of his baritone, and the '70s, when Curtis Mayfield had Master Henry Gibson's bongos flying into the clouds of his falsetto.

Textures thus became even richer as the full arsenal of percussion was deployed. What bongos, timbales, wood blocks and bells, all of which featured regularly in the work of War, Mandrill and Cymande, brought to the sound canvas was an array of higher, sharper pitches that could strike vivid contrasts with the lower, more felt-like tonality of the kit drum. In many cases, they also injected a significant degree of urgency into the main beat through a range of subdivisions.

Adding a percussionist to a band marked a highly significant development in the transition from 1960s to '70s soul and its flowering into funk – primarily because the new musician increased the polyrhythmic possibilities of the music and brought more diversity to the measures of sound that might be heard in the course of an arrangement.

Congas and bongos have smaller, lighter timbres than a snare or kick. So when their pulse is added to that of a kit, a thinner, more pinched element is introduced to the tonal palette and, if the instruments are properly mixed, the combined effect is almost a mirror of the difference between the single notes and block chords of a piano.

Furthermore, percussion imparts more fluidity to the rhythmic identity of a band. In the hands of a skilled player, a conga or bongo will wind its way around the central groove laid down by the kit drummer. And in bands where the musicians really understand the importance of ensemble playing, the two elements will come to complement one other astutely rather than playing exactly the same patterns.

Many funk bands also gave more prominence to hand drums when the concept of the 'breakdown' was introduced – meaning keys, horns and voices would drop out, leaving the drums, congas, bongos and often timbales to run riot. These passages were important because, by presenting several types of drum and highlighting their individual tone, they inadvertently harked back to marching-band traditions in which bass, snare and cymbals were separated, rather than being brought together in a single instrument that would later become the drum kit or trap set.

This combined attack of drum kit and hand drums amounted to a form of percussion orchestration in which rhythm instruments prevailed over harmony instruments, so that for lengthy stretches of a song the onus was on invention with pulse rather than trickery with chords.

The song's geography became more craggy, the energy more primal.

It also became a convention for soul bands to introduce bongos or congas on the second verse or chorus of a song, because they upped the dynamism of an arrangement, bringing aggressive energy to the already established beat and also changing the tonal quality.

Percussion as an organising principle, rather than a simple embellishment to the rhythm section, could be heard on more and more tracks in the 1970s. An obvious highlight was Candido's roaring club smash *Jingo*.[6] But perhaps the ultimate recognition of percussion's importance came with go-go, a brand of hypnotic, shuffling funk that evolved in Washington, DC.

Go-go is hugely important in reinforcing the complicity between African American and Caribbean forms of popular music. Its creator, Chuck Brown, was a soul vocalist-guitarist who decided to make hand drums the focus of his music after playing in an Afro-Cuban band, Los Latinos, during the mid-1960s. His aim was specifically to bring together the rhythms of Latin music, rhythm and blues and funk. Brown, whose early aspiration to be a jazz guitarist can also be heard in his music, had one overarching concern when he developed go-go: to keep people dancing throughout an entire performance. As a member of Los Latinos, he had noticed that audiences were particularly receptive to congas and bongos. If they were constantly rolling, Brown reasoned, then the unbroken momentum would up the energy of a performance. Go-go gigs can be marathons in which the percussion keeps cranking as one song segues into another: the net result a carnival of sorts.

'Because that's what people want', Brown told me in 2011:

> Even if there ain't no music playing, they just wanna hear that beat, you know what I'm saying? Everybody moves to the percussion. Because before that people used to come to our shows, they'd sit around at tables, dance off a couple of slow songs, but they didn't really get into it until they got a little tipsy. After we started go-go, the tables and chairs moved out of the places we played and there was nothing but dance floor, and all the mink coats and suits and ties came off because everybody wanted to dance. When you hear go-go, you gonna start moving.
>
> Everybody likes percussion, people move off that beat. They had go-go girls and go-go clubs, so I called it go-go music because when you put that together, you don't stop, you just keep playing. We might play three hours without stopping. That's go-go, it just goes and goes and goes.[7]

Just as interesting is that in go-go the percussion is often hit with sticks to produce crisp, tubular tones. This raw, edgy sound can dominate for epic passages of one particular piece, leaving the horn section to make darting interventions for just a few bars.

Hence the usual hierarchy of instruments is inverted. Go-go bands often forgo a 'breakdown', in which a frontline rhythm and horn section would stop playing to strip the track clean to drums and percussion. Instead they perform a kind of 'break-up', in which the relentlessly churning percussion essentially forms the frontline, while horns and keyboards shimmy in momentarily, playing a few tense, jolting power chords before being duly banished, beaten back down by the savage beast of a beat.

Such rhythmic primacy and uninterrupted groove made go-go highly relevant to hip hop. The whole principle of the mix in the latter genre is a constant flow of sound. A Chuck Brown gig practically replaces the DJ and turntables with a live band.

Tellingly, several rappers attended Brown's gigs in the late 1970s. It's not hard to imagine them standing in the crowd and silently freestyling over all the percussion bustin' loose on the stage. Kurtis Blow's use of a fiendishly funky go-go beat on 'Party Time' just made it official.

More West Indian

Relevant as it was to hip hop, go-go had strong transcultural ramifications. The percussion brought a distinctly African-Caribbean quality to soul, precisely because these instruments were so pivotal in salsa, samba, calypso and merengue, And if, as was argued in Chapter 4, Latin beats were common currency in soul and jazz, then the use of hand drums could only strengthen and enhance any putative kinship.

Certainly as funk groups in the 1970s started to write longer, more layered arrangements, there were more and more passages in which the vocals would withdraw and the bobbing, busy percussion and stabbing, strident horns would be used in a manner not dissimilar to the Latin jazz minted by legends such as Dizzy Gillespie, Chano Pozo, Machito, Perez Parado and Mongo Santamaria.

Determining the *precise* nature of the rhythmic relationship between African American and African-Caribbean music would require doctorate-level research. But what is perhaps relevant to our discussion here is the fact that the two cultures, or the one culture spread over different geographical locations, do indeed have some kind of relationship.

Many are the funk drummers who have talked about the importance of studying Caribbean music and who, even though they may be speaking in vague terms, have acknowledged that their approach to rhythm is not divorced from traditions in Jamaica, Cuba and Trinidad.

Explaining the origins of his kind of funky rhythmic patent to British writer Geoff Brown in 2000, Bill Curtis – kit drummer and percussionist in the group with the hugely symbolic name for this chapter, Fatback (previously The Fatback Band) – stated rather thought-provokingly: 'It's more West

Indian than anything else. I used to tell drummers, just think of calypso. That's where the beat really comes from.'[8]

Fatback went on to become a very progressive funk band in the 1970s, but Curtis's comments are more than borne out both by their sizeable commercial hits in the middle of the decade, such as 'Wicky Wacky' and 'Bus Stop', and their earlier songs such as 'Soul March', where there is a clear calypso sensibility in the fizzing, insistent hi-hat patterns and the implication of a fast triangle beat. Both of these facets became key components of disco, and it is precisely through a group like Fatback that one sees how the sub-genre that turned into a major event in popular music was a Caribbean sound filtering through American funk – which saw its tempo upped and its character become crazy frantic.

Listening to Trinidadian steel bands in the 1950s, where percussion had considerable strength in the ensemble because it was often assigned to one musician in the absence of kit drummers, one hears a clear prototype of disco. And it is when an artist with a firm grasp of both West Indian and American musical history brings the cultural cross-fertilisation to a creative peak that soul can spring tasty surprises.

Ralph McDonald was born in New York to the Trinidadian calypso singer Macbeth The Great. After taking up percussion as a boy, he became a highly sought-after session player and producer-songwriter from the late 1960s onwards, working in soul and jazz-fusion with anybody from Roberta Flack and Grover Washington Jnr to Aretha Franklin and King Curtis. McDonald also started to develop his own career as a solo artist, and by the middle of the 1970s he was recording albums like *The Sound of A Drum*.

Although McDonald's songs featured a full electric rhythm section, mostly comprising the crack Atlantic Records session players he had worked with, they afforded generous space to hand drums – and occasionally to instruments that were not instruments at all but household objects deeply rooted in Trinidadian musical folklore: namely the bottle, often a timekeeper in very old calypsos.

Featured on the aforementioned album is 'Calyspo Breakdown',[9] a hugely important piece for the way it conjoins several strands of black pop and art music, inflecting a calypso beat towards funk, embellishing it with several jazz improvisations (notably by a New Orleans clarinet) and implying disco in the process. The tune feels relevant at once to the open-air jump-up, the *bacchanale* of carnival, and to the enclosed delirium of a club.

Standing as a symbolic intersection of Caribbean and American music, 'Calypso Breakdown' served notice both of disco's huge popularity in places like Port Of Spain, because the local population could relate to the pulse that was coming back at them from across the Atlantic, and that songs with a more explicitly West Indian flavour would find favour under the strobe lights of New York. Furthermore, another substratum of Afro-Latin disco, often leaning towards salsa, evolved around this time and made its presence felt in

America in no uncertain terms, especially when the lyrics were in Spanish rather than English.

In any case, it is often forgotten that tucked away on the soundtrack to *Saturday Night Fever*, struggling for attention amidst the banshee crescendo of the Bee Gees' vocals, is a piece of bewitched and bewitching instrumental music: Ralph McDonald's 'Calypso Breakdown'.

Breaking the beat

One instrument that McDonald often used was a 'syndrum', a kind of electronic bongo that produced a high-pitched ray gun effect. At times it was entirely appropriate to the colourful, almost burlesque nature of carnival music, the oddity of both sights and sounds experienced by the reveller in Trinidad's Fredericks Street. At times it would land somewhere between the plain corny and the humorously futuristic.

In any case, this instrument was a reminder that technological innovations in the field of percussion, the use of drum machines and devices to programme rhythm, had been deployed in soul since the late 1960s. The best-known example was the Rhythm Ace used by Sly Stone in his work with The Family Stone and his production for the female vocal group Little Sister – notably on their hit single 'Somebody's Watching You', a song with a wonderfully warm gospel verse that was artfully dimmed, in true Sly fashion, by a sinister stalker-for-ya lyric.[10]

Put simply, the Rhythm Ace sounded strange in a charming, almost effete way. Its pitch was relatively high but it had a dampened quality, almost like the burr of an African log drum, and there was also a mild hiss of electricity behind the notes that made the machine sound similar to a generator or some external supply of electrical current.

Yet its presence was meaningful. It altered the texture and rhythmic identity of a song through the greater rigidity of the pulse, which had none of the slight gradations and accents played by the steadiest, most 'in the pocket' drummers. This more mechanical, slightly austere character stood in contrast to the fluctuations in pitch and timbre that were a defining part of vocal performances in soul music.

Certainly in the case of Stone's work, the use of the Rhythm Ace is important because its unerring metronomic quality contrasts not just with the activity of the singers, who flit frequently between wide and close harmonies, but with the ever-changing additions to, and subtle variations on, the rhythm parts played by the bass, guitar and keys.

Stories abound of Stone, a visionary of pyschedelic soul, replacing entire tracks of live drums with his own simple programming. But on many of the cuts both man and machine can be heard simultaneously, making it clear

Stone was interested in how technology could be integrated into the band tradition instead of supplanting it wholesale.

Throughout the 1970s, drum machines were used intermittently, or sometimes keyboards were programmed to create drum-like sounds that could bring an extra surge to what the kit drummer and percussionist were already doing. These technologies were still not conceived as an outright labour-saving device that would threaten the existence of a drummer offering more than pre-set patterns.

By the early 1980s, however, it was becoming harder to keep bands together, due to declining profits and record company budgets, and the quality of drum machines increased through new models offered by companies such as Roland. So it was now possible for musicians to create their own drum lines, rather than using the pre-programmed options offered hitherto. One could act as a virtual drummer with a keyboard.

Drum machines became much more prevalent among studio artists who were making singles rather than touring albums, and eventually there came a new model of singer + keyboard player-drum programmer that loosely mirrored developments in other genres. So in soul-funk there was the duo D-Train and in pop music there was the twosome Soft Cell.

Turntable scratches also became part of the percussive arsenal of the new music known as hip hop. It was especially interesting to hear how early expressions of the genre – which were sometimes skeletal in construction, presenting a beat as the bare bones and the rapped verses as the flesh – dovetailed potently with go-go, precisely because the music devoted such lengthy passages to nothing but the edgy percolations of voice and drums.

We should not be rash in assessing all this. There were extremes. One simple truth stands out, though: some of the drum programming was far too loud and clunky, especially for singers who did not have the tonal depth or strength of attack to make themselves heard over the thunderous maelstrom. This is precisely why rappers, with their art of 'spitting' a line with more aggression and thrashing velocity, could fare better in this context.

Yet it would be a grave mistake to write off completely the use of the drum machine in 1980s soul. Once again, a simple truth stands out.

Many of the producers and keyboard players did not just programme drums, they – crucially – programmed percussion or, perhaps even more crucially, programmed one or several drum lines *percussively*.

Reach right back to Sly Stone's use of the crude Rhythm Ace and one hears that loud and clear. For the most part, the figures are either straight Afro-Cuban clave time or variations thereon. The deployment of new equipment underlines that a major part of the vocabulary of soul that emerged in the late 1960s, namely the clatter of hand drums and Latin rhythms, did not instantly vanish with the arrival of state-of-the-art technology. It was transferred to it.

Precise cut-off points between eras of music don't really exist anyway.

Soul had been an electric genre for many years, and for it to become a more electronic, more programmed idiom was not so much revolution as evolution. Moreover, there were trained musicians who lived through that transition. Hence some of the two- or three-musician units playing keyboards in the 1980s, and replacing the eight- to ten-piece funk bands of the '70s, naturally attempted to retain the detail of the percussionists. The continuing presence of a Caribbean pulse in a machine-based setting produced very interesting results in the hands of a group like Cameo.

'Candy', one of their big hits, may be aglow with bright, shimmering synthesizer chords yet its percussive patter, though spangled with electronic distortion, is not far removed from the realm of soca. This is something borne out by the seamlessness with which the piece mixes with 'one dollar wine' tunes played at West Indian dances in London.

One of the most interesting features of the drum programming heard in a lot of soul from this era was the fact that the electronic cowbell was dramatically high in the mix, presenting a uniquely odd timbre close to the wood blocks used in Cuban clave. 'Real' percussion such as congas and bongos was still used – Larry Blackmon of Cameo was a competent hand- and kit-drummer – so there was a kind of straddling of the man–machine divide that again harked back to Sly Stone.

Machines have since become an increasingly regular feature of soul-funk and its more recent derivatives such as house music, where the programmer is often the one-man-band creative focal point. When even more sub-strands, such as Afro and Latin house, came into being around the early 1990s, a wildly interesting primal percussion fest materialised. As heard in the prolific output of MAW (Masters at Work), Joe Claussell and Jerome Sydenham, it was often enriched by the input of several hand drummers.

Around the late 1990s in London, yet another new sub-genre brought yet another colour to the mosaic of music rooted in the prehistory of the beat and the modern history of beats: broken beat.

At the centre of this movement was Ian Grant, whose *nom de scène* I.G. Culture said much about both his Jamaican origins and his deep roots in reggae. Grant's initial creative stirrings as a teenager in the 1980s saw him debut as a 'chatter' on local sound systems in West London.

His initial recordings during the early 1990s were in hip hop, as part of a duo known as Dodge City Productions. But I.G. started to experiment extensively with rhythm patterns when he went solo and worked under a range of monikers such as New Sector Movements, Likwid Biskit and Quango. What started to emerge in his productions was a staccato, stuttering approach to the pulse that became known as broken beat.[11] The central fragmented rhythm was often surrounded and thickened by several layers of percussion and detonations of electronic flange.

Broken beat has been one of the most idiosyncratic developments in modern black music simply because of its great pluralism. I.G. has always maintained that the two principal raw materials in his work are hip hop and reggae. You can hear both the breeze-block weight of the former and the incisive, offbeat slur of the latter.

Yet broken beat is complex in its construction and its Afro-Latin character is strong. An enormous number of drum tracks can be stacked up to create a polyrhythmic thicket. A Cuban clave pulse sits with occasionally heavily displaced snares that may land in very odd places in the bar. Meanwhile, a bass drum is used to produce the kind of rapid-fire rolls that might be expected from bongos or congas.

On other tracks, one loose, springy snare rattles rapidly through a whole measure, while another stays tight on the 'one' and a third smacks down forcefully between beats late in the bar, giving the impression that several drummers are playing pinball. Broken beat is ultra-sophisticated rhythmic displacement, organised jerks, jumps and jolts.

With that in mind, the fact that I.G. is also conga player is telling. Some of his music could almost pass as a kind of Afro-techno, given the prevalence of machines. Yet the other decisive element in the broken-beat story is the enormous influence of 1970s jazz-funkers like Roy Ayers and the input of contemporary jazz soloists and soul singers such as Frank McComb and Eska Mtungwazi. Their presence made the genre an even more hybridised entity, whose substantial rhythmic ingenuity was leavened by a certain melodic and harmonic finesse.

Broken beat flourished between the late 1990s and 2005, with producers like I.G., Bugz In The Attic, Afronaught, Colonel Red and Mark de Clive-Lowe creating similar levels of energy to drum and bass, thanks to their harnessing of violence through percussive ignition and agitation. The great force of their work was magnified by powerful speakers pumping out a rush of dense tones in small clubs like Plastic People in East London.

Soul, both rhythmically and texturally, has undergone significant change since the introduction and growth in importance of hand drums. The advent of a new strand such as broken beat is simply a logical progression of this heritage. Created by a computer-literate generation, the idiom did not sacrifice Afro-Latin sensibilities. Nor did it, crucially, forego live drums, congas and bongos alongside the latest digital music-making software. In fact, its percussion-centric character made broken beat an indirect but imperious successor to go-go music.

That said, broken beat is practically a summary and scrambling of many strands of rhythmic traditions in soul. Elements of James Brown's funky drumming, the 'island' sensibilities of anyone from Candido to Ralph McDonald, and even the tambourine-led groove of gospel house are encoded in this music. Yet they are configured with much imagination and a wholly rigorous attention to textural detail.

10 Four tablespoons of boiling Memphis guitars

No, I don't solo. (Melvin Ragin, aka 'Wah Wah' Watson)

Three up to clean up

Following his demand for half a teacup of bass and a pound of fatback drums in his introduction to 'Memphis Soul Stew', King Curtis hollered for 'four tablespoons of boiling Memphis guitars'. Two guitars sparked into life and, as befitted the nature of the request, immediately set about stoking another rhythmic fire to join those of the drums and bass crackling under the leader's hearty, buoyant voice.

R. F. Taylor and Reggie Young were the guitarists who obliged. They had both worked with Curtis before and were part of a large aggregation of crack Memphis and New York studio musicians that the saxophonist frequently dipped into throughout the 1960s, as he assembled bands with continually shifting line-ups. Among the guitarists alone, these counted the likes of Al Casey, Hugh McCracken and the quite outstanding Cornell Dupree whose relaxed, almost laconic sense of time was combined with a sharply piercing tone that was hugely expressive yet never overbearing.

'Memphis Soul Stew' has one guitarist playing a bright, brisk single-note figure with a lovely spiralling quality, dancing lightly on the pulse, while the other delivers a series of chords at a slower speed, their gravelly resonance sounding very different to the slender timbre of the first line. The two guitars thus contrast with and complement each other as the tenor and baritone singers do in a street-corner doo-wop ensemble.

This arrangement had precedents. Blues songs reaching back to the 1930s and '40s often featured a two-guitar frontline, as exemplified by Papa Charlie Jackson and Blind Blake. They were deployed in a similar fashion, one player creating the string of spindly single notes and the other the fat roll of chords, so that the guitar palette combined different characters or sizes of tone. Nineteen-fifties R&B largely upheld this principle.

What emerges first and foremost from many of the records of that period, and in the black pop of the subsequent decade, is the range of different roles the guitars played: from straight, dead-on-the-beat rhythm to full-on, roaming solos to concise, melodic motifs that acted almost as a fleeting second voice to either a singer or saxophonist.

The organisation of the guitars could vary considerably from one band to the next. While the principle of a lead guitarist who could neatly lay down a one-bar or two-bar fill that directly served the singer, extending or finishing a line they had just completed, was commonplace, there were also many cases in which the soloist would shuttle between short extemporisations and repeated rhythmic patterns. Some of these patterns, as on several John Lee Hooker sides, slanted into flighty, ska-like offbeats.

Attacking the instrument with an entirely different mindset, Bo Diddley was all bludgeon and blunderbuss.[1] Many of his classic 1950s tunes feature Diddley and a second guitarist absolutely mangling chords with such ferocity – often in a sustained headlong rush to the end of the piece, without the slightest pause between verse and chorus – that they create an all-consuming noise detonation which engulfs the whole song.

This was one of the reasons why Diddley's music often had such a wild, theatrical quality that was also a clear forerunner of pyschedelic sounds. Diddley's chords snapped and snarled big cat-style, and when he named one of his pieces 'Mumblin' Guitar', it was a case of metaphorical description, a figurative image, acquiring an almost literal meaning.

Gradually, this kind of proto-punk splurge became less common. As soul turned to funk and in the late 1960s – when the guiding principle, rhythmically, was to pump both drums and bass to create a form of percussion – the idea of using two guitarists to make a range of smaller, thinner sounds, in serpentine, busy figures rather than blasting out one power chord after another, started to gain ground.

That is not to say that one guitarist alone could not produce a superlative blend of rhythm playing and occasional improvisations, as was thrillingly demonstrated by such as Teenie Hodges, celebrated for his fine work with Al Green, or Steve Cropper of Booker T. & The MGs. Yet a rhythm section with a single six-string wasn't the sole model to which groups gravitated.

As the 1970s dawned, bands either used two or more guitarists, or they overdubbed lines to boost the polyrhythmic richness of a piece. Often this made a virtue of combining several short, pithy phrases which, in the best case, could be positioned inventively within the metre, sometimes by quite subtle means.

In 1971, four years after King Curtis cut 'Memphis Soul Stew', Betty Wright recorded 'Clean Up Woman', the monster-seller that guaranteed the Miami-born singer a place in the pantheon of soul divas alongside the likes of Etta James, Carla Thomas and Aretha Franklin.

This superbly rendered admonition to a sister to beware the other woman as man-thief both served notice of a vocalist with a compellingly dramatic charge and provided an object lesson in how to arrange multiple guitar lines successfully. From the linkage of three wiry, extremely precise figures played by James Knight, Snoopy Dean and Willie 'Little Beaver' Hale, all noted local session warriors, came an unassuming but memorable chain mail that wrapped tightly around the leader's vocal.

The guitars offer masterful contrasts. The central riff, a sunlit pentatonic figure that strongly evokes a child's carefree whistle in a playground, sets a breezy ambience. After just two bars, though, this is abruptly modified by the entry of a faster, steely eleven-note pattern, tapped out forcefully ahead of the beat. Then a third riff sneaks in, just behind the beat, to shift the energy, its slow-moving, fey chords a pacifying cushion to its spikier predecessor. Softly strummed, the line is felt rather than heard.

The sound mosaic is enriched by a simple but devastatingly effective strategy: the entry of the second and third figures in odd places, the first anticipating the 'one' and the second dragging after it to create the sensation of lines tripping over one another or staggering forth. With the several discrepancies in phrase length, the sound of the guitars is like a system of precisely activated levers or pulleys, with some speeding up and others slowing down on the pulse of the song.

There is a remarkable structural finesse at work here. It is not just the sleight of hand *vis-à-vis* tempo but the range of attack and tonality across the three figures, the meeting of gruff bluesiness with urbane jazziness, that demonstrates a desire to use guitars as intricate rhythmic embroidery by stitching together several lines.

Everything gels in steadied tension. The simultaneous deployment of five lazy clacks and eleven busy clicks prompts vividly contrasting sensations, so the listener feels the entwining lines as droopy and nervy, casual and purposeful, a groove holding back and striding forth.

'Clean Up Woman' is a high watermark in six-string arrangement in black popular music. It exerts a subtle yet haunting hypnosis, a closely calibrated bubbling and brimming of sound that acts as an astute foil to the no-nonsense, arresting character of the lead vocal. In many ways the piece stands as a manifesto, a template for musical complexity arising from the amalgamation of relatively simple components. Here is a sonic whole that is infinitely greater than the sum of its parts.

Throughout soul in the 1970s and beyond, this principle was taken up and applied extensively, so that the meshing of several finger-picked lines, often in staggered tempos and with a wide range of thin and thinner tonalities in line with the Wright model, became something of a norm.

Raising the stature of an instrument in an ensemble is not just about multiplicity of voices, about having two or three guitarists instead of one. The presence of one instrument can benefit from the absence of another. Something that should be noted in any discussion on the prominence of the guitar in soul is that several exponents of funk, particularly its grittiest brand, did not use pianos.

Hence the electrified strings – both the guitar and the bass guitar – were a conspicuous feature of the rhythm section, providing both a surge of power and a sprinkle of detail in an arrangement without vying for attention with the power chords of a keyboard.

Pianoless, guitar-led funk has a dry, grainy, grinding quality. Certainly James Brown made this a prime feature of much of his work, using between two and three guitarists in the company of three to six brass/reed players, so there were heavy horns in conjunction with heavy strings, and with no keyboard acting as a buffer between them. On 'Talkin' Loud And Sayin' Nothing', 'Give It Up Or Turn It Loose' and 'Soul Power', the guitarists bring more punch and kinetic energy to the table. The interlocking, tightly knit single-note lines played by Phelps 'Catfish' Collins, Hearlon 'Cheese' Martin and Jimmy 'Chank' Nolen criss-crossed *à la* 'Clean Up', but they were faster and had a sharp, flinty resonance that significantly ratcheted up the tension in the rhythm section. The guitars acted as coils that were constantly wound tighter and tighter and tighter.

Polyrhythm is essential here. The whole success of the endeavour hinges on weaving together several repeating motifs that create a kind of organised entanglement, so that the lines, by dint of each having a different measure of sharpness and a different life cycle, curl around the beat in myriad ways.

Rugged is the most appropriate word for the textures created by this thicket of guitars in the absence of a keyboard. Other than James Brown, one artist who availed himself of the technique well was Curtis Mayfield, particularly on his classic 1971 performance at The Bitter End club in New York's Greenwich Village.

All the above cases highlight a noteworthy development in the conception of guitar players in soul, their role and function, that differs considerably from those in other forms of pop. Where rock fêtes the guitar hero as a soloist who will stand as a single entity under the spotlight, arm wheeling ritually, soul makes a virtue of *rhythm guitar heroes*, with two or three of them pooling resources in a carefully synchronised operation of collective rather than individual flourish. King Curtis asked for four tablespoons of boiling Memphis guitar on 'Memphis Soul Stew'. It was a large helping for the mix, a code for not just one but two players to step up and put down their thing – together.

What's on the Wah-wah?

Such are the vocal gifts of the likes of Curtis Mayfield and Bobby Womack,[2] artists deserving the hype of soul legend, that it is often forgotten what fine guitarists they are. Mayfield had a beautifully precise, delicate manner of articulating his chords, some of which could be almost ethereal yet with enough body to support a singer ably – as can be heard on Mayfield's work in the early 1960s with Jerry Butler, his colleague in the gospel-soul vocal group The Impressions.

Womack, on the other hand, the man who was mentored by Sam Cooke and debuted in the vocal group The Valentinos, had a gruffer, rougher tone. He earned his living as a session guitarist in both rock and R&B, playing with anybody from Elvis Presley and Ike Turner to King Curtis, and eventually finding a stolen moment to be a soul singer.

Although his contribution was uncredited, Womack played on Sly & The Family Stone's 'There's A Riot Goin' On' in 1971. Listening to this and Womack's own solo albums from the period, such as *Facts Of Life*, one can hear him and the other players whipping up an inordinate amount of rhythmic excitement through fast, fractured chords whose sound has a kind of scraped or 'chicken-scratch' quality to them, a technique that was being used with increasing sophistication in funk guitar.

Adding to all the ricochets and explosions of sound these players were capable of producing was a device unveiled to the general public in 1967. Although initially embraced by rock players like Frank Zappa and Jimi Hendrix, it was adopted by more of their peers in soul and funk. By the middle of 1970s, it had played a large role in defining the textural lexicon of those idioms.

The wah-wah was an effects pedal. Its manufacturer, Vox, had originally conceived the device as an attachment for brass and reed players, offering a new form of sound modification to supplement the long tradition of using mutes in classical music, jazz and R&B.

Several guitarists found great joy in the wide range of modifications in timbre that the wah-wah afforded, and none more so than the weeping, wailing 'cry baby' quality it could bring to a chord. In the hands – or rather, under the feet – of many funk players, the device could fashion a bizarre, prehistoric birdsong, with the reverberations glancing away from the pitch, deviating and then receding into the distance, much as a pterodactyl's cry might do in its deathly swoop.

Contrast was another reason why the wah-wah pedal was valuable. When used aggressively, it imbued the guitar with a scratchy, grainy tone. This artifice of roughness was diametrically opposed to the smooth, silken quality of the large string sections that were often prevalent in 1970s soul, increasing the whole dynamic range of the music.

Dennis Coffey of Motown's Funk Brothers band proved an astoundingly creative exponent of the wah-wah. But literally making his name with the device was Wah Wah Watson, aka Melvin Ragin. The Detroit native became a fine studio player for Motown and other labels between the early 1970s and mid-1980s. His list of credits, from The Four Tops and Marvin Gaye to The Jackson Five and Herbie Hancock, to name but a few, is really quite astonishing.

A neat, nimble player who constructed concise figures that brought substantial muscle to a rhythm section without being excessively dense, Watson enriched the wah-wah vocabulary through the daring amount of sustain he applied to some lines. This gave them a wildcat purr or a harder resonance that was close to the greasy sizzle of a Fender Rhodes electric piano – which, in many cases, was also having its whirlpool of sound heavily adulterated by the use of several new pedals.

Watson was greatly interested in novel timbres, and he deployed a lot of state-of-the-art hardware to assist him in his explorations. One of his best performances as a sideman was on Hancock's 1975 set *Manchild*,[3] where,

Guitarist 'Wah Wah' Watson with his foot on the pedal that made his name (photo courtesy Gijsbert Hankeroot/Getty Images).

in addition to the wah-wah, Watson used a Maestro Universal Synthesizer System and a Maestro Universal Sample and Hold Unit. And a voice bag. All this parallels the way in which Stevie Wonder and other keyboardists were embracing technology in the pursuit of uncommon sounds.

Depending on the way the wah-wah pedal was pumped by the guitarist, it could also leave a chord to reverberate in the manner of the echo-chamber techniques often favoured by dub reggae producers. At its best, the device could create highly vocalised phrases that either hiccupped on rapidly executed rhythms or whispered, almost horn-like, on more legato figures. The guitar could thus be presented in a state of near emotional tumult.

Some of the great wah-wah moments are not just about the guitar, though. They come from the way the instrument is cast against the fabric stitched from other elements of a band. The work of Watson and a coterie of grade A guitarists that included Robert White and Joe Messina on The Temptations' 'Papa Was A Rolling Stone' is a fine example of sonic ingenuity wrought by the union of horn and guitar.

As on 'Clean-Up Woman', the piece employs a skilful staggering of tempos. The bass is dispensed in slow two- and three-note trails marked by tense, eerie pauses, the whole statement teased out over four bars. The last of these has no notes whatsoever: it is a resignation to silence, the sad surrender of the low end. Through this gloomy, floating cloud of notes comes a cascade of furious, desperate wah-wah licks in double time, a choppy sea under dark heavens, while a trumpet blows doleful mariachi-like phrases, bleak puffs fluttering in draughts of moist reverb.

Speed of sound and stillness of sound are thus dramatically juxtaposed.

There is something utterly haunting and slightly surreal about the blend of the wah-wah guitar and echo-heavy brass, because both instruments are essentially weeping: the former in a flood of short, spiked, hurting sobs, the latter in longer, hopeless sighs. The combined effect is the perfect doom-laden prelude to the crushing fatalism of the opening lyric: 'It was the third of September, the day I'll always remember'.[4]

Roger & Rodgers

From Watson's heyday in the mid-1970s, when horns and strings reigned, to the rise of more keyboard-led soul in the '80s, there came to prominence a number of other brilliant guitarists who either played in bands or worked as 'axes for hire' on one-off producer-led projects.

The long lineage of studio players who occasionally stepped out as leaders would include David T. Walker and Ray Parker Jnr, notable first and foremost for their work with heavyweights such as The Crusaders and Stevie Wonder throughout the 1970s. But one man from the '80s whose name should really not be overlooked is Ira Siegel, a guitarist who laid down quite stupendous rhythm and lead lines for many singers – two good examples being Evelyn 'Champagne' King and Tashan Rashad.

Also to be considered are two players whose contribution to the vocabulary of the guitar in soul music is often overlooked because their respective groups produced such epochal songs: Nile Rodgers of Chic and Roger Troutman of Zapp. The former hailed from New York, the latter from Dayton. Rodgers was nurtured on militant political values, a member of the Black Panther party at the age of sixteen and graduate of the Apollo house band who subsequently turned into a creative lightning rod in funky disco. Troutman was a musician from the earliest available opportunity,[5] leading groups as a teenager before going on to enjoy the tutelage of George Clinton and become part of Parliament-Funkadelic's sprawling, ever-mutating extended family in the early 1980s.

Scanning their individual outputs throughout the decade, it's fair to say that Troutman revealed himself as more of a soloist, a wholly competent bluesy jazz player on albums such as 'The Many Facets Of Roger', where he improvised extensively. Rodgers excelled with very richly voiced chords, many of which were inverted, and his tremendous wealth of harmonic nuance entirely suited the tight, precisely layered, if not tapestry-like song structures of Chic, a group whose use of strings as both soprano voice and vehicle for rhythmic emphasis was peerless.

What actually aligned these two figures was their tendency to play predominantly in the upper register. They made an art of it. On the bulk of their output, there are some fantastically sharp, high-pitched rhythmic figures that are almost harp-like, such is the piercing nature of the sound: a rapier slicing through the warm, soft folds of the ensemble voice.

Heard in isolation, Rodgers's guitar is practically a bundle of fast, funky pizzicato violas, but with more body and consistency in their tone. His introduction on 'Thinking Of You', the piece that Chic wrote and produced for Sister Sledge in 1982, is one of the most expressive pieces of rhythm playing ever recorded. The crystalline clarity of the guitarist's chording is operatic in character – hence the superb effect created when the string section enters in counterpoint (the other instruments having dropped out) in a deeply moving interlude during the final stages of the song.

Benefiting from very limpid engineering, Rodgers is startlingly well-defined. But this is not only down to the people manning the studio. His composure, his physical command of the instrument is what counts. The weight, the motion, the laser sweep of Rodgers's hand on the strings is brilliantly controlled, his eye-of-the-needle deftness making him a cultured electric satellite to the mothership of the acoustic string orchestra.

Roger Troutman was perhaps a wilder card. In the 1980s he brought a tough, invariably raucous character to some of the licks that were harder and grainier than the 'chicken scratch' of the previous decade. The way in which Troutman's chords contrived to explode into life loosely evoked the likes of

Bo Diddley or Chuck Berry. But there was much more timbral richness and a surgical precision in their execution.

Making Troutman's work stand out above all else was the bold use of dissonance that marked so many of his lines. Rising right up to the high register, Troutman would imbue many of his notes with a grating, almost clash-of-swords quality that could be unsettling. It completely suited the atmosphere of some pieces, for as joyous as hits like 'Dancefloor' and 'More Bounce To The Ounce' were, they also – by dint of a vice-like tautness in the groove – summoned up feelings of marked excitation.

On top of that, offbeats were all over Zapp's guitar rhythms. The judder in the pulse that defined reggae, the feeling of the groove shifting slightly to one side, swaying just a touch without losing its balance: it was there in Troutman's playing. But again, there was a hardness in his touch that would surely make the nature rise in most rock audiences.

It's also worth pointing out that Troutman was a general sound adventurer who was interested in the use of technology and electronic gizmos as well as instruments such as the guitar and synthesizers. One of his distinguishing features was the 'talk box', a long tube that looked like a piece of medical apparatus, and into which Troutman would blow to alter the pitch of his voice, sometimes producing cartoon-like results.

This could be dismissed as gimmickry but it extended Zapp's sonic range and, most intriguingly, harked back to the harmonica, as if Troutman wanted to tip an iconic blues instrument into the future.

All of the tracks that Zapp and Chic recorded between the late 1970s and the mid-1980s were a substantial addition to the canon of funk guitar, being intelligent refinements of the work of previous players. The echo of Melvin 'Wah Wah Watson' Ragin was undeniable but it had now been supplemented with a wide range of daring new idiosyncrasies.

Tonally, the work of these players did not break decisively with tradition because the sound was still thin rather than thick. Soul-funk guitar was about the rapier, and rock the broadsword. Generally speaking, rock's exponents had a much heavier, brawnier voice, often cranked up by substantial levels of amplification that fed into the camp, ritual theatre of their music's screaming, stadium-filling stance: the collusion of big voice, big guitar and big hair.

Inevitably, the soul-funk bands that strayed into this territory could not help but stand out. Well-known examples would be The Isley Brothers and Funkadelic, whose guitarists played so loud and brash on 'That Lady' and 'Maggot Brain' respectively that they alarmed, if not completely repelled, some black music fans – who, by the time these pieces were recorded in the mid-1970s, would associate that sound with hard rock, if not heavy metal.

There is a huge irony at play here, since the coruscating guitar work on 'That Lady' and 'Maggot Brain' could obviously be traced back to the vocabulary of Jimi Hendrix – which itself was directly shaped by blues players like Elmore James and indirectly approximated Bo Diddley. So The Isley Brothers and Funkadelic were not so much crossing the line into 'white' music as reaching back to the R&B foundation on which soul was built.

Historical data of this kind were not really discussed at the time because the genre was too busy splintering into funk and disco, while arrangers and producers were also taking black pop into adventurous new territory.

Earlier incarnations of the music were thus easily forgotten. To a certain extent, the relentless demand for constant newness in the beat and the voracious appetite of African American artists for technology has meant that a blues lick from the past could be thought of as old, but clued-up, imaginative players would always reveal its relevance to the present.

Considered in purely sonic terms, rock guitar can be a very relevant instrument for soul music, and for a simple reason: its size, weight and volume can mirror the size, weight and volume of a church-bred voice.

Funkadelic indirectly acknowledged as much in their arrangements, where they pitted loud guitars against a small army of boisterous chorus singers.

Interestingly, rock guitar continued to crash into soul during the 1980s. Some of the electronic productions were cranked up to such high decibel levels, and the synthesizers, drum programming and sequencing became so tonally dense, that when a guitar chord or solo was deemed necessary, it had to assume a Hendrix-like force to cut through the meteor storm of machine-made snares and cowbells.

Two key examples here are the SOS Band's chart smash 'Just Be Good To Me' and Tashan Rashad's 'Chasin' A Dream'. Both are full-tilt speaker-shakers. The former offers not so much a wall as a skyscraper of sound, constructed on keyboards, bass synthesizer and programmed drums that churn away with substantial force for the best part of ten minutes. When the guitar enters to play some edgy, sustained licks in the latter half of the piece, it can only feasibly make an impact by playing with a loud, brash rock tone, and the combination of electronics and electrics makes for an interesting sound canvas.

Rashad's 'Chasin' A Dream' is even more extreme.[6] There are two drum kits, as well as percussion, keys, bass and a four-piece vocal group. The bottom end of the song is elephantine and there is no way that a light, Nile Rogers-style tone would have registered on tape.

Fittingly, two guitarists – Barry Vincent and Ira Siegel – lay down the kind of volcanic eruptions of sound that would blow the wigs off most heavy-metal poodles. Anger spills out all over the place. The scream of the guitars echoes the stark, bleak urgency of Rashad's voice and lyrics.

The piece is a powerful protest against inner-city decay that sets out to capture and convey the harsh realities of urban life for African Americans under then-president Ronald Reagan. It sounds a note of defiance that reaches right back to the vision of Dr Martin Luther King Jnr, a sample of whose voice is also featured. The civil rights icon might have been alarmed by the sonic barrage, but here was a song that brought a vital, socially conscious charge to rock, a black music deeply rooted in soul.

The guitar man of my dreams (don't solo)

Guitars, of course, are iconic instruments in rock and its forebear the blues, especially among practitioners who came from humble circumstances and could not afford the more expensive and cumbersome piano. Images of Robert Johnson, John Lee Hooker or Muddy Waters with guitar in hand enshrined the six-string as one of the primary pieces of kit that exponents of black popular music could use to accompany themselves. Classic songs by any of the above in which there is nothing more than voice and guitar do not sound denuded.

One of the defining features in the evolution of black pop, the transition from blues to rhythm and blues to soul, is the huge amount of sonic flesh wrapped around the bare bones of a melody, how the expansion of rhythm sections and the growing deployment of state-of-the-art technology substantially enriched the core vocabulary.

Other related forms of music, such as rock and heavy metal, made an overwhelmingly macho cult of the guitar in the 1960s, '70s and '80s.

But soul, during those same decades, set great store by a raft of other instruments, above all horns, strings, bass, keys and electronics.

It's not so much that soul suddenly fell out of love with guitars. It was more a case of the music having a harem of other sounds to deal with.

The status of the guitar in black popular music was thus somewhat ambiguous by the time 'Chasin' A Dream' was recorded. And regardless of how relevant the song's wailing chords may have been to the legacy of a certain Mister Bo Diddley, they were frankly out of step with the dominant, electro-leaning trends in black popular music at the time.

Tashan Rashad was something of an anomaly, anyway. He was a singer who signed to a hip hop label – Def Jam, home of Public Enemy – in 1986 and made soul music that was partly influenced by hip hop, or at least managed to render something both of its sonic brutality and its chant-down-Babylon rebelliousness. It's a shame that no impresarios actually had the vision to promote Rashad as the vanguard of hip hop soul, a tactic that paid dividends years later for singers like Mary J. Blige.

Within a few years of 'Chasin' A Dream', musicians would become increasingly marginalised in hip hop, fast emerging as the dominant form of black popular music. Hip hop asserted itself first and foremost as a DJ/producer-led movement in which samples and breaks, the hallowed 'perfect beat', supplanted the input of conventional instruments and their players.

Recordings by the founding fathers of funk became the raw materials with which new music was constructed. This created something of a dichotomy between tradition and modernity or, rather, framed in a novel way the whole issue of what constituted the past and present of sound, since hip hop was a largely non-musician's music.

Bridges could be built, though. Producers and rappers were not the only ones rediscovering the music of James Brown, Roy Ayers or Curtis Mayfield and using them to make beats. There were also musicians who, inspired by the instruments behind the records *inside* hip hop, set about reviving and recreating those sounds outside hip hop. As a result, certain stylistic particularities coexisted in a synthetic state as a sample and in an organic state as a riff played in real time.

Hence the revival of the wah-wah. Many of the groups that emerged in London during the acid jazz years of the early 1990s – and despite the name given to the scene, the '70s funk of Brown and others was the most salient guiding principle – reverted to the 'cry baby' effects pedal that had become much less common in the mostly electronic soul productions that prevailed in the '80s.

Acts like Push, The Brand New Heavies and Young Disciples were instrumental in propounding the idea of a band – with guitarists as well as horn players, for that matter – playing 'old school' yet interfacing with the new breakbeat generation through the input of rappers, beats and samples: sometimes nothing more than a snatch of Prince's spectral voice or a flute loop purloined from an old jazz disc.

Because a new generation of listeners had recently rediscovered the music of Brown, Mayfield *et al.*, both through hip hop producers and the championing of these artists' music by DJs at 'rare groove' clubs, the sound of a wah-wah guitar played in real time in a studio – or better still, on stage – did not seem as anachronistic as it might have done, had the whole trend of sampling and mining of old music not occurred.

Furthermore, an old warrior returned alongside a new gunslinger. In 1993 Me'Shell NdegéOcello made her debut with a startling album called *Plantation Lullabies*. A Washington, D.C. native who had moved to New York in 1989, NdegéOcello auditioned for Living Colour, a rock band who did more than rock, and recorded as Michelle Johnson with Steve Coleman, a jazz saxophonist whose early work leaned heavily towards funk. NdegéOcello was a brilliant bass guitarist, as well as a singer. And although clearly a progressive thinker, she constructed her work on solid historical ground.

Old-school funk was a building block for her, but that wasn't as significant as the edge of authenticity NdegéOcello gave her music through the input of none other than Melvin 'Wah Wah Watson' Ragin – a musician who had not been heard in soul for some time, or at least not on an album that garnered the kind of attention NdegéOcello's did.

Ragin's licks on tracks like 'Call Me' and 'Shoot'n Up And Gett'n High' were instantly recognisable. Hearing those rasping, guttural timbres in a sonic context that had, through its blend of live and programmed drums and its fine engineering, captured some of the brawn of a hip hop production, was an exciting and instructive demonstration of how compatible old and new methodologies and outlooks could be in black popular music.

Intriguingly, Wah Wah's presence also served as a reminder of the virtues of the rhythm-guitar hero in soul-funk and how truly relevant his ethos could be to a generation of music-makers who had made the loop their *modus operandi*. At several junctures on *Plantation Lullabies*, Ragin was to be found not so much doing very little as not doing any more than was necessary.

He understood proportion. He understood economy. He understood the potential for hypnosis in repetition – or more to the point, its potential for creativity, the fact that there is a fine art to playing a phrase with trance-like regularity and finding subtle shadings of new detail, rich incremental shifts in the character of the groove.

One of the reasons why hip hop was smitten with the music of James Brown and others was because these bands, guitarists included, had taken that lesson on board. The absolutely metronomic quality of the performances that were often sampled, as much as they lent themselves to looping *ad infinitum*, did not in the first place possess the bloodless, mechanical quality of a beat that had actually been programmed.

Generally speaking, the funk player has more of a proclivity for changeless groove playing, the jazz player less so. The latter's overriding aesthetic impulse will be towards a much greater breadth of expression, at least harmonically, whereas the former's is more likely to privilege concentration of expression – meaning less a barrage of new data and more a profound investigation of existing content.

Each point of view is valid and, crucially, they are not incompatible. One thing I have noticed over the years is that several jazz musicians have expressed a desire to be less 'note heavy' and to play the same line longer. They see the value of constancy. Funnily enough, when jazz musicians use a word like *ostinato* to denote a repeated line, they have a semblance of kudos because the term is drawn from European classical music. But when a funk player describes an analogous function with the expression 'same beat', the perception is different – the implication being that the funk musician's work has far less substance.

One might pause to consider the place of the audience, the partner, the accomplice of the musician, in this debate. Also featured on *Plantation Lullabies* was a talented young guitarist by the name of David Fiuczynski, who worked as a sideman with composer-theorist George Russell in the late 1980s and went on to form a band called Screaming Headless Torsos. This unit found an original way of playing rock with all the ingenuity of jazz, the hard drive of funk and the sashaying lilt of Afro-Cuban music. Fiuczynski has an interesting tale to tell about gigging with NdegéOcello and Watson:

> I remember being on stage with Me'Shell and I did this wild solo and people liked it and clapped, and then the band broke down and Wah Wah took over, and he'll tell you, 'No, I don't solo'. You know, he doesn't even stand up on stage; he's sitting down. Anyway, he just started doing his groove thing and he kept on, and he kept on … and on … and people *lost* it! I mean, they really lost it.

It got me thinking. When I was 19, I had three food groups that were important to me: they were loud, distorted, and fast and fancy. Luckily I outgrew that and realised, 'wow', rhythm and groove playing are just as heavy, at times maybe even *heavier* than soloing. I mean, if Hendrix hadn't taken a single solo he still would have been great, because his rhythm playing was, oh my god ... it was just ridiculous.[7]

Significantly, and sadly for that matter, this observation isn't made regularly enough. The cult of the lead guitar, the consecration of the soloist, has to a large extent come at the expense of the rhythm guitar hero, whose contribution to soul music has proved to be nothing less than essential over the course of the last four decades.

That doesn't mean there is no room for the guitar solo in soul, but great music can be made when lead and rhythm lines find some kind of balance. One important, overlooked figure here is the Philadelphian Jef Lee Johnson, largely a session man who has worked with anyone from George Duke to D'Angelo. Listen to his 1997 album *Blue*,[8] and you'll hear a fine mesh of complex rhythm, punchy solos and beautifully crafted counter-melodies laced around Johnson's wry and plaintive singing.

Johnson is often at his most effective when playing a short rhythmic fill at the end of a vocal line, pithily epiloguing it. And although *Blue* has some memorably cogent improvisations, many moments of magic occur when the guitar creates one spiralling rhythmic variation after another.

Indeed, there is a hugely important tradition of the guitar solo conceived and executed as a *series* of rhythmic figures, each one repeated for several bars, rather than a long harmonic-melodic undulation. All this presents the guitarist as a pivotal component of a band's percussive battery: another drummer, but one hitting strings not skins.

Certain bandleaders have recognised that there is a great deal of musical richness to be gained from the astute deployment of this member of the band. The obvious example is James Brown, whose arrangements generally invert the hierarchy and give prominence to the rhythm guitar, or rhythm guitars, while minimising lead guitar work.

That the rhythm-guitar credo is a key weapon in the arsenal of any contemporary soul musician is not in doubt, and the historical precedents for it are too strong to ignore. The big question is how much fine detail or novelty can be brought to the table when this credo is applied. With that in mind, one might consider lastly the 2008 album by Me'Shell NdegéOcello, *The World Has Made Me The Man Of My Dreams*.

In terms of song structures and deployment of guitars, it is a work of enormous concision and concentration, if not compression. It would not be inappropriate to describe this as advanced groove minimalism.

Unsurprisingly, given NdegéOcello's long-running engagement with improvising musicians, the album includes some of the strongest voices in contemporary jazz guitar – Brandon Ross, Hervé Sambe, David Gilmore and Pat Metheny – yet, bar a few fills here and there, *none* of them takes a solo.

Fiuczynski's Wah Wah Watson parable is played out to thrilling effect.

What counts is the distinctive sound of each player, presented both as pert rhythmic entity and as melodic and textural flickers. This suits the tone of the whole album, where the instruments are used practically as flashes of light against the dark, brooding sky of NdegéOcello's voice.

All through this quite wonderful piece of work, the master guitarists appear virtually to tightrope-walk through the songs, creating maximum impact through minimum volleys of notes, their discreet presence a kind of impressionism that nonetheless does not want for vigour.

Genre-wise, this work is very hard to classify. It is part of the soul–rock continuum discussed in Chapter 6. But the frequent slides into spacious, airy soundscapes say much about NdegéOcello's engagement with reggae, something made even more explicit on the 2003 CD *Comfort Woman*, where wafts of dream-state electronics betray an interest in machines and synthesizers – all kinds of keyboards, in fact.

11 Just a little pinch of organ

There's no doubt about it, the Hammond organ is the first synthesizer.
(Dr Lonnie Smith)

I found out about this guy named Tom Oberheim and I bought this ARP Odyssey, and I found out that I could bend the notes and I was like, 'man, I can play the blues on this thing'. Then I got interested.   (George Duke)

I took a credit card and blew it all on a keyboard that sequenced.   (M. Nahadr)

Ever since he switched from jazz piano

With guitars, bass and drums all conjoined in precise, tightly wound, almost spring-loaded movement in the prelude to 'Memphis Soul Stew', King Curtis then asked for a 'just a little pinch of organ'.

It was an interesting choice of words. He had previously requested 'boiling Memphis guitars', the sub-text of intensity in the sound and playing unequivocal. And the way his players duly cracked into action showed they understood exactly what Curtis wanted to hear.

'Just a little pinch' implied subtlety, understatement, though. Accordingly, organist Bobby Emmons, who had played rock and roll with the Bill Black Combo and would play country with Willie Nelson, pressed his hands lightly on the keyboard, somewhere in the middle register, and proceeded to make a chord gurgle over the rest of a rhythm section in joyous momentum. They were marching; he was ambling.

After sustaining his line for a few bars, tantalising rather than roaring, Emmons leapt to a higher pitch and played a thinner, sharper chord, the tonality almost boyish and juvenile compared with the much deeper, more manly resonance of his first statement. The shift between the first and the second lines makes a quintessential point about the organ: it is an electric instrument with a great richness of timbres.

Shrill and reedy, that was the upper register. The low, on the other hand, could often be treacle-thick, bolstering a rhythm section that was light and spindly or turning to cast iron one that was already steely.

Wurlitzer made organs as well as pianos but the model that became the fetish object in black music was the Hammond B3 – actually two keyboards set in a large wooden cabinet, which also had a bank of floor pedals for stomping out bass lines with the feet.

Visually, the instrument is striking for the powerful images it evokes. The sturdy case of brown teak with its wide, solid flanks loosely recalls the pulpit. This is entirely appropriate as the Hammond is tied first and foremost to the black church, being one of the few instruments accepted as a vehicle for producing a 'joyful noise unto the creator', given the general mistrust of the piano and guitar due to their associations with the immoral sporting-house denizen and the dissolute ways of the *hobo sapien*.

Houses of worship were not the organ's only setting. The Hammond had come into jazz at the same time as it arrived in black churches, from the late 1930s onwards. Fats Waller, who had recorded on the pipe organ, let his fingers walk tall on the Hammond, as did his erstwhile pupil Count Basie.

There developed a tradition of jazz players who explored the territory between jazz and blues on the instrument, chief among them Wild Bill Davis, Milt Herth and Bill Doggett. But it was Jimmy Smith who managed to combine harmonic flourish and bluesy warmth to really thrilling effect, modelling some of his lines on those of bebop saxophonists. Smith often played in a tight trio that featured electric guitar and drums, a format favoured by pioneers like Davis and Milt Buckner.

Smith's success with albums such as 1957's *The Sermon* led the way for other Hammond heroes: Jimmy McGriff, Richard 'Groove' Holmes and 'Brother' Jack McDuff. Blue Note and Prestige Records, both iconic jazz labels, had their stables of grits 'n gravy players whose music appealed to black audiences.

By dint of its tonality, there was a sonic hot flush, a burning sensation the Hammond could produce, particularly when notes were held in tremolo, that matched the intense wail of a gospel singer. It is revealing that the instrument was seen as a very step towards that genre.

For example, in 1967 Bob Rolontz, the manager of McDuff – a musician with a devastatingly funky rhythmic feel – declared: 'Ever since he switched from jazz piano to organ about six years ago, he has been playing in the soul groove.'[1] Incidentally, McDuff adopted the adjunct 'Brother' several years before James Brown. The organist's interest in rhythm and blues vividly materialised on *Double Barreled Soul*, a brilliant album cut with alto saxophonist David 'Fathead' Newman – who, though a fine leader, was also a valuable sideman to Ray Charles.

Inventor of soul was perhaps his most significant epithet, but Charles was also a skilled organist. And the presence of the instrument in his work paved the way for a strain of excellent R&B players, including Dave 'Baby' Cortez, Billy Preston and Booker T. Jones of Booker T. & The MGs, who chalked up a number of hits playing generally shorter pieces than their jazz peers. In fact, Jones made the B3 a major element of the whole Stax sound.

Hammonds were fitted with a Leslie loudspeaker/amplifier that greatly enhanced the impact of the notes. It created strong vibrato and tremolo by activating both a treble and a bass unit. The screams, cries, violent leaps and curls of sound that the Hammond generated also stemmed from its 'expression pedal' – actually a kind of prototype wah-wah that would vocalise phrases through considerable bending of pitches. Moreover, above the instrument's two keyboards was a panel with knobs called drawbars. When these knobs were pulled out, they changed the timbre of a chord, thinning or thickening it, and sometimes creating a kind of filter effect on the notes, as if the crackle of a telephone line were bleeding into the sound. So Hammond players could perform a simple remix mid-song, while continuing to play. The instrument offered real-time, albeit relatively crude, sound engineering.

Dr Lonnie Smith, a Blue Note artist who initially worked with guitarist George Benson and alto saxophonist Lou Donaldson in the mid-1960s before going on to cut several very funky soul-jazz albums as a leader for the label, explained this capacity when I interviewed him after a performance with Donaldson at London's Jazz Café in summer 2008.

> One keyboard has a softer sound. I keep it at a different type of setting where it's not as percussive. The top keyboard is more percussive and almost like a big-band sound. If I really wanna stretch out and give it that whole orchestra feel, I get that big sound with the drawbars.
>
> I pull those out and everything is suddenly a whole lot fuller and fatter. The thing is, I can change things as I go along. I've got *options*, which is really what a synthesizer is about, so in my mind there's no doubt about it, the Hammond organ is the first synthesizer.[2]

If I had a hammer

Favoured though it was by soul artists, the B3 organ was eclipsed by an influx of other keyboards, namely electric pianos and synthesizers manufactured by the likes of Fender, Wurlitzer, Moog, Roland, Prophet, Korg, Oberheim and Hohner between the late 1960s and early '70s.

Just as James Brown, also an organ player on occasion, and several other funk groups he influenced were banishing the keyboard from their line-ups to fashion a raw, increasingly harmonically denuded sound, other musicians boldly headed in the opposite direction, embracing the new instruments to expand considerably their tonal palette.

While the rhythm section, horns and strings remained a key part of the soul-music lexicon, keyboards began to play a significant role in shaping and colouring the sound of many productions. Several keyboard players made a marked contribution as freelancers to bands and singers in the 1970s, the most notable being Greg Phillinganes and Dexter Wansel – the former doing great work with anybody from Stevie Wonder to Michael Jackson,[3] the latter one of the key arranger-producers as well as players affiliated with the TSOP label, the mighty creation of Gamble & Huff.

There were two distinct poles in black pop: stripped down and dressed up; keyboard lite and keyboard heavy. As related as it was rhythmically, the music of two artists playing soul could be very different sonically, and it is precisely this range that gave the genre its richness. Soul maintained certain core values, namely incendiary gospel phrasing and the central dynamo of call and response. But it welcomed the sound of something like the Fender Rhodes electric piano and made the instrument a crucial new element in the ongoing evolution of soul vocabulary.

Technology is a vague term. It conjures up an image of white coats in a lab, greater minds bringing something of tomorrow to the lesser minds of today. Beyond that cliché, though, it can be argued that the high-tech hinges on a desire to effect change in an existing piece of apparatus, regardless of how basic the means with which it is done.

There had been an artisan-bricoleur impulse running through black music – and black culture, for that matter – that was an important prelude to the gusto with which soul strapped on synthesizers. An obvious precedent was the use of mutes like coconut shells and hats to distort the sound of brass instruments in the 1920s.

What is more relevant to the immediate discussion, though, is the example of a musician like Maurice White, drummer with Ramsey Lewis in the 1960s and then leader of Earth, Wind & Fire in the '70s. He took a time-honoured African instrument, the kalimba, and saw in it more than a miniature xylophone with a limited range of pitches. Although its tone is activated through the use of the thumbs rather than fingers, the kalimba is nonetheless a keyboard with a richness of timbre – or perhaps more significantly, from White's point of view, it had the potential to be transformed into something that sounded like something else.

Options, according to Dr Lonnie Smith, are the *raison d'être* of a synthesizer. So White engaged in some basic mechanical engineering, building his own electric pick-ups for the kalimba, which he often distorted heavily to produce insanely spooky tonalities, shuddering vibrations that blended fascinatingly the thud of wood and the ping of steel, endowing Earth, Wind & Fire with considerable sonic idiosyncrasy.

Driving aesthetic choice is thus a desire to modify and customise sound, to shape it according to what a particular musician may hear, or wants to hear, in his head, before the world of instrument makers catches his coat-tails. There is also the pragmatic issue of volume. White was increasing the amplitude of a kalimba note to compete with the bass guitar, percussion and drums. So to a certain extent there is a parallel with the evolution of slap technique on the bass, which also sought to clear the hurdle of compensating volume.

Synthesizers could only serve and enhance this way of thinking, this pursuit of new sounds. Pictures of Stevie Wonder or Bernie Worrell hemmed in

Dr Lonnie Smith explores 'options' on the Hammond organ (photo courtesy David Redfern/ Redferns/Getty Images).

by half a dozen or so state-of-the-art Moogs, ARPs, Rhodes and clavinets are the strongest symbol of the increasingly bold steps soul music would take on an electronic Yellow Brick Road.

Through his ability to combine the most novel sounds with precise rhythmic and counter-melodic flair, Worrell, who received classical training at the Juilliard School of Music in New York, proved himself to be a vital cog in the Parliament-Funkadelic machine lubricated by the vision of George Clinton. From *Chocolate City* to *One Nation Under A Groove*, sonic expansion was an organising principle, and guitars, drums, percussion and voices all contrived to gain in weight and density. This was something the keyboard player duly matched by playing multiple parts *à la* Stevie Wonder, who was wont to stand in as his own orchestra on occasion.

Setting off a minefield of electronics, the tonalities approximating hiccups, sneezes and scratches in between slithery, curling motifs, their pitches often rudely bent, Worrell made his aesthetic a cross between the baroque and burlesque. His synths were invariably choral in nature, a wry, distorting mirror to the merry riot of the P-Funk singers.

Well versed as he was in music theory, Worrell gave the impression that he also knew how to think sonically, *extra-musically* as well as musically. As such, he could create audio effects and textural quirks crucial to the complicity between his ever-shifting sonic rainbow and that of an industrious vocal ensemble that constantly changed its configuration.

The singers would move between doo-wop close harmonies, gospel hollers, solo lines, cartoon character yelps and exclamations, and other oddball tonalities. That range was paralleled in the use of synthesizers that would switch from thick, rich block chords to piping single-note melodies to snatches of otherworldly or Machine Age sound.

Worrell's work on Parliament classics like *Motor Booty Affair* exerted an influence on a number of soul ensembles in the 1970s, who simply stacked up synthesizer figures in expansive arrangements to the extent that sometimes the keyboard player functioned as a small self-contained unit, almost as a 'section' had done in the days of a jazz big band, with its highly active cells of saxophones, trumpets and trombones.

There was a degree of overlap between developments in soul and jazz during the early 1970s, in so far as both genres underwent considerable sonic changes due to the impact of new synthesizers. The likes of Worrell and Stevie Wonder were of primary importance because they straddled these schools, making soul with an undeniably marked jazz sensibility. Conversely, there was a coterie of jazz pianists making soul with funky inclinations, and gleefully embracing the latest keyboards in the process. Herbie Hancock, an 'early adopter' of Apple Computer software in the 1970s, is arguably the most iconic of these players. But Ramsey Lewis, Charles Earland, Lonnie Liston Smith and George Duke are other keyboardists who made music so defined by the novel sounds of synthesizers that at times it toppled into a kind of hot-gospel electro.[4]

There were two points of similarity between Hancock and Duke. They cut their teeth on acoustic jazz and they were also greatly driven by an interest in technology and advances in sound manipulation. In Duke's case, this was consolidated by a course in electronics at San Francisco State University during the 1960s. 'They taught you how to take two- or four-track tapes and you construct sounds ... a door knock or a chair sliding across the floor', Duke recalled:

> Any sound that you could record with a microphone and put on there and develop into a piece. You could use normal sounds like piano or trumpet but basically they were looking for something in nature, or something *non-musical*. You know, I felt like an engineer. It was strange but I learnt something.[5]

Duke would put those lessons into practice most fruitfully on albums such as 1977's *Reach For It* and 1978's *Don't Let Go*, which spawned the sizeable hit single 'Dukey Stick' – a track betraying the clear influence of Bernie Worrell, Bootsy Collins and the whole Parliament-Funkadelic aesthetic, especially in the juxtaposition of puckish, at times abrupt rhythmic riffs and dramatic, hard-hitting but tightly marshalled solos.

There is a balance of quirkiness and dynamism in the above that reflects some of the rich experience Duke gathered as a sideman fortunate enough to be working in the early 1970s, a time when the dividing lines between genres of music were not so rigid. He toured with jazz saxophonist Julian 'Cannonball' Adderley, recorded and toured with rock avant-gardist Frank Zappa and also co-led a band with the drummer Billy Cobham, who was a member of the Mahavishnu Orchestra – a pioneering ensemble that infused the energy of stadium rock into arrangements whose barqoue grandeur referenced jazz and classical music.

Essential as these experiences were, they did not wholly account for George Duke's embrace of electronics. One might assume, given that he had studied the use of 'non-musical' sounds at college, that Duke had an unquenchable curiosity for previously unheard tonal colours, for any timbre that might lend originality to an arrangement.

While that's certainly true, there was a more elemental concern. Duke wanted to wring as much feeling from any modern kit as he had done using the equipment previously available – namely, the piano or organ that had provided so much emotional depth as well as harmonic and textural richness for decades before a new arsenal of space age synths was introduced. He still had to tap into the foundations of African American folk expression. He still had to obey a fundamental cultural as well as musical impulse. He still had to play the blues.

Duke began seriously to switch on to the new keyboards after lending an ear to a young Czech musician, Jan Hammer, the synthesizer whiz kid with the aforementioned Mahavishnu Orchestra. 'I heard this record by the Mahavishnu Orchestra and said, "What the hell is this?" Well, Jan Hammer was playing some strange, real funky keys', Duke remembers.

> I was like, 'this is not a guitar … that's a synthesizer', but I'd never heard anybody play it like that. It turned out to be an Oberheim.
>
> I found out about this guy named Tom Oberheim and I bought this ARP Odyssey, and I found out that I could bend the notes and was like, 'man, I can play the blues on this thing'. Then I got interested. I knew before that I could get all these weird sounds and all the 'wooh ooh ooh' and stuff but when I found out that I could bend the notes, I tried to make the synthesizer sound like Yusef Lateef playing the flute. That's what drew me to synthesizers …. because I found out that I could play the blues on them.[6]

All systems go

Soul music was rooted in the doctrine of the group, the ensemble, the pooling of resources so that a certain magic emanated from the blend of personalities and the differing touch and feel on their instruments. But there were nonetheless instances of the one-man band asserting itself in no uncertain terms. The key examples here are Stevie Wonder and Prince.

Running through their work, from the 1970s to the present day, has been a creative tension between autonomous music-making, greatly facilitated by all manner of new keyboards, and faith in the dynamics of a band – be it Wonderlove or The Revolution – in which the different personalities of individual musicians reveal themselves as absolutely essential to the success of the overall artistic endeavour.

Both Stevie's and Prince's ability as multi-instrumentalists has also come into play. They can perform most of the parts in a song themselves, yet there is nonetheless a recognition that they cannot do certain things other musicians can do. And maybe that ongoing relationship between the personal and the collective creative praxis has been essential not just to keeping their music interesting but to soul in general over time. It is both an individual and a team sport.

That said, it must be noted that Wonder's spellbinding work with synthesizers in the mid-1970s was decisively facilitated by the input of electronics polymaths and programmers Bob Margouleff and Malcolm Cecil (of the pioneering Tonto's Expanding Headband), as well as by sharp-eared engineers such as John Fischbach and Gary Olazabal. Hence there was an exceptional individual surrounded by an equally exceptional team.

Enormous amounts of state-of-the-art analogue equipment were deployed like futuristic, Star Wars weaponry on albums such as 1973's *Innervisions*. All the same, crucial timbral detail was added by any number of top session guitarists (e.g. David T. Walker) and percussionists.

The band would expand when the sounds in Stevie's head multiplied.

Declines in sales of soul music by the end of the 1970s, and the reluctance of record companies to continue bankrolling ambitious projects and the large bands – with horns, backing vocalists and strings – that Wonder and Earth, Wind & Fire had used to such powerful effect, played a part in the influx of keyboard-based soul during the early '80s. But the thirst for new sounds in black pop was already so strong that chances are several artists would have eased on down that road anyway.

Financially, the benefits were substantial. One skilled musician handling several keyboards could – certainly in a studio rather than on stage – play enough lines to compensate for the absence of two to three costly brass and reed instruments, or even the sacrosanct drums, percussion, bass guitar and electric guitars of a rhythm section.

Many examples of synthesizer-led soul recorded in the 1980s are laced with polyphonic figures that closely evoke the horn stabs, the sax and trumpet harmonies, that were so prevalent in the preceding decade. And it is clear that some keyboard players were, either consciously or subconsciously, referencing that vocabulary.

As was noted in Chapter 9, the model of the singer + keyboard player-drum programmer gained ground, as it did in pop, due to both the pragmatic solution it offered in difficult economic circumstances and the room for creative manoeuvre it gave to songwriters or players who perhaps did not feel as comfortable working in the context of a full band.

More fascinating still was the way in which some synthesizer players/producers would keep faith in the most traditional, if not simple, sounds in the midst of a barrage of state-of-the-art keys. On many occasions real handclaps would crack against heavily reverberating electronic chords, possibly because the crispness of palm on palm was actually very hard to emulate with a machine and possibly because the artists in question – Wonder and Greg Phillinganes did this a lot – wanted to retain a sound so redolent of the black church.

Keyboards and electronics in general are an absolutely fascinating component of the history of soul during the 1980s because their deployment produced such wild extremes, making the music both resoundingly funky and jarringly soulless. Even though there was a dramatic change in the textures of the music compared with soul in the '70s and certainly the '60s and '50s, synth-led soul was nonetheless in the continuum of what had come before it. Rhythm and blues musicians had always displayed a fascination

Stevie Wonder plugs in and grooves out (photo courtesy Michael Ochs Archives/Getty Images).

with machines and with any devices, both manufactured and improvised, that afforded opportunities to manipulate, adulterate, personalise, customise and generally create excitement – or, in some cases, to create a kind of beguiling, chameleon fantasia in sound.

These musicians liked to play with sound. They liked to mess with sound. They liked to electrify or distort. In that respect, the example of Maurice White's home-wired kalimba is appropriate. But one should also remember that New Orleans legend Professor Longhair was significantly altering the sound of his piano back in the 1940s by doing nothing more than strategically placing a drumhead on the underside of the body and jamming a microphone between his legs to make the notes shudder when he bashed the ivories with those hammer-hands. Over a loose, calypso-style beat with double or treble time implied, the result was hypnotic.

With the range of keyboards expanding and the opportunities for textural invention increased by greater use of overdubs and programming, soul music became a crazy rainbow of sounds as time went on. And as much as its exponents applied harmonic discipline, there was also – as was the case with Funkadelic and Worrell – a sense of several artists taking liberties with new timbres and striving definitely towards zany pitches that suggested both the fairground and the video game.

Some 1980s recordings made with electronics sound very anachronistic today, though. In several cases, the songs were simply undermined by synthesizer tapestries in which tonalities – sometimes garishly bright polyphonic chords – assumed a crude, if not childish music-box quality with overly glossy motifs or bell-like harmonic embellishments that lacked the velvety fuzz, purr and whirr of older analogue keys.

Coupled with harsh, whiplash-like drum programmes that were so *fortissimo* and shuddering, they just killed the lead vocal, the results were mediocre and would have kept the delete button warm had such tracks been made in Mac-able, downloadable, iPod-able times.

There is no more pungent symbol of electronics contriving to stifle soulfulness than *Electric Universe*, the dire all-synthesizer album cut by Earth, Wind & Fire in 1983. It cries out for the humanising holler of horns. More importantly, it represents the kind of rhythmically stiff and texturally plastic lexicon that would eventually give other artists, hankering for the days of a band replete with brass, reeds and rhythm section, something to react against. There was no soul in the machine.

Yet too many interesting records were made for 1980s electro-soul, for want of a better term, to be summarily dismissed. One of the great triumphs of the music from this period is precisely that trained musicians did not adopt a Luddite posture and refuse to engage with technology. Rather, they welcomed it while keeping faith in solid songwriting values and arranging sensibilities that reflected soul's roots in the fertile ground of R&B. Crucial examples of this trend were producers and musicians Nick Martinelli, Jam &

Lewis, Jimi Randolph and Eric Matthews, or the groups One Way, Cameo, Aurra, Kleeer, Fatback and The Gap Band, who confected aggressively funky and sonically adventurous work by way of a wide range of new keyboards.[7] There was soul in the machine.

In fact, it is highly symbolic that the electronic, synth-heavy brand of post-disco 1980s soul should have been dubbed 'boogie' by many DJs. The term referred to a generic idea of dance in black culture but it reached back further to boogie-woogie, the shuffling, pumping, piano-based blues of the '20s that was essentially about the energy rush generated by the keyboard with a surge of movement in the low register – something that filtered through to '40s big-band jazz and '50s R&B. So maybe the application of the term 'boogie' to '80s electronic soul-funk was really saying that effervescence - rhythmic bustle and momentum – remained a core value in black music, regardless of whether orchestras, bands or machines were the order of the day.

In any case, jazz sensibilities still prevailed amid the synthesizers and sequencers. Indeed, a fair amount of electronic-led soul had rich harmonies or solos. Certainly the likes of Hubert Eaves (of D-Train) or James Ingram (of Ingram) could trace their formative years to the 70s, when the 'fusion' move-ment brought together jazz, soul and rock.[8] Tellingly, Ingram was a saxophon-ist as well as a whiz on keyboards. Electro, in his hands, did not mean less sophisticated arrangements.

What it could mean was the addition of the textural hardness and percus-sive drive that had helped to distinguish funk from soul. Through extensive layering of mostly short, punchy rhythmic motifs and counter-melodies, key-board players created collisions, like bumper cars of sound with all the agi-tation and febrile energy common to the vocals and bands of James Brown, George Clinton *et al*. Deprived of a band, keyboardists nonetheless looked at four beats in a bar and thought about how to map their squelches and squiggles between, as well as on, those signposts in ways that would electrify dancer and listener alike.

Many of the tightly coiled keyboard figures were punctuated by a slurred legato chord or a sharp, staccato single-note blast – think Jam & Lewis's lethal arrangement for Thelma Houston's 'You Used To Hold Me So Tight' – that increased the overall tension of a piece, particularly when complemented by bounces of moog bass and ricochets of bass guitar. Two- or three-note explo-sions went off all over the rhythm section. Keys, bass and drums were laid down like a veritable minefield of sounds.

In any case, some of the best productions from that era question the demarcation between soul and techno, the putative hot and cold of pop: music with a bump and flexibility or music with a grind and rigidity.

Alternatively, as with The System's 'You Are In My System', they show how soulful techno can be, or rather how much techno soul music can accommodate.

Comprising vocalist-guitarist Mic Murphy and keyboardist-programmer-producer David Frank, The System were a duo who wrote fine love songs and presented them in a sonic context that used bang-up-to-date digital as well as analogue sounds and recording techniques. They scored a sizeable club hit with 'You Are In My System', enough to warrant radio play and a pop-courting cover by singer Robert Palmer.

Cut in 1983, 'You Are In My System' is a blueprint for dot-matrix precision in music-making, a glimpse of a hip hop future in which notes would appear almost as chess pieces on a computer screen. Everything about the song – the roadside drill of the bass and drums, the miniature detonations of sound in the slipstream of Murphy's plaintive vocal in the verse, the way chords swell up like surf in the chorus – points to the tightly mapped audio collages that would later be made with yet-to-be-invented software such as Pro Tools, Logic and Reason.

Defined by the sharp, clipped nature of its keyboard licks, the piece has a devilishly funky undertow, simply because Frank, a classically trained pianist, was smart enough to position his array of glowing tonalities in some off-kilter positions not unrelated to the cogent use of polyrhythms in R&B traditions. Many of his predecessors had shown how the tight interlocking of riffs in an arrangement or the crash-landing of sounds at various points in a bar were the key to the door of excitation, the circular movement within movement of funk. And when this stagger-stutter combined with clever textural ideas, the results were superb.

Syncopation remained a guiding principle in the one-man orchestra, and although the notes and beats from Frank's keys and drums were executed with a perceptible curtness, there was nonetheless enough internal motion in the arrangement to make it clear he had understood or, better still, fully absorbed the dynamics of a decent live rhythm section.

To a certain extent, the keyboards on 'You Are In My System' echoed the shrewd placement of two or three guitars in classic soul and funk, where in many cases rough and smooth sounds – heavy, grainy chords and slender finger-picked notes – would make for a wide textural gamut, all the while accented at several strategic points in the song's metre.

So Frank makes a bulky, rock-hard synthesizer spark into life like a wah-wah just before beat three of each bar. And in the third measure of the verse, he has a wave-like chord rise up between the two and the four to create a miniature flood, a glancing roller of energy. As for the chorus, it vividly releases tension through a stream of whispery, string-like tones that ripple sensually under the vocals. A wealth of liquid and solid sounds coalesce. Warm blood flows in the silvery body electric of the music.

Contrasting note lengths are used to great effect. The verse is mostly pinched staccatos that drizzle around the vocal before becoming a flood of legatos that swirl over no fewer than sixteen bars in the chorus. So there is a slow wash of sound coming to the fore, engulfing the busy percussion.

Of equal importance is the fact that the central harmony of 'You Are In My System' does not break with past models. Whether or not he was heeding

George Duke's edict about the need to be able to play the blues on his Moog, David Frank was making the blues on his own synthesizers, and 'You Are In My System' was a seminal example of just how fruitful the application of new sonic skin to old harmonic bones could be. So right in the middle of the verse, he plays a robust IV chord change. The shift from the A-sharp to the E-flat packs a huge emotional punch because it ratchets up the suspense of the narrative, lends added traction to the vocal and futuristic keyboard licks, and reasserts the tried and tested structural model of countless 'old' James Brown tunes. Through this brilliant conflation of familiarity and novelty, The System thus teach us that a techno lament with a BPM (beats per minute) of 110 can also be a blues in A-sharp.

Black pop did much more than investigate electronica. Black pop consumed electronica. Black pop produced electronica.

B-3 bounce-back

By and large, The System's music could be termed synth-soul and is usually categorised separately from hip hop. But what the likes of David Frank were doing was not on an entirely different plane from the work of producers such as Man Parrish, whose high-tempo, staccato sequencing and programming offered a curtain raiser to the age of rap. Frank was beholden to melody and rhythm, while Parrish hinged more on rhythm.

New York-based Parrish became part of the 'electro' movement in the early 1980s, when he scored hits with insanely catchy songs such as 'Hip Hop Be Bop'. His work essentially showed how the core vocabulary of a funky backbeat and an accompanying barrage of percussion could acquire an entirely Computer Age resonance when several lines of rhythmic agitation interlocked in an ultra-precise organisational grid system and were given tonalities leaning towards metal rather than velvet.

Throughout the latter half of the 1980s and the first part of the '90s, the years in which hip hop asserted itself as an artistic and increasingly commercial force to be reckoned with, significant advances were made in music-making technology through the invention of sampling devices, digital equipment and software that offered a limitless supply of synthesizer sounds as well as passable approximations of anything from drums and bass to strings and horns.

House, garage and electronic music generally brought a deluge of new keyboard sounds into popular music, and the praxis of synthesizer programming, sequencing and looping gained further currency.

Producers such as Teddy Riley sought to bring hip hop beats into alliance with vocal melodies through a strand of black pop called New Jack Swing. To a large extent, this marked the moment when a new definition of R&B lost some of the flavour of old-school R&B, primarily due to melodic impoverishment and the lowering of the blues coefficient in arrangements and textures which at times had a day-glo shininess leaning squarely towards mainstream pop, where boy and girl bands were becoming a humungous chart-bound juggernaut.

Yet in the midst of this wild explosion of new sounds, there were still references, if not returns, to both tonalities from another era and musicians who'd also played them in another era – players who knew about the art of dynamics and arrangements in a song, as well as how to programme beats that were fa … resh.

David Frank came back. In 1994 he made a significant contribution to one of the best albums recorded that year, British soul singer Omar's *For Pleasure*, a set that had a very sizeable influence on the forthcoming crop of US 'neo-soul' artists like Erykah Badu and Maxwell.[9]

What was most impressive about this work was its blend of traditional and modern sensibilities through the use of keyboards that were either old Moogs or were programmed to evoke that sound, as well as razor-sharp programming from Frank that had the cut and thrust of sample-led music like hip hop.

Loosely associated with the acid jazz movement, Omar emerged in the late 1980s as the genius child of UK black music, chalking up a modest pop hit with 1991's 'There's Nothing Like This', and generally exciting audiences because his rich singing voice was supplemented by all-round musical ability (keyboards, bass, drums, percussion) that harked back to Stevie Wonder. Omar was interested in the potential interface between a classicist soul sound and a new soul sound for the hip hop age, one that did not completely eschew the use of old instruments and a band.

So Fender Rhodes, string synthesizers and, above all, the clavinet became a pivotal part of his aesthetic. A similar interest registered among others. Just as acid jazz brought back the wah-wah guitar to soul in the mid-1990s, it also contributed to the resurrection of the Hammond organ, certainly through the likes of bands like the James Taylor Quartet, who quickly carved out a reputation as a must-see live act in the UK through some quite incendiary performances in clubs.

Formerly part of an old-school R&B group, The Prisoners, Taylor was a B3 player who'd been inspired by Brian Auger, a vital force at the crossroads of blues, jazz and rock in London during the late 1960s, and by Auger's American role models: the two Jimmys, Smith and McGriff.

Leading a combo of drums, electric bass and guitar, Taylor had a taut sound that was equally effective on 1960s-style soul jazz and '70s funk. Although the music made no secret of classicist references, there was a verve in the execution, as well as a fair helping of decent original tunes, that made it welcome at a time when increasing numbers of reissued jazz albums featuring the B3 sparked interest in a band that smacked down on stage what hip hop jacked up in the studio.

Club performances by the group were hugely important because Taylor exposed the Hammond organ to teenagers who had never before eyed the instrument in its big, brown-box glory. By way of old black vinyl it had remained abstract, but now it was real, fulfilling the sacrosanct condition for an instrument's passage from one generation to the next: it has to be *seen* as well as heard, and preferably under the spotlight, in the warrior-arena ambiance of a gig.

This re-entry into popular consciousness may have led to the B3 becoming a less anachronistic and more viable option for the wave of post-acid Jazz soul artists, who would either use it or programme a new keyboard to conjure up its presence. A notable example is D'Angelo's 'Brown Sugar', the breakout single that swelled the speakers of many a jeep in 1995.

Decisively touched by Al Green's nuanced romanticism, D'Angelo's voice – that of a dyed-in-the-wool Southern soul singer from Virginia – was striking, but it was also brilliantly served by tonal contrasts on the above track. 'Brown Sugar' has a very heavy low end, with drums and bass solidifying into an airless mass of granite upon which the organ sizzles with a churchy heat. The piece pushes down to the dark of hip hop while rising up to the light of gospel, as D'Angelo pours out mucho good-rockin'-tonight lust, putting his own spin on the sacred–profane continuum.

Credit crunched

Contemporary soul's most talented keyboardists, such as Bobby 'Too Funky' Sparks, James Poyser (a vital member of the camp of players that gravitate around The Roots), Kaidi Tatham and Mark de Clive-Lowe – the latter two prime movers on the late-1990s UK 'broken beat' scene – have all distinguished themselves by the shrewd use of old and new instruments and their application within an aesthetic that recognises the value of sampling, looping and post-production as well as live playing.

Excitingly, a character like de Clive-Lowe, a London-based New Zealander, often programmes drums and keyboards in concert to create a virtual band that is then enriched by the input of other players such as a vocalist, drummer, percussionist or saxophonist.[10]

Beyond its imaginative use of specific keyboards, soul has also had a long-running fascination with odd, unheard noises and ways of manipulating instruments to produce these noises that are not divorced from the jazz tradition. The example of Earth, Wind & Fire's Maurice White (who stands right between the two genres), customising the kalimba to create a tonality in 1969 that sounds distinctly 2009, is instructive.

Black pop's engagement with this kind of sound treatment, as well as state-of-the-art keyboards, is too deeply rooted for there to be any great unbridgeable gap between acoustic and electric soul, strands that are distinct but not mutually exclusive. So Mister Stevie loves to bump his piano and Brother Wonder loves to grind his Electrone Polyphonic GX10.

Hence the fully electric flower of soul music is not so much an addition to as an outgrowth of its acoustic seedbed. Over the past five decades, musicians have explored all manner of entwinements between what might be deemed organic and synthetic sounds. With hip hop placing machines and the manipulation of pre-recorded audio at the forefront of its aesthetic in the 1980s, the prospect of post-hip hop soul having a different feel – whether due to the touch of a player who had grown up listening to beats as well as playing the beat, or to a more dissonant use of sounds, as could be the case in rap productions – was entirely logical.

What hip hop brought to soul from the 1990s and beyond was a certain hardness and bigness of sound, a greater bulge in the bass and sustain in certain chords that made them almost flood the stereo image, so that the voice was bathing in a sea of sound. This has definitely touched the work of keyboardists like de Clive-Lowe and it has made songs by vocalists Jill Scott or Raheem DeVaughn sound different when they share studios with hip hop producers such as Jazzy Jeff.

Occasionally, Jeff makes beats that display such fine textural sensitivity, where a muted tone is obviously informed by the breathy timbre of a horn or choir, that they can embellish a singer's trajectory without employing any complex harmonic movement or changes of key.

Nineteen-eighties electro-soul, its attention to detail partly shaped by the wily shadow play of Jamaican dub, mooted the possibilities of a chord's decay to silence, elongating and expanding sound to slide dramatic silhouettes into the mix. Hip hop production sometimes does that brilliantly, taking what appears to be the buzz of a fly or a human exhalation and stretching it, in the hands of a skilled producer like DJ Premier,[11] across several bars. This can be both oppressive and curiously seductive: one solitary strange noise could be at once act as an infinite scream of dread and an eternal swoon of delight, a lingering trail under the fast flight of rhymes.

Put simply, this is all about atmosphere, imagery in sound. And any advance in keyboard and production technology can only be a good, not a bad, thing for a competent soul singer. If the history of the music shows us one thing, it is that a proper gospel or blues voice can thrive against any sonic backdrop, be it made by man or machine, or indeed both.

Had black pop really believed that a Hammond organ and a tambourine could never be replaced, then the genre wouldn't have proved so rich. The continual appearance of soul artists who embrace rather than reject electronics is not so much progressive as a logical extension of a long-established order.

M. Nahadr's *EclecticIsM*, issued in 2009, is proof positive thereof.

An African American albino from Washington, D.C. who moved to New York in the late 1990s, became a performance artist and staged an opera, *Madwoman*, as well as multi-media installations, Nahadr has an extraordinary multi-octave voice and an ingenuity in her phrasing that reflect a direct engagement with the world of free jazz. She was mentored by avant-garde veterans Sabir Mateen and Daniel Carter.

Besides her intelligent use of this superlative voice, Nahadr plays keys and programmes beats with her son, Quynton Wright, to utterly beguiling effect. There is a startling dissonance in this music that cohesively binds hip hop to free jazz. The ambiguity of the whole sound canvas suggests anything from cut-ups of synthesizer chords to fragments of street noise that have been rinsed out with reverb and then reconditioned as unrecognisable strains of a weird, austere semi-industrial humming.

'I took a credit card and blew it all on a keyboard that sequenced,' Nahadr chuckled to me in 2009, keen to stress that using synthesizers to create a wide spectrum of sounds on *EclecticIsM* was of paramount importance.[12] Just as one hears with Stevie Wonder, just as one hears with David Frank, there is a great attention to detail in the use of electronics that betrays an interest in the finer shadings of the human voice, strings or brass.

Ultimately, it is the sumptuous, noble melodies that make Nahadr's songs beautiful, but they are brilliantly served by a savvy blend of natural and distorted sounds, some of which are lengthy, shadowy notes that reflect the uninterrupted muffle that she associates with life in an urban setting.

> I find that sometimes it can be interesting to have something running through the verse and chorus and bridge, and it's still very present, so it can stretch for many more bars and ... *trip* on. Trip is a good word.
>
> Imagine me by the kitchen sink having a coffee, humming a tune, and it comes to an end and then here comes the cab driver, and he honks his horn in perfect timing and perfect harmony and it becomes part of the piece. It is an amazing thing to see how much the world is singing *at* you... *constantly*. I'm trying to get that with the keys.[13]

The sonic originality of *EclecticIsM* is almost a 'You Are In My System' for the millennium, a dazzling display of audio collage that does not callously kill the blues.

Nahadr is as much a songwriter as a beatmaker, so the music is at times melodically minimalist and oddly configured, throwing one curveball after another at the listener. In the midst of this great ocean of electronics are not one but two bass guitarists – and a horn player, who blows just the right number of notes.

12 A half a pint of horn

I really don't think genres are that deep. C major is C major. The point, is what are you gonna do with that?   (Kenny Garrett, alto saxophone)

A saxy road runner

Horn is a general term. It refers to both the brass and reeds that, throughout the history of black pop, have featured either as solo instruments or in combination. The brass section has been as distinct an element of the ensemble as drums, bass and other members of the rhythm section.

There are arguably fewer horns featured in soul music today than in times past. But when reeds or brass blast out a note, like the spectral electric trumpet played by Meg Montgomery on M. Nahadhr's 2009 masterpiece *EclecticIsM*, a long lineage is evoked and it could include anything from Bobbi Humphrey's flute in 1989 to Fred Wesley's trombone in 1978 to King Curtis's saxophone in 1967.

In the intro to 'Memphis Soul Stew' (cut that year), Curtis, after calling for bass, drums, guitar and organ, announced the need for 'a half a pint of horn' and proceeded to blow his tenor for four bars, repeating a short flicker of a phrase with minimal harmonic variation before it faded into silence. The riff was discreet but not inconspicuous for it.

Curtis's sax was the last instrument to be named in the introduction. Once he had demonstrated to the listener what the half pint sounded like, he told the band, somewhat theatrically, to 'beat ... well' and then took full control of the piece, stating the melody before going on to improvise some busier, choppy lines on the set chord changes.

Although he generously gave each of his musicians the spotlight in the prelude to the song, 'Memphis Soul Stew' was very much Curtis's track.

He was the lead voice, the wordless singer. By the time Curtis recorded the piece, he had already carved out a highly successful career as a supremely versatile artist: producer, arranger, musical director for the likes of Aretha Franklin, he was a respected figure in the world of soul music who had also proved a master of the short solo. Curtis would pop up in the middle of a song to supplement the vocal with a new burst of tonal colour and skilful line construction that enhanced the already established narrative and provided a change of focus for the listener.

For example, his appearance on Franklin's 'Respect' is one of the great displays of expertly *measured* improvisation on record. In the space of just eight bars, Curtis attacks vividly but soberly, keeping his phrasing buoyant and bouncing without toppling into lengthy phrases or excessively rapid volleys of notes. Emotionally, he generates heat but mostly simmers, exactly as the singer does in a performance of marked intelligence, one in which she demands equality with firm self-possession rather than screaming for it in frantic desperation.

Complicity of voice and saxophone was a recurrent feature of the R&B era in which Curtis served his apprenticeship during the 1950s. Listening to some of those recordings, one is struck by the considerable amount of space the horn was sometimes afforded to solo by some of the leading singers of the day – or at least by the producers and arrangers in charge of directing the sessions.

'Jim Dandy' by the estimable Lavern Baker, one of the significant early signings to Atlantic Records, featured a blazing twelve-bar solo from Sam 'The Man' Taylor that was assigned a clear metaphorical as well as musical role in the piece. The horn acted as the titular hero, the man who comes to the rescue of a girl named Sue who was 'feeling kind of blue'.[1] As the tenor sax rips into its improvisation, Baker chants 'Go Jim Dandy!' with a hot tone that suggests she is urging a chivalrous knight to sweep a damsel in distress off her feet. The horn break is conspicuously wild.

Contexts such as these present the horn player as more than a perfunctory sideman. The musician is making a contribution to the dramatic subtext of the piece, either reflecting or, in the best cases, showily embellishing the atmosphere created by the singer.

Other 1950s R&B tunes were practically singer-saxophonist duets, featuring horn breaks that lasted as long as twenty-four bars. The tenor player, usually equipped with a hard, rugged tone, would either play constantly behind the voice or make a fleeting two-bar intervention to finish off one of the singer's lines before he or she moved on to the next – a convention that had existed in jazz and blues, mostly with a guitarist in the accompanying role, for several decades.

To the question of why these strategic choices were made, why a horn might be given a prominent role on a singer's track, one could cite a strand of instrumental R&B, mostly sax-led, that was a successful commercial proposition, thus narrowing the distance between vocal and non-vocal tunes in black popular music. Saxophonists like Sil Austin, Red Prysock, Jack McVea and Joe Houston had all chalked up hits playing highly energised, often raucous music that bounced between R&B and a slightly more frenzied rock and roll, their songs tapping into the myriad rhythmic variations on the blues, be they boogie, shuffle or 'twist'. These players honked out catchy melodies and relatively simple, forceful solos that moved many a dancehall crowd.

By and large, they were all influenced by Louis Jordan, who enjoyed star status between the early 1940s and late '50s. Although he sang heartily on the bulk of his tunes, Jordan was also a very good saxophonist. He was capable of delivering precise, pithy solos that brought a great surge of excitement to his songs, and when he added more horns on pieces like 'Caldonia' and arranged them colourfully, the results were excellent.

Because he had spent his formative years in Chick Webb's big band, Jordan understood the basic mechanics of playing in a horn section and he applied that knowledge to a small-group setting. Jazz orchestras were thus an important training ground for a future generation of R&B players, who would retain elements of swing in their music while incorporating new rhythms and eventually a new range of instruments.

Making the link between the eras even clearer was a piece like Jimmy Forrest's 1961 track 'Night Train'. Although it was rock-solid R&B, built on a mild boogaloo groove with a spiralling, windmill-like central rhythm, the piece had a raucous holler of a sax-led melody, derived from a combination of various motifs that were used in Duke Ellington's 'Happy Go Lucky Local' and 'That's The Blues Old Man'.[2]

A few years later, James Brown got hold of the song and made it one of the key items in his repertoire. That one of the most significant exponents of black popular music, the man who would soon become a prime architect of rhythmic innovation, should have Ellington encoded in his music was arguably one of the strongest symbols yet of the proximity between jazz and R&B that would carry over into the world of soul and funk.

Different genres of music have better chances of interacting if there are influential figures who embrace them and lead the way for others. And if Brown was inclined to give some space to horn players in his work, then he could not possibly have ignored the recordings of another role model, Ray Charles. His orchestra featured two brilliant alto saxophonists, Hank Crawford and David 'Fathead' Newman, both of whom made a string of excellent solo albums throughout the 1960s.

Charles was also a passable alto saxophonist, and pictures of one of the principal creators of soul music on stage with a beatific smile and a shiny horn around his neck made a clear and meaningful historical link with Louis Jordan. They reminded us quite emphatically that an epochal song like 'I've Got A Woman' probably would not have swung into life without the instructive precursor of Jordan's 'Caldonia'.

Like Charles, Newman and Crawford signed to Atlantic Records, and although their work was categorised very much as soul jazz, it was not that far removed from the output of their label mate King Curtis. 'Soul Serenade', the big hit Curtis scored in 1965, was, in its wonderfully yearning melody and ripe, joyous gospel-heavy refrains, a piece with obvious parallels to the work of the three aforementioned artists.

If Atlantic had a formidable soul sax star in Curtis, then Motown, the other iconic label of the decade, had its own answer in Junior Walker. Originally signed to Harvey, a label owned by Harvey Fuqua that was acquired by his brother-in-law, Motown boss Berry Gordy, Walker was a saxophonist who made waves locally with 'Cleo's Mood', a very sultry, moody blues that performed the impressive sleight of hand of making a middle tempo sound, or rather feel, languorously slow and all the funkier for it.

Although Walker wasn't generally as effusive as a bebop jazz player, he nonetheless made a virtue of contrasts in timbre and his shifts from very high, piercingly thin notes to guttural lows and a liberal smattering of overtones brought considerable character to his solos.

As was the case with King Curtis, Walker's *oeuvre* demonstrated how effective an improvisation could be when it was concise and concentrated. Walker's timing, his sense of when to make a line ascend or to hold a note for maximum climactic effect within the limited space of just four bars, was a skill that serves as a lesson to any musician.

Many of his big hits – 'Shotgun', 'Pucker Up Buttercup', 'Walk In The Night' – featured lead and backing vocals. This meant the spotlight was not continually on Walker as a soloist, yet his impact as a leader is arguably greater for what he could do within this format. 'Roadrunner', a brisk number set to a stomping, heavily blues-oriented beat in which a ringing tambourine brought the sound of the black church into earshot, only had two eight-bar solos from Walker in the main body of the song and one lasting twelve bars in the coda. But in each case, particularly during Walker's opening statement, he played with an articulate holler, maintaining a firm grip on tone and inflection within his bubbling stream of notes.

Walker's upper-register shrieks also showed that some of the wild exclamations that were becoming common among jazz avant-garde players such as Pharoah Sanders and Albert Ayler were by no means absent from the world of R&B. The common denominator between the two schools may well have been a desire to attain some of the ecstatic heights of a gospel singer or, more to the point, the timbre of little-heard church saxophonists like Vernard Johnson – who, according to some observers, exerted a decisive influence on Ayler.[3]

More than twelve bars of soul power

Walker often had other reeds accompanying him and certainly 'Roadrunner' would not have delivered the same kick without the virile baritone saxophone that pumped away behind the tenor. King Curtis, too, would cast his tenor saxophone against a backdrop of assorted reeds and brass that could boost the harmonic richness of his arrangements.

'Memphis Soul Stew' featured a ballsy four-piece horn section consisting of one trumpet and three saxophones – two tenors and one baritone.

Saxophones, trumpets and trombones are wind instruments and it is principally through lung power and breath, the raw materials of the vocalist, that they produce a note – one completely different in character from the note that crackles into the world of sound through an amplifier.

Traditionally, the electric–acoustic divide in music, something that has been a major issue in both jazz and folk, pits the guitar that is plugged in against the one that is unplugged. Horns are usually ruled out of the conflict, and that is a huge oversight. They are acoustic instruments, something that – in the hands of a skilled player, particularly a saxophonist or flautist – can be clearly heard and felt. It means a soul band with keys and horns is actually an electro-acoustic ensemble, combining two very different modes of sound. Breath is thus flowing between, and binding, the vocalist, brass and reeds.

Non-musical reasons also lend importance to these instruments. This takes us into the realm of stagecraft. In concert, horn players hold – if not point – their instruments into the air, at head height, catching the light because the horns are gold or silver. But guitarists mostly wield their axe at waist height, unable to achieve the same degree of elevation, their eyes usually cast down-wards. So the combination of both types of musician greatly increases the visual stimulus for the audience, giving two distinct levels at which the focus, the sight line, can be directed.

Footage of old funk bands reveals how aware the horn players were of this distinction, of the dramatic impact that they could make. They are often seen leaning right back and holding the trumpet or sax very high in the air, so that musician and instrument grow even taller. In this way, the players gain more stature in the eyes of the audience. It's super theatre.

Visual flair notwithstanding, horns represented, above all, power. When a section moved in unison, and three or four instruments combined to play a chord with a rich voicing, sustaining it with the right intonation, the effect was substantial, the blast akin to a pit-of-the-stomach scream from a vocalist with the magnitude of an Otis or an Aretha.

Often backing the above and the likes of King Curtis were the Memphis Horns, a now legendary section co-led by trumpeter Wayne Jackson, a col-ourful character who was a one-time stunt pilot, and tenor saxophonist Andrew Love, son of a local reverend. Trombone as well as second and third reeds were also on hand, to be deployed in a variety of configurations: each one, even a two-piece, packing a formidable punch.

Classic 1960s Stax songs, from Eddie Floyd's 'Knock On Wood' to Sam & Dave's 'Hold On I'm Comin', benefited markedly from the input of these players, whose skills were – and this is something that parallels Walker's work – dispensed with considerable economy. Often the rhythmic drive of a pass-ing burst of brass and reeds had the immediacy of the best blues-guitar riff.

A great deal could be achieved within strict confines, though. 'Hold On I'm Comin'' had a wrangling, circular central horn line built on just three pitches, yet it was a perfect expression of the forthright promise in the song's title. The brass and reeds conveyed a striding and confident forward motion, even though their tuning sounds questionable on the second chorus. In the song's middle eight, the trumpet drops out for four bars, leaving a salty tenor unaccompanied. This substantially modifies the texture and weight of the whole band, since the reed in isolation breathes much more air and levity into the piece.

Finally, the whole section returns to play four bars of slow chords that ascend with steady purpose. The alteration in the horns' character and movement – the slide from the rhythmic bustle of the solo reed to the stately glide of the reed and brass together – is highly effective as it underscores a bold shift in the emotional centre of the vocals.

Every note serves a purpose. In just two-and-a-half minutes, the horns give a brilliant display of using simple light and shade in timbre and line construction. Arrangements such as these, focused in their brevity and precision, were the norm for a number of labels in soul music during the late 1960s. Chess, Hi and Motown all turned out smart horn charts that used a variety of small and large configurations, according to the ambitions of a particular arranger. With the latter resource including talents such as Wade Marcus and David Van De Pitte, there was always scope for a lush orchestral sound. That yielded fine results when the score was for a singer like Marvin Gaye, whose ingenious phrasing suggested the sigh of reeds or the swish of strings.

One thing that stood out in the work of the Memphis Horns for both Stax and Hi was the darkness of the sound, its relatively dense and low pitch. There were never more brass than reed instruments in the sections. Tenor and baritone saxophones were preferred to the shriller sound of the alto. In many cases, this ensemble voice could buttress a rhythm section reinforced by new electric instruments. That said, as the 1970s dawned, funk bands played with all kinds of permutations in the horn section, sometimes to achieve even heavier, sturdier resonances than those heard on the Stax tunes. Some used just saxophones while others opted for trumpets that often imparted the flavour of salsa, where brass is predominantly the order of the day. As many groups also featured a great deal of percussion, they brought – like Fatback – an authentic Afro-Latin sound to the table.

James Brown was constantly shuffling the cards in his pack of horn players, and there were many aces. Prominent among them were alto saxophonist Maceo Parker, tenor saxophonist Alfred 'Pee Wee' Ellis and trombonist Fred Wesley – although the likes of St Clair Pinckney, a very good baritone saxophonist, are also worthy of mention.

Typically, Brown deployed three or four instruments at a time: usually at least two brass and one reed, although he did not adhere strictly to any one model. While 'Give It Up, Turn It Loose' featured two trumpets and one tenor sax, 'Get Up, Get Into It And Get Involved' added a baritone sax to that combination. Musical directors Nat Jones and Pee Wee Ellis were constantly experimenting with the tonal palette of the horns. That led to a very muscular six-piece (three brass + three reeds) within an eleven-piece ensemble on 'Funky Drummer', while the relatively unknown 'It's A New Day' had two tenors, one baritone sax and no brass at all.

Finding the right timbral combination for the horns was not the only thing on the agenda. Brown's faith in repeated phrases, the liberation from chord changes so that rhythm could take pride of place over harmony and, to a certain extent, melody, had led to his string players holding the same line for lengthy periods. Eventually the same principle was applied to the horns. Nineteen seventy-one's 'Soul Power' featured a four-piece section (three brass + one reed) stating the same figure for twenty-six bars before playing a change for sixteen. So the first statement had a better chance of taking root and growing in the listener's subconscious, in the same way as other repeated riffs did.

Comprising rapid three-note lines delivered with a full-blooded punch, the seesawing horns were clearly conceived as a form of rhythmic contagion, and the extended duration rammed the point home that brass and reeds could be effective when maintaining tension in the most primal of ways. One expects the figure to swerve through some kind of chord change much sooner. It refuses to. It acts like a bass.

Stripped of piano, the piece had few cushioning or liquid sounds. 'Soul Power' offered a stark, dry, almost parched tonal palette. Guitars were crackling, congas rumbling and horns raking away for this extended stretch of repeated riffing that practically bullied its way to a climax.

Elsewhere in Brown's *oeuvre*, the brass and reeds were deployed with much more complexity. To some degree, it could be argued that Brown was intent on exploring extremes in his arrangements. If 'Soul Power' was about maximum impact from a minimum amount of notes, then the way the horns attacked in longer, more fluid, fluttering lines on 'Get Up Offa That Thing' showed that Brown's years spent listening to jazz solos still had some pull with his inner sorcerer.[4]

Or rather, the musical directors Brown appointed were able to bring a certain tonal flourish to the table because some were still directly engaged with the world of improvising musicians – none more so than Pee Wee Ellis, who could be found writing charts and conducting for Sonny Stitt, a bebop and soul-jazz player of considerable stature.

Two possibilities for horn charts, two distinct poles, emerged in the music of James Brown and others throughout the 1970s. On the one hand, brass and reeds could be used as energy boosters in a piece, great depth charges of sonic power that could push a song's steady cruise into overdrive if the players attacked the phrases – usually short and incisive, for this very purpose – with enough intensity.

Alternatively, lines could be much more elaborate, acting as a countermelody in some cases, adding a harmonic complexity that kept alive the close relationship soul had enjoyed with jazz in previous decades. Generally, saxophonists and trumpeters had a grasp of music theory and were competent sight-readers, which did not always hold true for musicians in rhythm sections.

Hence there could be varying degrees of education and culture within the same ensemble. This coming together of different types of musician could yield a productive exchange of ideas, a running dialogue between the so-called 'school' and 'street' players.

Furthermore, many horn players in funk bands were kids in the mid-1960s, when soul-jazz artists such as Lee Morgan enjoyed hits with singles like 'The Sidewinder'. They had heard this music on their parents' record players, possibly with John Coltrane and Miles Davis to boot. Horn players had thus absorbed a degree of improvisatory energy alongside the funkiness of James Brown, which they were liable to imbibe both mentally and physically through the experience of dancing at parties. So horn sections in funk maintained a vital connection to the lexicon of jazz.

Out of Brown's own circle of musicians emerged the JBs (Parker, Ellis and Wesley), who would excel as a group in their own right and later as The Horny Horns for numerous P-Funk productions. Meanwhile, Kool & The Gang, Earth, Wind & Fire and Brass Construction all emboldened funk through the muscularity of their horn scores as well as their rhythm tracks.

'Soul Power' was tough but a piece like Brass Construction's 'Movin'' was plain brutal.[5] The way the trumpets spat out swift two-note allegros, and then proceeded to leaven them with a single scary legato that bordered on an overtone, injected a menace perfectly suited to the rabble-rousing quality of the vocal – for there was no single lead singer, just several members of the band chanting. The aesthetic was militaristic: many horns; many voices; many grooves. The sound of a funky battalion.

Straight-ahead Chinese Middle Eastern funk

Eventually the army demobbed. By the early 1980s, as was noted in the previous chapter, horn sections were becoming increasingly scarce.

Synthesizers were much cheaper to run than three or four saxophonists or trumpeters. This prompted a marked change in the sound of soul music over the decade, certainly in terms of the many studio projects that were able to survive through sales of twelve-inch singles.

Occasionally, though, echoes of the past could be heard. While Cameo can be cited as the archetype of a large horn-led band shedding its brass and reeds in favour of a battery of electric keyboards that completely reshaped its sound, the group nonetheless reverted to their former tools when deemed appropriate.

So although tracks like the minimalist 'She's Strange' set the agenda for Cameo's work in 1985, the group took it upon themselves to hire horn players as supplementary personnel for other pieces. Of these, 'I've Got Your Image' was a jazz ballad with a series of ornately arranged interludes serving as a reminder that Cameo's leader, Larry Blackmon, was a Juilliard graduate who knew the art of arrangement.

With hip hop taking a sizeable share of the market away from soul, and enshrining the principle of programmed and sampled beats as opposed to performed music, this kind of approach became increasingly cost-defective by the end of the decade. It also represented an anachronism to some. Perhaps no better indication of the fundamental sea change in mentality could be found than in the comments of certain 'breaks generation' producers and DJs, who went as far as to describe several ailing live bands as being 'too musical'.

Alternatively, it could be argued that these bands were not the right kind of musical, that their hardness quotient was inadequate. Moreover, hip hop was essentially about reconditioning fragments of a musical past, as well as giving non-musical noise a chance to be musical. Such was its revolution. In this climate, it was difficult for trained players of instruments to be relevant: the idea of a band reading sheet music was at odds with the modernist image of a man with two turntables, reviving, manipulating and modifying sonic ghosts in the machine.

Acid jazz was therefore important because it both challenged and attempted to make peace with this aesthetic.[6] As discussed in previous chapters, the UK-based movement, taking its cue from James Brown's 1970s funk, helped to bring back old instruments like wah-wah guitars, Hammond organs and, last but not least, horn sections. Groups such as The Brand New Heavies built a major part of their sound around brass and reed players, some of whom were noted British jazz musicians. What was perhaps more significant, though, was the fact that the group's peers, Young Disciples, made a direct connection with the source of inspiration by asking Maceo Parker, Pee Wee Ellis and Fred Wesley of Brown's band the JBs to guest on their sole album, *Road To Freedom*, a worthy nomination for the 1991 Mercury Music Prize.

Parker, in particular, sounded superb. It was easy to see why he was so valued by Brown when he and his brother, the guitarist Bernard Parker, were recruited from their home town of Kinston, North Carolina in the mid-1960s. Although he initially played tenor for the Godfather, it was on the alto that Maceo Parker excelled, drawing from its higher pitch a shrill, piercing tone that, when he took solos, cut through the horns and rhythm section like a strong beam of light emerging from dense cloud.

Greatly symbolic of Parker's value to Brown is the fact that he was among the few band members whose *name* the Godfather actually called out to solo. The drilling, staccato nature of the saxophonist's phrasing often reached a fever pitch that seemed to echo the sheer urgency of the bandleader's hyperventilating stage persona.

Funk is Maceo, as much as it is Brown. And yet a narrative intelligence that also reflected a very real understanding of the jazz tradition defined Parker's improvisations. In 1990, the year before he took part in the Young Disciples session, Parker was turning in a highly spirited rendition of Charles Mingus's 'Better Get Hit In Yo' Soul' on his own album *Roots Revisited*.

There was a duality in Parker's artistic identity that served as a reminder of the long-running and ongoing entwinement of soul music and jazz. And if Parker was indeed one of the definitive funky horn players, then he was not alone. There were many other saxophonists with similarly strong rhythmic sensibilities, but they presented their music in much more produced, less raw settings. The obvious examples are Grover Washington Jnr and David Sanborn.[7] Both became commercially successful by inflecting their oeuvre towards highly melodic and at times, unfortunately, anodyne material that would eventually be dubbed 'smooth jazz' – for the most part, a wholly misleading spin on the term 'easy listening'.

Yet these artists' work should not be summarily dismissed. Both of them had deep roots in jazz that reached back to the 1960s, and they were capable of imbuing their performances with very affecting blues and gospel tonalities. Indeed, some of albums Washington Jnr and Sanborn recorded throughout the '70s and '80s were essentially soul or funk records *without* vocals. They stood in the lineage of instrumental R&B that Parker could also claim as his own. He and others all owed a debt to Ray Charles's horn players.

With its vast array of different schools, sub-genres and approaches to the improvisatory tradition, jazz is one of the most difficult genres to keep track of at any given point in history. It can move in several directions simultaneously, but its roots in the blues mean jazz always has the potential to be soulful – or that, more pertinently, its exponents can become soul artists if and when the creative muse calls for it.

Alas, there is a political problem, though. Because jazz is perceived first and foremost as art music and soul as pop, it does not suit market categorisation or a simplified version of history – something becoming more and more apparent as the internet age puts everything on expedient quick-time – for a jazz musician not just to play soulfully but to *be* a soul musician. It's a confusing, undesirable notion.

Some critics already get disorientated by an improviser's decision to move from an electric to an acoustic setting, and the abandonment of a swing pulse for a backbeat can cause even more consternation. Jazz also has such prestige as a category these days, there is a mistaken assumption that the ability to play it will automatically lift the incumbent away from the muddy waters of populism. That's lie no. 2.

What all this means is that some of Maceo Parker's successors are to be found precisely where they are not expected to be these days: at jazz festivals, often in large open air venues rather than in smaller soul clubs.

A case in point is the Detroit-born alto saxophonist Kenny Garrett, who to a large extent is a living embodiment of many intersecting strands of soul and jazz horn-playing. He was mentored by the trumpeter Marcus Belgrave, a very significant figure for his work as an educator in the Motor City. Given the deaths in 2009 of both Hank Crawford and David Newman, Belgrave is a cherished surviving member of the esteemed soloists in Ray Charles's classic 1950s orchestra.

Garrett has an ability to play complex improvisations that draw on non-western scales and modes, and these make his work attractive to jazz audiences who want to hear virtuosity.[8] But he also has an enormously bluesy, driving propulsion and a skill with concise riffs that strike a chord with soul crowds, precisely because there is a hard edge to Garrett's playing that sits as well with a backbeat as it does with swing.

His notable career breakthrough came as a member of the Miles Davis band in the early 1980s, when Garrett was essentially playing off muscular funk grooves set by a loud, brash electric rhythm section. Since that time, though, he has gone on to play the music of John Coltrane in a mostly acoustic ensemble and also to work with pop artists like Sting.

Perhaps most significantly, Garrett has shown in the last decade that, when on stage, his jazz group always has the option of morphing into an R&B combo through an understanding of the rhythmic data shared by both genres: namely, fundamental, age-old beats like the 'second line' derived from the New Orleans marching band tradition.

Similarly, if Garrett starts a tune in a funk groove, the jazz musician in him may well decide that, once the drums and bass have stoked enough tension through a repeated backbeat, he will have them release it through a fluid, rushing swing pulse. What Garrett is essentially doing is showing that the intensity of a performance can be maintained regardless of the way the beat is handled by the rhythm section.

That said, I don't think Garrett is attempting to create a pluralistic form of music with any conscious missionary zeal. It is more a question of all the particular strands of his training and areas of interest being constantly available to him. When I discussed this with Garrett in 2008, he was keen to stress that his ultimate goal was to keep his options open. 'I really don't think genres are that deep. C major is C major,' he argued. 'The point is, what are you gonna do with that? How can I do what I love to do with the music, regardless of if it's straight-ahead jazz, funk, Chinese, Japanese, Indian or Middle Eastern?'[9]

The year 2000's 'Happy People' shows this statement is not for effect. It is one of the best tunes in Garrett's songbook and has proved a huge crowd-pleaser because it has a danceable, very uplifting quality to it.

Yet it is a structurally ambitious piece, its melody built on an Eastern scale over a driving funk groove that eases into a joyous gospel chorus – the part that moves the crowd, even if the flesh is weak.

Dancing to horn players is deeply rooted in black popular culture. Armed with their brass and reeds, the marching bands of New Orleans have been inspiring revellers at the city's fêted Mardi Gras celebrations to loosen their limbs since the 1890s. It is telling that many soul-funk combos conversant with that culture will sometimes finish their sets by having the saxophonists and trumpeters leave the stage and walk through the audience. They thus turn the gig into a kind of parade. Such is the power of horns. They are acoustic, portable instruments. They are mobile.

Although brass bands have not been a major commercial force in recent black popular music, they have nonetheless continued to resurface periodically. The latest wave of ensembles that mix the New Orleans marching tradition with hip hop, soul and funk has been welcome. Young Blood, Hot 8, Hypnotic and Soul Rebels are all noteworthy examples.

In fact, their emergence has been of considerable importance because they are partially filling the gap created by the demise of the horn section in contemporary soul. It is now entirely feasible that younger audiences may see saxophones, trombones and trumpets in a pop context for the very first time at a Soul Rebels concert, where the reprises of material by anybody from Eurythmics to Stevie Wonder ensure that the music is not intimidating, even though the ensemble playing is impressively sharp.

While brass bands have combined New Orleans traditions with rapping and chanting, relatively few horn players – certainly virtuosi – have sought both to improvise and perform freestyle emceeing with any conviction or competence. In Britain, however, the expatriate American trumpeter Abram Wilson and alto saxophonist Soweto Kinch have done as much.

Born in London to Caribbean parents, Kinch has shown himself to be an excellent bebop player. But the other substantial element in his work is an engagement with hip hop, through the use both of beats that he programmes and rhymes that he writes and raps. This is more in evidence on Kinch's second album, 2006's *A Life in the Day of B19: Tales Of The Tower Block*, in which he paints an interesting portrait of life on a council estate in Birmingham, offering thoughtful, often insightful observations about the lives of local characters that make the work a worthwhile sociocultural and political document.

Kinch remains problematic for some commentators and promoters because he is constantly switching between the roles of virtuoso saxophonist and rapper. Given the substantial perceived distance between jazz and hip hop in both the media and the music industry, his duality stands very much against the grain. In fact, Kinch is simply extending a vocal–instrumental continuum that reaches right back to Louis Jordan, an artist who both played the saxophone and used his voice. The difference is that hip hop did not exist in the 1940s, so Jordan sang then, whereas today Kinch raps. But the result is essentially the same: a horn player giving vent to creative impulses that are manifested sometimes as words and sometimes as musical notes.

Scanning the history of soul and funky-jazz horn players, one sees this phenomenon is actually not as rare as one might imagine. Maceo Parker also sings. Kenny Garrett has recorded raps. King Curtis, before blowing a note on his tenor sax on 'Memphis Soul Stew', narrates a short but very engaging introduction. It might be interesting to reflect on why he did this and how this spoken-word tradition functions in soul music.

13 We gonna tell you right now

Before we get into it, I wanna rap a little bit.   (Maceo Parker, alto saxophone)

Word up at the cook-out

King Curtis's tone on tenor saxophone was solid and substantial, liable to become thunderous at highpoints of a solo. His 'other' voice – the one he spoke with – was also forthright. As heard on the opening narration of 'Memphis Soul Stew', it is commandingly deep and poised, quite authoritative in the way African American male voices, particularly those from the South (Curtis was a Texan) often can be.

Given the role-playing element of the text, which portrays Curtis as a musical master chef detailing the necessary ingredients to cook up a dish of soul music, chances are that the words were written out, and that he was reading out his metaphors – from 'a half a teacup of bass' to 'a half pint of horn' – from a manuscript in the studio.

However, it is the asides that catch the ear. What brings the monologue to life is the passing affirmations Curtis slips in between the main points of the cookery lesson. The way he says 'We gonna tell you right now' implies that Curtis and his team of trusty assistants are responding to urgent enquiries about the making of soul, while 'This gon' taste alright' gives the impression that Curtis is dipping his finger into the boiling gumbo of sounds and giving it a discreet lick, to ensure the stew is thickening up to be plenty tasty.

Script or no script, he remained conversational, and that ease in front of the microphone would surface on many other occasions after the recording of 'Memphis Soul Stew' in July 1967. In August and December of the same year, Curtis recorded spoken-word introductions to 'Cook-Out' and 'This Is Soul', then in 1969 he did the same on 'Instant Groove'.

Hearing the saxophonist speak on these tunes is important because it has a humanising effect. It demystifies Curtis. Musicians who express themselves on instruments rather than with the voice can touch a listener, especially if they have great soulfulness. But they cannot produce literal meaning as words can, so the big advantage of a narration, be it four, eight or twenty-four bars, is that it overcomes the abstraction of instrumental music and provides a far clearer intellectual signpost.

Bursts of oral expression such as Curtis's lyrics on 'Memphis Soul Stew' enabled the player to become a more concrete communicative entity for an audience. Instrumentalists, particularly jazz musicians, can become cloaked in mystique, partly because their speaking voice is mute. When that silence breaks, a personality – and sometimes it is an underwhelming but nonetheless real entity – comes forcibly to life.

The voice with which an artist sings is not always the same as the voice with which an artist talks, but the timbre usually remains unchanged. Rappers, in general, chant their verses with intonations that can be very close to the way they converse naturally, away from performance. This may be one reason why their rhymes strike such a chord with some listeners. They feel that the artistry isn't filtered through any artifice.

Rap, in any case, once meant talking rather than setting rhyme to rhythm.

From the 1920s onwards, a number of jazz musicians became well known for their use of spoken word in performance, 'rapping' at length to the audience at gigs as well as, in shorter passages, on record. Among the most celebrated of these figures were Fats Waller, Cab Calloway, Slim Gaillard, Louis Jordan and Dizzy Gillespie. One who came later was the alto saxophonist Julian 'Cannonball' Adderley, a prime mover in the soul-jazz movement of the late '50s that was not entirely unrelated to the rhythm and blues played by Curtis. Adderley stood tall for the brilliance of his improvisations. Yet he also launched into lengthy monologues or 'Cannon raps' during a number of concerts released as live albums such as 'Music You All'. These raps completely changed the atmosphere of the performance, because Adderley was making a direct connection with the listener through his treatment of philosophical, sociocultural or political subjects.

Such was the liveliness and generally rousing nature of his discourse, Adderley came across almost as a community leader or minister. Photographs of him with a microphone in his hand are therefore as meaningful as those that depict Adderley cradling a sax on the mound of his considerable midriff. He has the same intensity in both scenarios.

Spoken word is thus direct self-expression: an assertion of the individual, a point of view conjugated in the singular that could have a resonance in the plural. It is the 'I' that may hold meaning for 'they' and possibly 'we'. The recognition of the soloist, either in the form of musician or orator, is part of the bedrock of ancestral black culture that values a single voice within a framework of free assembly.

Speaking one's piece, the act of testifyin', is a deeply rooted element of African American and African-Caribbean *art de vivre* that flows from the pre-eminent status of the preacher in local communities and from a more general love of verbiage, banter and lyrical jousting that reflects the essential primacy of oral culture. Word is indeed bond.

Backdrops to these vocal excursions could range from the porch of a house to the stoop of a brownstone or, perhaps most symbolically, the barbershop – as much a place of social intercourse as it is of the tonsorial arts.

Curtis's 'This Is Soul', more so even than 'Memphis Soul Stew', is worth noting because it presents the artist as an individual speaker who has articulated his convictions in a quotidian setting.

Curtis does not sound stilted here. He is talking, rather than reading, and a very significant structural characteristic of 'This Is Soul' is the way his spoken words are split into two passages. Curtis opens the piece with speech and then, after taking a six-bar saxophone solo, returns to elaborate on the theme. Far from being relegated to an introductory role, the text frames the main body of the song. A commentator plays his horn, then a horn player commentates. There is a semblance of parity.

Spoken word is thus not a superficial stylistic element in this particular case. What it effectively does is moot the possibility that a lengthy narration could become a defining element in a piece of music, that it might occupy the space usually allocated to a melody, regardless of whether that melody were sung or played by horns.

In fact, this had already happened. In the 1950s, two monuments of R&B and rock and roll – the bassist-songwriter Willie Dixon and the singer-guitarist Bo Diddley – recorded 'Signifiyin' Monkey' and 'Say Man' respectively, two songs that essentially celebrated the tradition of 'the dozens', whereby street-corner denizens attempt to trump each other's insults. The object of the exercise was to deploy imagination and imagistic prowess at the expense of a figure held in great affection: usually a mother or girlfriend who might be so uneasy on the eye that she'd 'have to sneak up on the glass to get a drink of water'.

All this showed that verbal dexterity, a praxis that had existed in African American popular culture for decades, could be transposed to a formal musical context. There were plenty of genuine sermonisers and preachers whose work appeared in the catalogues of 'race records', starting with Calvin P. Dixon in 1925 and going on to include the Reverend J. C. Burnett, whose *Downfall of Nebuchadnezzar* became a best-seller. Religious or sacred speech, by way of the sermon, was considered important enough to be treated as a commodity by record companies. A key historical entry was Motown's release of several lengthy soliloquies by Martin Luther King Jnr in the early 1960s.

Solomon say, Solomon sing

Whether through kickster, prankster jibes rooted in the profane or through civil rights allocutions raised on the sacred, spoken word was gradually spreading and seeping into the world of recordings. The scene was set for the interaction and hybridisation of various forms of expression employing the human voice, be they the sermon or the song from the soul.

As it holds that cliché is often reality, a soul singer is the son of a preacher man – or a preacher man in waiting, a child with the good book in his hand. Behold Solomon Burke, a colossus in every sense of the word; a father of many children, a big man with even bigger business acumen. Burke was someone who, as a resourceful young man in the 1950s, could see the profit to be made from running a funeral parlour or selling sandwiches by wandering the aisles of the Apollo Theatre, before he stepped on stage to take his place in the pantheon of great voices that included a young James Brown and an even younger Bobby Womack.

An intensely moving, not to mention arresting, baritone singing voice was not the only gift Burke had been given. Dubbed 'the wonder boy preacher' in his youth, he held forth to the masses at the House Of God For All People and also presented a religious radio show before going on to make his recording debut, cutting gospel albums by the time he was fifteen.

'Just Out Of Reach (Of My Two Open Arms)', an astounding record of intense emotion and skilled phrasing, revealed Burke to be as important to the future of soul music as his celebrated peers Ray Charles and Sam Cooke, both of whom had also drawn heavily on the ways of gospel performers. But another song, made in 1964, was even more significant.

Chorus is all in popular music. A song can hook a listener and reel them in with the refrain because this is the explosion after the crackle of fire in the verse. 'Everybody Needs Somebody To Love' has one of the best refrains ever written. From its use of internal rhyme in the first and third words, to its teasing elongation of syllables, to the stark rhythmic summons of 'you … you … you' that concludes the chorus, it is a work of great structural craftsmanship.

More important, though, is what happens before the chorus is reached. The evangelist in Solomon Burke takes centre stage. He sermonises on the most universal of themes: the life-enhancing soul mate craved by even the most independent of spirits. What is remarkable about this arrangement is the inordinate amount of space granted to the monologue. Burke speaks for a mammoth thirty-seven bars.

That's just under a minute. Considering that the recording lasts 2:43 mins, the spoken-word introduction accounts for over one third of the performance. All this means that enormous value is attached to what is said as well as what is sung. Burke the commentator, the thinker, the minister, has roughly equal billing with Burke the singer.

'Everybody Needs Somebody To Love' is thus not a song *per se*. It is a sermon that *evolves* into a song, an extended bout of heated testifyin' relieved by a commensurately hot verse and chorus, the melodies bathed in the milk of horns and sweetened by the honey of guitars.

Given that introductions, whether sung, narrated or played on a saxophone, usually lasted no more than eight bars at the very most, the decision to present Burke in monologue for this extended period – in which, crucially, he gave the impression that he was speaking his piece without keeping an eye on the clock – proved that spoken word, the voice in isolation, engaged in either confession or philosophy, was an asset in African American popular culture that could feasibly co-exist with a singer and band. And with its tight rhythm section and chipper fanfare of horns, 'Everybody Needs Somebody To Love' was by no means a song kitted out with a disposable arrangement.

Hence, in the 1960s came records that featured spoken-word passages either at the beginning or in the middle of tracks. The best of these were Lou Rawls's 'Dead End Street',[1] or songs with intertwined talking and singing, as in Ike & Tina Turner's 'It's Gonna Work Out Fine', or the extended riffing of a raucous stand-up comedian over a funky backbeat, as exemplified by Pigmeat Markham's 'Here Comes The Judge'.

Burke's *chef d'oeuvre* and these and other songs demonstrate two key points: first, spoken word is a creative asset *available* to a singer or, in the case of King Curtis, a horn player; and second, exponents of oral culture, be they funny backsliders or serious preachers, often have very rhythmic, if not swinging, musical speech. That allows them to place their art in the world of song and musicianship at any given moment. The other crucial exponent of this trend was the radio DJ-turned-singer. Among the strongest symbols of that transition was Rufus Thomas, a Memphis broadcaster who became a successful Stax recording artist.

Possessed of decent singing pipes, Thomas could carry a hit tune such as 1963's 'Walking The Dog' purely as a melodist. But it is not without significance that in the middle of the piece he broke into a swaying variation on a nursery rhyme that essentially deflected Thomas towards the dynamics of rap. The change in delivery, although fleeting, totally altered the 'flow' of his voice.

Ain't sh--t happening

The voice is a malleable entity. Its delivery is open to mutation. The spoken word is, after all, a vague, flexible term that is distinct from the written word. But what the likes of Thomas were showing was that it could be shaped by musicality, by the property of rhythm, in unpredictable ways. In African American communities such as those of Chicago or Detroit, the vernacular was richly complex and evolutionary. Soul music in the 1960s gradually reflected the permeation of this rhythmic speech through the work of several renowned artists.

During the final three years of the decade, Thomas's 'Soul Food', King Curtis's 'Cook Out' and James Brown's 'Say It Loud (I'm Black And I'm Proud)' all implemented either a moderately or fast paced rhyming-couplet scheme in 4/4 that provided a clear glimpse of what rap would become when formalised as hip hop in a fast-approaching future.

The solidly on-the-beat delivery of another radio DJ, Gary Byrd, is also noteworthy.[2] But the most significant development in this period is that a musician, a saxophonist who did not sing on any of his other performances – King Curtis – rhymed on some of his material after having delivered narration elsewhere. What this tells us is that there were certain R&B-soul musicians, both instrumentalists and singers, who were receptive to an oral culture that was as protean as it was dynamic, and able to manifest itself in a number of different ways according to the specific needs of the artist in question at a given time.

With some of Brown's 'message songs', for example, it is clear that a rap – meaning both a recital and a series of rhymes – is more appropriate to the context than melodic or rhythmic singing, primarily because Brown wrote a rather voluminous text. This is certainly the case with 'King Heroin'. When he had many points to make, Brown would simply talk or rap rather than sing.

His guest appearance on Maceo Parker's 'The Soul Of A Black Man', arguably one of the highlights of the saxophonist's 1974 album *US*, provides further evidence of this tendency. Clocking in at just over ten minutes, this spine-tingling, gospel-tinged ballad starts with an extended monologue from Brown, occupying the producer's chair, in which the singer pays tribute to the man who plays 'exceptional horn'. It is a ceremonial prelude to Maceo stepping up and declaring: 'Before we get into it, I wanna rap a little bit'.

Compliments are duly returned. Parker talks of the value of Brown's 'teachings' and how much he has learned from his association with the Godfather, before asking him to address the social issues of the day and administer a reality check to 'the people living in the big houses'.

Formality frames the whole exchange, with both men showing great respect for one another, and there are moments when the tone skims an almost cloying solemnity. Yet the dialogue is made eminently listenable, if not soulful, by the fact that Brown invests his vocal performance with immense feeling and enriches it through changes in form. He starts talking and finishes singing. It's exactly what can be heard in the rhythmic modulations of a black Baptist preacher, with Dr Martin Luther King Jnr an iconic example. Essentially, Brown's sermon cements the continuity between gospel singing, sanctified talking, singing soul and talking soul – or rather talking blues, which is what 'The Soul Of A Black Man' really is. The song is a reminder that in black churches, preachers recite *over* the music just as easily as they do without it, so there is no great divide between the sound of an instrument and that of the human voice. In his monologue, Brown croons the title of a song Parker has played and occasionally draws out a phrase like 'I be…liee…eve…uuuh' before the sax breaks out. In the process, spoken word, sung melody and horn bind in a unifying dance.

Each agent of creativity is available to the other. Speech can call on song at any time, which appears to be a major part of Brown's artistic mindset. Eventually, and with enormous symbolism, he says, in an almost weary tone,

'I don't wanna talk no more ... so come here quick and bring that funky lickin' stick'. This final summons for Parker's sax makes explicit what was implicit in the fine solos he took on several landmark Brown numbers, such as 'Papa's Got A Brand New Bag' and 'Cold Sweat': the horn is kith and kin, ally, support and relief to the human voice. Or maybe the human voice is kith and kin, ally, support and relief to the horn.[3]

Through the myriad forms of vocal expression he used, and more importantly through the tension between his singing, talking and rhyming and the frequent improvised instrumental passages in his work, Brown set up a creative minefield in which words could explode into life in ever-changing ways, or indeed be aided and abetted by a saxophone.

This duality of voice and instrument, and the way the starring role in a song could swing back and forth between spoken word, sung melody and horn, piano or guitar solo, was by no means new. The reason why there is so much weight, so much resonance when Brown makes that dramatic declaration, 'I don't wanna talk no more ...', is because it is something with deep roots, a praxis reaching all the way back into blues, gospel and folk music.

Sonny Terry and Brownie McGhee were one of the greatest duos in black popular music during the 1940s and '50s. North Carolina-born Terry played harmonica while Tennessee native McGhee played acoustic guitar and sang. Together they made country blues that swayed gently but powerfully between secular and spiritual texts, so that one song would find McGhee singing praises to the Good Lord, the joy of being 'In His Care', while another, 'Raise The Ruckus Tonight', hailed ungodly living.

Both pieces were featured on the duo's classic 1952 album *Get On Board*. Throughout most of the songs, Terry would solo freely on harmonica while McGhee sang and strummed, so there was a sense that the two men were really musical equals. Even more thrilling was 'Mama Blues', because it marked the moment at which McGhee recognised the limitations of his guitar and called on Terry's harmonica for assistance. 'I'm tired of playing, now call your mama for me, boy...call again now!'[4]

With these words, Terry answers back with his harmonica, trilling to simulate weeping and wailing, vocalising his tone almost like a trumpeter with a mute. A dialogue ensues. McGhee prompts Terry to 'speak' as if he were a child in need of his 'mama'. What becomes clear is that an instrument, be it a guitar or voice, can lay out at any time, so that the other instrument takes over, just as Maceo's saxophone would take over from James Brown two decades down the line. The effect is to create a range of lead voices within a changing configuration of sound.

Spoken word, singing and playing are thus presented as fluid rather than fixed entities within the overall creative palette, which becomes richer still if a large portion of improvisation is brought to the table by an instrument constantly roaming behind the voice. Hence a musician from the 1960s or '70s who was aware of this historical foundation, who saw its dramatic potential, could clearly create interesting work through a blend of poetry, song and music.

Politics, an interest in civil rights and a desire to comment on the lived experience of black America were also important ingredients thrown into the pot. The struggle for equality that continued after the assassinations of iconic figures such as Martin Luther King Jnr, Medgar Evers and Malcolm X touched artists determined to reflect the harsh realities of life in 'the projects', the dismal housing estates and debilitating ghettoes to which many African Americans were consigned.

Artists such as The Watts Prophets from Los Angeles and The Last Poets from New York crystallised this energy and, in the uncompromising, thought-provoking, rabble-rousing nature of their work – no more so than in the latter's 'Niggers Are Scared Of Revolution' – one can hear the riptide fervour of Malcolm X in full flow on the podium.

One thing that stands out in works such as these is the raging torrent of ideas, observations and feelings, all of which are thrown into very sharp relief by the pared-down musical setting. Many of The Last Poets' early recordings feature just bongos, congas and cowbells.

The relentless, combative delivery of the vocals comes through extremely clearly against the pummelling beat from the percussion.

Angry, abrasive songs such as 'Black People What Y'All Gon' Do' stand in stark contrast to earlier examples of spoken word set to music, because of the staunch rejection of melody or a fuller rhythm section that might put some form of melodic or harmonic flesh on the bare bones of the song. Casting voice against percussion in such a stark, primeval way was a very non-western conception of arrangement.

That said, The Last Poets also experimented with form. One of their most intriguing techniques was to supply a prelude to a piece, no more than a minute long, in which three poets sang a chorus rather than recited any verse. Hence 'Black People What Y'All Gon' Do' was announced by 'Black People What Y'All Gon' Do Chant', which served as a kind of fleeting ceremonial fanfare to the lengthy poem in question.

Any artist who could embrace both The Last Poets' raw, robust soliloquies and a verse-chorus song structure, an artist who could make music with similar inflammatory rhetoric and with intricate, soulful and jazz-inclined arrangements, could not fail to be interesting. And especially if they had wit and poetry as well as burning indignation.

Gil Scott-Heron was one such artist. Although greatly inspired by The Last Poets, the man who has been christened 'The Godfather Of Rap' also wrote two novels as a teenager. His literary leanings, his interest in Harlem Renaissance authors such as Langston Hughes and Claude McKay, as well as his admiration for jazz musicians like Duke Ellington, Ron Carter, John Coltrane and Billie Holliday, made for an astounding artistic package. Here was a spoken-word artist, proto-rapper and highly accomplished songwriter.

He spoke and he sang. In 1970, Scott-Heron recited the blistering mono-logue 'The Revolution Will Not Be Televised' and crooned the deeply moving lament 'Pieces Of A Man'.

Scott-Heron's ultimate significance resides in his multiplicity, the potential for a black creative spirit to *navigate* between several forms of expression, so that no single definition can pin him down. A great deal of artistic freedom and conceptual imagination is displayed in his work, and it resonates with an ideal many jazz artists evoke.

Jazz, in the sense that Scott-Heron's appearances on stage came with a question mark. He might sit down and play the Fender Rhodes piano while a saxophonist improvised. Or he might throw down a series of comedy skits *à la* Red Foxx. Or he might sing a song in which his silken baritone recalled Lou Rawls. Or he might set the chorus of Marvin Gaye's 'Inner City Blues' to a defiant poem that chanted down government hypocrisy.

Throughout the 1970s that very tactic – perhaps applied with less verve than by Scott-Heron – surfaced intermittently in soul and jazz, where spoken-word monologues were deployed either as a means to express politi-cal insight, as in the way Syl Johnson moved seamlessly from singing to talk-ing on 'Is It Because I'm Black?'; or, more commonly, as a device for analysing tempestuous affairs of the heart or romantic entanglements. Isaac Hayes, with his long-running series of raps on the vagaries of the love game, reigned supreme here.

Fêted first and foremost for his enormous success with *Shaft* in the early 1970s, Hayes is another example of the protean, free-wheeling spirit in black music, a man wont to shuttle between forms and genres. He started his career as a songwriter for the Stax label in Memphis, partnering with David Porter to pen anthems such as 'Soul Man' for Sam & Dave. But on his 1969 debut album, *In The Beginning*, Hayes revealed a wide stylistic range. Gospel and blues sensibilities were conspicuous but above all he showed an interest in jazz, strikingly embodied in a medley that offered decent reprises of Count Basie's 'Going To Chicago Blues' and Errol Garner's 'Misty'.

Instead of simply adding a lyric to the melody of 'Misty', which was origi-nally a popular piano-led instrumental, Hayes launches into a monologue at the start of the piece. It is a long rap. He creates a romantic prelude to a love song, making it clear that Misty refers to the feeling of joy his main squeeze brings him.

There is a marked informality in his delivery that suggests a certain amount of ad-libbing, even if the text has been worked out beforehand, and the relaxed spontaneity with which the words flow recalls some of the monologues Lou Rawls, quite possibly a source of inspiration for Hayes, had recorded several years previously. The parallels are clear.

Spoken word invariably takes a singer into the realm of theatre. Both Rawls and Hayes are compelling because they sound natural and believable when they are in rapper mode, but they are also adopting something of a persona or character. They launch into a narrative, no matter how brief or sketchy. They create a scenario. They tell a story.

Given the dramatic dimensions of a rap, it stands to reason that any exponent of black music, be it pop or art, with an understanding of theatre and literature might create an *oeuvre* of some significance.

Like Lou Rawls, Oscar Brown Jnr hailed from Chicago. He was a man of letters as well as of jazz and blues. Although originally enrolled in a law course at a local college, he switched to English and began acting in plays. That interest in theatre and literature never waned as Brown Jnr made his way as a singer. He was a consummate storyteller.

Furthermore, he was unabashedly political. His engagement with the civil rights movement was perhaps best encapsulated in the lyrics he contributed to Max Roach's seminal protest album *We Insist! Freedom Now Suite* in 1960. Also significant was the exposure Brown Jnr gave to African American poetry through his astute adaptation of works by Paul Lawrence Dunbar and Gwendolyn Brooks.

Hence Brown Jnr's *oeuvre*, especially the early 1960s albums *Sin & Soul*, *Between Heaven And Hell* and *Tell It Like It Is*, highlights a certain interactivity in African American culture, whereby song, written text and recital intermingled and, in the hands of such a skilled practitioner, paid real creative dividends. The beauty of Brown Jnr's rendition of Brooks's 'Elegy (Plain Black Boy)' lies in the pronounced melodicism and bluesiness the singer brings to some highly political words.

If he could take a written text and reveal its underlying melodic swing, Brown Jnr could also break up a swinging melody with spoken word inserts. The epitome of this approach is the superb 'Signifiyin' Monkey'. Throughout the piece, an adaptation of a folk tale, Brown Jnr moves liberally from sung phrases to declaimed lines. The performance comes alive because he switches between the characters of Monkey and Lion, altering his vocal tone accordingly, as a stand-up comedian would do to engage an audience.

Not every soul or jazz singer who came after Brown Jnr was quite so theatrical, but he greatly contributed to the ongoing evolution of role-playing in black music. A wide range of personae could come to the fore, the most common of which were the joker, the fighter and the lover. In each case, there was a statement of opinion and an explanation. There was the expression of an individual's point of view. There was also anecdote, image, metaphor and exaggeration for effect.

Listen to Isaac Hayes performing his raps on *Live At The Sahara Tahoe* (Stax, 1973). You can hear a clear echo both of Brown Jnr and those who preceded him in the spicy humour with which Hayes picks over the bones of an exploitative relationship in the short but memorable introductory rap to his rendition of Bill Withers's 'Use Me'.

One of Hayes's friends is madly in love with a 'broad' who, in return, plays him for a patsy. 'She would go off, say she's going shopping today … and come back the day after tomorrow', the singer states casually before adopting a decidedly affected, grand thespian tone to give the man's justification for staying with a woman who 'puts on a lot of tricks'.

Hayes pauses dramatically, then enters the realm of Shakespeare: 'Well, if I am to be considered an instrument of pleasure ... then ... so ... be ... it!'[5]

Raucous laughter breaks out as he hits the punch line, and at that moment the whole atmosphere in the auditorium is comparable to the exuberant, infectious energy of a comedy show. The audience has become fully involved in the story, possibly because they recognise something of the 'cat' and the 'chick', and the way the latter might beguile the former with what she has, knowing full well what he wants.

One of Hayes's significant peers was Millie Jackson.[6] During the 1970s she recorded a string of startling love-triangle dissections, of which *Caught Up* was the highpoint. Here, she alternated conventional song with spoken word and then varied the form within a single piece. Hence the beauty of the tellingly titled 'The Rap', a lengthy soliloquy on the state of mind of 'the other woman', stems from the skilled way Jackson fans a scorching emotional fire through recited passages, some stretching to twenty-eight bars, before burning up with a hotly sung line. Melody thus functions as a form of release from the tension of spoken word.

Spoken word thrives as a medium for expression precisely because it can accommodate anything from sexuality to spirituality to politics. And, as Hayes, Jackson and others showed, it is wholly effective as a platform for extended analysis, for a detailed 'breakdown' of a theme that will last as long as the speaker deems necessary.

Most artists want to communicate. The question is how to do it. Objectively speaking, there is no such thing as an ideal vehicle to achieve that goal, because the definition of what is interesting or moving usually differs from one listener to another, even within the same constituency. Yet saying something, in the figurative sense, may be the shared goal of the bulk of artistic expression, whatever the form.

Saying something in the literal sense is a device that has actually become something of a binding force, a kind of common denominator between high- and low-brow forms of expression in black music. Spoken word essentially unifies rhythm and blues, soul, jazz and hip hop.

Furthermore, the content of verbal expression in the above contexts is vast.

Although a great deal of the monologues in jazz, particularly during the 1970s, were of a spiritual, philosophical or political bent, it should be pointed out that comedy also cropped up from time to time and that – in perhaps the most telling indication of the unpredictability of African American oral culture – an accomplished, learned and experimental improviser could actually function as an X-rated stand-up.

Chicagoan saxophonist-vocalist Eddie Harris's 1976 set *The Reason Why I'm Talking S--t* is a case in point. It is essentially Harris *à la* Richard Pryor, the terrific and tormenting *enfant terrible* of black and blackenising humour, who himself announced through his deep profanity the parental advisory status that would come to define hip hop.

Operating in full-on gutter-mouth mode, Harris cannot refrain from expletives almost every other word and, although abundantly puerile, his raps on anything from the perils of breaking wind in public to the more serious but no less rib-tickling subject of life in a ghetto 'project' have real verve. He revels in his own slop of profanity. And part of the set, ironically, was recorded at a club called the Amazing Grace.

Rooted though Harris is in black culture, one could also argue that this provocative tiptoeing on, if not graceless fall from, the tightrope of what is socially acceptable was part of the spirit of the age. For example, British comedians Peter Cook and Dudley Moore pushed the decency envelope as Derek and Clive at the same time as Harris.

Extreme as Harris's album may seem, especially in the canon of a musician who, with 'Listen Here', created brilliant instrumental soul jazz and also pushed the envelope in using electronics with his saxophone, it is not a complete departure from a number of traditions. What Harris was doing was taking the notion of 'funky', in the sense of risqué, off-key, boastful thinking and behaviour, to a logical conclusion – one in which sexuality and social issues could all be aired in a tone of voice coloured by both frivolity and profundity.

'Talking shit', shooting the breeze in ways that could be both worthless and worthwhile, is an essential part of the soul 'ethos' and of soul music. And as long as that dynamic is in the air, then it creates a gamut of formal possibilities for the voice, be they thespian-like declamation, the straight monologue or highly cadenced rhymes.

Hip hop crystallised just a few years after Harris's album. One of its main creative strategies, the wave upon wave of tripwire rapped verses, was evolutionary in so far as it built on the intermittent use of rhyme in black popular music that had preceded it. Yet it was also revolutionary, or rather subversive, in so far as it largely banished the other forms of vocal expression, such as melodic singing and non-metric narration, that had hitherto coexisted in soul, jazz and even uncensored stand-up comedy.

Historical accounts of hip hop's genus overwhelmingly highlight the precursor role of singers, radio DJs or comedians, all of whom are hugely important for the way that they foreshadowed the form several years in advance. But the fact that spoken word was such a pervasive force in African American art and culture, that it could nudge three saxophonists, Harris, King Curtis and Cannonball Adderley, down the road towards different forms of rap as early as the mid-1960s, is both exciting and thought-provoking.

Curtis's status as a proto-rapper – or maybe passing rapper would be a more appropriate term – should not be overstated, since in the wider context of his recordings this side of his artistic persona was not prominent. Nevertheless, it existed and to a large extent it symbolised the possibility of a black-music practitioner rechanneling his expressive nature in ways both familiar and not so familiar.

Spoken-word interludes, especially political addresses and romantic monologues, have been so integral to the fabric of black music for decades – with singers in particular breaking into speech, sometimes at random, in the middle of song – that the idea of a form like hip hop, in which rhyme is more tightly marshalled, was almost inevitable.

Throughout the 1980s, hip hop appeared so antithetical to soul and jazz because of its use of technology, its anti-instrumentalism, its lack of formal musical education and its supposed lack of culture, that the notion of the three genres having shared roots and any potential for cross-fertilisation seemed to have very little, if any, credence.

Yet the tree from which all these branches have grown is blues. Not just the music but the culture, which essentially means an expressionistic urge that can materialise in a variety of forms, be they talking of logs and thangs, singing of a lonesome room, evoking an elder through a straight horn, or rhyming on the dangers that are inherent to life in 'Crooklyn'.

The now widespread use of rappers on the middle eight of a soul singer's track may reflect a desire to hit the lucrative hip hop target market. But the conjunction of these two forms also reflects the richness, the plurality of blues culture, and it formalises the informal praxis of James Brown or Millie Jackson moving liberally between melody and rap in the course of a single arrangement.

To hear a tune start out as a sung melody and then turn to rapped verses is to hear the human voice as both calm waters and choppy sea. It demonstrates the essentially fluid character of blues culture.

At the same time, this phenomenon largely negates a deeply-rooted tradition. The rap replaces rather than supplements a horn solo. As we know from recognising the importance of Maceo Parker to James Brown's aesthetic, this is a cause for regret, particularly because the distance between the worlds of improvisation and popular song widens in the process. Parker is, lest we forget, relevant to both soul and jazz.

Given these developments, the existence of an artist who is not necessarily intent on weaving together all these historical strands, but who understands their relationship, understands the flexible nature of spoken word in black music, understands the potential for movement between rhyme, narration and solo (be it vocal or instrumental), is key.

Me'Shell NdegéOcello is that artist. Since her 1993 debut *Plantation Lullabies*, the Washington, DC native has continually navigated between spoken word, melody and improvisation in a manner that effectively condenses many of the legacies thus far discussed in this chapter. Certainly the way she uses her voice, which frequently blurs the line between recital, chant, cadenced whisper and verse-chorus, reflects the marked interest NdegéOcello has in a vast repository of oral culture and literature, be it recorded or published poetry and prose.

Alto saxophonist, rapper and vocalist Maceo Parker (photo courtesy Clayton Call/Redferns/Getty Images).

Of great significance is that NdegéOcello is a superlative musician, a bass guitarist, who also welcomes solos, from keyboards, reeds or brass, in her aesthetic. Although committed to vocal music, she is also clearly wedded to the principle of letting instrumentalists express themselves on her projects, something that has actually led to barracking from fans intent on hearing her sing rather than play.

Cookie: The Anthropological Mixtape, NdegéOcello's 2002 album, is a significant piece of work in contemporary soul because it is a multifaceted creation that recognises the compatibility of the many forms outlined above. Featuring singing and narration, improvisation from bass clarinetist Marcus Miller and saxophonist Jacques Schwarz-Bart, as well as excerpts from recordings of Gil Scott-Heron, Angela Davis and June Jordan, the set is 'an homage to the power of the word written and spoken' that does not negate the beauty of either voice or instrument. It is a celebration and extension of a historical continuum.

Maceo on the mike

While few soul records issued during the last decade or so have explored the relationship between vocal, spoken-word and playing traditions with as much verve as NdegéOcello did on *Cookie,* one can still hear clear echoes of the strength of oral culture among a number of singers today. To a large extent, the 'rap' as exemplified by James Brown, Millie Jackson or Isaac Hayes, during which the artist lays bare an emotional truth – usually a meditation on a failed love affair, a cultural or sociopolitical observation, or indeed a taunt aimed at a rival of some kind – remains an essential organising principle for song. It is often used as a prelude, an appetiser or short scene-setter before the main body of the verse-chorus.

Also worth bearing in mind is the fact that many soul artists will deploy spoken-word strategies on stage, where the relative lack of time constraints prompts either spontaneous skits or testifyin' that can be much more substantial and intense than a pop artist introducing a piece with of a few lines of banter. In the best cases, the soul artist often treads the line between storytelling and stand-up. While directly invoking the tradition of the comic, this also serves as a reminder that the likes of Bill Withers and Gil Scott-Heron were able to bring an added communicative dimension to their live performances, with highly engaging bouts of sometimes madcap humour.[7]

Through a figure such as Scott-Heron, one can see an amalgamation, a collision of creative forces and traditions that is terribly important, because this openness inspired new voices to emerge and prosper. If Scott-Heron represents the place where poetry, jazz, blues and soul meet, then the last decade or so has been significant for the emergence of scenes or collectives of artists in London, New York and Philadelphia that have enabled a comparable intermingling of forms. Crucially, these scenes have added hip hop to their set of formative references, but they have not entirely negated song form in the process. What this means is that spoken-word artists such as Saul Williams, Carl Hancock Rux and Ursula Rucker have achieved a structural flexibility in their work that allows frequent shifts from recited text to melodic singing, and that a vocalist like Jill Scott can dot a set of songs with spoken-word interludes or skits.[8] Scott has also made the explicitly political declaration that she was 'born a poet and will die a poet'.[9]

What has been more problematic is the legacy of horn players or instrumentalists who will avail themselves of either spoken word or vocal when they see fit. For the most part, there has been no real successor to the likes of King Curtis or Junior Walker – although, as was pointed out in the last chapter, it is really in the field of jazz that the heritage, or at least an understanding of that heritage or partial reference to it, can be discerned. As previously mentioned, Britain's Soweto Kinch is important for the bridge he has built between improvisation, rap and song. His use of the very accomplished vocalist Eska Mtungwazi on several compositions has added to this plurality of form.

At this point, there are no rappers who can play the alto sax as well as Kinch does and no alto sax players who can rap with comparable skill, so he stands as a rare proposition in black music: an artist right on the cusp of art and populism. Kinch's location in a spoken-word–music continuum is noteworthy because his use of the voice, as well as his cultural and linguistic idiosyncrasies, have been largely informed by hip hop, a genre that did not exist at the time of his precursors. To a certain extent, he is an update of Louis Jordan.

Whether or not Kinch inspires a successor in years to come – something that is vital for the sustained growth of the continuum – remains to be seen. However, what should be pointed out is that the sixty-six-year-old alto saxophonist Maceo Parker is still active, and that he has continued to engage with spoken, sung and rapped word in a wide variety of contexts over the last two decades or so. This has meant the use of emcees in the bands Parker leads himself as well as a quite brilliant collaboration with celebrated American rappers De La Soul.

Gifted saxophonist though he may be, Parker – and this is especially clear from his live performances – sees the voice as an essential complement to the horn. While 'The Soul Of A Black Man', the 1974 classic on which he traded reverent soliloquies with James Brown, is a song Parker rarely performs these days, the piece stands as a kind of liberating force in his whole aesthetic, marking a point of departure for the use of his voice.

It eventually led to *Roots & Grooves*. This 2007 album was a live double that saw Parker augment his own trio, a group anchored by the exceptional drummer Dennis Chambers, with the fourteen-piece WDR Big Band from Cologne. The programme featured reprises of classic JBs material such as 'Pass The Peas' as well as an entire sequence dedicated to Ray Charles, in which Parker played beautifully hard swing on 'Hallelujah, I Love Her So' and sang a bracingly gruff blues on 'Hit The Road, Jack'.

During the set, Parker shared an interesting thought with the audience.

'I've always wanted to be in a situation where I could be in front of a big band and *sing* Ray Charles.' This is perhaps the revelation that marks out Parker, fine improviser though he is, as an R&B artist to his bones. That great desire to enter directly the world of song, through the vehicle of one's own voice, is a vital dynamic in the genre.

This is something increasingly rare in contemporary jazz, where the horn virtuoso, especially the saxophonist, has become so sacrosanct that embracing a lead vocal role may be seen as frivolity. Yet hearing Parker sing on 'Hit The Road, Jack' is as rewarding as hearing him blow and rap on 'The Soul Of A Black Man'.

14 One final ingredient

> Whether he was playing piano or writing string charts, there was something unique about the way he heard things.
>
> (Earth, Wind & Fire's Maurice White on Charles Stepney, arranger for Ramsey Lewis, Minnie Riperton and Rotary Connection)

Higher and higher

Ambling somewhere between low and mid-tempo, Maceo Parker's 'The Soul Of A Black Man' calls for restraint from the rhythm section. Bass, drums, guitars and organ stroke rather than drag the song forward. Parker's alto saxophone and Brown's voice are the lead instruments, vividly entwining in a lengthy narrative that flows like a strong, almost dangerous current into the still waters created by the band.

Another very important instrument eventually ripples into life. Instruments, to be precise: strings. At roughly the three-quarter mark of the arrangement, they make a tentative, bashful entry, gently rising into existence, deliberately fading up from zero decibels rather than storming straight in at the same noise level as the rhythm section. There are just three chords, set almost in hazy, slow-motion waltz time against the determinedly creeping four-to-the-bar pulse of the band. These chords repeat over and over, gaining more sustain and body as the track progresses before they draw discreetly back to silence, thinning down in the final bars and disappearing, like an evaporation.

Air is what the string section brings to mind most vividly. It exhales into life and then inhales into non-existence, gently streaming or hovering off the ground rather than scraping on a hard surface, as the guitars in particular do in 'The Soul of A Black Man', a piece predicated on the deep complicity between voice and alto saxophone.

To the quality of air one might add light. The strings, whose arranger is not credited, introduce a brightness that gradually becomes a glow, spreading outwards in a pool instead of tightening up in a vice – which is exactly the role of the guitarists playing single-note lines. And perhaps more importantly, the violins offer a smoothness that stands far apart from the decidedly hoarse outpourings of both horn and voice.

The presence of strings can create contrasts in texture. If the voice often embodied sass and grit, the strings were yearning and wistful, a more delicate presence to the explosive drive of an electric rhythm section.

Generally speaking, strings had leant towards that character in the bulk of black pop preceding 'The Soul Of A Black Man'. Rhythm and blues in the 1950s and '60s often featured string sections defined first and foremost by the romanticism that they could impart to a song, the creaminess of the sound evoking intimacy on a ballad, underscoring the whimper of a voice weighed down by a broken heart.

Doo-wop vocal groups often used this kind of backing, and in certain cases the strings could be more important than a rhythm or horn section, precisely because of the melodramatic emphasis they provided. Some arrangements had more substance than others. The danger of a score subsiding into a mire of overly sentimentalised tones – usually long, lush legato phrases – was not always averted. The Platters's 'Twilight Time' and Brook Benton's 'Fools Rush In' both have brilliant vocal performances vulgarised by deeply saccharine strings. But it would be rash to level this accusation wholesale, particularly when one listens to groups like The Drifters or The Tams and hears an artful synthesis of singers and strings, the finesse of the voices – usually between four and five – moving from high tenor down to bass, mirroring the ornate orchestra.

Complexity in the construction and developmental movement of a chart was not always the golden fleece arrangers were pursuing. The masters of the art understood that the synergy of vocal and accompaniment was crucial, and that a singer's verses had to be veiled with suitable textures. Gauzy, wafery chords served the useful purpose of cushioning voices, creating vital dynamics when those voices were particularly deep and bluesy. Hard edges were swathed in silk.

Whether the strings were playing a more overtly harmonic or melodic role, one thing they often did to great effect, particularly when a large orchestra was involved, was expand the breadth of sound, giving the impression that all the space around the vocal was opening up.

Jackie Wilson's 'Your Love Keeps Lifting Me Higher' is a great example of this, the chorus potently elevated and transported into a wide open sky by the dazzling jet stream of violins that rushes through the track, pulling it irresistibly high into the air – as befits the song's title.

Successor to Clyde McPhatter in The Dominoes, Wilson was, along with Sam Cooke and Ray Charles, one of the defining figures of solo male R&B. His performance on this 1967 anthem was transcendent, the monumental power of his tone unleashing an emotional ardour that did not undermine the regal poise in Wilson' delivery. But it was the great intelligence of the string score, the way the notes were left constantly brimming and bubbling against the insistent throb of the bass, that enabled the music to take off so stirringly in beautiful symbiosis with the singer's captivated heart.

Sadly, there are no credits indicating who wrote this chart. But most of the progressive labels in R&B recognised the value of string writing enough to make an arranger-conductor a key part of their staff, as was the case with Arif Mardin at Atlantic. After joining the imprint in 1963, Mardin had a substantial impact on its history. To a certain extent he was an essential lubricant in the artistic engine powered by a series of quite outstanding singers and players.

Jazz was Mardin's core vocabulary. He graduated from Berklee on a scholarship organised by Quincy Jones. The two had met when Jones was on tour with Dizzy Gillespie's band and arrived in Mardin's home town of Istanbul. After landing an arranger's job at Atlantic, Mardin scored for the likes of The Persuaders and Aretha Franklin, bringing rich chord voicings to string charts in the concise format of the three-minute love song or dance tune.

Of greater significance was the fact that Mardin, on becoming a major component in the development of soul during the 1970s, was still able to give vent to his composer's impulses, making an ambitious and quite deftly executed solo album, *Forms*, on which his arrangements for an instrumental ensemble magnified the colour and stealth that marked his work in pop.

This was exactly why the presence of strings in soul was important: not only for their sonic richness but for the canvas that they provided to strong personalities – an arranger who wanted to sketch an interesting backdrop for a singer's voice, a musician who realised that a tone like Aretha Franklin's, for example, could be enhanced by a score with sufficiently expressive textures.

Marcus Comedown

Motown had equivalent figures in its fabled Detroit studios between the late 1950s and early '70s. David Van De Pitte and Wade Marcus were two exceptional arrangers who brought similar timbral flourish and attention to detail to the charts they wrote for many of the label's icons, notably The Temptations and Marvin Gaye.

As with Mardin, these arrangers had a great ability to alter the emotional tenor of a piece through the additional harmonies of a string or horn chart. Certainly Gaye's *What's Going On* would be significantly impoverished without the spectrum of finely shaded chords that entrancingly shadow the singer's movement through his tremulous highs and lows.

Van De Pitte proved himself a superior 'listening' collaborator as well as a writer. This is one of the most underrated aspects of both soul and jazz, the latter a genre in which soloists, with their flurries of notes, are perhaps lionised at the expense of accompanists or, in an orchestral context, arrangers, the shapers of narrative.

Gaye's *What's Going On* is an album that, while not jazz itself, owes a lot to the genre. It compares to Duke Ellington's method of writing jazz pieces that were not dependent on improvisation, but where the ensemble scoring created excitement equal to that of an improvising artist through the tapestry-like textures wrought from astute use of the orchestra. The magic is in the extreme attention to detail.

What also made Motown strings special was the gamut of other sounds around them. Because percussion was a prominent element of the label's house band, the strings could create original juxtapositions in timbre, such as when a blues voice as fathomless as that of The Four Tops's Levi Stubbs was allied to the crisp, curt roll of congas, which then gave way to the sharp attack of a comet tail of strings.[1]

Bringing even more sonic idiosyncrasy to the table was the combination of bongos, tambourines, strings and woodwinds, such as oboes, bassoons and flutes, that could be heard on several of the iconic tracks in the label's songbook. All this achieved a weird subversion of classical-music traditions, as if a passing fragment of Ellington's swish arrangement of a Grieg concerto had been usurped and set against a surging barrage of heavy drums and heavier gospel voices.

Creative energies of a wide variety were circulating in the Motown camp. As much as they were engaged in making pop songs, the arrangers had too many ideas not to imbue their work with the kind of quirks that often define art music. Just as with Arif Mardin, one might mention the jazz credentials of an arranger like Wade Marcus to explain the excellence of his soul-funk work.

Marcus wrote charts for double bassist Ron Carter, penned the soundtrack of *The Final Comedown* performed by guitarist Grant Green, and also scored the brass section fleetingly featured on trumpeter Miles Davis's *On The Corner* in the early 1970s. There was a clear interest in composition and harmony that was not instantly relinquished in Marcus's work with the likes of singers Marvin Gaye, Eddie Kendricks or Stevie Wonder.

The fact that a mind as adventurous as Marcus's was willing to embrace experimental settings as much as more radio-friendly contexts says a lot about the ongoing interaction of jazz and soul, even though the audiences for each of these genres, and the way they were represented and perceived in the media, became increasingly distinct.

One of Marcus's finest moments was actually recorded for Atlantic. His arrangements for Wilson Pickett's 1971 set *Don't Knock My Love* are striking for their large intervals, insistent flights in the upper register, unconventional counterpoint and swish frenzy in some of the phrases, suggesting that Marcus had been slyly moonlighting in Bollywood.[2]

Charlie Soprano

Deployed with as much muscularity as they were in the above example, strings were almost like a second guitar, busy, bright and bustling. Yet in many other soul-music arrangements they acquired a kind of poised majesty, a strong sense of grandeur and scale.

Above all, when used in conjunction with horns, strings imbued soul with a stately, epic quality. This orchestration often created a good deal of drama.

The expansion of the sound palette coincided with extended song durations in the case of producers and arrangers like Norman Whitfield and Paul Riser. These were brilliant Motown staffers who played an important part in shaping a sub-genre dubbed 'pyschedelic soul'. Typical of this trend were the Whitfield-produced The Undisputed Truth, an act whose combination of rock bombast, gospel intensity, funky explosiveness and orchestral flourish cohered in spectacular fashion on albums such as 1971's *Face To Face With The Truth*. Yet Whitfield enjoyed many fine moments elsewhere, notably with his productions for The Temptations. 1973's 'Masterpiece' represents a seismic shift from the days of orchestral R&B. Whitfield dared to allow himself just under fourteen minutes for the arrangement, as opposed to the standard just over three minutes, meaning the introduction alone was a song in itself and all the elements of the orchestra, from harps to French horns, could be highlighted periodically. More time equalled more ideas, or rather more space to develop those ideas in much greater detail. There was also a jazz dynamic at play: the manifestation of conceptual ambition, if not audacity, that would take the artist out of his or her comfort zone – in this case, a radio-friendly pop format based on the core values of verse and chorus.

'Masterpiece' may well have pushed the tolerance threshold through the roof. Fourteen minutes of a single piece, more suite than song, may have been perceived as self-indulgence, practically as a 'pomp soul' moment at which creative impulses ran riot in defiance of commercial imperatives. The debate was complicated because much of the funky and soulful disco recorded just a few years down the line, some of which was highly successful, also tended towards lengthy tracks with ambitious arrangements. But from the 1990s onwards, more rigid formatting became prevalent, to the extent that contemporary R&B is largely held under the yoke of the three-minute track. It might well be possible to challenge that norm and still sell records, as Donna Summer did with all fifteen minutes of her dewily aroused self on 'I Feel Love', if music-industry and broadcasting powerbrokers decided that attention deficit disorder was an affliction to be treated rather than tolerated.

By today's norms, where the vocalist and the all-important hook enjoy a mostly unchallenged hegemony, Whitfield's subversive streak on 'Masterpiece' was an extreme gesture, a grand 'freak out' impulse in all its glory.

Indeed, the most impressive thing about 'Masterpiece' is that the strings, horns and rhythm section take overwhelming precedence over the singers, thus inverting the usual hierarchy whereby the orchestra is scored in deference to the voice: a star vehicle driving all before it.

There are just forty bars of vocals here, split into three short segments – two of sixteen bars and one of eight – in a score totalling some 420 bars.

What is more, the Temps are not even given the simplest of hooks to work with. The score rules. The vocals are really just flashes of colour on a heavily embroidered backdrop, daringly subjugated to the shimmer of the violins and woodwinds. These instruments' tonalities are often starkly non-western: in several passages of the lengthy piece the feel is principally Arabic.

Adding to the newness of this sound palette, and distinguishing it fundamentally from early 1960s R&B, is the fact that the strings are conjoined to electric not acoustic instruments. The presence of bass guitar, wah-wah guitar and Fender Rhodes piano creates an entirely different mood from that of the double bass and acoustic piano that were the norm in the previous decade. So there is a conflation of traditional and modern tonalities. A temporal continuum thus carries an old sound device, the orchestra, into a new world in which the band plugs in and proceeds to distort stridently its range of timbres.

'Masterpiece' is a dark, lugubrious song. And it is cruelly ironic. The title track of one of The Temps's best albums is not about a beautiful painting but a picture of decay and social deprivation, a ghetto nightmare in 3-D. What the strings do is render the atmosphere all the more sinister and fraught, stalking the central ostinato bass line and attacking it in a series of cruel, cutting flurries, whipping around like winged harpies tormenting the blind sinners of Greek mythology.

Throughout, the violins are prominent but for the most part they do not rival the guitars or vocalists in decibel levels. And this was another key advantage strings afforded producers/arrangers working with soul artists. The orchestra could provide great richness of sound, but it was miked so as not to drown out the singer or band. A slew of elements could increase timbral detail without excess volumes.

Of particular significance here are the aesthetics of the mix. As noted above, strings, and particularly the lower cellos, could be cast well to the fore by an engineer and made highly conspicuous. But in the majority of cases they were laced, almost like a fluttering veil, around the audio so that they did not overpower the other elements. Brass was much noisier.

Charles Stepney took decisive advantage of this distinction. His scores were marked by enormous precision, very high pitches that occasionally became dissonant, and dramatic changes in tone. But they never detracted from the vocalists Stepney worked with. There was a heightened sense of drama in his charts that nonetheless avoided the excessively theatrical.

Born in Chicago in 1945, Stepney started his career as a staff arranger-producer at Chess, doing sessions with vocal group The Dells and pianist Ramsey Lewis in the late 1960s, and writing killer scores for pieces like Lewis's 'Eternal Journey' before reaching a creative zenith in the early '70s through his work with Minnie Riperton and the group Rotary Connection.

'Whether he was playing piano or writing string charts, there was something unique about the way he heard things.' So said Maurice White, percussionist, vocalist, songwriter and founder of Earth, Wind & Fire.[3] White was as qualified as anybody to make that claim because he played a fair number of jazz gigs with Stepney, a competent pianist, and had the opportunity to see him bring complex charts to life in the studio when White held the drum chair in Ramsey Lewis's band.

Significantly, Stepney arranged for voices and strings on the bulk of his work. The unique nature of his output stems largely from the mirror effect he could create with these two elements, something that had occasionally happened in doo-wop. Stepney's scores had a stark edge. He favoured piercingly high soprano rather than tenor sounds.

In Minnie Riperton, the singer who was once a receptionist at the Chess Records office in Chicago, Stepney found a musician whose multi-octave, operatic voice had a startling and at times very eerie quality that he complemented potently with his scores on pieces like 'Les Fleur'. Even better was to come with Rotary Connection, a group in which Riperton shared lead singer duties with Sidney Barnes and Mitch Aliotta, all casting their voices against backdrops that blended rock and classical music. While resoundingly soulful, Rotary Connection's songs also had a folk-like agelessness.

Formed in 1966 and essentially the brainchild of Marshall Chess, son of label boss Leonard, the band was very much in line with the flower-child ethos of the time and drew parallels with Sly & The Family Stone, as much for its multiracial line-up as its rock proclivities. Stepney was drafted in as arranger-producer on the strength of his mid-1960s work. Over six albums in five years, Rotary Connection built a sometimes patchy *oeuvre*, its occasional descents into tawdry melodies more than salvaged by a piece like 'I Am The Black Gold Of The Sun', where a magnificent theme was brilliantly served by a series of intricately written parts for rhythm section, vocals and orchestra.

Perceptions of time are scrambled here. The unsettling, eldritch character of the piece derives from its juxtaposition of eras: the acoustic-guitar prelude is so close to a mandolin that it evokes a Middle Ages ballad, one abruptly shattered by a belligerent fuzz guitar pulled straight from 1960s pyschedelia. This blur of history, its promiscuous time travel, is glazed over by the shifting of light in Riperton's voice, which becomes as thin as a piccolo flute on its ascending lines.

All these sounds swirl around the central harmony like escaping substances in a chamber, before vaporising in a hail of violins. The resulting sonic cloud is almost like a spooky Gregorian chant. As such, there is a clear parallel with the work of David Axelrod,[4] the highly idiosyncratic producer of jazz artist Julian 'Cannonball' Adderley.

Love Jones

Sophisticated as Stepney's arrangements were, they did not really embrace the other aspect of string scores that marked a major breakthrough in the 1970s: rhythm.

During the previous decade the role of strings had been conceived largely as harmonic or counter-melodic, providing pads for the vocal or passing motifs that enhanced the horns. The idea of violins moving as energetically as bass or drums wasn't common.

Slowly but surely, though, charts were written in which the string parts had the same kind of forward thrust as a band's electric instruments. This was primarily because the whole concept of funk was one of rhythmic pervasion. As the idiom gained ground, its overarching principle was applied to the orchestra, with scores by Isaac Hayes, Gene Page or Barry White notable for their dynamism.

In these contexts, the fast, furious slashing of the violins synergised effectively with the heated detonations of wah-wah guitar and congas.

Because tempo was a vital distinguishing mark in disco, as the genre began to take hold of black popular music in the middle of the decade, strings upped their velocity accordingly. The orchestras that found particular favour with dancers under the mirror balls – White's Love Unlimited, Salsoul and MFSB[5] – were those with the febrile, electric-shock attack of rhythm sections that were wholly percussive.

Hearing a string section slice frantically through the air as a band cooked underneath, its congas, bongos and wood blocks sending continual tremors through the moving earth of the music, could be enormously exciting, with the rhythm spreading across a wide range of textures. It's intriguing that funk, which virtually banished strings during its genesis in the late 1960s – mainly because raw and rugged rather than smooth and polished were the tonal and conceptual order of the day – re-embraced them several years later as black pop expanded its range of technical resources.

Strings were once weepy-soppy. Now they were reborn as sexy-groovy.

When a disco-funk band broke down, leaving the drums and percussion in isolation before the other elements of the rhythm section made their entrance one by one, the appearance of a busy, bustling string motif was just another turn of the handle for agitated and agitating energy.

Light and heavy sounds were thus conjoined. If the emergence of hand drums accounted for a major evolution in soul by thickening up the rhythm section, then strings offered a counterpoint. They were able to bring levity to the sonic subtext because they so strongly evoked weightlessness, the bobbing of ribbons against the metallic clunk of the cowbell and the punishing medicine-ball bounce of the bass.

Love Unlimited Orchestra's 'Strange Games And Things', a 1976 classic that became a key rare-groove or revival tune in the 1990s, was proof positive that strings could be both savage and soothing. Against a foundation of menacingly funky drums and bass, the violins and cellos were cast in alternating roles: one to create extreme tension through a series of darting, hissing, thin upper register motifs; the other to release it through long, lush, broad middle register tones that flooded right across the rhythm section like a welcome air stream on a hot day. The strings made the song first climb, twirl round and roll, and then calmly straighten and glide. They pressed feathers to the drums and bass.

Not every arrangement was conceived with such artistry, though. The downside was that disco strings, especially as the sub-genre burnt out creatively, were easily subject to cliché, where the high-register rhythmic drive of the line became, in many cases, a ludicrous squeal that lacked the subtlety distinguishing the work of Stepney, Marcus, Van De Pitte *et al.* In the hands of a lesser arranger, the orchestra also could be abused, its range a licence for vulgarity if not reined in with a degree of control or harmonic variety.

Yet without strings, artists such as Quincy Jones and Chic could not have created their superlative musical mosaics. Many of the highlights of their respective *oeuvres*, from the former's 'You've Got It Bad Girl' to the latter's 'I Want Your Love', are rich because the strings are assigned harmonic and rhythmic roles, offering a velvet glove to the spiky chords of the guitar while matching them for drive and effervescence. Because they were softer than horns, strings could also be deployed in double or treble time over a rhythm section to simulate a sharp whistle of wind – one that did not blow over and disrupt the drums and bass as trumpets or saxes might have. The cultured use of *all* these instruments together produced outstanding results, as the talented Mr Jones made abundantly clear on many an occasion.

Mad about Osborne

The problem is, strings don't come cheap. As previously noted, the large soul-funk groups of the 1970s started to scale down in the '80s. If a horn section was a luxury they could ill afford, then a string orchestra was simply out of the question, especially for artists who had not proved their profit-making potential to a major or reasonably successful independent label that might have been willing to bankroll such a substantial expense in days of old, when the marketplace returned healthy sales for Hayes and White. The latter was depicted on the back cover of many of his album covers as a rock in a sea of besuited violinists.

Synthesizers became increasingly prevalent in the 1980s, as they offered a new tonal range in addition to their cost-cutting advantages. Combinations of keyboards and drum machines dominated. It could be argued that their use was almost a necessary evil, since it broke with what had previously been the norm. A production built solely on electronics could be tremendously creative, especially when a skilled producer, engineer or mixer was part of the 'band'. Or it could yield mediocre results if an already poor song was further compromised by the absence of advanced dynamics offered by strings and horns.

Interestingly, many keyboardists made good use of the ARP Odyssey string synthesizer, creating chords or pads that were sometimes muted and flimsier, precisely to conjure up something of the delicacy of a violin and raise the level of contrasts in the sound palette. Even more interestingly, many artists made records where the use of a string section on one piece was followed by state-of-the-art keys on another. In the process, the music became a kind of oddball bridge between two epochs. One could clearly hear the sound of one era and that of another juxtaposed on the same recording.

Jeffrey Osborne's *Stay With Me Tonight* was a case in point. Blessed with one of the great voices in soul, a tenor whose well regulated finesse easily warranted comparison with Luther Vandross (arguably the key male soul voice of the 1980s), Osborne was the drummer and lead vocalist for L.T.D., precisely the kind of large ensemble that thrived in soul music during the '70s. They made a sequence of albums with funky playing and quality arranging, penning the wistful anthem 'Love Ballad', which was subsequently reprised by guitarist-vocalist George Benson.

When Osborne went solo in the early 1980s, his initial efforts were produced by keyboard player and vocalist George Duke, a man with a long track record of engagement with jazz, rock, soul and Latin music. *Stay With Me Tonight* opened with an absolute killer melody, 'Don't You Get So Mad About It', a mid-tempo ballad brilliantly arranged by Duke, who set Osborne's voice over a burble of percussion, slinky guitar and bass riffs as well as a neatly measured string score, moving from discreet melodic sighs to urgent rhythmic cries as the song, guided by its majestic lead vocal, rose from reflective verse to climactic chorus.

And then came the title track. In place of the orchestra were hefty, chunky synth chords and a broad-toned rock guitar that grated away while Osborne hollered for his paramour to come into his kitchen for all kinds of cooking. It's an example of keyboards undermining rather than enhancing a song. The basic blues riff would have been much better served either by orchestration akin to that on the previous track or, moving in an atavistic direction, by a honky-tonk band that liked it rough and ready.

Negotiation and resolution of the discrepancy between 'Don't You Get So Mad About It' and *Stay With Me Tonight* was one of the key steps soul music had to take to keep on evolving in the years following Osborne's release. It was obvious, especially with the growing artistic and cultural impact of hip hop, that the use of machines would be of irrevocable importance. So the advent of an artist who showed an understanding of and affinity for electronics while keeping faith in past templates could be nothing less than interesting. As jazz had frequently demonstrated over time, a temporal continuum could pay artistic dividends. Old School needed to meet New School.

In fact, it happened on both sides of the Atlantic in exactly the same year.

In 1989 a group from Chicago named Ten City released a superb single, 'That's The Way Love Is', while a collective from Camden, North London by the name of Soul II Soul issued an equally fine song called 'Keep On Movin''. What linked the two songs was that they augmented a predominantly keyboard/drum machine-based sound with live strings and in so doing effected a smart segue from a past of played soul-disco to a present of programmed hip hop and house.

While both acts were important because they boasted excellent vocalists among their ranks – Byron Stingily in Ten City and Caron Wheeler in Soul II Soul – they also benefited substantially from the presence of Marshall Jefferson in the former set-up and Jazzie B in the latter. Both men were producer-mixers who had extensive knowledge of the roots of black pop but were also conversant with the nascent aesthetic of sampling, electronic production and the audio sculpture of Jamaican dub techniques, their shrewdly poetic use of ellipsis and caesura, their cinematic editing and shadow plays. Bolstered by the essential input of another producer-mixer, Nellee Hooper, Soul II Soul made great contemporary rhythm and blues that acknowledged both the liberating energy and the limitations of hip hop: that a song could be a highly effective patchwork of recorded or sequenced sounds yet it could not match the artistic integrity of an orchestra in real-time performance. So both ingredients were thrown into the same pot.

Between them, 'That's The Way Love Is' and 'Keep On Movin'' brought back to the credits of album sleeves a word that was anachronistic to some new music makers, a term with historical significance that had been more or less excised by the advent of hip hop: arranger. Byron Stingily and Marshall Jefferson scored string parts for Ten City and Mykaell S. Riley scored string parts for Soul II Soul. This language, this function predated a time of programming, yet here they were, back to cause mayhem, proof that writing still had its place in a world of sampling.

An even more delicious twist in the tale was that the violins gracing epochal Soul II Soul tracks like 'Keep On Movin'' and 'Back To Life', pieces that made soul music sound truly of the 1990s, came from a unique entity: a black classically trained ensemble, The Reggae Philharmonic Orchestra, brainchild of Riley, a talented multi-instrumentalist who had started his career with the seminal British reggae band Steel Pulse during the '70s.

Soul music's strings had traditionally been supplied by freelancing classical players who were predominantly white.[6] The mere fact that The RPO was made up of people of colour, several of them sporting dreadlocks, their association with Rastafarianism still strong and non-mainstream friendly in the early '90s, simply added to the sense of empowerment that Jazzie B's ethos represented for black Britain.

What this music did was make strings a viable option for contemporary soul birthed in the age of beats and samples. It placed the orchestra back in the realm of possibility, although the key question of budgets had not been fully resolved and several soul artists, on major labels in particular, voiced frustration at the lack of funds allocated to them to cover these expenses. This was symptomatic of a wider reluctance in the music industry to sign up and invest in any prospective new exponents of soul.

There were reasons to be cheerful, nonetheless. The Reggae Philharmonic Orchestra had some important sequels. In the mid-1990s, their cellist Stephen Hussey went on to lead his own ensembles and to work across a wide range of British soul and hip hop. He did several sessions for Incognito and D'Influence, groups that took their cue from the likes of Earth, Wind & Fire, and he also recorded with Attica Blues, a three-piece who sought to apply the lessons of classic soul orchestration to an electronic, beats-based setting. This they did very well on 'Blueprint'.

Most histories of a particular genre or scene feature a producer or musician for hire who works quite tirelessly in the backroom and remains largely invisible, yet whose influence is clearly felt. In the violinist Everton Nelson, another very talented RPO graduate, British black music found just that figure.

Two pages, four heroes

Nelson was the significant link between Soul II Soul and 4hero. It was he who appeared with other string players on the latter's 1998 album *Two Pages*. This sprawling and ambitious piece of work made the statement that two producers who had established their name in drum and bass, Dennis 'Dego' McFarlane and Mark 'Marc Mac' Clair, actually had roots running very deep into soul and jazz, in much the same way as Jazzie B. McFarlane and Clair had also come up through record-collecting culture and knew the footnotes as well as the main chapters of black art and pop culture. It was obvious from their work that they had listened to a gargantuan amount of music.

Two Pages was interesting because it dared to reveal 4hero's education amid their graduation. Alongside drum and bass and electronica came soul that, in its orchestral sweep and saturnine ambiences, drew explicitly on the lexicon of Charles Stepney and Rotary Connection. As with Soul II Soul and Attica Blues, an entirely postmodern stance framed the whole wildly mutative venture, jumbling up resonances that suggested man's command of the machine with those evoking the machine's command of man in an austere future.

Sonically, it was a shock to hear the soaring violins on the soul tune 'Starchasers' and the molten drum-programming of 'What They Do' on the same album, but the conjunction said much about the capacity of black popular music to throw curveballs. Further increasing the novelty of the sound was the use of acoustic rather than electric bass on the orchestral swirl of 'Loveless', a manoeuvre that both recalled Stepney's work with Ramsey Lewis and brought in something of the flavour of hip hop, where samples of the instrument were particularly prevalent.[7] Hence the span of references in the music was substantial. This created a thrilling openness and ambiguity in 4hero's putative musical identity. Regardless of whether they were conversant with state-of-the-art drum machines, Dego and Marc Mac were not about to negate the history of 'old' instruments such as drums, keys and guitars. Their use of a string section seemed all the more radical because it represented a certain romantic, melodious heritage in soul, apparently at odds with the stark, dissonant sounds of the club culture they were associated with.

Image was important. Few imagined that 4hero would make 'Loveless' *after* they had delivered the pneumatic drum and bass of 'Cookin' Up Yer Brain', not least because the use of the strings brought them into a world of sheet music and supposed musical literacy that, so the classic highbrow-lowbrow dichotomy holds, runs decidedly counter to the supposed musical illiteracy of beat-making and programming.

Two Pages was thus a challenge to more than the partitioning of genres. It was effectively a symbol of black popular music, no matter how far into the future it reached, being able to access its past simultaneously and make the two poles intersect, without any loss of artistic credibility or cohesion in the process.

A few years later I.G. Culture, the prime instigator of broken beat, the London-based dance idiom, showed a similar scope. Although his music's marks of distinction were ultra-busy, jerk-and-judder electronic beats, I.G. Culture also had a marked interest in song form and orchestration, indicated by the presence in his West London studio of classic jazz vinyl albums like Wayne Shorter's *The All Seeing Eye* among great stacks of New York hip hop or JA dubplates.[8] Just like Jazzie B and 4hero, I.G. Culture had an education as wide as it was deep.

Hence the deployment of strings in broken beat was not surprising but predictable, given the formative references of its practitioners. With its surfeit of drum programming, the idiom is part of an electronic music canon. Yet I.G. Culture, whether making beats or not, modelled himself on Quincy Jones, *not* on hip hop producers, much as he admired them. So the desire to use violins was an entirely logical development.

Strings, like horns, is a vague, general term. A section can vary tremendously in size and configuration, either scaling up to a twenty-five-piece or down to a two- to four-piece, or using overdubs to make a two- to four-piece sound like a twenty-five-piece – all of which can dramatically alter the sound palette. I.G. Culture and Kaidi Tatham, another key figure in broken beat, brought a certain idiosyncrasy to their work through the use of just a couple of string players. Even more distinctive was their use not of strings but of just one string instrument, namely the cello. Its thick, grainy tone invested a song like Tatham's 2004 single 'Betcha' Did' with a brooding, heavy timbre. It was a reminder that the cello had enjoyed key moments in 1960s pop, such as in The Beatles' 'Eleanor Rigby'.

The single cello on 'Betcha' Did' provides a subtle boost to the bass, and this suits the substantial low end of post-hip hop soul. It increases tonal density and resonates with the words of a take-no-nonsense woman who tells a take-too-much loverman she will 'kick him to the kerb'.

15 A recipe not from Memphis

The man is his own instrument. The instrument is an orchestra.
(Sleeve notes, Stevie Wonder, *Music Of My Mind*)

When I saw this digital device, I was very happy because I could create the band and the backing singers all in one lovely little box. (M. Nahadr)

It's not your sign, it's your mind

Playing the cello on Tatham's 'Betcha Did' is Izzi Dunn. Along with violinist Stella Page, she formed a string duet, charmingly dubbed Chix with Stix, in the late 1990s and appeared on a number of works by British producers I.G. Culture, Bugz In The Attic and Wookie. Among Dunn's other notable credits is an appearance on *The Chancer*, a 2001 CD by Nash, a quite excellent London soul combo with hip hop leanings who, sadly, never made the commercial impact their talent warranted.

Dunn is also a very good singer, producer and songwriter in her own right who cut a strong solo album, *The Big Picture*, a few years after the Nash sessions. The fluid, serpentine cello melodies that adorn this album point indirectly to Dunn's background as the daughter of an opera singer who took up the instrument at the age of eleven. Yet the strident use of subsonic bass lines, spring-loaded drum programming and well calibrated blues harmony evidence a thorough grasp of a wide historical range of black popular music, from soul and funk right through to hip hop and broken beat. The big picture, indeed.

Essentially, the record is by Dunn and assorted guests. There is no group *per se*. Guitarists and keyboard players appear on most of the songs but the backbone is really the singer-cellist playing her strings and various keyboards as well as programming beats, with the input of these other players lending additional harmonic colour. Tellingly, each track credits Dunn with 'all other instruments', as if she were a self-contained creative force, a *bona fide* one-woman band. This is an increasingly prevalent model in soul. Many are the albums on which either the artist, if sufficiently multiskilled, will make all the rhythm as well as the vocal tracks, or the producer(s) will create all the beats for a singer, perhaps with the input of a few session musicians when necessary. The point is that the definition of the word 'producer' has altered significantly in the last four decades.

Up until the 1970s, generally speaking, a producer meant somebody who steered and oversaw the music-making progress, usually working with a singer or band and, crucially, an arranger-conductor if string or horn parts were required. Producer was always a highly ambiguous term, in so far as it could mean an individual being directly involved in the composing process or could denote conceptual input, whereby the producer would take a singer or pianist's naked melody, imagine a fabric of sound to clothe it in, and then draw together the necessary elements to make the ideas materialise as notes. Above all, producers were thinkers.

Even though there are still producers who act almost as midwife to the birth of a song's sound, to produce now largely means creating the music rather than nurturing its development, and this chimes strongly with the beats + rhymes *modus operandi* that defines hip hop. Furthermore, the reduction in the costs of home studios, audio software and sampling and sequencing equipment has made it much easier for a relatively gifted musician to create a virtual band. It would, however, be historically inaccurate to ascribe this development exclusively to the advent of the beat-making generation of the 1980s, as several notable figures were drawn towards autonomy many years before that. They could do nearly everything themselves. So they did.

Consider this quote: 'This album is virtually the work of one man. All the songs are composed, arranged and performed by Stevie Wonder on piano, drums, harmonica, organ, clavichord, clavinet, and ARP and Moog synthesizers. The man is his own instrument. The instrument is an orchestra.' Sleeve notes are invariably characterised by hyperbole but this text, taken from the jacket of Stevie Wonder's 1972 album *Music Of My Mind*, is anything but overblown rhetoric. The words ring true.

Though smart enough to avail himself of the talents of several members of the Motown Records house band, Wonder laid down many tracks himself. He was an accomplished multi-instrumentalist, and an integral part of his creative development was asserting this versatility.

Had Wonder not actually become the orchestra that his mind, or rather his inner ear, was steering him towards, there is every chance he would not have been able to achieve what he did in that remarkably fertile period between the early and mid-1970s, during which albums such as *Innervisions, Fulfillngness' First Finale* and *Talking Book* became expressions not just of his artistic independence but, bar the appearance of a few contributors, his ability to *be* a whole ensemble.

Arrangement and performance carried out by a single hand can go one of two ways. The work in question can suffer due to a lack of musicianship, with a very stilted delivery of the various parts, or it can acquire extra cohesion due to one central personality pervading and driving the whole endeavour. As such, all the keys, drums and other instruments will benefit from the same *touch*, a quality evoked *ad infinitum* in jazz.

Whether playing piano, percussion or harmonica, Wonder had superlative rhythm, great textural richness and, particularly on the last instrument, a scorching blues sensibility. All this enabled him to create the illusion of a collection of different players who had been well run in and moulded into a crack unit. The absolute triumph of a piece such as 'Higher Ground' is that the marvellous alchemy of the keyboard and drum tracks suggests the optimum state of a band that has either gained a serious studio tan from a hard slog of rehearsals or has come in to record after gruelling months on the road. And all that from one mind.

Moreover, Wonder was carving out this extraordinary legacy as a Renaissance soundman at a time when a number of equally extraordinary bands – Earth, Wind & Fire, Kool & The Gang, Parliament-Funkadelic and groups led by singers such as James Brown or Marvin Gaye – were also at something of a creative peak. So two distinctly different models were posited in soul, the solo captain and the full crew. An important subtext in the bigger story of black popular music over the decades has been the ongoing push and pull between these two poles.

Technology has played an intriguing role here. Because soul artists have always had a fascination for new synthesizers, electronics and novel ways of manipulating and distorting sound imaginatively, intricate advanced orchestration has been a possibility even in a small set-up, as Wonder proves. His keyboard tapestries relate to the profound insight of organist Dr Lonnie Smith, who argued that the Hammond B3 provided 'options'. Most artists with imagination welcome options.

With their high level of all-round musicianship, Prince, Omar and Me'Shell NdegéOcello are important successors to Wonder and have proved adept at constructing entire tracks on their own. Another model that has emerged is the multi-instrumentalist-producer + vocalist, as embodied by Hubert Eaves-James Williams in the 1980s, I.G. Culture-Bembé Segue in the '90s and Jazzy Jeff-Jill Scott in the new millennium.

By and large, soul bands – as in the unit, the team – have become an increasingly rare phenomenon in 2010. One thing that has undoubtedly taken root in the popular consciousness is a grand divide between the group, which is almost exclusively the preserve of the guitar-rock domain, and the solo artist (either a rapper or singer) who has become the prevalent norm in hip hop and R&B. The repercussion of this development is that new audiences are becoming increasingly detached from the history of artists such as Earth, Wind & Fire, so that the very *idea* of a whole group playing soul is anomalous. Today, black pop is largely defined by individuals, not collectives.

From a political, cultural and visual point of view, this is a totally regrettable state of affairs. The band model, complete with the all-important horn section, is a link to a jazz tradition. And although few punters may think of this when they hum Earth, Wind & Fire's 'Let's Groove', the fact of the matter is that the piece stands in a lineage which can be traced back to the orchestras of James Brown, Ray Charles and Count Basie. Yes, it's nothing more than 'One Mint Julep' for mirror balls. It is a union of dancing brass and scatting vocoder. It is modernity plugged into tradition. And tradition switched on to modernity.

Of mints and masks

Wherein lies the great need for Mint Condition. A four-piece soul group is enough of an oddity, but one that has been around since the mid-1980s scores extra points in the strangeness stakes, simply because there is such a huge turnover of acts, both real and manufactured, in the world of pop these days or a name is used clinically as a franchise while the group members come and ago like a roster of temporary employees.

Mint Condition hail from Minneapolis, Prince country no less, and in their formative years they were partly nurtured by Jimmy Jam & Terry Lewis of The Time, a group that was also active on the local scene. After debuting with *Meant To Be Mint* in 1991, vocalist/drummer Stokley Williams, bassist Ricky Kinchen, guitarist Homer O'Dell, pianist Larry Waddell and saxophonist Jeffrey Allen went on to enjoy a string of hits throughout the decade, sometimes leaning slightly towards pop but always retaining a high degree of soulfulness, before their deal with Elektra ended and they went quiet for some years. They re-emerged in 2005 with *Livin' The Luxury Brown* on their own Caged Bird label.

Whether success tailed off because Mint Condition failed to move with the times or not is a moot point. One thing beyond contention is that they always took a hard line when it came to their identity, refusing to name a front man in the rock tradition. Hence Mint Condition was unerringly about a collective of strong individuals rather than one star around which several subservient backing members gravitated, something that was intensely problematic in terms of marketing the group in a music industry resolutely tied to that very model.

Commercially, this may have been costly in the end but artistically it is a distinct premium. Performing live, Mint Condition, in their moments of true inspiration, approach the cohesion and, most importantly, the imagination of a jazz ensemble. Which means they solo extensively in between songs, they groove as hard as a funk or rock band, and they pull left-field moves such as singer Williams, whose excellent pipes testify that he actually worked with gospel sensations Sounds Of Blackness as a youngster, jumping behind his *own* drum kit and proceeding to trade fours with the regular drummer.

Bravado. Audacity. And above all, surprise. When they did that at London's Jazz Café in 2008, a tremor of disbelief ran through the audience, followed by an eruption of excitement that said much about the enormous artistic dividends awaiting a band that pursues a simple but very meaningful strategy in performance – namely, it deigns to give the paying public what it *didn't* think it wanted.

Coming through loud and clear at that gig was how much the musicians all loved to play and how important the unity of the band experience was. Writing songs, recording albums and performing them live is only half of the *raison d'être* of a group in the pure sense of the term.

Any impresario, producer or promoter can throw together several musicians on stage and have them play an impromptu or rehearsed gig. But that doesn't necessarily make them a group in which the whole is greater than the sum of the parts. Personalities have to cohere.

Players have to rely on each other. They have to know their respective strengths. That's what makes a real band. It is doomed without that complicity, that recognition of mutual need.

Which is why the following statement matters: 'I'd just cry if he left us'. So confessed Jean-Paul 'Bluey' Maunick of drummer Richard Bailey.[1] There was absolutely no sentimentality in his voice when he said it, around summer 1999, the time of *No Time Like The Future*, Maunick's best work to date.

He leads Incognito.[2] He is Incognito. A Briton of Mauritian descent, Maunick began making music in the late 1970s and was a prime mover in what became known as 'Brit funk', co-founding groups such as Freeez and Light Of The World as well as Incognito, an outfit that was initially dedicated to playing soul and instrumental jazz-fusion.

Since its inception Incognito has, with Maunick as its fulcrum, built an aggregation of players, a family as he calls it, that includes some of the best session musicians on the British black music scene. A man like Bailey is a seasoned and highly respected veteran of that scene. This is a very different scenario from Mint Condition: it involves a large volume of musicians, yet at the same time it is a camp or a circle that retains a strong character and continuity, even though it has expanded over the years to incorporate excellent singers like Maysa Leak and Karen Bernod as well as several gifted horn players.

Another reason why Incognito is an important group is sociocultural. Maunick is a patriarch, an elder statesman who has brought younger musicians into the fold. So at any given time the band represents several generations, several different mindsets and outlooks on life. This set-up can pay creative dividends, simply by blending levels of experience and energy. It is also a means of safeguarding musical skills and folklore through oral culture, as the elders pass on pragmatic information about technique and stories about lifestyle to their younger colleagues. History thus filters through spoken word.

Finding a potential successor to the likes of Incognito and Mint Condition appears a daunting task today, but there is another important reality to bear in mind. Several jazz musicians lead soul bands, the most high-profile being Roy Hargrove's R.H Factor,[3] and a jazz band can turn into a soul combo, just as it can a funk or a rock group at any given moment. But this eventuality is largely overlooked because it may complicate market segmentation.

Even more worrying perhaps is the notion that modern soul music is all about singers rather than bands. The genre was largely defined by the former, but it is a mistake to think that Earth, Wind & Fire, The Isleys, Kool & The Gang or The Commodores were the only memorable exponents of the latter. Cast an inquisitive eye over the history of the music, particularly in the 1970s, and one will find a lot of bands that sold a lot of records – from the well-known Cameo, Gap Band, Chic, Fatback, Mandrill and War to the more obscure Brick or B.T. Express. There were more: The Ohio Players, Dayton, Lakeside, Slave, Confunkshun, One Way, Dazz Band, Tower Of Power, Crown Heights Affair, Rose Royce, Pleasure, The Meters, Zapp, Trouble Funk. These were not fly-by-night affairs.

Each recorded between half a dozen and ten albums in their lifetime.

We believe soul is all about singers because the likes of Aretha and Otis are such forceful, defining personalities in the whole history and mythology of the music. Yet bands have been legion in soul. And they have been creative.

The aforementioned examples are not the whole story either. Other groups that have made their mark include Kleeer, Heatwave, T-Connection, L.T.D., FBI, The SOS Band, Cymande, The Average White Band and Light Of The World. And what is the name of one of the great soul-funk combos of the 1970s, bridging the surrealism of Parliament and the majesty of The Miracles? The name of that band is an inspired one: Bloodstone.[4] All the above made a contribution to the evolution of black pop, but they are largely relegated to footnotes in the history of the music.

As noted above, their successors are really few and far between today. This is regrettable because the mechanics of a group are very different to those of a singer with a hired backing band or team of songwriters. In a band context there can be creative exchange across a range of personalities. Interesting music can come out of a singer co-writing with a drummer and then a keyboardist arranging with a horn player. In the best cases, the net result is an informal democracy that can enrich the whole aesthetic. Obviously tensions may arise within the camp, and Lord knows many groups have imploded because at least one ego runs out of control. But there is nonetheless something essential about four or five individuals 'working things out', be the issues musical or behavioural, in the pressure cooker of a rehearsal room. And it is the process of negotiating and resolving artistic differences that just might distill moments of magic. Fractious parts are not pleasant but they can produce a phenomenal whole.

Furthermore, groups are hugely important because they can prompt hero worship of different instrumentalists, which helps to ensure that a new generation of musicians is born. Impressionable teenagers need to see and revere a drummer, bassist, saxophonist or guitarist as well as a singer, because not everybody has it in them to be the next Marvin Gaye. Talent can therefore be spread across a wider range of outlets. This is crucial because no myth is more destructive than the one about all the brothers and sisters being blessed with a heavenly larynx. Had the late Paul 'Tubbs' Williams of Light Of The World not been inspired by Paul Jackson of The Headhunters, British soul music would have been robbed of one of its premier bassists in the 1980s.

It is hugely important that Williams's name is not forgotten, and that a new generation is made aware that he is as much a musical role model as a producer or rapper. If not, there won't be another Light Of The World.

Developments in black pop during the 1980s were arguably the most intriguing and confusing, if not plain paradoxical, in the music's history. Hip hop was a blessing and a curse. Its praxis of sampling and its emphasis on studio production and inventive sound manipulation, best encapsulated by the birth of the scratch from the womb of black vinyl, brought a great energy boost to black pop. But the price of that energy was the relative decline of the band and the desire to play instruments, already set in motion by reduced availability of music lessons due to substantial cuts in funding at many inner city schools in America during the Reagan years.

Nostalgia is a key word associated with the heyday of the live band in rhythm and blues. Younger listeners sometimes accuse its proponents of living in the past and of refusing steadfastly to get with a rapidly changing, technologically driven programme. But a real understanding of both new-school production and old-school instrumentalists would recognise the advantages and disadvantages of both options.

Not every 1970s soul group pushed the envelope. One thing that is undeniable, though, is that many of them covered a relatively wide amount of stylistic ground, since a basic apprenticeship in piano or guitar usually leads to the investigation of styles *other* than R&B. Many of the aforesaid bands were great because, standing on the shoulders of Earth, Wind & Fire, who themselves were standing on the shoulders of The Beatles as well as Booker T. & The MGs, they included an element of rock in their aesthetic that made their output admirably multifaceted.

Music industry, media and broadcasting gatekeepers do not usually welcome artists who make a mockery of the dividing lines between genres.

Black and white is far easier to see than grey. Adding very stubbornly to the confusion is a handful of musicians who are hard to define, or rather who are continually changing context or revealing another aspect of their creativity, rendering easy summaries of their art null and void.

M People

Me'Shell NdegéOcello is an archetype of this shape-shifting nature, having emerged in the early 1990s as an artist largely inspired by '70s soul-funk, even though her sensibilities – political and sonic – were self-evidently shaped by hip hop. She would go on to make folk, jazz, reggae and, latterly, a beguiling form of soulful rock that also incorporates African vocal melodies and state-of-the-art electronic soundscapes.

It is accurate to call NdegéOcello a soul artist because rhythm and blues remains a core element of her vocabulary. But the impressive idiomatic scope of her output to date has shown that she will not be constrained by that definition in any way. In other words, she is a musician who, despite the specific nature of her education, responds to whatever new sounds, beats or voices catch her ear, regardless of how 'exotic' they may appear.

Each project NdegéOcello has embarked on has brought not just changes in personnel but discernible modifications to the arranging and production techniques deployed, so that the sonic backdrops in which she swathes her voice and bass guitar are ever subject to change.

To a large extent, she epitomises the contemporary soul artist as creative being with a touchstone that is both self-op studio *and* band. Hence if NdegéOcello shifts from a keys/drum programming/voice set-up to drums/bass/keys/horns, there should be no great surprise involved, even though she has met with resistance from fans on those occasions when she has decided to forego entirely the use of her own voice.

Given the enormous range of synthesizers and programming/sequencing equipment now available at affordable prices, figures like NdegéOcello can make interesting music with completely electronic backing, or they can supplement the drum machines and keyboards with an array of guests. This essentially shows the prescience of Stevie Wonder's *modus operandi* in the 1970s. While *Music Of My Mind* is a great solo album, it is also one on which the singer recognises the need for input from instruments beyond his capability, none more so than Art Baron's frothy trombone.

Steeped in nostalgia if not mythology, the band – the set-up of drums, bass, guitar, organ and horn – according to King Curtis's 'Memphis Soul Stew' template has proved to be just one available model for black popular music from 1967 to the present day. It has not been the only template. Much of what is interesting about the genre's history stems from the variations found for the blueprint of a soul combo, as well as creativity in the recording process: even Curtis, although he believed in real-time playing, multi-tracked his tenor in 1969.

His faith in the basic rhythm section + horns model was more or less unwavering up until his death, but Curtis also consistently experimented with different line-ups, searching for new textures and sources of percussive drive. This led him to vary frequently the configuration of his brass and reeds, and to deploy conga players in addition to his kit drummer. Curtis's use of spoken word also brought a certain zest to his work.

There is thus no single, definitive, all-purpose template for an R&B band, no classic recipe for a soul stew, even though the use of rhythm, horns and, in many cases, string sections has been prevalent over the years.

Artists did not stick slavishly to the same instrumentation but there was enough of a core line-up to create a generic historical model that makes an interesting point of comparison with the *modus operandi* of multi-instrumentalist + guest *à la* Stevie Wonder. All this means that soul music has been able to assume a wide range of sonic guises.

Wonder's autonomy was a monumental breakthrough. He showed that a group could be contained, captured and encoded in not one but a series of synthesizers which, when programmed with skill, yielded quite ornate tonal mosaics. These often had a harmonic gleam and shimmer that made abundantly clear the desire to view parts almost as 'sections' of a big band.

More intriguing is that this self-contained praxis never entirely replaced the group aesthetic. Wonder still drew on the services of the best session musicians Motown had to offer throughout the 1970s. Several of his albums were characterised by the alternation of completely solo and full band tracks. The most successful example of this approach is *Songs In The Key Of Life*, where the input of rhythm players, horns and choirs provides a valuable contrast to futuristic synthesizers like the Electrone Polyphonic GX10. Coming through loud and clear on that album is the connection between Wonder's solo electro proclivities and his implied big-band leanings. He is doing the 'out of many keyboards, one mind' thing with all the experience of someone who has closely listened to and skilfully orchestrated myriad sounds for many different voices. He is making electronic music *after* a lengthy immersion in electro-acoustic music.

Since that time, the originality and strangeness of the sound of soul has been determined largely by the imagination players have brought to their 'axes' and by the fine-tuning of keyboard-based orchestration through the integration of other instruments. Woodwinds have been particularly important in this respect. For example, many artists have incorporated the flute – still a relatively rare beast in jazz and more so in pop – into their work, reminding us that other 'classical' instruments like oboes and bassoons were featured on several of Motown's best arrangements in the 1960s and '70s. Hence also the use of bass clarinet on two anthems from the past fifteen years: Marcus Miller's 'Rush Over' (1995) and Omar's 'Syleste' (2003).[5]

Omar's desire to use a skilled musician like Ben Castle on 'Syleste' shows his affinity with the culture of the player in soul, and a steadfast belief in the absolute need for specific musicians in specific circumstances. Synthesizers can imitate the sound of horns. But they can't be horns.

M. Nahadr's 2009 set *EclecticIsM,* one of the great new works in the canon of contemporary black popular music, stands directly in this lineage. The core sound is the singer, keyboards and programming, yet brilliant timbres are added by a heavily distorted trumpet and by two bass guitars, one often playing high and wiry like an electric guitar, the other low and bulbous like a Moog synthesizer with more glissando.

Orchestration is once again at play. This music is underpinned by a clear quest for textural intricacy that suggests the artist has previously engaged with both improvised and composed music, and has thought carefully about how her own songs can be conceived as a series of closely interlocking parts that wrap tightly around her voice, as various instruments would do were Nahadr fronting a much bigger group of musicians.

Tellingly, she said of the first sequencing keyboard she bought: 'When I saw this digital device, I was very happy because I could create the band and the backing singers all in one lovely little box.'[6]

Had *EclecticIsM* been made several decades ago, had Nahadr's talent been transplanted to a time of bigger budgets and deeper investment by record labels, it would have – and I've no doubt here – materialised as a large production with horn and string sections and backing vocalists.

That time is mostly over, and especially for a creative being who will not submit to prevailing formulae. That holds resoundingly true for Nahadr, just as it does for the likes of Me'Shell NdegéOcello or several other artists, for that matter. That Nahadr found novel options to serve her muse, beyond the synths + voice template, says much of her strength of character and guile. Any artist with vision, inner visions even, is bound to say 'here is the music of my mind' with honesty to the world. And the world has always been more than a place that, according to bad boys white and black, drinks and goes home and eats its young: America.

16 Universoul sounds I

[Cymande's] The Message … that was one of the non-reggae tunes that crossed over into sound system [reggae] world. (Dennis Bovell)

De la soul

Soul music has travelled throughout the world – or more precisely, it has greatly affected listeners outside its birthplace in America. First and foremost, one might think of the adulation that greeted the first Motown and Stax revues when they hit Britain in the mid-1960s. But that was always on the cards, given the intense love affair with rhythm and blues the country's youth had embarked on several years previously.

If Britain took to black popular music in no uncertain terms, then other territories in Europe showed a similar 'fever for the flavour'. France emerged as a major constituency for soul music in the 1960s and '70s. Sold-out gigs by the likes of Ray Charles, James Brown and Aretha Franklin at prestigious venues such as L'Olympia in Paris made it clear these artists had cleared the language barrier while the struggle to haul themselves over the bigger, bloodier hurdle of civil rights raged on.

Foreign audiences liking soul is one thing but perhaps a more interesting subject for debate is foreign artists making soul. Can a singer born outside Memphis or Detroit hope to attain the same degree of artistic authenticity, the same credibility in soulfulness? Can a francophone holler out R-E-S-P-E-C-T with all her heart and make you care about what it means to her in the same way Aretha does?

Furthermore, how would you feel if those lyrics were translated into French, so that the phonetic sounds of 'Are-Eee-Ess-Pee-Eee-Cee-Tee' became 'Air-Euh-Es-Pay-Euh-Say-Tay?' This might be called Gallic soul. Could it really work, though? Soul is the music of an anglophone country with a precise vernacular: the way in which black people, once denied access to education, have inflected English towards something unique. So the question of how much substance can be retained when the bare bones of soul music – lyrics, melody, vocal performance, words brought to life – are clothed in new language is an intriguing one.

In May 2009 the American soul vocalist M. Nahadr travelled to Paris to work with French producer Vincent Beyard on a show called *Meme*, a serendipitous linguistic approximation of her own first name, Mem. That Nahadr should be heading for Europe to venture into something she herself could not at the time describe to me in any great detail said a lot about the unpredictable, incident-packed course her artistic life had followed thus far. She was happy to embrace the adventure.

Prior to making her debut album *EclecticIsM*, released a few months before her trip to France, the Washington-born singer immersed herself in the myriad music scenes New York had to offer and, hungry for as many adventures in sound as possible, took part in 'anything from crazy improvisation to Tibetan music to huge gospel choirs'.[1] When I interviewed her during the Paris sojourn, Nahadr was keen to talk about the universality of her work, its potential appeal to lovers of any kind of music who appreciated an expression of honesty. The logical corollary of this appeared to be Nahadr's own liking for songs that she *felt* were predicated on similar values, regardless of whether or not she could literally understand their lyrical content – like Tibetan music.

Nahadr found this music, along with many other genres, soulful. To the question of how soulful soul could be when one of its primary components, the English language, was removed from the equation, she answered by referring to a vocalist called Sandra Nkaké.[2] 'She's really incredible … whether she's singing in French or English, I don't think it really matters. She is really, fantastically soulful.'[3]

Any track on Nkaké's debut album, *Mansaadi*, released to relatively little fanfare in 2008, bears this out. She has a voice of immense range that she handles with fine precision and control, her timbral ingenuity placing her as much in the lineage of great jazz singers as that of soul divas. Listening to an anglophone piece such as 'Happy' next to a francophone number like 'La Mauvaise Réputation' is a curious experience. Nkaké, who was born in Paris to Ivorian parents, essentially retains the same sonic richness and, more to the point, the same character and emotional depth, recalling ever so slightly the steely grace of Carleen Anderson.

Just as Nahadr suggested, there is no loss of soulfulness in Nkaké's performances, regardless of whether she is telling a lover 'don't ask me' or 'ça va de soi'. One might observe that her declamatory 'woah' *en français* has the same impact as her declamatory 'woah' in English.

Historically, French has been adopted more frequently by jazz than soul singers, key examples being Louis Armstrong, Nat 'King' Cole and Nina Simone. When handled by the above, the florid language of Baudelaire and Brel is appropriate for a fluid, airy swing pulse, perhaps more than for a relatively static, tougher backbeat groove.

Still, as previously mentioned, soul has been big in France more or less since its genesis, and the fervour with which it was embraced by the local population has birthed a strong culture of appreciation for black pop. The

French are soul and blues connoisseurs. This explains to a certain extent why Sandra Nkaké sounds as 'authentic' as she does.

One local artist who was an important antecedent to Nkaké was the Toulousain vocalist Claude Nougarou. He wasn't a soul singer but he had a strong jazz pedigree that also encompassed a gruff bluesiness. In fact, Nougarou is a fascinating example of a singer with a European folk sensibility that vividly and very engagingly connected with African American blues.

Over time, there have been very few major breakthroughs for French soul artists singing in their native tongue in America. To a large degree that reinforces the notion that there really is a kind of linguistic hegemony at play, one stating quite resolutely that there is no room for soul texts in an 'Old World', or indeed African, language.

Such charges could be levelled at the world of cinema and pop culture in general. There are still relatively few non-anglophone movies that make an impact in mainstream America and Britain. This overall climate may make it hard for any foreign-language artistic endeavours, be they audio or visual, to travel beyond their local borders.

Having said that, the great international success of Brazilian bossa nova music, with its mellifluous Portugese lyrics, is an example of a non-anglophone art form moving extensively beyond the beaches of Rio.

When it comes to suitability for soul music, French has a major advantage over the Northern European or Scandinavian languages due to the melodious softness and feline nature of its tonality. It is spared the harsh, cutting sounds of German or Dutch. With that in mind, French can more feasibly accommodate and convey some of the romanticism that has always underpinned soul, a characteristic equally relevant to jazz.

This may explain why Les Nubians enjoyed some success in America. And In French too. Les Nubians are two sisters, Hélène and Célia Faussart, of French and Cameroonian descent. Their 1998 debut album, *Princesses Nubiennes*, was a somewhat dreamy blend of soul, funk, hip hop and understated African rhythms. It turned out to be a surprise hit on American college radio after it was ignored, in true stranger-in-your-own-land fashion, back home in the sisters' native Bordeaux. 'It was really the campus DJs who got behind the album', Hélène told me during a promotional trip to Paris in 1999. 'People were phoning up to say that they didn't really understand what we were saying but it sounded good.'[4]

Boosted by this interest, Les Nubians went on to play festivals stateside. The most successful of these was a New Orleans event, where they were programmed after a raucously funky ensemble that had the audience on its feet, the high-energy pulse a huge contrast to the largely down-tempo, gentle slant of Les Nubians' songs. Both sisters admitted they almost succumbed to a major attack of nerves before show time.

Given the integral place of francophone culture in the history of New Orleans, the audience may have been well disposed anyway. But the fact of the matter is that the content of Les Nubians' lyrics very much addressed life as the sisters lived it in Bordeaux, rather than life on the Bayous.

The crowd's love shower underlined that people are, or at least can be, more open-minded than one might imagine, if the right elements come together in a piece of art. The Faussart sisters have a strong 'Afropean' image, a sassiness and natural grace, and above all a certain strength of character that may well have facilitated any communication beyond language barriers. One could argue that their whole 'vibe' as much as their songs did some talking too.

Then again, no assumptions can be made about exactly why they struck the chord they did. Whether Americans, black or white, saw something of, say, Erykah Badu in Les Nubians that they could relate to is a moot point. They may just as easily have been taken by the exoticism of a foreign language and the escapism of unfamiliar words and accents.

Soulfulness is not exclusive to American singers. Similar depths of feeling can be achieved by many artists around the world, and certainly by exponents of a local equivalent of the blues, be they African, Turkish or Vietnamese. The question is how willing a listener accustomed to English-language lyrics that address fundamental emotional, political and spiritual themes – 'I'll Be There', 'Sign Of The Times', 'Have A Talk With God '– is to accept a canon of francophone songs that may be reduced purely to feeling through sound rather than literal meaning through words.

One of the great clichéd observations on soul music is that it is all about the heartstrings, that great outpourings of emotion will be enough to satisfy everyone. This is a grave insult to a lyric as insightful as 'We're all sensitive people' or as wry as 'I'm more serious than the price of gas'.[5]

We are moved by Marvin Gaye in the first instance and tickled by Amp Fiddler in the second because of their intellectual honesty and artful command of language, skills deployed to crystallise a response to, respectively, the sexual liberation of the 1970s and fear of spiralling oil prices in the new millennium. When one considers how closely major geopolitical interests are tied to 'black gold', the lyric has a profound resonance.

Hence feeling, through the sonic beauty of voices, is allied to meaning, through the substance of the word. And it is perhaps a mistake to assume that, while there are some banal texts in black popular music, its adepts make few demands of the genre's lyricists. Hence anglophone audiences, or audiences who are wedded to the *idea* of soul as anglophone music, will welcome the fact that some excellent European groups, such as Dutch artists Tasha's World and the Franco-Belgian ensemble Soul I:D, as well as the superb Sandra Nkaké, have opted to sing in English – something that is not an issue for their counterparts to be found a groovin' on the other side of La Manche.

Korner shop

If you were asked to name an artist who was the best representative of contemporary British soul, then Omar Lye-Fook would probably be the obvious choice. For the best part of twenty years he has made consistently high-quality music, as exemplified by albums such as 1994's *For Pleasure*, 1997's *This Is Not A Love Song* and 2005's *Best By Far*, all works on which Omar's skills as a singer are matched by his great ability as a multi-instrumentalist, songwriter and producer.

Standing to a large extent on the foundation of Stevie Wonder, Omar has developed a distinctive vocal and sonic identity, especially in his use of keyboards and drum patterns. That makes his work fairly easy to identity, and his influence on the newer American soul artists is widely acknowledged. When Omar made his debut in the early 1990s, he was perceived first and foremost as a member of the 'acid jazz' scene that also included the likes of The Brand New Heavies, D Influence and Young Disciples. These groups made a point of re-asserting the 'band culture' of the '70s. To a certain degree, they were also trying to build a bridge to the sampling aesthetic of a younger black music called hip hop.

The most important thing they did was to bring a sense of newness and reinvigoration to the UK soul scene that had not really been seen since the substantial but fleeting commercial successes chalked up by Soul II Soul in the late '80s and Loose Ends a few years before that.

Certainly with Omar picking up the baton from these groups and sounding so confident and accomplished both in the studio and on stage – his early gigs often featured a dazzling sequence of solo scat vocal, where he layered up body rhythms by slapping his chest and distorting his tone, revealing the clear influence of virtuoso jazz vocalists like Bobby McFerrin and Al Jarreau – there was a sense that British soul had really come of age. Here was an artist more than able to cut the mustard stateside.

It mattered because the UK take on the American tradition of black popular music had long been maligned by the domestic press, who dismissed it largely as an inferior dilution of the 'real thing' – paralleling attitudes that had been prevalent for many years in the jazz world. In fact, prior to Omar, Soul II Soul and Loose Ends had both significantly undermined that prejudice. No better symbol of their new entitlement was to be found than on hip hop records that deigned to name-check them alongside US legends.

There was another reason why an artist like Omar was important, though. He was steeped in the history of British soul. Back in the early 1970s Omar's father, Byron Lye-Fook, a drummer and activist, co-founded the Black Music Association with the singer Root Jackson, thus creating a vital platform for black artists resident in London. Most of these were Caribbean immigrants who had grown up with popular local genres like calypso, mento, ska and reggae as well as imported R&B from America, something that had proved enormously popular in many former British colonies such as Jamaica, Trinidad and Barbados. Hailing from St Vincent, Jackson fronted an influential combo called F.B.I., but his first break came as a member of Batik, a group that backed visiting American soul singers like Eddie Floyd in the 1960s.

Concerts such as these were in demand due to the huge impact of the Motown and Stax revue tours in the UK. Yet prior to this, there had been a lively UK blues scene spearheaded by guitarist Alexis Korner, his zeal fired above all by Muddy Waters, whom he saw in concert in 1958. A key mentor to many fledgling players, Korner, born in London to a Greek mother and an Austrian father, founded Blues Incorporated with Cyril Davies. The band had a revolving door of personnel that welcomed various members of future rock supergroups such as the Rolling Stones and Cream, as well as progressive folk ensembles like Pentangle.

The dividing lines between blues, R&B and jazz were not so rigid then and, with Korner as a galvanising figurehead, there was an openness that led to gatherings of musicians from diverse stylistic and ethnic backgrounds. Hence a session might pair the Bajan trumpeter Harry Beckett with English guitarist Eric Clapton. In any case, it appears there was a definite 'core' vocabulary of blues chords and vocal inflections that a plethora of musicians absorbed, using American role models before attempting to define an artistic voice of their own.

Generally speaking, the evolution of any genre of music is by no means linear or clear-cut. There is usually a complex prehistory that reveals several individuals searching for a novel sound, experimenting with new and old instruments and with approaches to form, or perhaps applying the principles or lessons of another idiom to the style they are working in. Some kind of 'fusion' always unfolds.

Overall, soul music in the 1960s was about the integration of electric sounds through guitar and keyboards, more percussive, funkier inflections in both bass and drum patterns, and the use of 'hot' gospel vocals that facilitated a decisive shift away from the R&B base that had held sway in the '50s. Soul gained a harder, tougher sound.

In the UK, local musicians assiduously kept pace with this trend and a distinctly British sound emerged, gradually distilling into a tasty local brew through the intermingling of a wide range of personalities with very specific artistic and cultural identities.

So there was Graham Bond's heavy, muscular organ-guitar-horn combo; there was the grinding of two very different organs – breezy Georgie Fame and bulky Brian Auger – and there was the fiery presence of several American expatriate singers, like Geno Washington,[6] Herbie Goins and Madeleine Bell. One should perhaps also note that, with his innate, deeply rooted bluesiness, Jimi Hendrix – although drawn to the noise-heavy realm of a burgeoning rock scene – was another artist entirely relevant to the whole history of British R&B.

Last but not least, there was the contribution of African and Caribbean immigrants who formed bands such as The Equals, The Funkees and Matata, all of which were adding new inflections, rhythmically and vocally, to a live R&B circuit that also boasted impressive acts such as Zoot Money.

London venues that have since become storied – chief among them The Half Moon, Upstairs at Ronnie Scott's and the Q Club – were some of the key locations for the development of British soul, in so far as they provided a platform for certain of these myriad forces to interact.

What really counted was the sense of stylistic possibility and mutability in the music of many of those mentioned above. The wide range of elements bubbling away in the communal melting pot – a term that is far from clichéd in this instance – meant these musicians could shift from rocky soul to soulful rock to Latin soul or jazzy soul at will.

Listening to the music of a band like Gonzalez, for example, one hears a clear desire to exert good musicianship and launch into fairly lengthy improvisations and all-instrumental pieces, as well as to write more radio-friendly tunes. Because they were listening to R&B, Gonzalez didn't stop listening to jazz, Brazilian or Cuban music. Their work makes that plain.

It should also be pointed out that there was a much higher proportion of multiracial bands on the London scene than was the case in America at the time. This alliance of black and white musicians in UK soul also distinguished the genre quite substantially from the largely monoracial ensembles in jazz and rock.

Message in the music

However, the formation of an all-black band like Cymande in the late 1960s was hugely significant because it brought to bear on British soul possibly its boldest Caribbean character, something indicative of the greater cultural impact West Indian migrants would have on mainstream British society in years to come. Symbolising this clearly was Cymande's use of creolised English – the very name of the group can be heard as a variation on the patois 'see man deh' or 'see man dem' – in their song titles. This artistic decision has to be seen as audacious when one considers that black artists and the black community in general were ridiculed for the idiosyncrasies of their language on prime-time television as well as in the public domain, be it the classroom, the high street or the shop floor.

Passages of spoken word and chanted vocals on the three albums Cymande recorded in the early 1970s – their eponymous debut, *Second Time Around* and *Promised Heights* – made it clear the group were West Indian and that their identity in the fullest sense, right down to their speech rhythms and vocabulary, was not about to be played down.

Comprising musicians from Guyana, St Vincent and Jamaica who assembled in Brixton, South London and started to jam in basements, Cymande had a line-up mirroring that of contemporaneous American funk ensembles such as Kool & The Gang, War and Mandrill, in so far as they used a rhythm section, percussion, horns and vocals.

Among their key influences were Rahsaan Roland Kirk's post-modern jazz, Miles Davis's 'fusion' and James Brown's funk, and faith in these pathfinders largely explained their blend of extended solos and tight groove playing. Into this pot were thrown Caribbean idioms like calypso and mento, prompting the group to either weave percussive lines around R&B licks or to alternate straight soul tunes with songs that had a West Indian folk flavour. Several tracks were stripped right down to a series of heady vocal chants over barrages of rolling hand drums.

Part of the appeal of Cymande's music to funk fans was its raw, rugged quality, something that was heightened by the absence of a piano in the rhythm section – a key parallel to the music of James Brown. But above all, there was a hazy, floating quality in some of their rhythmic execution not that far from the music of Bob Marley. So what Cymande effectively did was to make soul music that managed to have a similar *feel* to reggae without being reggae *per se*.

Furthermore, in their percussionist Pablo Gonsales, Cymande had a musician who had adopted the Rastafarian faith and whose input into the lyrical and philosophical content of the band was substantial. Hence the politicised African-Caribbean character of the group was far from covert. It was obtrusive, despite Cymande being first and foremost exponents of soul music, an African American genre.

Although Caribbean immigrants in Britain listened to a wide range of black music, there were marked boundaries between the reggae and soul scenes. At social functions where one idiom was championed, chances are that the other might not be welcome, and often soul was perceived as much less 'manly' and militant than reggae.

Cymande bridged the gap. '"The Message" ... that was one of the non-reggae tunes that crossed over into sound system [reggae] world', said Dennis Bovell of Cymande's first single from 1971 when I interviewed him in 2000.[7] Leader of the roots reggae band Matumbi and producer of dub poet Linton Kwesi Johnson, Bovell was perfectly placed to see the impact of the group. He was a vital force in British reggae at the time and knew what songs earned approval at West Indian dances where 'sound systems', with their turntables and selectors spinning a deluge of the latest 'pre-release' singles shipped 'from yard', held sway.

Bovell is also a pivotal character for his versatility. Not only did he collaborate with post-punk outfits like The Pop Group but he also contributed to 'lovers rock', a mid-1970s strain of British reggae whose overtly romantic inclinations were directly inspired by both American soul and Jamaican pop. Janet Kay's 1979 hit 'Silly Games', a song Bovell produced, was obviously informed by the artfully told tales of heartache that were the trademark of American soul labels like Philadelphia International, even though it was set to an evanescent reggae pulse.

Lovers rock was significant because it showed a changing face of black British culture, in which reggae and R&B could collide in interesting ways. Although not soul, the resulting music exuded soulfulness. Furthermore, it showed an impressive musical discipline that made it a formative language, a useful staging post for future generations of soul singers like Caron Wheeler and for jazz musicians like Cleveland Watkiss and Steve Williamson.

Things moved on, in any case. Other new voices made themselves heard. Indeed, a key point to bear in mind is that any music genre or scene needs a change of generation to ensure continued vitality as well as a degree of evolution. A particular year group of musicians cannot go on forever and, more pertinently, its successors will have a different outlook, energy and possibly culture from those who inspired them.

The new crop may draw on different music as their formative influences. They may have distinct shibboleths and ways of expressing themselves. And above all, they may feel they have an identity of their own. All these factors come into play with the acts that were mainly classed as 'Brit funk' in the late 1970s: Hi-Tension, Incognito, Light Of The World.[8] These musicians were not Caribbean immigrants but were mostly the sons of Caribbean immigrants, born and bred on Her Majesty's soil. So they were specifically black Britons rather than blacks resident in Britain. This detail is not at all anodyne.

To a large extent, it could be said that these acts had a less overtly West Indian slant than their immediate predecessors. That is an inevitable and logical state of affairs, as the new crop of musicians were as much prone to the generation gap and a certain culture clash as their white peers who were not essentially drawn to the music of their parents. There is perhaps more of an expectation for ethnic-minority artists in the UK or America to make explicit their non-western 'backstory'. Yet it could be argued that in a truly enlightened society these artists have as much right as anybody *not* to reference that backstory if they see fit.

Exactly how this relationship is managed is complex. One thing that should be underlined is that Afro-Latin pulses were very prominent in the music of that 'second wave' of UK soul, reflecting an interest in jazz fusion, This in itself struck a chord with the Caribbean background of many of these acts' members. Percussion and horns were also a major part of their sound. What the music conveyed above all else was a sense that it *could* take a turn towards 'island sensibilities' at any given moment. Central Line's 'Lovely Day' did just that in fine style.[9]

Ocean eleven

There were also several very talented white musicians working in soul who exported their skills to America, none more so than pianist-songwriter Rod Temperton, a member of floor-filling funkateers Heatwave who also penned

'Off The Wall' and 'Rock With You', arguably two of Michael Jackson's best songs.

Of perhaps greater significance, though, was the keyboard player and synthesizer specialist Malcolm Cecil. This largely unheralded figure has pursued one of the most interesting career paths of any figure in pop or art music in recent times, debuting as a double bassist with dance bands before joining a bebop jazz quartet – the EmCee Four, led by pianist Mike Carr – in Newcastle in 1959. Carr's older brother, the trumpeter Ian, would later join, making the EmCee Four the EmCee Five.[10] Cecil eventually left and became the house bassist at Ronnie Scott's club in London, working with Americans like Sonny Rollins before co-founding the beguilingly abstract electronics duo Tonto's Expanding Headband.

His ability to programme keyboards and his mixing and engineering skills attracted the attention of first Stevie Wonder, with whom Cecil worked extensively in the 1970s, and then Gil Scott-Heron, a number of whose albums he produced for Arista Records. Cecil's wide-ranging musical knowledge, curiosity for new sounds and deep roots in jazz culture made him an obvious creative foil for singers of this stature.

Wonder and Scott-Heron represent in no uncertain terms soul music that is closely wedded to jazz, given its structural sophistication and the high standard of playing in the bands both men led. Yet it should not be forgotten that their work had such wide appeal because they managed to retain pop sensibilities: a certain simplicity of form and, certainly in Wonder's case, a deeply communicative sense of melody, all of which made these artists part of a tradition of great songwriting that would include Broadway traditions as much as folk or church music.

Soul is a form of pop. Pop is not necessarily soul, or indeed soulful. Yet the two genres are bound by the principles of melody, narrative and a desire to communicate – a double-edged sword, in so far as it yields themes that can be tawdry if their catchiness appears too calculated, or emotive if the developmental arc has guile and grace.

With that in mind, it should be noted that there have been some very good musicians who have trodden the line between soul and pop, leaning arguably more towards the commercial-artistic rather than the commercial-commercial. The fact that these musicians make radio-friendly fare on occasion should not detract from their overriding artistry.

Guyanese singer Eddy Grant, whose long history runs from 1960s R&B combo The Equals to his easy-on-the-ear reggae efforts in the '80s, is one example and Trinidad-born Billy Ocean, who once worked as a tailor in London's Saville Row, is another. Ocean typifies an artist who was able to build an audience through appearances at the capital's clubs, and then translate that popularity into commercial success by way of well-written and -performed songs that were melodically rich. Ocean notched up a string of hits in the '70s and '80s, several of which – such as 'Love Really Hurts Without

You' – betrayed the clear influence of a classic Motown sound, the swinging arrangement recalling Marvin Gaye's 'How Sweet It Is To Be Loved By You'. That may have given some ammunition to critics intent on deriding UK soul as a lesser derivative of 'the real thing' born on the other side of the Atlantic.

The charge would be excessively harsh. First, Ocean has a unique voice. It is soulful but not so gospel-oriented. He has impressive subtlety in his middle range, uses his low range sparingly and his high range gymnastically. Above all, Ocean retains a subtle Trinidadian tinge in his inflections, making it clear that a kind of transcultural hue has permeated his timbre.

Second, there has not been a total marginalisation of West Indian music in Ocean's work. At times this is rhythmically implicit, at times explicit. It functions really as one of several creative elements available to him, as are R&B and jazz. 1982's 'Caribbean Queen' may represent the pop slant on these roots but 1979's 'Calypso Funkin'', decisively powered by steel pan virtuoso Annise Hadeed, brings an altogether more ambitious spark to the table. The result is robust, rampaging 'island' funk.

Dred system

British soul music doesn't always need these resonances to be interesting. London's Loose Ends and Manchester's 52nd Street made a significant step forward for the genre in the mid-1980s by engaging creatively with electronics and the latest production techniques, while retaining good compositional skills, a degree of jazz finesse and strong vocal arrangements. Those elements are just as important.

Yet there is no denying that manifestations of a changing black British identity, something with distinct Caribbean-inflected speech patterns and vocabulary as well as a unique sartorial style, impacted on soul music during the Thatcher years. Loose Ends set the wheels in motion with Afrocentric threads and Jamaican patois like 'broadhead', while Soul II Soul ostentatiously took things to the next level a few years later.

Soul II Soul are quintessential figures in British black popular music because they managed to capture and crystallise something that went far beyond song and dance. They became a leitmotiv for a confident, evolving black British identity, sufficiently self-possessed to fuse the American soul-funk model of the group with the West Indian template of the 'sound system': a collective of singers, players, producers, DJs and dancers that could function as effectively in a club, spinning records, as it could on stage, performing as a full band.

Jazzie B, the fulcrum of the unit, was a DJ from North London who had been a major part of the city's club scene, playing at parties along with the likes of Norman Jay to develop a 'rare groove' policy – reviving the early 1970s funk of James Brown, Curtis Mayfield and Cymande among others – that would play a crucial role in educating listeners and exposing the source of the 'breakbeats' that were largely shaping hip hop.

This culture of record collecting had been key to both the soul and reggae scenes. To a large extent, Jazzie B stood as a bridge between the two, understanding something of the aesthetics both of funk grooves and dub production. As such, Soul II Soul embodied a running dialogue across the range of idioms to be found in black America and the black Caribbean.

Language was key too. Soul II Soul called themselves the 'Funki Dreds', in reference to a unique tonsorial style – fashion being another strong element in the mix. And while the band possessed in Caron Wheeler one of the great singers of the decade, a supreme presence on the 1989 number one 'Back To Life', Jazzie B's spoken-word interventions on a piece like 'Jazzie's Groove' greatly defined the Soul II Soul aesthetic, because he had an audible Black British resonance in his voice. He did not shirk from using terms like 'sound system', one of many elements of the Jamaican vocabulary that was entering the lexicon of the mainstream.

Gradually coming to the fore, then, was a localisation of the UK soul identity that highlighted the cultural realities of a changing society. Or rather, there was an assertion of the right to reflect one's origins, be they African or Caribbean, when appropriate for a given composition.

Flower child

Echoes of this standpoint have reverberated in Soul II Soul's successors. At times they are subtle but perhaps the more effective for it. They may manifest as a creolised title – such as Young Disciples calling a 1991 piece 'Mek It Funki' as opposed to 'Make It Funky' – or in the use of creolised English within a stanza otherwise constructed in standard English. Omar Lye-Fook did this superbly when he guested on Galliano's 'Golden Flower', released a year after the Disciples song. In the second verse, Omar clearly slips into patois – 'chil'ren cyaan find no bed' – and there is a strong tinge of Jamaica oral culture.

Young Disciples and Galliano were two of the groups that came to prominence in Britain in the early 1990s under the banner of 'acid jazz'. Under the impulse of DJs such as Chris Bangs and Gilles Peterson, this was a short-lived London scene that revived old-school funk in which wah-wah guitars, Hammond organ and horn sections took pride of place. The trend stood largely in opposition to an increasingly prevalent template in America whereby a keyboard player-producer would lay down backing tracks for singers. Acid jazz, however, kept its faith in 'old' instruments, although some of its exponents such as Young Disciples did liberally deploy samples and beats in conjunction with real-time playing.

As was argued in the previous chapter, the tension between these two models has been a key element in the history of soul music. The resurgence of bands that presented half a dozen personnel on stage, creating a degree of interaction between vocalists and soloists, was an exciting counterweight to the ongoing fascination black pop had with electronics, especially in the new sampling culture of hip hop.

Acts like Young Disciples, The Sindecut and Galliano conjoined rappers, singers and a live band – in the case of the latter a very competent rhythm section that still backs visiting American jazz players to this day. This combination said much about the post-modernism that was instrumental in shaping British black music, leading to novel collisions of sub-genres and a range of possible approaches to writing, performance and production.

Despite initial media interest, acid jazz – which really denoted funk rather than jazz – didn't hold its own in the marketplace. The only group that has survived as a more of less viable commercial entity today is The Brand New Heavies, primarily because they are a good live act, have employed quality vocalists and have also written enduring songs.

Moreover, The Brand New Heavies had an influence on many of the American 'neo soul' artists during the mid-1990s.

Since that time, British soul has proved itself diverse in content and character. And to a certain extent, it is Omar Lye-Fook who remains the strongest symbol of that pluralism, his classical training, strong Afro-Latin sensibility and grip on the flurry of urban life, its tough, hard 'street beat', creating music of considerable richness.

Many others have done good work, though. Don-E, Ola Onabule, Alyson Evelyn, Shaun Escoffery, Noel McKoy, Mica Paris and Paul Johnson are just a few of the excellent vocalists whose careers have not reached the commercial heights commensurate with their talent. One might legitimately question whether the British music industry has a problem with the very idea of an older black artist – the above-mentioned are all now in their late thirties if not early forties – making a form of pop that is not an obvious draw for the pre-teen demographic crucial to the urban scene.

One of the great tragedies to befall British soul in the last decade was the death of singer/multi-instrumentalist Lynden David Hall. Having emerged to justifiable excitement in the late 1990s with the album *Medicine 4 My Pain*, he passed away in 2006 after succumbing to a form of cancer called Hodgkin's lymphoma. Hall was just thirty-one years old.

British soul in 2012 feels like something of a cottage industry, in which a handful of artists are chipping away at ever-diminishing returns while healthier investments are made in the world of pop-flavoured R&B, where the likes of Taio Cruz, Jay Sean and Estelle hold sway.

It could be argued that Omar, along with such as Jhelisa Anderson and Siji,[11] two absolutely fascinating singers who have made very creative albums in the last decade or so, are part of a coterie of UK soul artists whose *raison d'être* is to retain a classicist R&B form, all the while engaging with anything from electronica to Afrobeat to jazz.

Somewhat paradoxically, soul the music isn't at all confined to soul the genre. What I mean is that a significant number of very good performances in the idiom are possibly discounted from the modern-day canon because they are classified elsewhere in the marketplace. The obvious examples are jazz and the less well known 'broken beat', a sub-genre that emerged in London during the mid-1990s and has largely been lumped in with electronic dance music.

It is a drums-heavy genre that makes creative capital out of a deep history of West Indian as well as African rhythms. Essentially it synthesises and reconfigures these rhythms using the latest music-making software as well as analogue instruments. Its practitioners are computer-literate and fascinated by the tools that preceded computers.

To understand broken beat, one has to understand the formative influences of its prime movers such as I.G. Culture – who, although voraciously enthusiastic about new audio software, has never denied his love for the jazz of Quincy Jones, George Duke or Roy Ayers.

Yet another genre has been crucial too. Its rhythm is regular. But they use a different word for regular on a proud, loud island in the Caribbean.

17 Universoul sounds II

I've always heard reggae as Caribbean soul. (Amp Fiddler)

Salsoul is an album in which I have tried to capture the sound of Latin and soul music combined. (Joe Bataan)

Soul Makossa was not a direct reference to American soul music. Not at all. (Manu Dibango)

Caribbean soul

A West Londoner of Jamaican descent, Ian Grant uses the moniker I.G. Culture as a clear indication of the pre-eminence given to reggae, the creolisation of the word 'regular', in his creative mindset and worldview. This is a very meaningful *nom de scène*, not just for its jaunty catchiness but because Culture is the name of one of the superlative groups in the reggae genre. On a more philosophical level, it denotes an awareness of heritage that makes it a key suffix to the term 'roots'.

Under a variety of monikers such as New Sector Movement, Likwid Biskit and Quango, I.G. Culture has made an important contribution to soul music in the past fifteen years, yet he has always been vocal about the importance of Jamaican music as a core creative value. He was 'toasting' on West London sound systems when he was a callow 'yoot'.

Reggae is a music with a diverse, complex history that takes in a number of styles, from roots rock to dub and dancehall. It is largely defined by the crisp, stubbornly sharp offbeat, that, when well executed, lends a bewitching swagger to the central rhythmic thrust of a song. This sway and saunter makes the word 'rock' appropriate as a description of the sensual movement that the genre both contains and induces.

There are distinct parallels between the rhythmic identity of early Jamaican pop and of old-school 1940s American R&B. The influence of New Orleans pioneers such as Dave Bartholomew and Professor Longhair is generally acknowledged to have been decisive in creating the shuffling, slightly tipsy character of the beat in Kingston.

Louis Jordan's blues, as well as Charlie Parker's bebop jazz, also had an impact on local musicians like guitarist Ernest Ranglin who helped to fashion ska, a form dominant in the 1950s and characterised by stabbing, busy lines from a horn section and the influence of local folk rhythms that brought a lilting, breezy quality to the music.

Reggae is what happened when ska slowed down and switched from an acoustic to an electric music and absorbed some of the new energies emanating from black pop in America. It did not lose its primary rhythmic character, namely the razor-sharp offbeat, but the tough drive and constant pressure of the hard-punching 'one' of funk came into play.

With the offbeat guitar in reggae such a resonant and attention-grabbing feature of the audio landscape, it is easy to overlook the richness of many of the bass patterns. They often closely approximate some of the figures that anchor the music of James Brown, in so far as they perform a drum-like function, often busily pounding out a long line over just a few pitches. Hence funky reggae or reggaefied funk appears not so much a question of deliberate 'fusion' as the consequence of partially shared data between the two genres.

Certainly some of the bass work from brilliant Jamaican musicians like Aston 'Family Man' Barrett and Robbie Shakespeare on songs by the likes of Bob Marley and Black Uhuru in the 1970s and '80s achieves the same hard-edged hypnosis as any number of great groove combos from New Orleans, Detroit, Memphis or San Francisco.

Blues changes were still predominantly the building blocks of reggae, so this state of affairs was logical to say the least. Moreover, the relatively spare harmony and the faith in fewer chords offer another important parallel between popular music from America and the Caribbean. Rhythmic pulsation, often repeated for many bars, ran right across the two regions.

There was further complicity between reggae and soul because many of the significant vocalists in Jamaican music, led by Marley, took their cue from Americans such as Curtis Mayfield and The Impressions. The infusion of a gospel-blues sensibility, a certain delicacy in the use of falsetto tone in particular, can be discerned in fine reggae vocalists like Freddie McGregor and Gregory Isaacs. The same can be said of classic harmony groups like The Paragons or The Heptones.

Also worth considering is the long-standing tradition of reggae artists 'versioning' popular soul tunes, a very important way of maintaining a kind of informal artistic dialogue between Jamaica and America. The result is an essential contribution to the wider praxis of the remix that lies at the very heart of hip hop culture.

As roots reggae peaked creatively in the 1970s, scores of timeless songs recorded by the above and many other artists were founded on extremely focused playing of instruments that were also prevalent in African American music – namely, drums, bass guitar and guitar, as well as the all-important percussion and horns. This vast canon of tunes thus possessed a degree of either soulfulness or funkiness, without necessarily being soul or funk music *per se.*

For all its referencing of an American model, though, reggae became *something else*. The lyrical content evoked specific local politics, society and culture, there was a gradual influx of vocal inflections that were distinctly made in JA, and the music was underscored by the unique way drummers had of feeling a song's pulse. Few of their counterparts outside Jamaica could set a beat exactly as they did.

US soul musicians have occasionally drawn on reggae precisely because they want to bring a different quality to their own work, even if the 'prehistory' of this foreign idiom has roots in rhythm and blues. In some cases the results can be stilted and mismatched, but there are several compelling examples of the American–Caribbean rhythmic continuum working to very fruitful effect.

Standing tall here is The Staple Singers's 1972 song 'I'll Take You There',[1] which is nothing other than ripe, rock-steady reggae infused with a typically surging and heated vocal performance from Mavis Staples, one of the great purveyors of gospel-soul. Significantly, it mixes to the manner born with the classic Jamaican groove of 'Liquidator' by Harry J's All Stars.

'I'll Take You There' is a soul-reggae 'mash-up', the mischievous grafting of melody from one genre onto rhythm from another. Its artistic triumph is that the union appears in no way contrived, the implication being that both elements actually belong together. It moots the possibility of a music that is as much soul reggae as reggae soul.

No tune in this vein is more iconic than Stevie Wonder's 1981 hit 'Master Blaster'. But what is arguably more interesting is the coherence of Wonder's collaboration with reggae giants Third World just a year later. 'Try Jah Love (Jah Jah Love)', which Wonder wrote and produced, is a magnificent song rooted in an intensely emotive verse and chorus that are very well executed by Third World's lead vocalist Rugs Clarke. More significant, though, is that Wonder managed to write a piece which fits so well into Third World's songbook.

Massively successful in the 1980s with anthems such as 'Now That We've Found Love', Third World always had a strong disco-funk overtone in their work. It gave some of their tunes a touch more bustle than most of their Jamaican counterparts, and Wonder maintained that energy in his song through an aggressive drilling of bass and drums.

Added to that were bustling, scything piano chords that infused a raucous churchy flavour, so the physical groove became pure gospel ecstasy while the lyric consecrated 'Jah' as a salutary new faith.

What all this meant was that soul and reggae could exist and entwine in the same space if the musician in question possessed sufficient understanding of, or affinity with, both genres. Wonder's firm grasp of Afro-Cuban music, whose pulse is not entirely divorced from that of Jamaican pop, undoubtedly furthered the synthesis.

Because reggae, soul and funk are related through a common historical foundation of rhythm and blues, there is always the possibility that the peculiarities of one genre may become more explicit within another at any given moment, that a groove may appear more Caribbean or American depending on the context in which it is delivered. When a DJ drops a reggae tune, the right reggae tune, in the middle of a soul set, it can highlight the music's funk rather than expose a lack of it.

Personalities also count. Some Jamaican musicians are characteristically soulful or funky, just in the way they touch an instrument. Sometimes it takes an American musician to make that point. The meeting of Amp Fiddler,[2] the Trinidad-descended, Detroit-born keyboard player-vocalist who debuted with Funkadelic in the 80s, and Sly & Robbie, the hallowed 'riddim twins' who have played a huge role in shaping Jamaican music since the early 1970s, is instructive in this respect. Although the combo's *Inspiration Information* set, recorded in Kingston in 2008, is just a touch inconsistent melodically, it has some absolutely brilliant performances from all the players, effortlessly marking out an idiomatic space that functions as a very coherent and organic JA–USA continuum.

'They just put it down and it hit like they were from Conant Gardens where I'm from', Amp Fiddler said of Sly & Robbie. "I was like, 'damn', this is so soulful. But I've always heard reggae as Caribbean soul.'[3]

Calypso blues

Caribbean soul is a broad term. Reggae is by no means the only music the region has produced. The other significant idiom that has always maintained a relationship with soul is calypso, whose heartland is Trinidad, an island lying very close to the coast of Venezuela.

Calypso – roughly speaking, an entwining of African rhythms with Spanish and French melodies – is a genre of music with a great deal of swing in its pulse, the airy, dancing feel of the arrangements producing an entirely different sensation from the punch of a backbeat. It should come as no surprise, then, that calypso has enjoyed a long relationship with jazz.

An acoustic music in which double bass, piano and percussion define the rhythm section, calypso often has intricate horns weaving in and out of the vocal melodies. Certainly in the case of classic exponents of the genre such as Lord Kitchener and Mighty Sparrow, these horns have a fluid bounce that lend a good deal of grace to the aesthetic.

It is also important to understand that calypso performs an essential function as a vehicle for social commentary, be it of a universal or specific nature. It is a formula that can be applied to any subject and in that respect is a type of blues, an eminently adaptable outlet for feeling and meaning. There are calypsos broaching subjects as diverse as politics, sexuality and relationships.

Storytelling, the performance of tales that can veer between profound psychology and frivolous bedroom farce, is thus a dynamic common to calypso, blues and blues-derived music, be it first rhythm and blues and then soul. Certainly there is both a sonic and a lyrical kinship between these genres, in the rolling, sashaying riffs and the salty, pithy humour. More to the point are the parallels between the characters of Louis Jordan and Lord Kitchener. They both serve as symbols, signposts, vividly illuminating specific local cultures and lifestyles in the black diaspora.

Throughout the 1940s and '50s, scores of excellent calypsos were written in Trinidad and other Caribbean islands that generally reinforce these parallels. And given the huge popularity of American jazz and R&B recordings in the region, it is entirely logical that there would be echoes in its music of Jordan, Fats Domino and Cab Calloway, who successfully toured right across the Caribbean and South America in 1952.[4]

R&B changed, though. It moved from an acoustic to an electric music: soul. A new generation of Trinidadian musicians in the late 1960s chose to reflect that by creating soca – a highly significant concept and word, in that it amalgamated soul and calypso, making it clear the brief was to embrace the keyboards, synthesizers and bass guitar shaping the evolution across the sea.

Soca presents a much tougher, louder sound than calypso, and a greater degree of funkiness as a result of this rhythmic muscle. There are times, though, when it cleverly retains some of the swing of its predecessor in the character of its rhythm. There is still a bounce.

Yet soca can have a frenzied, if not slightly hyperactive, feel, ramming home the point that the music's roots foreshadowed American disco, whose fizzing hi-hat and triangle patterns can be traced back to calypso. So there has been a great infusion and hybridisation of Caribbean rhythms through US black pop.

Explaining exactly how this came about would require extensive research. But what is significant is that numerous Stateside musicians have emphasised the cross-fertilisation, none more so than Fatback drummer Bill Curtis, who cited West Indian beats as a primary source for the band's music. Listen to some of the group's early 1970s music and you clearly hear both the future of disco and the past of calypso.

Hence an exciting intersection and exchange of rhythmic information has unfolded across pop in the Americas over time. That means a single piece of music, such as 'Funky Nassau' by the stupendously groovy Bahamas combo Beginning Of The End, can be heard simultaneously as one man's funk, another's soca and another's disco.

Black British soul artists of West Indian descent have retained this sense of mutability perhaps a little more than some of their American counterparts. It is one of the marks of distinction that surfaces intermittently in their work when the creative muse calls for it. A group like Central Line is a case in point. Part of the early 1980s wave of acts that included Linx, Freez and Level 42, Central Line enjoyed minor hits with songs such as 'Walking Into Sunshine'. These were defined largely by an electronics-led sound not far removed from what was prevalent on the other side of the Atlantic, although they suffered from relatively poor sound engineering and production values.

Central Line came into their own towards the end of their existence in the late 1980s, when they wrote a quite stunning single called 'Lovely Day' that drew heavily on calypso rhythms, used a gorgeous steel-pan motif and featured some very soulful, evanescent harmonies. It remains an essential entry in the catalogue of recent black popular music recorded in the UK.

Rooted as the song is in the beat of Trinidad, it has a whirring percussive figure in its breakdown that exudes a novel pan-Caribbean flavour, the pulse hovering quite tantalisingly between calypso and salsa.

Of all the artists to have emerged in soul on both sides of the Atlantic over the last two decades, the figure who has most consistently reinforced this connection is Omar Lye-Fook, a skilled drummer-percussionist as well as a bass guitarist and keyboardist. While the music of Stevie Wonder has arguably served as the essential building block for his work, Omar has incorporated strong West Indian sensibilities extensively into his writing and arranging. They bring considerable richness to the rhythmic and metric content of many of his songs, where congas, bongos and cowbells often play prominent roles.

On occasion the source material may be Jamaican. Pieces such as 'Best By Far' and 'Revelation', a startlingly beautiful song Omar wrote for fellow British singer Vanessa Simon, are shaped decisively by a firm grasp of dub. At other times clear Cuban and Brazilian rhythms come into play. But Omar's creative peaks are perhaps those arrangements in which there is no precise cultural definition of the beat but rather a meshing of several rhythmic vocabularies.

'It's So' is one example. An immensely popular track in clubs on its release in 2007, the song has a percussive base that is stridently Cuban, its potent drums emphasised by a daring absence of bass in the verse. It then saunters into a chorus with a bold calypso resonance, the horns and bass heavily shaped by a swing pulse that reiterates the close interaction between jazz and calypso in the latter's early history. The result is a piece of bracing, very danceable soul music that is resolutely Caribbean. Others might well call it Latin music.

Cha cha king

Latin music principally denotes a wealth of Cuban, Puerto Rican and Brazilian idioms, anything from son and bomba to samba and bossa nova, as well as a whole host of very specific sub-genres or derivatives thereof, amounting to an inordinately rich repository of sounds.

As was argued earlier in this book, Latin music has been a common denominator between soul, or rather rhythm and blues, and jazz since the 1940s. And if great importance is attached to the principle of the 'Spanish tinge' in the art strand of African American music, then it should not be forgotten that there is a loose parallel in the 'south of the border' character that has often surfaced in its populist cousin.

New Orleans R&B, for example, invariably had a strong rumba sensibility, which resonated on through the genre in the decades that followed. And certainly a singer like Bo Diddley, even though he recorded for the most part in Chicago, retained a similar slant in his work. In fact, Diddley made the maracas an essential fulcrum of many of the great songs he wrote in the 1950s.

Furthermore, the craze for mambo and cha-cha-chá, the music and dances that had swept America during the previous decade, added to the interest in non-western rhythms that may have shaped the thinking of R&B players or arrangers, as it did in jazz. The fact that several musicians were moving between both idioms increased the interaction.

How a song comes to life can be an unpredictable process. Some singers invariably recount how melodies just pop into their heads, whether they are sleeping or travelling by train, plane or automobile. Others claim that tunes are moulded by the casual exploration of a certain chord sequence, an interval or a scale.

Because Latin rhythms were in 'circulation', both through their presence in New Orleans pop and their deployment in jazz – which R&B musicians were closer to in the 1950s – it was inevitable they would add to the information that could be drawn on in the songwriting process. Latin rhythms were part of the soul artist's creative arsenal.

Images matter here. When defining R&B, one seldom considers its non-western content – possibly because, from a cultural-political point of view, it is much easier to view the genre as a purely African American phenomenon rather than as a pan-American idiom into which a vast number of rhythmic influences have flowed over the decades.

Yet the fact of the matter is that Ben E. King's 1960 masterpiece 'Stand By Me' is nothing other than a cha-cha-chá, or strongly implies the genre. Were the scraper a touch louder and a curt, clipped horn line added, this would be clear. But even without these elements, the Latin rhythmic root of the piece is undeniable.

Songs such as this were by no means isolated cases, and the appearance of Cuban and South American percussive figures in R&B and then soul was not in itself a new development within a stylistic continuum. The interesting question was how explicit or implicit these non-western musical data were going to be, with how much subtlety they would be absorbed into an orchestral form that was making highly creative use of strings, horns, vocals and an electric rhythm section.

Answers vary according to the particular artist, but it's not really an either/or scenario. Latin rhythms have been both explicit and implicit in the history of soul and funk, and the music's prime movers have realised it is precisely the integration of a Cuban or Brazilian pulse alongside other idioms, be they rock, folk or African music, that can render their work interesting when a mosaic of styles emerges.

Stevie Wonder and Earth, Wind & Fire spring to mind here.[5] Both have set great store by either son or samba rhythms in the songs they have written. But these rhythms have not dominated their aesthetic, so that the input of other elements – of which there are many – becomes marginal. Wonder can be heard simultaneously as a Latin singer-player and a soul singer-player on a number of superb performances. The obvious example is 'Don't You Worry 'Bout A Thing'.

Young, gifted & brown

As Wonder was enjoying his breakthrough hit in 1963 with 'Fingertips', a piece of instrumental son with burning blues harmonica that resoundingly illustrates the above point, several New York musicians of either Puerto Rican or Cuban parentage – residents of the fabled 'Spanish Harlem' area, with its substantial immigrant community from those countries – started to incorporate R&B horns and English-language lyrics into songs with a mambo or son rhythmic architecture.

Exemplified by big hits such as Ray Barretto's 'El Watusi' and Joe Cuba's 'Bang! Bang!', this new 'Latin soul' sound certainly had a distinctive flavor, primarily because the vocals were conveyed in audible Spanish accents and were clearly not African American. So these tracks were a statement of identity for a relatively new community that was growing up in a bilingual and bicultural world, where the music of Ray Charles and James Brown registered alongside that of Tito Puente and Celia Cruz.

African Americans, Cuban Americans and Puerto Rican Americans were all ethnic minorities, struggling for the enforcement of civil rights, and it is feasible there was solidarity in their common resistance to a hostile majority that would have led these groups to embrace each other's culture. But that point would need a wealth of watertight and substantial sociological research to gain credence.

What can be noted, however, is that a singer such as Joe Bataan, an Eastside Harlemite who was half-black and half-Filipino, made his breakthrough with singles like 'Subway Joe' because of their popularity on R&B radio stations with largely African American listeners. As such, Bataan came to encapsulate a certain cultural duality by shuttling seamlessly between anglophone and Hispanic songs, several of which were reprises of big soul tunes by the leading vocalists of the day.

To a large extent, Bataan is a symbol of New York's hugely exciting openness and of the city's evolutionary musical identity. He initially made Latin soul tunes, some of which were very jazz-inflected. But Bataan would go on to record for Fania, the seminal record label that documented the birth of salsa, a genre blending sharp, stinging son rhythms with full-blooded vocals and brass lines that often swung hard.

Significantly, the great percussionist Ray Barretto, another original exponent of Latin soul, also signed with the label. Fania was very much a manifestation of a new creativity and self-assertion in Spanish Harlem, drawing liberally on funk, rock and jazz to produce a sprawling, consistently high-quality catalogue that was highly relevant to the wider history of black popular music. Many called it 'the Latin Motown'.

Such parallels were not meaningless. Great musicianship, an adventurous approach to instrumentation and a desire to embrace new technology, particularly keyboards such as the electric piano, meant the label struck a boldly progressive stance, marking it out as an expression of New York as a quite unique cultural melting pot.

In any case, it is apparent that artists like Bataan engaged with African American culture while staying true to their Latin roots, proving that the empowering ideal of the lyric 'Young, gifted and black' could find a coherent echo in the no less uplifting premise of 'Young, gifted and brown'. Nineteen seventy-six's *Salsoul*, one of Bataan's best ever albums, made clear this intention to uphold some form of idiomatic plurality. '*Salsoul* is an album in which I have tried to capture the sound of Latin and soul music combined', he said in the record's liner notes.[6]

Salsoul was the inaugural release of the highly influential label of the same name, which would enjoy much success with a funky disco sound that drew extensively on Latin rhythms throughout the 1970s and early '80s. The extended and often very rhythmically aggressive breakdowns afforded by the twelve-inch single format used for many releases found favour with African Americans and immigrant communities from all over the Caribbean, whether the island was Cuba, Puerto Rico or Trinidad.

Essentially, Salsoul's catalogue emphasised that disco was a catch all-term which could encompass as much a rhythm and blues as an Afro-Caribbean heritage, with a wealth of push and pull between the two genres. The relationship was typified by a piece such as 'Jingo' by Candido, the master conguero from Havana who had played with Charles Mingus and several other jazz legends back in the 1950s.

Slotting this music into too precise a category would be misleading, if not pointless. For if this was disco, it was not that far removed from the music of a number of funk bands of the day whose rhythmic sensibilities were Latin and who often engaged in extended percussive riots. An explosion of hand drums would take the music very close to the frenzied barrage of bongos that defined Candido's piece. In other words, Cuban and African American artists could reach similar musical conclusions, even though their point of departure had been very different.

Hence any debate on the essential meaning of the term 'Latin soul' has to take into account the far-reaching historical connectedness of the elements in question. Latin rhythms were *inside* soul before Latin soul was coined as a sub-genre. Even after the Barretto/Bataan wave of the 1960s ran its course, Latin rhythms could still be found within soul and funk. The emblematic exponents were the likes of War and Mandrill, both of which functioned as effectively as Latin jazz ensembles as they did as straight R&B bands.

Also worthy of note is the contribution of superlative freelance non-American and Caribbean-descended percussionists to American soul in the 1970s and '80s, through their absolutely prolific studio work. From Trinidad came Ralph McDonald, from Puerto Rico Lenny Castro and from Brazil Paulinho Da Costa.[7] Between them, they energised literally hundreds of sessions for all of the A-list singers in black music, jazz as well as soul. Through their great musicality and authentic knowledge of a wide range of ancestral and folkloric instruments, these musicians were able to enrich the R&B lexicon decisively with rhythmic and tonal detail.

Despite the influx of drum machines and programmes into soul during the last two decades, Latin grooves still permeate the music, whether played live or sequenced on a keyboard. And it is precisely the conjunction of these two approaches that makes a black British idiom such as broken beat so exciting both to listen and dance to.

Music from Cuba, Puerto Rico and Brazil remains immensely relevant to black pop because it offers metrical and textural options that the music has always thrived on. When a group switches from a funk groove to a Latin rhythm, or proceeds to negotiate an undefined space between the two, the effect on the listener can be enormous. The character of the beat is shifting, the narrative of the sound deftly evolving.

This rhythmic esperanto is as stimulating as the moment when a Latin soul singer twirls his or her tongue around English and then Spanish – or, in a flicker of inspiration, around an especial form of 'Spanglish' all of their own making.

Speak Lo

Musicians using a foreign language can be immensely charming.

Nat 'King' Cole, for one, lost none of his suave manner when singing in the language of Cervantes, Marquez *et al.*, and there are many examples (notably Stevie Wonder) of other vocalists doing the same.

Personality, as well as linguistic skills, is what counts here. If a musician has a degree of gravitas in his voice and persona, he can sound as much a leader of men as musicians in any tongue.

And so we come to Manu Dibango in concert in 1974, the year when Wonder was redefining soul music with Latin rhythms and electronics aplenty. With characteristic authority, Dibango addressed the crowd at the Coliseo Roberto Clemente in San Juan, Puerto Rico in duala and then Spanish, his 'buenos noches' conspicuously accented. The Cameroonian, smooth bald head shining like Isaac Hayes's, then proceeded to draw a distinctively rasping, guttural sound from his tenor saxophone as he performed his own 'Soul Makossa', while a battery of congas, bongos, timbales and cowbells, rhythm and horns, rang out around him. All this was supplied by the Fania All Stars, which counted Ray Barretto, Larry Harlow and Celia Cruz among a large cast spread out across the stage, like a jazz big band without uniforms or music stands.

Dibango's appearance at this historic concert was important because it confirmed his international status. 'Soul Makossa' had been a worldwide hit two years previously, finding favour in America as well as Europe. Its tightly coiled bassline, strident hand drums and rugged, raucous, pneumatic horn melody seemed to epitomise a union of African folk and US R&B that was dizzyingly rhythmic, robustly funky. It kicked hard.

This was just one among hundreds of bracingly danceable pieces of groove music recorded between the late 1960s and early '70s across the African continent, from Kenya and Ethiopia to Ghana, Benin and Nigeria. Many of these tunes were never released beyond their local borders and are only now coming to light in the West through the extensive research of journalists, broadcasters or independent producers.

Some artists broke though internationally, though. Along with Dibango came South Africa's Hugh Masekela and Nigeria's Fela Anikulapo Kuti, whose outlandish charisma, highly subversive and uncompromising political stance, and sprawling *oeuvre* make him one of the essential characters as well as artists of any twentieth-century musical history.

Masekela is perhaps best known as both a jazz and an Afro-pop artist, primarily because of his skill as a trumpeter/flugelhorn player as well as his vocal performances on songs that often use South African township idioms like marabi and kwela. However, rhythm and blues, funk and rock have also been major weapons in his musical arsenal and it should not be forgotten that, when in exile in America during the 1970s, Masekela spent a lot of time hanging out with the likes of Stephen Stills of Crosby, Stills & Nash fame. Whether or not he was consciously looking to incorporate a funk-rock element into some of his work to achieve greater commercial success is a moot point. But if you listen to a piece such as Masekela's 1984 anthem 'Don't Go Lose It Baby', you can hear a blend of African and funk rhythms that is anything but contrived and admirably presages certain types of 1990s house music.

Masekela, Dibango and Kuti serve, to a large degree, as emblems for any discussion on the possibility of an African form of R&B. Their influence was pervasive throughout the continent and their respective works, though different in many respects, were bound by moments of extreme polyrhythmic intricacy – bordering on hypnosis – and by a hardness in the pulse, to the extent that they lean much more towards Afro-funk than Afro-soul.

Listening to pieces such as Dibango's 'Weya' and Kuti's 'Roforofo Fight' makes it clear that percussive phrasing, sometimes expressed in stark, shuddering staccato lines, is an organising principle in every area of the music, from drums and bass to horns and vocals. Every component of the overall sound is emboldened and hyper, the guitars constantly wrangling, the wood block relentlessly clacking.

Funk is everywhere in the music. Yet to claim that what these artists were doing was 'fusing' African music with that of James Brown *et al.* is to simplify their education and evolution. For both Dibango and Kuti, jazz was an essential part of their formative musical culture – perhaps more so for Dibango, who remains a soloist of considerable stature. And it is the complex relationship between improvisation, ambitious, at times symphonic, arrangements, and the dynamics of local genres such as makossa and hi-life, that brought great richness to the work of each.

Dibango cut his teeth in clubs in Brussels during the 1950s, while Kuti studied music in London and between July 1969 and March 1970 toured America, where he would have had ample opportunity to imbibe the music of Brown and Sly Stone. Resonances of both these artists are discernible to varying degrees in Dibango's own *oeuvre*. However, the artistic triumph of his work is that it transcends a fusion of motherland and diaspora sounds, and remains resolutely African, showing the relevance of the continent's vast rhythmic resources, scales and modes to any form of western funk.

Africa's relationship with American soul cannot be reduced to one artist. And if Fela Anikulapo Kuti is a rightful symbol of cast-iron success in creating an aesthetic that is incontrovertibly local, even though it has been partially shaped by external elements – a kind of Made In Lagos with hints of Rolled In London and Smoked in L.A. – then other players did go USA all the way. They had every right to do so.

For example, many Soweto musicians like Sipho Mabuse fell under the spell of Stax artists in the 60s,[8] and formed groups inspired by the prime movers of that label, because – and this is a crucial political point – they could not *relate* to local mbaqanga styles, a state of affairs that points to a generation gap or cultural divide of some kind. This mirrors the refusal of young Trinidadian soca exponents to play classic calypsos, to the extent that some went as far as to heap ridicule on the most popular 'old-time' tunes, such as 'Yellow Bird'.

All this means the very notion of African soul is a pluralistic one that encompasses a wide range of models, from artists exposing the funk latent in local rhythms to those who chose a more explicit American template. Furthermore, there were groups that could shuttle around the two possibilities or find some space in between. Osibisa, whose hi-life base often slid into rock as well as jazz, were proof positive of a thrilling multifaceted strain in African music.

Formed in London in the late 1960s, they were one of the great examples of resoundingly multicultural, stylistically open music made in Britain.

Comprising African and Caribbean musicians, Osibisa developed a signature sound with a highly percussive foundation, to which were added aggressive funky basslines, rock-edged guitar and swinging horns. Although their music was highly pluralistic, Osibisa were a band nonetheless defined by Africanness – from their flowing dashikis to their choice of name, which few British DJs ever pronounced correctly and which actually derives from the Fante word for hi-life: 'osibisaba'.

Language remained a key issue for artists of Osibisa's generation because it automatically set them apart from mainstream Western pop artists. Fela Kuti's decision to sing in pidgin English was hugely important in creating an unapologetic mark of distinction, far removed from a Western soul vernacular and to a large extent symbolising self-empowerment. It also reinforced Kuti's rejection of terms like 'Afro-funk' or 'Afro-soul' in favour of his own coinage, 'Afrobeat'.

Then again, when Africans do use the s-word, it might be rash to assume they are automatically invoking Otis, Aretha, JB *et al.*

'You know, 'Soul Makossa' was *not* a direct reference to American soul music,' Manu Dibango told me in London in 2008. 'Not at all. It's about a *new* take on makossa rhythms. I was after the soul of the makossa.'[9]

This anecdote is noteworthy because it reflects an artist's complexity of thinking. It also exposes how susceptible music is to misinterpretation based on our own preconceptions of words equated with particular categories. Soul does define a genre but that doesn't mean the use of the word inevitably signals a kinship with the music, even if the artist in question has his funk down pat. The dialectic is not a simple one.

Hence one has to recognise that, among the plethora of African groups that dubbed themselves 'Black Soul' and variations thereof in the 1970s, some but not all were explicitly adopting an American model. For example, South African group The Soul Brothers claimed the s-word on their own terms, playing local mbaqanga even though a Western-centric response to their name raises expectations of sonic echoes from Stax.

Conversely, an absence of words like soul doesn't mean the music isn't drawing on its guiding principles or achieving the same artistic effect. With that in mind, it is important to realise that a number of African musicians – both singers and players – making music today, decades after the first flowerings of Fela and Dibango, have as firm a grasp of James Brown's lexicon as any of their American counterparts. The obvious example is Senegalese singer Cheikh Lo. He has turned in some of the funkiest gigs I've ever seen.

Perhaps the reason this is overlooked is because Lo is classified first and foremost as a World Music artist and largely partitioned away from soul in the marketplace, possibly because he is deemed too exotic or incomprehensible for an audience inured to anglophone lyrics.

Then again, promoters, broadcasters and radio programmers have to ask themselves not just whether audiences reared on the English colloquialisms of James Brown could relate to Lo's observations in Wolof, but whether they could tune into his rhythmic sensibilities. I think there may be many soul fans who could easily feel Lo's music, especially given the input of saxophonist/horn arranger Pee Wee Ellis, a key contributor to the *oeuvre* of a certain James Brown.

That said, World Music audiences are denied a great deal of percussive electronic music being made in America, since it is crafted largely on machines and the World Music genre sets great store by 'traditional', largely acoustic instruments. It is ironic, because some of this electronic music is very African in its rhythmic identity and soulful in its vocal content – although that may not be what most people associate with the word 'house'.

18 Soulful house, techno soul, hip hop soul

The word House should be put on a block in the Grand Canyon, they should cover it up with cement and then explode it!   (Peven Everett)

Dance … dance, dance, dance …

House is indeed an uninspiring, vibe-less word. Make your nature rise it does not. Jazz once connoted sex. Salsa, literally and figuratively, is hot sauce. Soul is an ingenious use of metaphysics. Next to these terms, 'house' suffers, its blandness undeniable as it refers to accommodation, living space, a dwelling, something functional and physical rather than an element of culture, cuisine or a belief system.

It is quite simply the where you live to the how you live of jazz, salsa or soul.

Granted, that is what house music sounds like, what it evokes. But it's not quite what house means, for there is a history in the word that is actually intriguing. House is, according to some, a reference to Warehouse, the Chicago club that was a seminal venue in the music's genesis during the late 1970s. Others argue, though, that the word essentially evokes the home-made nature of the genre, one in which autonomous producers or DJ-programmers as opposed to a group of players are the *modus operandi*.

Musically, house has one of the most distinctive identities in modern popular genres. It is essentially a bass drum forcefully marking every beat of a fast 4/4 pulse, over which hiss and snap sharp, open hi-hats, usually in eighth notes and often more prominent in the mix than the snare, which is mostly used on the second and fourth beats.

Because this core vocabulary is programmed as opposed to played live, there is a perceptible rigidity in the music's pulse, and when the basic formula is applied with little imagination, the results can be tedious to say the least. But the history of house includes many skilful producers who have constructed drumming patterns that bring a degree of complexity to the template. More to the point, they have also used percussion extensively in their arrangements, the result being a decidedly rousing and occasionally more sensual sound.

Predominantly a twelve-inch single rather than an album genre, house often features extended breakdowns in which lengthy passages of hand drums induce the same tranced feeling that some of the great Cuban congueros or Senegalese djembe players can achieve in their solos.

Masters At Work, Osunlade, Blaze and Joaquin 'Joe' Claussell are just a few of the excellent producers who have made this a key part of their aesthetic. What may be of some significance is the contribution made to their body of work by percussionists who have played at the highest creative level either in Latin American folkloric music or in jazz. Notable examples are Luisito Quintero, Daniel Moreno and Mino Cinelu, the Martinique-born player who was a part of Miles Davis bands in the 1980s.

Percussion is not the only live input into house, and the use of session musicians who play anything from bass and guitar to keyboards and horns has also enabled the music to gain a certain textural richness. A key point is that these musicians are often given space to improvise since, generally speaking, house tracks last between five and ten minutes. With contemporary R&B and hip hop largely eschewing any instrumental showcases in their slavish observation of a three-minute format, this means house is one area of black pop in which solos aren't strangled at birth. That's essential. It maintains an umbilical cord to jazz.

House history is diverse. While the late-1980s wave of acid and 'jack trax' marked the hegemony of 808 drum machines, bleeps and blips, the music's roots ran deep into '70s disco – important, because that was an idiom with a plurality of form.

Four-to-the-floor kick drums and strident percussion were its salient characteristics but disco leant equally towards electronic backdrops and orchestral settings, in which large horn and string sections were deployed to give the music a certain richness in its sound palette and a sense of epic scale rivalling that of classical music.

Labels such as Salsoul and TSOP, with their fine 'house' bands and oft-deployed orchestras backing very good singers, represented the high watermarks of this model, while groups like Chic were instrumental in steering funk towards a melodically rich, texturally delicate palette on monster hits such as 'Good Times', 'Le Freak' and 'Dance, Dance, Dance'.

Disco referred first and foremost to a place, a location – the discotheque – rather than any specific musical style. When record labels dubbed a song a 'disco hit', that didn't necessarily mean the music *was* disco, but rather that it had been able to fill floors *in* a disco. A key case in point was War's 'Galaxy', which was aggressively marketed using those very terms, even though it was a quite glorious piece of pneumatic, Latin-tinged funk.

Disco is thus a relatively vague, imprecise term, as genres can be in general. Some of the juggernaut chart hits characterised as disco were not at all comparable, in terms of invention with the beat and funky ingenuity, to the music of bands like War or, above all, Chic, which clearly had the creativity to match their popularity. Their music was work of enormous detail.

There was a marked difference between the lyrically inane commercial strand of disco, which reduced string and bass lines to rushing high-tempo clichés, and the more explicitly Caribbean- and gospel-flavoured strands with an advanced polyrhythmic and choral substance. Disco often achieved the same frenzied sense of heat as rock and roll, the same emotional core that was at once ecstatic and delirious. But it was transposed to a different sonic context, one in which orchestration and percussion were more dense. The point is that the first disco diva was not Donna Summer. It was a ravishingly queenly king called Little Richard.

Jazz, funk and West Indian music fed into disco and could be played at discos, because they affected people *physically*. Hence the title of Chic's 'Dance, Dance, Dance' was significant. It designated a social function, the impulse to 'get up and get down'. And that reinforced a continuum with 1950s rhythm and blues, where the trope expressing the same idea was to 'shake a tail feather', and with calypso music, where the equally fruity manifesto for any willing reveller was 'wine yuh waist'.[1]

Each image implies community, shared experience, eroticism. It evokes a release of inhibitions or self-consciousness, and if house music creates new shibboleths such as 'move your body', 'jack your body' or 'slam your body', the end result is still the same. Soul had to evolve into disco, which had to evolve into house, because blacks like to change regularly how they dance, how they move, how they exercise their imagination through nothing other than the poetry of the body.

Counting *all* the dances that mark out the history of black popular music is a mammoth task that would take years of research to complete with any semblance of authority. But perhaps the real point is that the creation of a new step effectively underscores the creation of both a new rhythm and a new vernacular in the ongoing evolution of R&B, soul and funk. So if Ray Charles, in a bid to express his sexuality spontaneously and shamelessly, hollers for the 'girl with the red dress on', then he has to complete the impulse with a reference to the specific way that girl gyrates – 'she can do the birdland all night long'.[2]

She can dance 'til sunrise. She can probably do other things as well.

That was 1959. In 1999 house music, intent on finding new imagery, evoked anything from Jinga Boogie to Boombada, yet the underlying current remained the same. The crowd moves. Bodies rock.

Somebody looks good on the floor, it inspires a singer to sing a song.

'One of the reasons house music is important is because people dance to it', argues Peven Everett, an intriguing talent in contemporary soul for the range of his output. 'It's that simple. Dancing is a huge part of our culture. The hip hop generation is a generation that's more bling-oriented. The hip hop generation doesn't dance ... it, erm, *profiles*.'[3]

Singer, multi-instrumentalist and producer, Everett is one of the great mavericks of contemporary black music, a Chicagoan with jazz training who worked with Wynton Marsalis in the early 1990s before playing trumpet and singing on a hugely popular track, 'Gabriel', by the producer Roy Davis Jnr that epitomises the sub-genre known as soulful house.

Everett's *oeuvre* to date is significant because it shows there are no clearly defined boundaries between soul and house music, and that the latter emerged from the former via the specific strand of disco.

If disco came from soul and house from disco, certainly in terms of the prevalent drumming patterns, then it makes sense that an artist who understood the history would not find the idea of house music that could make these far-reaching roots explicit too much of a stretch for his imagination. With a firm grip on both black pop and black art music, Peven Everett is ideally placed to use this continuum creatively.

Roughly speaking, soulful house denotes a marked gospel or blues flavour by way of a strong lead vocal and the same charged minor piano chords that might be found in the music of Gaye, Wonder and others. And although Everett's first two solo albums, 2002's *Studio Confessions* and 2005's *The Latest Craze*, leaned more towards soul, his third set, *Power Soul*, is an excellent recent work of soulful house.

Intriguingly, as much as Everett liked the energy, the danceability of house music, he objected to the name, primarily because he saw it as a needless secession from rhythm and blues. 'The word House should be put on a block in the Grand Canyon, they should cover it up with cement and then explode it! It's just something else to call it instead of R&B old school. The evolution of instrumentation is the only thing that determines house. They use beat-machines instead of a drummer and a bass keyboard instead of James Jamerson. It's like, whatever, dude.'

Everett's observation is valid because there is, as this book has set out to demonstrate, a long-running electro–acoustic continuum in black popular music that should make the use of synthesizers and sequencers much less of a subject for debate – or at least the premise for a new sub-genre – than in rock or certainly folk.

Soul has been made with machines since the early 1970s, and if a decent singer adds a strong theme to a beat and then performs with a bold gospel inflection – a Michael Watford, Barbara Tucker or Marc Evans – the result can tip into soulful house in an instant.[4] A big enough voice, such as Evans's, will dominate the pulse and spread heat all over it. If vocal house sounds soulless at times, it is not always due to any supposed coldness in the programming. Sometimes the voices are simply too thin and insipid to compete with the mighty barrage of crashing kicks.

Sticky fingers

In any case, not all soulful house is reducible to a *modus operandi* of man + machine. Marc Evans, a Baltimore singer who made the excellent 2008 album *The Way You Love Me*, struck a fruitful creative partnership with the highly respected house producer DJ Spen, as well as a collective of studio musicians called the Muthafunkaz. It is precisely the conjunction of programming and live playing, both elements tied together by the singer's very commanding baritone, that makes this collaboration so impressive.

Similar praise could be heaped on Blaze, the New Jersey duo of Josh Milan and Kevin Hedge who have been making consistently good dance music since the late 1980s, when they released their debut, *25 Years Later*, on Motown. What jumps out above all from their catalogue is the incredible audio quality. The tracks are so brilliantly engineered, mixed and produced that they sound as if each frequency in the low, mid and high range has somehow been sketched into the air with a fine-tip pencil, rather than produced by instruments or machines.

Certainly a piece such as 'Directions', with its purring, almost vocoder-like synth bass, truncated, upper-register keyboard chords and flinty drum sound, employs advanced and refined electronic colours. To a large extent, it is techno. But that doesn't mean it's not sho' nuff funky. And maybe the point of a group like Blaze is that they have found an idiomatic space where they can fulfil simultaneously the criteria of several genres that, on paper, may appear opposed.

Techno implies machines and rhythmic rigidity: stiffness, if you will, a lack of swing, due to the prominence of programming rather than playing. While this is largely true of the genre, it is not entirely untrue of funk, which evolved away from jazz precisely through a certain staccato backbeat and more repetition in the bass and drums. These characteristics also prefigured, to a great extent, a future of machine-based beats.

Hence the potential for funk to become techno, to appeal to the same senses, is clear enough and was already announced in the early 1970s by Stevie Wonder, the difference being that Wonder did generally show a lot more swing in the way he played his moog bass, drums and percussion. Yet the genius of a piece such as 'Pastime Paradise' is that it is eerie in the extreme, austere and refined in its matrix of cello-like keyboard lines, in a manner approximated by well-composed Techno.

Attention is greatly distracted from the sounds in this piece because the lyrics, which so stridently denounce society's delusional behaviour and hypocrisy, the headlong rush 'to the evils of the world', powerfully represent Wonder as a New Age prophet, one who is able to blend biblical tropes and secular language. Mystic revelations reinforce the vibrations.

Take away all the words and heavenly incantations, remove the Hare Krishna singers and the West Angeles Church Of God Choir, filter in a touch of Herbie Hancock's vocoder, and you have proto electro-soul for a crafty future producer to exploit.

Larry Heard did just that. To a certain extent the celebrated Chicago technophile drew, either consciously or subconsciously, on Wonder, the more abstract synthesizer-oriented jazz developed by Hancock in the early 1970s, classical music, and a wide range of '80s keyboard-pop. As Mr Fingers, Heard created 'Can You Feel It?', a moodily decelerated, spaced out paean to spiritual fulfilment. Swathed in string-like chords and plaintive instrumental passages, it announced 'deep house' but was really an intelligent extrapolation of the fraught, questioning mood of 'Pastime Paradise'. 'Can You Feel It?' is potently ambiguous. The inquiry could pertain as much to a negative as a positive vibration. Can you feel the stimulus of the city? Can you feel its stress? Can you feel a life force?

Released in 1988, the single really appeared to capture something both of the bleakness of inner-city life for African Americans in places like Chicago, Detroit and New York, and of the attraction to distant planets and the sanctuary they might offer. This had been a theme among funk groups in the previous decade. Heard's music was very contemporary, yet it had clearly audible traces of a black pop heritage.[5]

Earth, wind & wired

The sound of Heard in the 1980s and beyond showed that soul-funk, through its engagement with new technology, had for a long time been carrying the potential to become fully machine-based. It could push the aforementioned pastime paradise into a future-groove war zone.

How soulful or funky this music would remain as it spiralled off into any form of house or techno was a moot point. And Heard is perhaps the perfect example of an autonomous musician-producer whose music might drag him as much towards an entirely electronic palette as an electro-acoustic one, in which vocals, horns and a live rhythm section would be deemed appropriate to serve the arrangement in question. The parallel between Heard and Wonder is strengthened by the fact that both men also sing.

Along with Heard, several highly talented electronic producers have emerged from iconic cities in the R&B–soul continuum, such as New York, Chicago and Detroit, over the last two decades. Their work has shown enormous variety in form and content, both developing the historical templates of Wonder or of jazz musicians like Herbie Hancock, who gleefully embraced electronics, and moving resolutely away from them. In some cases, these artists opt to do both on the same recording.

Whether or not a sound becomes so hard as to be industrial is not the issue. Just as interesting is how notions of techno as a very European idiom might be undermined by the overwhelming blackness that can still emerge in a heavily programmed, machine-dominated piece of music, precisely because the artist has absorbed and danced to rhythm and blues, understands its contagious, coursing physicality and still uses its predominantly backbeat-led vocabulary as a foundation.

Hence the killer funkiness of some of the music of Carl Craig, Moodymann and Stacey Pullen. Pullen's 'Futuristikfreakqueen' is an intricate nexus of programmed and sequenced lines that have enough syncopation and percussive aggression to achieve the same energising effects as the music of James Brown or George Clinton.

A highlight of Pullen's 2001 set *Today Is The Tomorrow You Were Promised Yesterday*, the song exposes the mindset of producer as aural sculptor as well as composer, where the manipulation of sound, down to the slightest of reverberations or slivers of noise, becomes a form of narrative not strictly beholden to harmonic movement.

Interestingly, in his sleeve notes Pullen, who studied with Derrick May, refers to 'old jazz recordings and the way they used to pan each instrument'.[6] He also cites Earth, Wind & Fire, an influence on numerous house artists. Regardless of the differences between studio producer and live band, the common denominator is attention to detail and faith in orchestration, be it Pro-tools, horns, strings or beats.

Pullen talks about Earth, Wind & Fire doing 'reprise mixes, a different vibe of the same song'.[7] In so doing, he reminds us that the very idea of constantly reinterpreting a given theme is something with really deep roots in black music. One could trace this further back to the whole concept of the jazz standard, where the principle is creating inventive musical ideas from a given theme or set of chord sequences.

Reinventions or reprises are essentially forerunners of the remix. This key notion of a potential change in a composition's DNA, or the idea that the process through which elements are conjoined and alchemised can always be altered and enhanced, are building blocks of much modern black popular music in the Caribbean and America. Dub, disco, electro, hip hop and house all share this state of adaptability. It makes nothing untouchable. In dub the voice can die, the keyboard chords melt into passing whispers. In disco the percussion can become a lead voice, its stature bolstered by the breakdown. In electro the drum machines can morph into the sound of a video game. In hip hop all the above, or a Broadway tune or a French lesson or clashing swords, can become music.

Equally common to these genres, even in the most crude yet ingenious use of four-track tapes in Jamaica during the 1970s, are editing and sequencing that reveal a desire to map out a piece almost as a grid system – one on which the various sounds, this collection of pieces on a chessboard, could be shuttled, or rather nudged into darkness or light, hide and re-emerge. There is a form of trickery in the music's geography.

Though generally set at a much higher tempo, electro, the early 1980s forerunner to hip hop, also shifts and shimmies its constituent parts, often dramatically altering the pitch of a voice or a keyboard figure to create the impression that the tape machine used in the studio was mischievously speeded up by gremlins during the recording process.

If there was a certain artificiality in these genres, then it was a planned, consciously manipulated artificiality. And hip hop simply took the aesthetic to a logical conclusion, using the ultimate commercial music format, black vinyl, as the gold from which to extract high-grade audio crude. The key is to edit to the essence of a sound, to drill with precision.

That DJs and producers went as far as to sample the crackle of the needle on a record, as well as the drums and bass stored in the scratched shellac, was the ultimate manifestation of the self-consciousness and reflexivity of the hip hop aesthetic – as if the magician were charming you by showing not only a rabbit and a hat, but how his savvy manipulation of the two elements created a merry illusion. Nothing is thus inscrutable.

This kind of demonstrativeness fits into a deeply rooted lineage in black pop. As I argued in Chapter 7, there is a strand of songs that unveil the anatomy of a band – epitomised by King Curtis Jr's 'Memphis Soul Stew' – and the audible crackle of the vinyl is essentially just a more playful, teasing, opaque example of this didacticism. But you have to know about the culture of vinyl, about the charm of worn grooves, to get it.

Hip hop is mostly about undoing what has been done, taking the finished and devolving it to the unfinished, its fragments, so that it can be finished again in a manner not originally intended by its innocent creators. In other words, sampling a record and looping one of its breaks is shrewd reinvention by way of destruction and subversion.

At its most creative, sampling can make a bad record sound good.

And it can also make a good record sound not like a record at all.

The rapper is cast against a backdrop of worthy of Dr Funkenstein.

DJs and producers who started to do this in the late 1970s were possibly more aware of the 're-edits' and 'versions' of disco and dub than they were of the reprise in soul or the standard in jazz. But there was still a discernible continuum that enshrined music as an evolutionary and dynamic rather than a static process. The 'bridge' was over, but only for a moment.

Hip hop too, through the anarchic liberties it takes with context, blurs the boundary between mechanical and human sound or, rather, shows how the former may be modelled on the latter and, in the best-case scenario, can meld the two. The best example of this alchemy is KRS One's 1993 anthem 'The Sound Of Da Police', which derives its immense emotional power from the central 'wooh wooh!' vocal hook. It is not just a human scream imitating a police siren but a dramatic reminder that a police siren is an imitation of a human scream. Sound is sensory. It is a shifting story.

Whether or not the use of any audio source – vinyl album, film or television dialogue, environmental or urban noise – to make hip hop was also prompted by the relative decline of bands in black inner-city areas during the early 1980s, or just by the pure imagination of 'the street', is perhaps less important than one thing.

That is the fact that the results anchored and formalised the primacy of myriad spoken-word and oral traditions in African American culture.

It offered a new vision of theme or melody, one that essentially posited talking as a force equivalent to singing. Hip hop tracks can sound not so much like songs as excerpts from a black radio show, cut to fit a three-minute pop format rather than an hour-long segment.

Humour and anger are absolutely essential dynamics in hip hop because the expression of these feelings can gain enormous lyrical and performative invention from a talker/testifier/rapper. Take the humour out of hip hop and hip hop will be all the poorer for it, as there is less escapism and characterisation. Take the anger out of hip hop and hip hop will be all the poorer for it, as there is less realism and urgency. In the late 1980s and early '90s, De La Soul, The Pharcyde and Freestyle Fellowship managed to keep both elements in brilliant balance, charming you with a childlike jocularity before delivering an unexpurgated uppercut of ghetto reality, be it the scourge of drug addiction or the desperation of homelessness.

Rhythm is ubiquitous in hip hop. It pervades every stratum of the musical rock. To the beat of the music, on the bottom, is added the rushing stream of rhythmic speech, on the top, instead of the still waters of melodic singing. Hence there is a logical prelude to hip hop in funk, a genre in which a relentless punishing groove, the stinging attack of the 'one', often took precedence over a sung theme.

James Brown's embrace by hip hop producers makes sense because it is a testimony to the richness of the arrangements in his 1970s funk and the brilliance of their execution by his band. But Brown's value also resides in the way he implied a future music in his grand belief that rhythm + rhythm actually matched melody + rhythm as a worthwhile creative strategy.

Jacked off

Finding common ground between soul and hip hop is naturally a much more problematic notion, since melody is such a key element in the former's aesthetic and such a marginal notion in the latter's, where the 'hook' is the only vehicle for a burst of singing – ironically, often delivered by vocalists who tend towards mediocrity.

Whether hip hop *needs* melody at all is highly debatable. On the one hand, one could argue against it because the alliance of rhythm, sound effects and inventive manipulation of noise, be it a turntable scratch or the crackle of worn vinyl, has already yielded superlative results.

On the other hand, the blend of a verse-chorus structure and the sampling process may produce something fresh in departing from the beat-rhyme norms that have prevailed for close to three decades. It mostly depends on who the practitioner is.

Sampling is not the evil that killed soul music. It is an inevitable and perhaps necessary reflection of a world in which changing technology and perceptions of the history of any art challenge the notion that something recorded or documented is sacrosanct. In that sense, the breakbeat is practically a forerunner to virtual reality and role-playing, where reference and recontextualisation are all. It's up to soul, or any genre of music for that matter, to deal with sampling, just as any rappers or lyric writers have to engage with both current events and the ongoing evolution of language, society and mythology.

If the sample creates a rhythmic dynamism and zest that capture the imagination of the listener, then musicians have to pick up the gauntlet and match the use of technology, if not exceed it. And in the best case scenario, those musicians will expose the limits of the machine rather than those of their own technical ability or lateral thinking.

Hip hop will then flatter the same musicians by immortalising them as breakbeats.

Singing over samples, in any case, is not a radical idea when one considers how valuable a force repetition and reduced harmony have been in black popular music since the 1950s. Yet there is a marked difference between a programmed loop and a band playing the same line over and over again. The band, if they are worth their creative salt, will be able to introduce slight but effective accents to colour their performance, even when they are locked right 'in the pocket' of a song. You will feel a human touch.

For the most part, melody over beats is a stock working definition of contemporary R&B, a genre that sometimes has a tenuous relationship with the original rhythm and blues template. The link is not completely lost, as some singers retain a marked gospel edge in their work. Yet in many cases the deployment of backing tracks built purely from samples or of short, sugary keyboard hooks can yield soulless results.

This template was posited largely by producers like Teddy Riley, spearhead of the so-called New Jack Swing era in the early 1990s, when James Brown breaks or derivatives thereof formed backing tracks for a new wave of singers or vocal groups like R. Kelly, Guy or Bell Biv Devoe.

These acts were significant because they acknowledged hip hop as a musical force too powerful to ignore. The very idea of attempting to build a bridge between a new praxis like sampling and a tried and tested tradition of songwriting was philosophically admirable. Registering change is much more honest than simply denying it.

That said, these artists did not produce a body of work defined principally by great songs. Bell Biv's 1992 hit 'Poison' was a fun tune and still presses an enjoyable nostalgia button, as it prompts us to do the dance of the day called 'The Running Man'. But the song has neither a well-mapped theme nor a very commanding vocal. It is underwritten.

There's something insubstantial about the tone of both the lead vocals and harmony singing, a juvenile lightness, that has become more marked in R&B over time, in line with its appeal to a pre-pubescent demographic.

If soul is the baritone of a man, then today's R&B is the soprano of a boy.

More worrying still is the fact that so much of the contemporary incarnation of R&B actually has little or no blues harmony as a base, to the extent that it could feasibly be regarded as pure pop made by black artists, rather than a body of work rooted in a black music tradition.

Back in the 1950s, rhythm and blues was dubbed R&B. But in the first decade of the millennium, R&B isn't always necessarily rhythm and blues.

Is R&B now so hollowed out and dumbed down that the legacy of its progenitors is imperilled? When you listen to any number of today's exponents of the genre, do you hear an empowering echo of the masters or is there nothing more than a faint, adulterated residue?

Songwriting, orchestration, arranging and vocal excellence were the core values of classic R&B. Those tenets are not always upheld today.

By and large, the onus is on immediacy. Songs have to hit home from the first two bars, and while some of the music of Ne-Yo, Beyoncé and the late Aaliyah is appealing for being so insanely catchy, I worry that contemporary R&B leaves little or no room for subtlety or surprise.

The music maintains a tradition of functionality in so far as it serves a purpose on the dance floor. But one has to ask whether this hasn't now resulted in the triumph of the formulaic over the fantastical. A lot of the aforementioned artists are essentially models of efficiency.

Interestingly, Beyoncé has a jazz saxophonist Tia Fuller acting as the musical director of her live band. Fuller was more than happy to point out that one of the singer's hits, 'Déjà vu', was in the same key as Charlie Parker's 'Ornithology' and that the two pieces could segue during a concert. Does the singer want to use this tasty potpourri as a way of bringing her core audience to bebop? Does she feel the need to champion art music when the pop world apparently can't get enough of her hits?

One imagines that the onus is still very much on radio-friendly material.

There is a real skill involved in writing a catchy tune that captures the imagination of young ears, yet believing such mass appeal can only be achieved at the expense of musical substance is a myth. Back in 1962, Ray Charles achieved a compelling funkiness by way of vocal hooks that are still being rebooted today. But when he wrote the line 'She gives me money when I'm In need' on 'I Got A Woman',[8] he didn't decline to include horn parts and an eight-bar sax solo. Charles enriched the narrative of the song. He did not forgo musical ambition.

The golden age of soul, the 1970s as epitomised by Stevie Wonder, came about because all Charles's ingenuity was ingested by his musical children. Wonder extended that ingenuity; he did not destroy it. The point is that there was evolution from *within*. You can hear the sacrosanct tenets of 1950s and

'60s R&B – busy brass scores, lengthy, tricky improvisations *and* pop-friendly vocal hooks – amid the embrace of electronics, synthesizers, strings and state-of-the-art recording kit.

What the music of many contemporary R&B singers suggests is a desire, either conscious or unconscious, to bring a mainstream pop, boy-band sensibility to bear on what they do. As such, it is inevitable that both the inclination towards ambitious arrangements and the gospel quotient in these artists' work will ebb decisively away.

To all intents and purposes, the actual structure of today's R&B is less of a problem than its execution. Were a singer to produce a great melody over a great loop, there would be no cause for complaint. The problem is that, for the most part, the genre has brought forth few great singers or melodies over the last decade. Indeed, it is legitimate to ask whether R&B today needs alteration, either through better standards of musicianship or the kind of structural changes soul underwent in the 1970s, to further its evolution – if that is in its interests.

Many record industry execs contend that young ears can't take too much complexity. I'd argue that their intelligence shouldn't be insulted.

One thing I've noticed when talking to fans of soul and original 1960s rhythm and blues is how they will actually sing musical interludes, or short keyboard or guitar solos, as well as vocal lines from their favourite songs, simply because they've been sensitised to that form of expression. It shows a real immersion in all aspects of a song's performance. It would be a crying shame if a new generation of listeners were to lose a similar appreciation of vocal-less sound.

Cooke out

R&B and hip hop are now both placed under the sign of 'urban' music, a kind of all-purpose umbrella for new black pop in which the video – preferably glossy – is crucial, as are songs that are instantly catchy. R&B and hip hop have merged extensively as exponents of one genre have guested on material from the other, occasionally creating interesting work if both the singer and rapper are strong. But many of these collaborations are conceived as a way of doubling audiences, rather than pushing the artistic envelope as far as it will go.

Today R&B and hip hop are essentially studio-based genres in which the producer makes beats for the vocalist, be it a singer or rapper, whereas in days of old a song might have been born by three or four members of the same band getting their groove on together. Those instrumentalists, even if their ideas were wildly progressive, had a more direct connection to the blues. But today a producer, thanks to the anarchic, exploded view of history fostered by hip hop, doesn't necessarily have a plug-in to that heritage. Sound is all, rather than the chords and intervals, or the riffs and harmonies built on them, that characterise another era. Manipulating audio is at a premium. What counts is an ability to nail a loop and find the right singer or rapper to ride it.

The advent of the loop in hip hop decisively changed the whole feel of black pop in the 1980s, because it pushed the idea of repetition to the ultimate point of infallibility, the sampler. Arrangements became much less beholden to harmony. Seventies funk had gone in a similar direction, stripping down song structures to one-chord grooves in some cases. By and large, though, there were still changes, and often an eight- or sixteen-bar bridge that conclusively altered a piece's trajectory. Hip hop boiled things down further to just one sonic component that came round and round again and again like a merciless train. It was an exciting and perhaps necessary evolution, since it elicited creativity in other areas of a song: namely, rhythm, texture and general studio production.

Furthermore, the birth of this new music was both disorientating and hugely stimulating because it scrambled any really linear sense of musical history. What we once heard as old was suddenly new, and the line between what was behind us and what was ahead of us on the creative road became a fine one, to say the least. History was being condensed, compressed and re-coloured in the form of a two- or four-bar sample of music. Fragments of the past were flying in the face of the present.

This scrambling, jumbling and collaging of historical sources of sound presented a challenge to the imagination both of artists who embraced hip hop and those who did not. When any paradigm shift occurs in art, incumbents can accept or reject, or perhaps find a way of negotiating both the old and the new model. And if the evolution of jazz tells us one thing, it is that musicians have regularly thought about how to organise sound in interesting ways, be it with chord changes, with even more chord changes, or without chord changes at all. The real point is that the smart musicians will say all the above, and possibly in a single composition.

Hearing a loop for the first time in hip hop felt as if music had been dramatically destroyed and reborn at the same time. The perfect, relentless, metronomic time, the shameless, unapologetic artificiality of it all, were both enticing and disturbing for their unerring precision.

That instantly threw down a challenge to both listeners and players. We want musicians to play as tightly as machines. We don't want musicians to *be* machines. The loop is from a machine. Yet man selects the loop. Hip hop can herald the triumph of editing skills, precise listening and distilling sounds as much as it is a victory for composing or playing.

Man vs. machine quandaries aside, the key question is this: does R&B, or hip hop for that matter, need more than a loop as its structural foundation? Is it time to revert to chord changes? Could something worthwhile evolve if a producer schooled in the new science of the loop embraced the old art of chord changes? Go figure.

Back in the late 1990s, a musician told me that, although the power shift towards DJs and producers had been partly detrimental to the 'traditional' soul he was pursuing, he nonetheless saw the value of their rise to prominence, because it encouraged him to 'hold the groove' more in his arrangements. He embraced greater repetition.

'It's kind of helped me not to get caught up in a "muso" trip, really.'[9]

Granted, that argument may be one side of a coin. Flip it over and the other side says there is something to be gained from DJs and producers going on a 'muso trip' themselves, taking themselves out of a comfort zone of four- or eight-bar samples and vocal hooks to explore how a song might be affected by a sixteen-bar horn solo or a six-bar instrumental introduction.

Old records, in any case, serve as an important reminder of how the populist and art strands of black music were once more closely entwined. There is arguably something to be said for singers putting the experience of performing Broadway tunes beloved of jazz soloists to good use in their own soul material. In real terms, that meant in 1958 Sam Cooke was recording 'Moonlight In Vermont' and in 1960 'You Send Me'. Two years later he was charming rowdy rock and roll fans when he went on a British tour with a certain Little Richard.

Cooke, lest we forget, was one of the progenitors of soul, a former gospel artist who went secular. He could do earthiness, emotion and an electrifying holler born of black church traditions over relatively simple song forms. But Cooke also set his voice to the more intricate structures that were used by many jazz musicians in the 1950s.

Forcing every contemporary R&B singer to record at least one Broadway standard and fining them for all the missed chord changes would be a tad fascistic, primarily because much of that canon is alien to them. But it is worth considering what these singers might gain from such an exercise, whether or not it might unlock something interesting that could potentially enrich their performances, rooted as they may be primarily in a beats-based culture that largely eschews any complex harmony.

Roots down

Time and again, harmonic ambition has produced beauty in soul.

The chords do not have to be the most complex but the way they can embellish a vocal performance, by providing rich colour and shaping the course of a verse or chorus, pays substantial creative dividends. For example, it is hard to imagine Marvin Gaye's 1968 anthem 'I Heard It Through The Grapevine' without the gorgeous glide of his voice prompted by the change on bar nine of each verse. The whole magic of the song hinges on the way the singer's pitch and timbre alter in line with the zig-zag of the chords. The story is rolling. Emotional news is breaking.

Changes in the musical score reinforce the tug at the heartstrings.

On the other hand, the entire foundation of Jill Scott's 2000 hit 'Slowly Surely' is a four-bar loop that rotates as regularly as a carousel. The beat just eases round and round and round, again and again and again. The harmonic movement is minimal. A snatch of an old song, a phrase in which a synthesizer and flute curl around each other, acts as a mantra of sorts. Scott's voice does relatively little, but her four-note lines on the chorus are absolutely dazzling. Right breakbeat, right voice, right vibe.

Maybe we don't need an either/or past-or-present dichotomy here, and the value of hip hop soul is that it might well build bridges between these poles. Instead of 'Slowly Surely' *replacing* 'I Heard It Through The Grapevine', the two might coexist peacefully and somehow organically blend. The changes model and the changes-free, changeless model have been applied for many years. Some tension between them may be good.

Black popular music's relationship with its past has always been a complex one. Perhaps one of the reasons why the canon is so fertile is because the artists have developed the idiom without wholly negating the models that preceded them. So although young 1950s R&B players were bored by the 'old' blues, they didn't entirely reject its harmonic or rhythmic foundation. They found a fresh, creative way of adapting it.

Since that time, musicians who really understand the blues have found ways of invigorating the form and bringing a novel edge to it. The blues demands great character and individuality, and its raw materials, its chord changes and rhythms, can create dramatically different sensations through variations in texture, tempo and metre.

Contemporary R&B doesn't always uphold these values. Functioning in the same space as radio-friendly pop, it puts a premium on the instant payoff of the vocal hook, rather than the advanced, graduated dynamics of an instrumental arrangement. Not that there isn't creativity. Occasionally, producers do cook up some beguiling beats – the likes of Darkchild, Timbaland and The Neptunes have all hit some worthwhile creative heights in the past fifteen years – but they work mostly from a rhythmic-textural rather than the melodic-harmonic base that has also been a key element in soul's lexicon.

Appreciations of black music often fall prey to the cliché that the groove is all 'n' all. Yes and no. It is, but rhythmic richness does not automatically preclude melodic invention. It is the coexistence of the two – a singer interpreting a great theme against the complex moving carriage of a great band – that creates real magic.

Rhythm is an absolutely pivotal part of rhythm and blues, soul and funk, but it has not always been at the expense of melody. The acid test of greatness in the canon is how beautiful a song can remain – obviously Stevie Wonder springs to mind here – if the beat, the thing that black pop had and white pop did not, were to disappear and the theme were left unaccompanied. If two of the finest ever soul artists, Al Green and Isaac Hayes, chose to cover the songs of Kris Kristofferson,[10] it was because they fell in love with the gorgeous melodies, not because there was a bad groove under their voices that could be made mo' better badder.

Great black pop can be reduced to the hop, skip and jump of the beat, but it is also the flight of melody as well as the somersault of rhythm.

To a certain extent it seems odd to assert as much, given that as this book has striven to point out, rhythm, repetition and the abandonment of changes have greatly governed the deployment of instruments in soul. But the fact remains that James Brown wrote songs. The magic of many of his pieces came from the inventiveness and sheer catchiness of the riffs. Nonetheless, Brown did not always eschew verse and chorus.

Melody is not associated enough with black pop. It is one of the reasons why my mother, and members of her generation who were weaned on Green and Hayes, don't like hip hop. There are too many words. She treasures the soar of a few syllables rather than the flurry of many. One artist capable of melodicism is R. Kelly, an undeniably talented singer-player-songwriter who can produce quality soul music and has done.[11] Yet he appears wedded to a core market that thrives on push-button saccharine ditties rather than pieces with compositional scope. So phenomenally successful has Kelly been at working a kind of formulaic, conveyor-belt R&B, the impact of which shows in the many imitators he has spawned, that it is hard for him to break with the music's strictures. A Gaye-like suite is now far too much of a market liability.

For the most part soul, especially when leaning towards jazz, is more harmonically complex than R&B and has melodies written with a sense of breathing space. This is because the singer's path is unfolding in line with chord changes either in the middle of a verse or between the verse and the chorus, the result being some semblance of a narrative arc.

Modern-day R&B, borrowing from hip hop's beats-led praxis, largely suffers from melodic impoverishment because a lot of singers are pumping out lines that do not have enough light and shade or twists in harmony to be interesting. If the bed of beats on which these lines rest is tawdry, then the results are mercilessly underwhelming, especially if the vocal performance is crudely, excessively melismatic.

Unfortunately, too many of the current incumbents don't relax and vary their note lengths. They excitedly spray out eighths and sixteenths, instead of holding onto a half or whole note to let the melody breathe, as they might do were they fitting the line to a thing called a chord change.

Such accusations could be levelled at some of James Brown's performances, which weren't about harmonic finesse. But Brown had extraordinary character in his tone and an extraordinary band backing him that fashioned an enviably rich rhythmic spectrum. Because, from the 1970s onwards, he was delivering longer pieces than the standard three-minute format of today's R&B, Brown was able to create light and shade through use of the sacrosanct bridge and solos, mostly by his horn players.

Brown could holler over one chord *ad infinitum* but he was astute enough to call on saxophonist Maceo Parker to take over when a tune needed a swerve. He would make way for the horn when he had to.

On the one hand, the idea that contemporary R&B should be reducible to a vocal hook and a sampled beat can be dangerous, because it precludes the possibility of a successor to the Brown-Parker tandem and makes quirks of song structure less likely. On the other hand, a reactionary approach to black pop that outlaws programming and machines is equally dangerous, since these tools can open up genuinely creative avenues that have proved worthwhile in the past.

To advocate a wholly Luddite stance that prohibits the use of electronics or of state-of-the-art technology would actually be a betrayal of the consistent spirit of innovation that has marked soul over time.

The genre should always maintain its relationship with electronics and music-making software, for the sake of modernity and the sense of sheer sonic newness these tools can impart when they are wisely deployed.

Over time, the funkier end of soul has set great store by an increasing hardness in its groove and rhythmic drive. Technology can foster that.

It should also be noted that a band who play 'in the tradition' of Marvin or Stevie, but slavishly ape their heroes without bringing any creative zest to the table, are just as unappealing and regressive as a talent-free producer making beats for a singer who can barely hold a wack tune.

Ideally, there could be a diversity of models in contemporary black pop: one favouring instruments, another electronics, and then several points in between those two poles, where the artist proves to be a musician with the curiosity and skill to programme or a programmer with the curiosity and skill to both embrace instrumentalists and deploy them effectively against beats. Curiosity might just save rather than kill any of the cats who hold the future of black pop in their paws.

Courageous, probing artists provide a clear solution to this conundrum. Listen to Stacey Pullen and it's clear that driving his sequencing and sampling is the mind of a man who loves jazz or, more to the point, has listened closely to jazz-informed soul groups like Earth, Wind & Fire. Listen to *Plantation Lullabies*, Me'Shell NdegéOcello's landmark 1993 debut, and it's clear she was affected by the hard, stark rhythms of hip hop even though she played 'traditional' funk. She sounded new but felt old. She felt familiar but came across real fresh. She was time travelling.

Standing over all these is Stevie Wonder. He came from the time of instruments, the early 1960s, and embraced electronics like a man possessed a decade later. And although Wonder's electro-acoustic work is essential, what is just as important is the fact that when he swings all the way to the world of electronics – check the underrated 'Skeletons' – he doesn't forsake his roots. You get the 'old' blues amid the new bleeps.

How to build on that example? How to reconcile the beauty of Stevie's playing with the programming of Premier or Pullen? How to make a song that is both a melody from above and a beat from below?

A melody from the heavens and a beat from the hottest of hellfires?

Perhaps another reason why today's R&B has become impoverished is the greater stratification in the music industry compared with the 1960s and '70s. Back then, there were a lot more Afro-Latin rhythms in soul, as exemplified by Mandrill, War *et al.* Today there are relatively fewer of these rhythms in R&B, and that may be down to the fact that straying into this kind of territory can confuse radio programmers and journalists, who will now have another category to contend with. It's called world music. It wasn't around in the 1970s. Whether or not this fairly new ground actively makes life difficult for any exponent of western black pop who ventures into it is a moot point. But there is sufficient distance between the markets for world music and urban music for an adventurous exponent of R&B who draws explicitly on African rhythms to be told by some disc jockeys that the music is too 'ethnic' for urban kids. If it's too jazzy, then it's too pretentious; too arty; too difficult.

Sadly, very few, if any, contemporary R&B tracks feature solos or instrumental breaks. The interesting push and pull between voice and saxophone heard in days of old, exemplified by the complicity between, say, Aretha Franklin and King Curtis, is absent.

Contemporary R&B has moved far away from jazz, in terms of both harmonic richness and improvisatory flourishes. So the idea of a song stretching beyond three minutes and including a complex horn break *à la* Earth, Wind & Fire is now more or less unheard of.

Instrumental black pop does exist but it has been pushed to the most extreme forms – either smooth jazz, a very distant outgrowth of 1960s soul jazz that has become so neutered and anodyne that it is really a new type of easy listening, or the occasional sax- or keyboard-led house or techno track, largely perceived as irrelevant to contemporary R&B because of the speed and hardness of the overall sound. Today's R&B is, for the most part, downtempo and ballad-based.

Actually, the nearest thing there is to a modern-day equivalent of a classic 1960s or '70s instrumental soul ensemble like the Bar-Kays, The JBs or Booker T. & The MGs is arguably The Roots, who turned in a quite brilliant rendition of the latter's 'Melting Pot' on their 2004 set *The Tipping Point*. It is a shame this track was not deemed single-worthy, possibly because of the commercial risk posed by voiceless cuts.

Being able to move convincingly from one discipline, one form to another, or to show not so much an understanding of as a genuine affinity with other genres, is almost a prerequisite for any kind of fusion. That is why the most important exponents of soulful hip hop are The Roots, who don't just make rap trax but *play* funk in the process.

Nearly two decades after its inception, the Philadelphia crew with the protean identity remains an almost unique entity in modern black music, having shown that a 'traditional' band with a core drums-bass-keys rhythm section can deliver the same explosiveness as the two-turntables-and-a-mike set-up that defines hip hop. The Roots' refusal to forgo a playing aesthetic places them firmly at the forefront of the funk–hip hop continuum.

The band is an absolutely crucial element of the modern black-music mosaic because of the way it conjoins various strands of history and offers living proof that beat-making need not be the only basis for hip hop.

It was precisely because they could play as hard and as funky as programmed breaks that The Roots were accepted by hip hop crowds.

Although they have used excellent rappers and beatboxers, in the form of Black Thought (Tariq Trotter), Malik B and Rahzel, and some of their most memorable tunes – 'Do You Want More?', 'The Next Movement', 'You Got Me' – are vocal-led, the use of instruments, as well as sampling, is of paramount importance in The Roots. They retain the potential to do without a voice, as with the band's sterling reprise of 'Melting Pot', at any given moment.

Sadly, The Roots' lone-warrior status highlights the absence of bands in contemporary black pop. From its genesis in the late 1940s right through to the mid-1980s, R&B set great store by the band and the input of musicians in general. But since the early '90s producers, acting as largely self-sufficient creators who put their faith in technology, have held sway. Whether the music can realistically equal the glories of its past – think Marvin, Stevie, JB – without competent instrumentalists is an important question and an urgent one.

Dreams to chase

Hip hop is organised noise: the eruption and manipulation of any sound from anywhere. It is the potential of the police siren, the car alarm or the clash of swords to become a component in a rhythmic matrix. As such, there should essentially be no precise stylistic definition of the genre. Hip hop is supposed to view the world, in all its sonic brutality and beauty, as a new orchestra. Timbres are not supposed to be restricted to instruments.

It's largely about non-musicians, people who don't have a formal understanding of keys, chords or intervals, exercising their imagination to distil sounds into interesting patterns that, at best, repeat to the point of hypnosis. The sounds can come from record collections, or daily life, or machines, and can have any characteristic, as long as they are *headnodic*.

Any audio, old or new, musical or non-musical, is a potential band.

Trademarks have emerged, though. Generally speaking, hip hop pushes the bass – the low-end theory, as A Tribe Called Quest would have it – towards very dark depths, a kind of murky, swampy mud. It uses a syncopated kick-drum and tends greatly towards dissonance, in line with its rejection of chords or a specific harmonic point of departure.

There is also a certain sharpness in the way sounds appear and disappear, as well as hardness and an overwhelming sense of tonal bulk. The object of the exercise is physically to affect listeners, to 'hit' them with the beat, often in such a fashion that if they don't dance, they'll at least bob their heads while striking a pose or 'profilin'.

Integrating these characteristics into a rhythm and blues tradition was supposed to create something new, a notion formalised by the moniker 'Queen of Hip hop Soul' that was bestowed with much fanfare on the New York singer Mary J. Blige in the mid-1990s.

Marketing-wise it was an inspired move. The title stuck and, more to the point, implied that creatively R&B had progressed since the days of the Queen Of Soul in the 1960s. But it didn't really tell the whole story of how certain artists prior to Blige had announced the 'fusion' of these genres and in some cases had done so with considerably more ingenuity. Blige is an important artist who did a lot to enshrine the idea that a singer who grew up with hip hop and really understood the culture could also strongly relate to past soul divas such as Chaka Khan and Anita Baker. Blige has turned out some very good songs since her 1992 debut *What's The 411?* but also many forgettable ones. She can be intensely moving but her discography to date is inconsistent. It suffers by comparison with her predecessors in royalty.

In America, few artists were more worthy of the title 'King of Hip hop Soul' than the singer Tashan Rashad, a New Yorker who signed to Def Jam, home of Public Enemy, in 1985.[12] His debut, *Chasin' A Dream*, offered a blend of surging gospel heat and the stark, primal sounds and ambiences that characterised the recordings of his label mates.

In fact, what the album did quite brilliantly was show that one of the links between hip hop and soul, informed by the black church, was a sense of immediacy, urgency and honesty. Both genres have reached creative heights because visionary practitioners have brought subtlety and restraint to the table, but telling it like it is, or keeping it real, is still a guiding principle. Essentially, it's about feelings, words and sounds not being contained at all, so they are externalised by shouting for the Lord or spitting on the mike – being moved by the spirit and moving the crowd.

Lyrically, hip hop has much more scope than gospel since it can, just as the blues does, broach profanity as well as sanctity. But the two genres can meet in their brilliance with image and metaphor, The Bible being a work of drama to match any tale of boyz in the hood. What Tashan does on the title track of *Chasin' A Dream* is to meld these two idioms sonically and lyrically, sliding a rock-rap backbeat and fiery Baptist harmonies under a text that moves from contemporary black urban vernacular – 'Got me chasin' a dream/ Find out what it means/Fly cars and a fancy bars/Seem to distract my mind/ Running here, running there/Always on the run somewhere' – to a quotation from one of the most enduring of all gospel standards –'No wonder I don't have time/But let me tell you somethin' baby/This little light of mine/I'm gonna let it shine'.[13] Hence street corner and church are brought into the same psychic space.

This is both reinforcement and updating of a deep-rooted tradition in black music. By bringing these two distinct registers of language into close proximity, Tashan is effectively saying that the struggle for daily bread, with all its glitzy material temptation, is not divorced from the presence of the divine and the invocation of faith, as embodied in the enduring gospel song 'This Little Light Of Mine'. The reference may have been lost on some, particularly younger listeners, but it is nonetheless important and recalls the way in which 1970s soul artists could talk of 'shaking she booty' in one line and taking 'a closer walk with thee' in another.

Some of their predecessors were just as daring. Back in 1927, Washington Philips's 'Denomination Blues' included in its verse a critique born of the great candour of the blues – 'Lot of preachers is preaching and think they're doin' well/An' all they want is your money an' they can go to hell'. The chorus was all gospel, though: 'An' that's all. I tell you that's all. But you better have Jesus now. I tell you that's all'.

Chasin' A Dream adds to the push and pull of these two forces. It is a work that resolutely broaches the subjects of tangible social deprivation, love and sex. Yet it also professes faith. It reflects a mind comfortable with both 'I love you, baby' and 'Thank you, Father'.

Sadly, *Chasin' A Dream* did not sell in significant quantities and, despite a good follow-up in *On The Horizon*, Rashad's career eventually dwindled – possibly because the world was not ready for the idea of hip hop and soul engaging in fruitful dialogue, at a time when a rapper like Chuck D appeared so antithetical to a singer like Luther Vandross. I also wonder whether America was ready for a soul man with a wholly non-western name like Tashan, which is the Punjabi word for style.

Generally speaking, the 1980s brought flashes of hip hop soul without ever really nailing it down formally as a sub-genre. British artists such as Loose Ends and Soul II Soul, the former active from the early '80s, the latter during the latter part of the decade, definitely evidenced a hip hop sensibility in the menacing, steely sharpness of their rhythm tracks, and particularly in the drum programming. Moreover, Soul II Soul's grasp of the dub aesthetic that had been so instrumental to the birth of hip hop predisposed them to a musical language that was decidedly trans-genre.

A good woman she be

A few years after Soul II Soul hit commercial and creative heights with their 1990 single 'Back To Life', a little-known pianist and singer from Macclesfield called Sarah Winton released one of the great albums in the recent history of black pop. 1993's *You Can't Keep A Good Woman Down* is a classic and has yet to be rivalled as a statement of musical creativity in which the harmonic fluidity of soul and jazz and the tonal solidity and sonic bulk of hip hop cohere with no sense of contrivance. Winton composed with considerable finesse, creating songs that included interludes, counterpoint and codas. Yet there was a starkness in some of her melodies and a bulge in her synthesizer bass lines that vividly captured some of the flavour both of the electro-boogie sound that immediately preceded hip hop and of hip hop itself.

Intriguingly, there was also a marked resonance of European classical music and an operatic use of the voice that chimed loosely with the seductive but sinister way producer RZA used strings in his beat-making for Wu-Tang Clan. The group's 1993 debut, *Enter The Wu-Tang (36 Chambers)*, significantly advanced hip hop's musical vocabulary by juxtaposing timbral ingenuity with extreme dissonance. What Winton managed to do was to create a specific ambience that evoked the melancholy and menace of the city without using clichéd 'urban' sound-effects.

You Can't Keep a Good Woman Down is a hard album to place geographically. It is overwhelmingly of the city but it is not exclusively *in* the city. Such is its achievement. There is both finesse and fragility, a gentleness to some of the piano and vocal tones that suggests softer, thinner, cleaner air in contrast with the punishing, almost concrete austerity of the bass and drum tracks. One might contend that the music, perhaps more by accident than design, is rural and urban.

This might be the essence of true hip hop soul, as the former is resolutely of the city and the latter of the country, or at least the country in flight to the city. And perhaps the intermingling of these sensibilities – the marriage of sensuality, gentility, slowness, and speed – is what can really bring the two ideas and lifestyles, as well as the two genres of music, into some form of constructive osmosis.

In his moments of genuine inspiration, D'Angelo, the West Virginian son of a preacher man who relocated to New York, touches a similar creative earth wire to Winton, as do Erykah Badu and the jazz pianists Robert Glasper and Jason Moran, all three of them loud and proud Texans.

There is a tough but particularly leisurely, almost unhurried character to the phrasing or touch of the keyboard in all the above that says a lot about African American culture in the Southern USA that has achieved a kind of tidy coexistence with the sharp snap of a Northern setting.

All these artists have, at various junctures in their careers to date, engaged with soul, hip hop, jazz and blues in a number of different ways. Whether it is D'Angelo casting his voice against the sophisticated harmonies of trumpeter Roy Hargrove (yet another Texan) or Badu rapping on one song and singing on the next, there appears to be a holistic and inclusive, rather than a partitioned, view of black music.

This doesn't always pay creative dividends. Erykah Badu's 2008 album *New Amerykah* was a mild disappointment, simply because there was a surfeit of distinctly average songwriting and an excess of below-average beat-making. But the very proximity of these disciplines, and the fact that an artist may be as open to samples and rhymes as they are to melody and live instrumentation, can only be healthy, since it brings different eras of black music into potentially creative collision.

That said, Badu's 2010 set *New Amerykah Part Two: Return Of The Ankh* was a return to form and seemed to strike a better balance between composition and production, even though it was an album on which studio ingenuity and manipulation of recorded material loomed large.[14] Seeing Badu in concert in London that year confirmed that, whether soul or hip hop is her *alma mater*, she is a vibrant creative being conversant with both the digital and analogue aesthetics of black pop, and that her spirit is largely dedicated to forming a continuum between the played and programmed.

Fusions of hip hop and soul aren't just about singers getting into beats.

The converse can be interesting too. A quite fascinating artist in black popular music, Cee-Lo Green, debuted in the mid-1990s as a rapper first and foremost. He was part of the Atlanta crew Goodie Mob and has also been a frequent collaborator with the mega-successful duo Outkast.

A skilled lyricist with a firm grasp of the element of surprise ('I think I'm gonna go crazy/Are you gonna go with me?'), Cee-Lo revealed himself as a singer with a surging gospel voice on his solo albums, 2002's *Cee-Lo Green And His Perfect Imperfections* and 2004's *Cee-Lo Green Is The Soul Machine*, as well as through his work with producer Dangermouse in the group Gnarls Barkley. Producer as well as rapper and singer, Green exemplifies a shape-shifting creativity, a muse that will take him into many different traditions of black popular music – as he himself declared on the track 'Sometimes' on the *Soul Machine* album: 'You know, sometimes I wanna rap, sometimes I wanna sing, sometimes all it calls for is a nice mellow groove, a little rimshot, you know … get you open.'[15] Being 'open' creatively can occasionally produce great work, and Cee-Lo is really at his best when moving between several forms, using a single piece like 'Sometimes' as a platform to mesh almost thespian-like declamations with rhythmic rhyme and soulful singing.

What an artist like Cee-Lo proves is that there is not so much a hip hop–soul continuum as a line that can be drawn from the talking blues of the 1920s to the rapping on a mike in the '80s and beyond; and that a quintessential aspect of black popular music is the option a singer may have to slip into speech at any time.

In that respect, Cee-Lo is actually a modern-day Leadbelly, the folk-blues legend who was known to interrupt song with story when the moment took him. If one accepts that hip hop is greatly concerned with storytelling as well as word play, it is logical that the genre should be a reversion to, and reassertion of, blues and folk culture that had become less prevalent during soul in the 1970s. Speech and song had always been closely related in black pop. What hip hop did was bring the stone down on the head of its soul brother, kicking all his sweet-boy singing and melody into touch. As liable to say 'I love you' as 'Fuck You!', Cee-Lo is a man big enough to house Cain and Abel in the same body.

Other rappers who have made the most soulful music include Mos Def, Pharoahe Monch, Common and Q-Tip, primarily because they are interested not just in sampling soul and funk but in attempting to graft the techniques that underpinned the work of its greatest exponents – that is, playing instruments, writing melodies, using changes – onto a rap aesthetic predicated on rhythm. The impressive thing about Q-Tip, for example, is that he occasionally subsumes his own voice – as can be heard on a 'Do You Dig U?', where the sound of the instruments is more important than that of the rapper. The music suggests that the rapper loves music. The rapper is thus willing to give space to musicians.

Soul, or rather jazz-informed soul, dominates Q-Tip's hip hop. On the piece in question, Tip rap-sings very little, instead giving the spotlight to two virtuosi, the flautist/saxophonist Gary Thomas and the guitarist Kurt Rosenwinkel. That is rare in modern urban music. But it is not a departure from soul's past. It is a throwback to old-school vocalists standing aside and calling on a horn player to step up to the plate. It is a form of musical lucidity. It is the singer's ego deflating in the cause of the song.

A great singer knows how to sing. A greater singer knows what to sing.

A really great singer knows when not to sing. A really great singer knows that elements other than the voice can enrich musical narrative.

A really great singer knows his or her absence can enhance his or her presence.

Again, history schools us here. Ray, Stevie and James all had great musicians behind them and recognised there was a need to let the band play.

Perhaps some rappers find it hard to make soul music for precisely that reason: their egos get in the way, tricking them into thinking that their song has to be defined by them and them alone, rather than being an exchange with other creative beings, the bounty of which is borne out by their predecessors. Few singers were as egotistical as James Brown. Yet Maceo Parker was given solos because they served the song.

Maybe what hip hop needs to do today is to ask itself whether it loves music and wants to serve the song. If it does, then it might keep its creative edge, because music is humanity and humanity is whimsical and subject to change. Younger producers and rappers, like Phuture Motion or Lupe Fiasco, do suggest that hip hop can love music and also be soulful.

Hip hop soul is actually something of a misnomer, since hip hop is so musically omnivorous that it doesn't necessarily need to be wedded to another genre to make it interesting. But perhaps soul can feel like hip hop if it takes on a certain rhythmic minimalism, a sparseness, stiffness or staccato quality that render the sonic framework tense or angst-ridden – which is so often the case with the best rap performances. For the most part, hip hop has also brought more bass into soul over the years.

Adrianna Evans's 'Reality', from her eponymous 1997 debut, is a paragon in this respect. Produced by the brilliant Dred Scott,[16] whose own 1993 set *Breakin' Combs* is one of the great hip hop albums of the decade, the piece has a wonderfully eerie, taut backdrop that suggests it could morph into Curtis Mayfield one minute and Wu-Tang Clan the next.

Scott unlocked something in his programming and the slightly discordant, slithery tonalities that skilfully pirouetted the arrangements for Evans's vocals, right bang on the cusp of hip hop mechanisation and blues incantation. The music is tough and tender. It's a crying shame the Scott-Evans partnership did not continue.

Listening to their work today, it is clear that musicianship as well as studio-as-instrument was on the creative agenda. Scott's production is really outstanding, but the input of the rhythm section – strings and horns, the bass of Sekou Bunch, the guitar of Craig T. Cooper and, above all, the flute of Rastine Calhoun III – is the absolute deal maker. It's not unlike the attention to detail that marks some of the best work of The Roots, a band that both plays funk and makes hip hop.

19 Divorcing neo to marry soul

If I go to a so-called neo soul show, it feels like I'm in a crowd of people who are trying to be hip. It's like some trendy shit. I'm already soulful … I don't have to try to be it.
(Amp Fiddler)

What's funny about neo soul is … I don't even know what it is … I don't reject it but honestly I didn't come up with it. I don't wanna be called the queen of it, 'cos I'm a change then everybody gon' be disappointed.
(Erykah Badu)

I leave it to those who need to give it a name … I call it soul music. (M. Nahadr)

Great Scott

Singer Jill Scott pays The Roots a huge compliment on 'A Long Walk', one of the outstanding songs from her award-winning debut in 2000, *Who Is Jill Scott?* Built on a couple of moist, almost liquefied electric piano chords, the piece is a hazy, graceful butterfly of a ballad in which Scott evokes the fathomless depths of her love for her partner by describing how the couple might connect emotionally, spiritually and culturally during a leisurely stroll in the park. They have options. They have things to do. They could see a movie. They could see a play. They could 'roll a tree'. They could eat passion fruit. They could cruise and listen to The Roots.

It is tempting to argue that Scott made the reference because of the kinship she felt with her homeboys: she is also from the City of Brotherly Love (Philadelphia) and she owed her breakthrough in no small part to the opportunity the band afforded her to sing the hook on 'You Got Me', a song whose success confirmed The Roots as a *bona fide* commercial force as well as a critics' favourite. To a certain extent, Scott owed them the props.

There was possibly much more to it than that, though. Scott's album is one of the most accomplished entries in the canon of twenty-first-century soul music. The enormous impact it made on release was partly down to the marked freshness and beauty of the arrangements, production and composition, as well as the singer's own performance.

Traditions were intersecting. On the one hand, there was in Scott's work a clear embodiment of the classic confessional soul or blues singer. On the other, there was a smart blend of live instrumentation and programmed beats with a subtlety often lacking in machine-based arrangements. The record's scope was encapsulated by the contrast between the simple structure of 'Slowly, Surely', which was nothing more than Scott singing over a loop (a discreetly effective one at that), and an orchestral piece like the stirringly dramatic 'It's Love', whose dizzying go-go rhythm was bolstered by high and mighty horns.

Who Is Jill Scott? thus carved out a space in modern black popular music where old and new methodologies could find some kind of equilibrium.

Scott was not alone. Bilal Oliver, a key collaborator with jazz pianist Robert Glasper, released in the same year a quite brilliant album, *First Born Second*, that evinced similar sensibilities, treading a fine line between soul composition and hip hop production to notable effect. Angie Stone's *Black Diamond*, cut in 1999 and India.Arie's *Acoustic Soul* were also accomplished sets with a similar array of formative influences.

Anybody taking a passing interest in black popular music could not have escaped the observation that the aforementioned had a definite revitalising effect on soul music through their individual artistry, above all the richness of their voices, and the arrangements in which those voices were cast. They were different from modern R&B artists.

Contemporary R&B, not solely but mostly glossy apolitical fodder, is geared to a teen video-led market where content vies for space with presentation. If the songs are melodically weak, then the counterweight is dazzling dance routines and super-sassed-out sets that are miniaturised Hollywood in an eye-popping three minutes.

Choreography has always been a major part of black music, no more so than on iconic labels like Motown. But there was a huge difference in production values during the 1960s: girl groups *à la* Supremes performed against orchestral, highly arranged backdrops in which the timbres were gilt-edged, even if the theme of the song was so bland as to be instantly forgotten. Kicking live drums or bass would groove you if words did not.

Because samples rather than a band with several instruments are deployed as backing tracks in contemporary R&B, all the details, dynamics and elements of improvisation that defined classic R&B are missing. And if the loop is tepid, a less than competent singer will be cruelly exposed. If she is a goddess in bootylicious paradise, this may not be so problematic. Moreover, if her face does not quite fit, chances are that another will shimmy along faster than a pimp in pursuit of his papers.

As attractive as she is, Jill Scott did not sell records on her looks. There was no gym-fit frame to distract attention from her voice. And what Scott, Angie Stone and India.Arie – who boldly empowered herself by *not* being 'the latest girl in the video' – did was effectively to make room for a more mature, subtle and substantial approach to lyrical content that matched a melodic richness and generally more instrument-led arrangements than in modern R&B. These singers didn't censor carnal issues but rather replaced overt sexuality with eroticism.

Scott's 'It's Love' was libido by way of culinary metaphor. It was tastefully tasty.

India's 'Brown Skin' was a subtle yet vivid tableau of physical union. It depicted the blend of two bodies rather than the bump and grind.

While the quality of their songwriting was a major factor in the success of all the above, listeners may also have been more receptive to these singers because several artists in the mid-1990s had pushed in a similar direction musically, reviving a soul-music template that harked back to the '70s, with wah-wah guitars, brass, reeds and Hammond B3 organs deployed alongside drum machines.

D'Angelo, Maxwell, Eric Benet, Erykah Badu and Adrianna Evans were among the prime movers in what was loosely termed 'neo soul' or 'nu classic soul' as a means of acknowledging the re-assertion of core values. The ethos dictated that a young pretender to the throne of Curtis Mayfield should try to *write* in his style rather than just sample him.

For those who had become disillusioned with an increasingly formulaic and synthetic form of R&B, dominant since the early 1990s, it was a mightily exciting time. Neo soul mooted the possibility of familiar musical vocabulary being revisited by a new generation who might bring to it inflections specific to their very own life experience.

Neo soul thus paralleled the so-called 'neo bop' revival spearheaded in jazz by Wynton Marsalis in the early 1980s. The thought of returning to a time when bands constructed songs through the process of playing, rather than by sampling hitherto recorded material, hit very large nostalgia buttons. Black pop was looking back for consolidation.

While the use of this buzzword created an all-important new narrative for the media, the full story of the relationship soul had with its past was much more complex. The 'neo' sub-strand implied that something missing – a more organic, live sound – had come back. But as this book has argued, soul music has extensively mixed the played and the programmed, the acoustic and the electric, throughout its history, making the genre a vast, anarchic mosaic of tonalities.

Artists were still playing instruments in the mid- and late 1980s. But they were doing so in conjunction with machines. The most important example of this trend is probably Tashan Rashad,[1] whose *Chasin' A Dream* managed to capture some of the nascent flavour of hip hop, all the while retaining a gospel charge that reached back to Ray Charles.

So there was a line that could be drawn from Rashad through to the likes of Soul II Soul, Omar Lye-Fook, D'Influence, Young Disciples and Sarah Winton, a string of young British artists who creatively engaged to varying degrees with the advent of sampling and beat-making.

Soul in the early 1990s had classic '70s resonances. Yet it was both enriched and nuanced by state-of-the-art electronics while perhaps, from a cultural viewpoint, being overshadowed by the excitement of a new rap-based paradigm, in which turntables became the cutting edge of modernity – not just for the scratching they produced but for the new visual focus they brought to music as a performance art.

A guy behind the decks was something new to look at and listen to.

Pop culture is so unerringly fickle and paradoxical that it can just as easily embrace what it apparently rejects. So a figure with a striking image, be it Me'Shell NdegéOcello wielding a bass guitar or Omar or D'Angelo hunched over a piano, can do wonders for a new bandwagon that says a band rather than a beatmaker is really where it's at.

Yet NdegéOcello obviously had an interest in hip hop and D'Angelo was a soul singer who appeared to catch the ear of hip hop fans. In the case of 'Brown Sugar', that may well have been down to the sound treatment as well as the songwriting or playing. Propped up on a very jazzy swing pulse, the piece and several others on the album of the same name benefited from hip hop engineering due to the input of Ali-Shaheed Muhammad and Bob Power, who had mixed for a wide variety of rappers. That input was crucial in so far as it brought a startlingly beautiful afterglow, an eerie purr and hiss, to the drums, keys and electronic effects that was the norm in most 'urban' music.

Engineers can be a crucial link between soul and hip hop. Somewhat unsung heroes, they can imbue the former with some of the audio quality of the latter. So even if one is listening to a verse/chorus structure with chord changes and a middle eight, organising principles that are far from the norm on rap records, an able mixer like Power, Russell 'The Dragon' Elevado or Mike Chavarria can treat frequencies so that they hit the listener just as the hardest, toughest breakbeats do.

Power's quite outstanding work on Erykah Badu's 1997 set *Baduizm* was proof positive of that. Whether it has The Roots or jazz-bass legend Ron Carter playing, the CD's audio quality is such that it lands like hip hop. The tonal weight and haze very much reflect a 'boom-bap' sensibility, one that is lyrically reinforced on 'Afro', a charming freestyle skit set to a mellow, musty blues riff. It pays tribute to Wu-Tang Clan, mad swordsmen then at rap's cutting edge.

Equating neo soul with a straight retro or revival strategy, one in which Gaye, Wonder, Hathaway *et al.* would have their licks dusted down and thrown back into the spotlight, was not wholly appropriate, given that some of the designated champions of the genre – from Badu to D'Angelo – were clearly not negating newer forms of black pop.

Be that as it may, what threw a massive spanner in the works for neo soul was these flag bearers' lack of consistency – none more so than D'Angelo, whose output in the thirteen years that have elapsed since 'Brown Sugar' amounts to a string of guest appearances on hip hop cuts and soundtracks, plus a second album, 2000's *Voodoo*, that failed to live up to the hype that has dogged D'Angelo since the release of his first. The set was somewhat patchy and jam-heavy, although the highpoints – 'Spanish Joint' and 'Africa' – were really quite majestic compositions.

Whether D'Angelo is or isn't neo-soul is no way near as important as the fact that he has yet to produce a defining artistic statement.

Because of the sense of deflation created by *Voodoo*, a work that was supposed to be a masterpiece, and the inability of D'Angelo to produce a follow-up, it really does feel as if neo soul has largely run its course. If he did come back strong, then the flag could always fly again, but it could become more limitation than liberation for an artist intent on growing.

One might also mention the inability of Lauryn Hill to match her excellent 1998 set *The Miseducation Of Lauryn Hill*, a record that stood quite intriguingly at the crossroads of soul and hip hop, announcing a great talent that has sadly not come to full fruition – something that might be ascribed to the artist's apparently turbulent private life.

As with D'Angelo, Hill became the source of immense frustration for soul fans. She showed she had the potential to be one of the pivotal figures in the genre, going into the millennium, but abruptly withdrew from the scene just as she seemed to be really getting started.

A reminder of Hill's brilliance recently came from an unexpected quarter: jazz singer Gretchen Parlato, who on her 2011 set *The Lost And Found* covered 'All That I Can Say', a gorgeous song Hill wrote for Mary J. Blige.

Hill's work did make the point that contemporary soul had more of a sociocultural or political edge than modern R&B, where the standard of lyric-writing was usually low. Certainly an artist like Me'Shell NdegéOcello has emerged as one of the most important commentators on the contemporary African American condition, by way of several uncompromising statements on quotidian realities. She has even dared to handle the generally taboo subject of same-sex relationships with the kind of explicit detail that the bulk of male hip hop artists have shimmied away from, be they straight or maybe not so straight.

The marriage is over

Any criticism of neo soul as a superficial hype vehicle has to be tempered with a few important pragmatic observations. The moniker helped to sell records because it created a story, or at least a semblance of one, for any media outlets that function primarily through trend-spotting, theme-identifying, the romance of the sea change, the arrival of the new school, the return of the old, the clash of new and old. Tradition versus modernity remains a timeless narrative.

To a large degree, the handful of soul bands that formed in the late 1980s and early '90s (mostly in the UK) were a reaction against the soul producer as one-man electronics fiend, and that tension was entirely healthy. That a group such as The Brand New Heavies, very much a stage-friendly outfit with their rhythm section and horns, contrasted so sharply with studio projects that were all keyboards, drum machine and vocalist was not a bad thing, since it revealed soul's idiomatic range.

Things get more complicated because any scene, school, sub-genre, call it what you will, must have its gatekeepers, curators and tastemakers, who effectively decide what constitutes the supposed art and what doesn't, who qualifies and who doesn't, which name is hip enough and which is not. Inevitably, there is a danger that some artists worthy of attention will be left out of the spotlight; or that, worse still, constraints will be placed on those who actually tick the right boxes.

Once tagged as neo soul, an artist would be expected to make neo soul or a working definition of it – which is fundamentally the problem with categorisation period. This was an issue for Jaguar Wright, who provocatively titled her 2005 album *Divorcing Neo 2 Marry Soul*, while the front cover of Erykah Badu's 2003 album *Worldwide Underground* featured the inscription 'Neo soul is dead'. When I asked Badu why a few years later, she pulled no punches.

'What's funny about neo soul is… I don't even know what it is', she told me at a press conference at the 2008 Barbados Jazz Festival.[2]

> I know what the two words mean but that term was thrust upon myself and D'Angelo by Kedar Massenburg, who was the president of the label that signed me. He was also managing D'Angelo at the time. That's what neo soul is to me. I don't reject it but honestly I didn't come up with it. I don't wanna be called the queen of it, 'cos I'm a change then everybody gon' be disappointed, so I feel that whatever it was that made him come up with that term, I thought it was brilliant but it's not me. It's *one* part of me. I mean, there's a whole lot of other stuff too.

Right underneath the 'Neo soul is dead' line on the *Worldwide Underground* sleeve, Badu asks a question that has important political ramifications for both herself as an artist and any audience old or new: 'Are you afraid of change?'[3] She then answers that question by equating change with *Worldwide Underground*. It now stands as a new aesthetic, one of her own making, as well as the title of an album.

The message is clear enough. Pigeonholes are for pigeons, not humans. Categories are not cool. Definitions are to be stretched, not tightened.

Echoing her sentiments is Amp Fiddler, the keyboardist-singer who made his breakthrough as a solo artist in 2002 with the excellent album *Waltz Of The Ghetto Fly*, after spending many years as a backing musician for George Clinton's P-Funk agglomeration, among others.

Interestingly, Fiddler evokes the danger of racial segregation along with an attack on artistic freedom. 'The term neo soul … I don't like to be called that because it represents something that has no possibility', he told me in London in 2008.

> It's very limiting. I want my music to have no limitations in who it reaches. I don't wanna reach a neo soul crowd, I know they're all gonna be black. I want a diversified crowd. If I go to a so-called neo soul show, it feels like I'm in a crowd of people who are trying to be hip. It's like some trendy shit. I'm already soulful, you know, that's it, man. I don't have to try to be it.[4]

How he would have fared in the marketplace, though, without the success of Badu, D'Angelo and other neo soulites is open to speculation. It's hard to escape the impression that their breakthrough was crucial in creating a receptive climate for Fiddler, and that in itself partly vindicates the existence of a bandwagon in the first place.

It doesn't alter the fact that Fiddler's music is much more wide-ranging than the neo-soul buzzword implies, and that his astute use of electronics, drum-programming and house rhythms has very little to do with the 'organic' 1970s-style sounds that are at such a premium.

We live in a time of hyper-categorisation in the record industry. Black popular music in particular is largely defined by its ability to birth new sub-genres on a very regular basis. The creation of a new sound or school of thought acts almost as a counterweight to the speed with which recent history is erased, especially in the realm of hip hop, where artist longevity is a relatively hard nut to crack.

What remains fascinating is the way in which new characters occasionally come along and seem so simultaneously old and new, or rather of times passed and times present. This is borne out by Erykah Badu's self-defining manifesto of the 'analogue girl in a digital world'.

There are a number of other figures to mention, and each differs considerably from the other: Aloe Blacc, Georgia Anne Muldrow, Van Hunt, Anthony Hamilton and Raphael Saadiq, formerly of the group Tony! Toni! Toné!, who seldom fails to produce interesting work, either as a solo artist or as part of the one-off project Lucy Pearl. But of all the artists to have emerged in the last decade or so, apart from Badu and Me'Shell NdegéOcello, the one who strikes me as having the most interesting relationship with both the history and the contemporary state of black music is Bilal Oliver. The thirty-year-old Philadelphian can legitimately be described as a jazz singer, as the finesse of his work with the likes of saxophonist John Ellis and pianist Robert Glasper attests. Yet Oliver has produced three fine soul albums, 2001's *First Born Second*, 2006's *Love For Sale* and 2010's *Airtight's Revenge*, that are entirely progressive in the way they leaven finely crafted melodies with the textural quirks, rhythmic brawn and sense of noise as danger, noise as affront, noise as assault, that define some of the best productions in hip hop.

Particularly on the last of these albums, there are intricate embroideries of electronic flange or subtle tonal distortions that often buck up against the hissing, offbeat grind of a guitar, the hard-ass drums and the controlled, seductive menace that Oliver brings to his middle range. As such, many of the songs nudge a Parliament-Funkadelic template towards a more distilled form with less density. It can still be baroque, though. It is music that recognises the value of production yet refuses to abandon the basic principle of verse, chorus and interlude. Oliver does key changes. Like Erykah Badu, he is also more than a singer. He writes and produces.

What is missing from *Airtight's Revenge* is woodwinds. The album would have been perfect had a flute, oboe, soprano saxophone or clarinet been used on some tracks as a foil to Oliver's voice, primarily because of the delicacy of his tone and the precision with which he modulates it.

Anyway, the reason why Oliver's music remains more vital than that of many of his peers is the breadth of the references that underpin it.

In concert, he might end a performance with a blues-rock take on Gloria Jones's northern soul classic 'Tainted Love', but before that he might spring another surprise or two on the audience. For example, the introduction to one of Oliver's most celebrated songs, 'Sometimes', could stretch into a ten-minute minor-key jam that culminates in a quotation of the melody from Wayne Shorter's 'Footprints'. This is a case of an artist upholding the soul–jazz continuum discussed earlier in this book.

There are extremes to Oliver's artistic persona. The two poles that largely frame him are George Clinton and Nat 'King' Cole, embodiments of surrealism and sophistication, the archetypal scoundrel and the nobleman of black pop-art music. Without a doubt, the fact that Oliver had a formal musical education, attending the New School in New York alongside pianist Robert Glasper, may account for his harmonic finesse. And when he really opens up his upper register, as on a piece like 'All Matter', he reveals a voice of operatic majesty. Then again, the same could be said of several great gospel singers such as James Cleveland.

Bilal Oliver strikes me first and foremost as a blues artist who really understands the urgency, immediacy and wildness/madness of its classic exponents back in the 1950s, as well as the urgency, immediacy and wildness/madness of life in the millennium. Hence he squares the circle between the urban music of then and the urban music of now.

There is an edginess, a volatility to Oliver on stage that seems equal parts natural adrenalin and irreverent, risqué theatricality that defines anyone from Little Richard to Richard Pryor to Prince Rogers Nelson.

In fact, Oliver often leans towards The Purple One in his songwriting sensibilities, particularly the kind of eerie, grave contemplation that Prince presented so compellingly on *Sign Of The Times*. There is a conjunction of beauty and austerity in many of Oliver's verses.

At times the 'that nigger's crazy!' stage antics, especially the swigs from a wine bottle, can be tiresome.[5] But they do not detract from one substantial weapon Oliver has apart from his killer voice: killer melodies.

It is a monumentally important part of his aesthetic that has perhaps been overlooked because of the quality of Oliver's voice. What is striking about some of his compositions, none more so than 'Love Poems', is precisely how well-crafted the themes are; how they glide and hover; how many more whole or half notes he uses than the bulk of R&B scream queens, intent on pumping out a hail of eighths and sixteenths; how relaxed his verses can be. Oliver knows when not to rush.

There is a melodic craftsmanship here that reflects both an engagement with a black-music tradition taking in anything from doo-wop to jazz balladry and an interest in European classical harmony.

What to call Bilal Oliver, though? How to market him? How to break him to the masses? Would it be viable to create a new sub-genre called 'neo soul jazz hip hop blues rock', or would it be better to say that he has soul, can write jazz and talk and sing the blues as well?

Do we have to explain the word 'blues' to a new generation of urban music fans who listen to R&B but rarely hear the term 'rhythm and blues'?

With new terms being coined to describe music so regularly, any genre with a pantheon that covers a few decades or more is in danger of looking like an anachronism, something of little relevance to a voracious youth market. Whether soul, jazz and blues are old forms of music is largely irrelevant. They are old brands, old images, old products.

Neo soul jazz hip hop blues rock could be a new sub-genre but it might not catch on. There are far too many words to say and, more to the point, to fit into the small box of iTunes classification.

Calling Bilal Oliver or even Erykah Badu or D'Angelo – assuming he makes another record in the next twenty years or so[6] – neo soul would be largely pointless now. The bandwagon that music became has largely ground to a halt, and there is no real sense of a concerted assembly of artists forming a whole greater than the sum of its parts – perhaps the greatest thing about any form of movement.

Guilty or not of creating a hype bubble that could only burst sooner or later, neo soul did nonetheless accomplish the simple but fundamental task of giving the s-word the highest profile it had enjoyed since the mid-1980s, when Bobby Womack dubbed himself – rather melodramatically – 'the last soul man'. That said, it was a prescient declaration, given that hip hop's rapid commercial ascendance was imminent.

Commercial free jazz? Just as long as it's grooving

If Womack was the last soul man, then could there be such a thing as the first neo soul man or the first man of soul reborn? Methinks not.

There was just another soul man who came along after the last one.

The idea of something being restored or reclaimed, the notion of a return to core values, is an extremely powerful one. Certainly black music, be it the populist strand of soul or the art strand of jazz, has seen many revivals over the course of its long and winding history.

What really makes these revivals interesting is not so much the re-assertion of either a type of sound or an approach to music-making that may hitherto have been lost, but the infusion of something novel into the process – so there is an acknowledgment that the world has shifted decisively since the birth of the music in times passed and the attempt to reinvigorate it in times present.

Neo music thus tells us that history is valuable and that it is ever-changing. Tradition can be a dynamic not a static force. Tradition does not have to die to be reborn. Over time, soul has evolved and taken on new resonances pre-cisely because artists with ambition, if not vision, have chosen to use time-honoured blues chords, gospel melodies and funk rhythms as a flexible body around which to wrap new sonic clothes, or to contort a limb in an original way through the input of other genres.

A very significant artist who has done just that recently is the Washington-born, New York-based singer-keyboard player Mem Nahadr, aka M. Nahadr. Her 2009 debut *EclecticIsM* is one of the best records released since the mil-lennium and a hugely important addition to the canon of soul. It resound-ingly acknowledges the music's roots while embracing several genres that lie outside it: namely, free jazz, electronica, experimental pop and opera, a key common denominator between Nahadr and Bilal Oliver.

Like Oliver, Nahadr does more than sing. She writes and produces.

Nahadr has a stunning multi-octave voice and has made extremely crea-tive use of synthesizers (see Chapter 11), but what really makes her music striking is its clear absorption of the spirits of two great artists, one black and one white, who are not usually mentioned in the same breath: Chaka Khan and Kate Bush.

Then again, Nahadr was mentored by the avant-garde clarinettist Sabir Mateen, so she has first-hand experience of the world of free jazz, where structures are generally more abstract than in soul. She dubbed her work 'commercial free jazz' as a tongue-in-cheek reference to the way it bridges the gap between populism and esotericism, with melodies that are easily retained and improvisations, particularly those performed with her own gym-fit voice, that are not.

On the thorny issue of categorisation, Nahadr is relatively indifferent. Although she accepts that what she does could loosely be described as 'alternative black music', she used the s-word with notable conviction when we spoke in 2009. 'This is soul music, literally as well as figuratively. I see the ancestry in my compositions. I guess I leave it to those who need to give it a name... I call it soul music.'[7]

Food for thought, indeed. Is there really a need for another term?

Frankly, just calling something soul music these days is not sexy, primarily because the attendant connotations are relatively staid.

Soul, for many, evokes the 1960s and '70s, and a suited and booted singer tied to a blues-gospel base, rather than an artist using that base as a point of departure for creative journeys that absorb other musical data.

What Nahadr, Oliver and Badu essentially suggest is the enduring nature of the blues. It is a devilishly flexible form. For a start, it has many structural possibilities. And although the most recognised template is the twelve bars, complete with time-honoured changes, the blues as a form without changes – where sometimes melody and spoken-word narration flow organically in and out of each other – is highly effective. The power of a John Lee Hooker or a Son House lies in their ability to move you so much while sometimes doing so little.

That blues evolved into rhythm and blues, rock and roll, soul, funk and rock demonstrates the huge potential of its base lexicon, and the beauty of an essential blues rhythm like a shuffle is that it invites myriad variations from a musician with imagination. Players with a modicum of curiosity will think about how the tension created by the use of two beats against three, how a conversation between the ride cymbal, snare and bass drum, can change from one day to the next.

Players with a modicum of curiosity will think about how the sense of physicality in a performance can alter if the emphasis is placed with relentless efficiency on the downbeat, or how the meaning of funk in African American popular consciousness – something dysfunctional, malodorous and uncouth – can translate into sound as something infectious, exuberant and energising.[8]

The story of black popular music is one of the original remix, of change and transformation. So one way of playing the blues is not definitive, although the underlying communicative value of the idiom is.

Which is why Jimi Hendrix, whether he was in the vanguard of rock or pyschedelia or whatever one cares to call it, described his music as 'today's blues' to a quizzical look from Dick Cavett on his popular chat show. Maybe he was dazzled by Jimi's azure kimono.[9]

That was not standard attire for a blues man. It was no visual cliché.

Hendrix's declaration was made in 1969. Yet as a concept or, more to the point, a profound insight or *modus operandi*, 'today's blues' has enormous meaning. Hendrix is essentially saying that life is not static and the deployment of sound to reflect that flux is also subject to change. But there is a concept, the blues – a place of confession, congregation and catharsis – that can underpin any journey through time. And at best, today's blues evokes a fantastic voyage that can be both backwards, to sounds that are known, and forwards, to sounds that are unknown.

Maybe the whole point of the blues is that it excels at the push and pull between the familiar and the unfamiliar. The chord changes and rhythms have been employed so extensively over the years that the listener can anticipate them. Yet the relative simplicity of the blues form allows room for structural and textural manoeuvre that can create a sensation (or perhaps illusion) of the new within the old.

Even Hendrix's most elaborately constructed songs can be broken down into constituent parts that were used in a time before he was born.

To this day, 'Voodoo Chile' is a work of both ancestral and futuristic beauty.

That's exactly what you have in the music of M. Nahadr and Bilal Oliver. It offers both the push of novelty and the pull of familiarity.

One of the reasons why is because, like Hendrix, these artists are obviously not content to listen to just one form of music. In both their vocal performances and their arrangements, Nahadr and Oliver evince a curiosity about sound in the widest possible sense, reminding us that, though you play the blues, you can still embrace every kind of music.

Recognising this fact is hugely important because it is the only way clichés and stereotypes about black artists will break down. Both the music industry and the media will be more receptive to these artists when they push the envelope towards any kind of sound or form that might be deemed unusual – and, dare one say, not typically black.

It is tempting to think that The O' Jays, those prince regents of vocal groups, wrote a love letter to soul with their 1975 anthem 'I Love Music'. But they did not. They wrote a love letter to 'any kind of music ... just as long as it's grooving'.[10] And maybe that kind of open-mindedness is not as readily attributed to exponents of soul because the genre has been identified so heavily with outpourings of emotion, if not divine inspiration, rather than with ingenuity in the use of instruments or detailed research of many genres of music.

Yet George Clinton, Stevie Wonder *et al* could not have made their work so rich without embracing a range of music other than the blues and gospel. And that same curiosity, perhaps one of the greatest assets for any artist, propelled a number of their peers and successors – which is why Latin music, folk, rock, dub and classical music were integrated into soul to varying degrees during the 1970s and '80s.

In fact, there has been plenty of pyschedelia in mainstream soul over time, since experimentation with both synthesizers and studio technology has been such a crucial part of the music. The fact that a number of artists made records anticipating hip hop in some way is also a sure-fire indication of a desire to broaden the lexicon of soul.

Hence the creative premise of M. Nahadr's *EclecticIsM* – as personal a credo as it is – tallies with the wider history of soul music. It is not necessary for soul musicians continually to trumpet their artistic achievements or artistic manifestos to the world at large. But it is telling that similar calls for diversity are encapsulated in a more politically confrontational manner by Funkadelic's bold rhetoric of 'Who says a funk band can't play rock?' and by Jill Scott's impassioned hymn to a musical church broader than Broadway: 'If it's hip hop, if it's bebop, reggaeton with a metronome …. if it's classical, country mood, rhythm and blues … if it's deeper soul, if it's rock & roll'.[11] These lyrics feature on the song 'Let It Be'. The Beatles it ain't.

20 Soul is stranger than fiction

Basically, you put it all in the blender; you see what happens.   (I.G. Culture)

I suppose that I have a real affection for sound.   (M. Nahadhr)

Place on the burner ... and bring to the boil ... now beat ... well.   (King Curtis)

Forty second fantasy

Jill Scott composed a quite beautiful piece on her 2007 album *The Real Thing: Words And Sounds Vol. 3* that saw her open her heart on the issue of solitude, detailing its insomniac side-effects and the way its attendant stresses and strains would come down hard on a girl prey to a 'gangster type of need'. The track is 'Celibacy Blues'.

History weighs heavy here. Psychically and emotionally, the blues has always been a functional platform on which to present and transcend any subject that nestles into the fabric of human life, from the most prosaic (Leadbelly's 'Packing Trunk Blues' [1935]) to the most tumultuously romantic (Ray Charles's 'I Got A Woman And Some Blues' [1959]) to the most political (Marvin Gaye's 'Inner City Blues' [1971]).

Anything and everything in life can be summarised, dramatised and alchemised by the blues. It is as much a system of mental and spiritual survival as it is a handful of chords, scales and riffs that can be deployed according to formulae potent enough to have underpinned significantly the evolution of many genres of music over time.

Soul, although substantially fired by gospel, has largely remained tied to the blues, because it offers both a basis for lyrical richness and great communicative power as a form. Soul is song. The principle is sacrosanct. A verse, perhaps with chord changes set in a twelve-bar pattern, perhaps with no changes at all, is followed by a chorus. The cycle is repeated, and a change of key usually occurs on the bridge before the verse and chorus make a return, striding forth to the conclusion.

Simple as that. Or is it? If this is a basic musical canvas, then – as hopefully this book has demonstrated convincingly – the spectrum of timbres, the rhythmic flourishes and the enormous wealth of detail in the *arrangements* of soul have not, since the genre evolved from rhythm and blues in the 1960s, been found wanting either in imagination or ambition. This is why classic and contemporary soul can sound and feel so different, even though there are constants – core values, if you will – that bind the two. One hears slivers of Stevie Wonder in Omar Lye-Fook's work but his 2006 set *Best By Far* has a rhythmic and textural sensibility, shaped by Jamaican and British music, that are his and his alone.

Jazz remains the most creative of existing genres because a number of its practitioners have consistently challenged any approach to form and narrative convention developed by their predecessors or peers, so that the aesthetic is in a constant state of animated debate.

Jazz musicians have, on many occasions, dispensed with song in their quest for an alternative route to creative fulfilment, one that removes the safety harness of verse-chorus-interlude and engages in lateral thinking, improvisation and sometimes classical orchestration.

There are few pieces in the soul canon that can match the suites of Duke Ellington for harmonic sophistication and structural invention. The lavish beauty created by the blend of many reed and brass 'voices' in his orchestra, as well as the poetic stealth with which Ellington's scores unfold, remain a thing of wonder. There is a restless, driving, questing energy here that has made jazz an innovative language.

At its peak, jazz questions itself. It then thinks of new lines of inquiry.

For the most part, soul music has not been through as many developments in form as jazz has, but it has proved to be an extremely creative genre. And one could argue, in fact, that soul's richness of expression is particularly impressive for having been achieved *without* taking the liberties taken by jazz. Instead, it has resigned itself to operating within the fundamental parameters of song.

Because many of the great forward thinkers in soul – Ray Charles, James Brown, Aretha Franklin, Stevie Wonder, Maurice White, Marvin Gaye – had either studied jazz or, as fledgling artists, performed the basic standards repertoire, it stands to reason that they were able to bring the degree of invention they did to their own form of sophisticated pop music.

Gaye's *What's Going On* remains a high watermark of creativity for the brilliance with which so many elements are handled on one set. Rhythm section, orchestra and complex vocal techniques all come together in an uninterrupted sequence that also has delicious grooves. That makes it a rarity among rarities in pop, a suite you can dance to, and if that isn't a feat for a concept album, then nothing is. And yet *What's Going On* is often missing from lists of historic concept albums, which are more or less perceived as the sole preserve of progressive rock.

Progressive soul, if such a maladroit term existed, could dampen the enthusiasm some might have for black pop. But it is an important notion to take on board, as within the pretensions of the maligned 'prog' lexicon there is often ambition. And that takes us back to jazz.

Ray Charles's formula of genius + soul = jazz, the title of his 1960 album, is still relevant today. It could be remixed into soul = jazz plus a different genius, a different complexity – or rather with those elements distilled. That is very true in the case of Stevie Wonder.

It is ironic, if not disheartening, that several critics have taken issue with Wonder's inclination towards lengthy solos and expansive arrangements in concert, instead of 'just playing the tune'. The reason why his melodies are so beautiful in the first place is precisely his extensive study of improvisation and classical music. Sadly, not one of the reviews in the British national press of a quite astounding gig that Wonder played at London's BBC Maida Vale studios in 2007 referred to the fact that, during a hits medley, he reprised John Coltrane's 'Giant Steps', a harmonic steeplechase liable to upend all but the most able of jazz thoroughbreds – the point being that its relevance to 'Sir Duke' is clear as a cowbell in a salsa number.

A friend of mine has been playing Wonder, soul and all kinds of music to his children for some time. One day I asked his eleven-year-old son what his favourite kind of music was. He spontaneously answered 'classical', which charmed me for defying the clichés of black kids not being able to relate to anything outside 'urban' music. Pressed as to why, he gave an illuminating answer: 'There are lots of instruments'.

Indeed there are. They fill a studio, cover a stage, flood a speaker. Throughout its history, soul music has also made use of lots of instruments. Rhythm sections have been fully electric since the early 1960s; all manner of percussion has supplemented kit drums; enormous arsenals of synthesizers and keyboards have been drafted in since the '70s; electronics have been used ambitiously since the '80s; 'old' instruments such as saxophones and trumpets, the almighty horns, have occasionally returned to the music in the '90s; string orchestras, or in some cases a single cello, have also been deployed.

Sounds have exploded. They have multiplied ten-fold. The genre is predominantly electro-acoustic, at times skeletal and at times orchestral. At its best, soul has crammed a fair amount of the stacks of kit listed above into a single arrangement.

Turn the clock back to 1977 and Earth, Wind & Fire's 'Fantasy'. It starts as a classical ballad, the four-bar string prelude vividly redolent of a baroque theme, with the faintest echo of a mandolin or harpsichord.

Then it bursts into life on bar five, the strings swirling into a liquid and otherworldly, space-age synthesizer chord against a hard pulsation of drums and bass guitar. Their low, bulky tonality contrasts potently with the high-register tingle of bongos slapped in double time.

Horns spit out glancing eighth notes like a car-chase theme, while a series of rapier-thin guitar chords ping and pow, ricocheting brashly into being as a second, single-note guitar line is aggressively finger-picked to create the taut, wiry timbre of a banjo.

In an instant the whole band – rhythm, horns, strings – gives the impression of a well-oiled engine in dramatic ignition, the cogs and pistons all pumping with startling efficiency. This mini-suite lasts just eight bars. Barely forty seconds are on the clock. Yet the level of musicianship, the finesse of the arrangement and the sheer breadth of artistic ambition rival what many groups would squeeze into three if not five minutes of music. The beauty of the work lies in the blend of acoustic classical resonances and electric funk tonalities, in the collision of an ancestral sound and a futuristic one, in the bridging of disparate worlds, in the creation of a great sonic expanse. As a smart black kid says, there are 'lots of instruments'.

Vocalist Philip Bailey makes his entrance after the instrumental intro and the piece progresses on a sumptuous melodic path as his falsetto is intermittently thickened by close harmonies, with more than a passing nod to the 1950s doo-wop era that coincided with Earth, Wind & Fire founder Maurice White's youth. Historical strands entwine quite gloriously.

Earth, Wind & Fire were more than accomplished musicians, not averse to complicating their music above what may have been perceived as the standard difficulty threshold for a pop audience – although one should bear in mind that mainstream charts included more instrumental songs in the 1970s to further the band's jazzophile cause.

Earth, Wind & Fire were actually very avant-garde thinkers. On 'Runnin'', one of the other outstanding cuts from *All 'n All*, the album that featured 'Fantasy', they put an Afro-Brazilian rhythm through a slalom of 4/4 and 6/8 time, with several key changes that could easily wrong-foot a musician not on his game. They also indulged in a bout of studio trickery that remains audacious in its very concept. At around the three-quarter mark of the arrangement, after a couple of burning horn solos, the band slowed the rhythm to a standstill and started to chant and wail, as if they were going into a full-on gospel trance, the voices hollering indecipherable sounds and cries caught tantalisingly between pleasure and pain. Then the chorus of a song is heard filtering into treble only, with no bass whatsoever, as if on a transistor radio or down a telephone line. It is 'Serpentine Fire', the piece that opens the album.

In the most crudely surreal fashion, Earth, Wind & Fire sampled themselves.[1] It's not hip hop as we know it, but this is 1977, several years before the process materialised in earnest. Earth, Wind & Fire provide an enlightening example of the omni-referential dynamic and the desire to treat pre-recorded audio as a building block for a song that would later inform hip hop. We have an inescapable truth. This is a band that has to be seen and heard by all and sundry, even though the day that rappers take Maurice and the boys as sartorial models has yet to come. You can decide whether that is a cause for celebration or lamentation.

Twilight zone

One of the reasons why artists like Earth, Wind & Fire made such interesting music was their awareness of 'schools' or styles spanning several different eras, their constantly self-reflexive and referential attitude to black music's heritage. They were looking back and forward simultaneously, which has also been a common trait in the jazz aesthetic.

Furthermore, some of the musicians who had come from one generation, from one era, carried their experience and expertise through to another. This explains why disco could never be an entirely adulterated version of soul. Many significant figures from the golden era of rhythm and blues contributed to the new genre.

So Sylvester's 'You Make Me Feel Mighty Real' has a marked orchestral finesse, great gospel rhythm and a lovely pace in its arrangement. It was produced by Harvey Fuqua, the man who mentored a young Marvin Gaye in the ranks of doo-wop legends The Moonglows.

Similarly, for all his highly idiosyncratic approaches to songwriting and production, George Clinton, the visionary force behind P-Funk, occasionally enlisted the services of David Van De Pitte, the genial gent who wrote the sumptuous string scores for Gaye's *What's Going On*. Look at another classic floor filler, Al Hudson's 'Spread Love', cut right in the middle of the disco boom in 1978. If the orchestrations sound majestic, it's because that man Van De Pitte again penned the charts.

Not all the creative richness in the soul music of this era and beyond can be ascribed to the guiding hand of a Van De Pitte or a Fuqua. But it's clear that the continuity they provided with the old-school set-up of producer, arranger, horns, strings and rhythm section paid superbly inventive dividends as new electric instruments and changing recording techniques came resolutely into play.

Since the 1960s and '70s also saw a large number of jazz musicians contributing to soul music, the standard of playing was invariably high.

In terms of sound alone, the diversity of soul as it entered the 1980s was astounding. The growing sophistication of percussive, highly Latin-inflected rhythm arrangements, as well as purely electronic productions in which keyboards and drum machines were deployed extensively to create a matrix of intricately sequenced grooves, were just two examples of musicians pushing beyond existing templates.

Quirks in arrangements, such as the use of a bass synthesizer and a slapped bass guitar to create a spectrum of tonalities in the low register, the enormous complexity with which multiple guitar lines were constructed, or the tantalising push and pull between sung melody and spoken word, made the evolving repository of sounds enviably copious.

These achievements may be overlooked because some fantastically creative moments were also great chart successes. They were sing-along hits with big vocal hooks, and that may have deflected attention from the ingenuity of the arrangements. It doesn't mean some of the playing and producing wasn't highly creative. One example that immediately springs to mind is Odyssey's 'Use It Up And Wear It Out', a single that soared to the top of the UK pop charts in 1980. Is this a frivolous piece of music? A trivial exhortation to dance your troubles away, like there's nothing left in this whole world you care about, apart from shaking your body down to the count of one, two, three? Could this really be art?

Possibly not. But that's not the point. It is artful pop. 'Use It Up And Wear It Out' has a devilishly astute blend of percussive and tonal characteristics that combine to lift the music way beyond the perfunctory role of a backing track that serves the surging vocals. The central rhythmic component is an Afro-Brazilian samba pattern, reinforced by a strange, very pinched synthesizer motif that sounds like a blast of hot air from a pipe. Set to the main beat, it acts as a sly aural shadow, eerily stalking the body of percussion.

One sound thus frames another. That happens again with the vocal line on the melody, which is doubled note for note by the most discreet clang of a glockenspiel. Hence the song unfolds against a backdrop of understated chiming bells, the effect of which is to lend a quite woozy, almost hallucinatory slant to the whole stereo image.

On the breakdown, the rhythm goes carnival crazy and a barrage of timbales, congas and sundry hand drums starts to run riot. Stylistically, the music occupies an undefined space between American soul, African folk and electro-pop. Its attention to detail and wide span of references make words like disco too vague a description.

Yet this is how Odyssey are often tagged. They have an image problem. Hipster epithets have not been coined for them. Terms like avant-soul or progressive soul have not been widely used over time. And while most people would probably accept that George Clinton and Bootsy Collins are the most relevant carriers of this putative mantle, there are many other artists who have proved themselves capable of thinking outside the box. Pop or not, Odyssey's music had moments of great creativity. Then again, with jazz musicians like bass maestro Marcus Miller contributing to several of their studio sessions, this should come as no surprise.

All this means that the instrumental passages in soul and funk, the fêted breakdown, where, for the most part, the vocals dropped out, were moments of high quality musicianship rather than tedious interludes that listeners had to endure before the star singer stepped back to the mike.

It is a major mistake to assume that these passages were bland or inconsequential. They gave the band a chance to display skills.

Another group, Maze, whose leader and vocalist Frankie Beverly was mentored by Marvin Gaye, is also worth considering at this point.

Very much the dyed-in-the-wool guitar-led soul band who were most effective when pumping out hits like 1980's 'Joy And Pain', Maze always had a proclivity for using synthesizers in an imaginative way, as can be heard in the growling wildcat keyboards that grace 'Southern Girl'. But only the most prescient of fans could have foreseen 'Twilight',[2] a song Maze cut in 1985. It is a mesmeric, mystic dreamscape of a composition that is both Afro-funk and techno-soul.

'Twilight' is machine music. It is both proto-ambient pop and deep house.

Texturally, it is aeons away from the strains of any horn-led 1960s soul.

Yet the immensely significant thing is that the track came from the minds and hands of artists who were completely tied to a rhythm and blues *playing* tradition. This was a proper band who had obviously learnt lessons from a long line of groups reaching back to Booker T. & The MGs, the Bar-Kays and the Motown and Chess house bands, all of which were predicated on the sacrosanct principle that the most simple of licks always had to be nailed down good and proper – as do the most complex of licks.

Maze applied this principle to their use of electronics. If 'Twilight' is one thing – and this explains the parallel with classical music – it is a consummate display of precision in writing and networking different parts for a song. From the opening string-like chord, a constant draft of air flowing in the background, to the potent gurgle of keyboard bass, the sharp raking of kalimba, the fleeting syncopations of organ prised straight from the Jimmy Smith book of licks and the rising swell of polyphonic synths, every component locks together with quite superb split-second accuracy at several strategic points within the basic 4/4 time.

Two- and three-note phrases jerk and jolt on the pulse to create a kind of robotic, assembly-line motion. Yet the underlying current of the song is a bassline which, although programmed, still has an aftertaste of swing, thus generating a real tension between stiffness and sensuality.

There is a huge amount of imagery in this piece. The evocative power of the music is such that the twilight of the title – the wistful fading of the sun, its segue into night – is rendered with great vividness by the range of sounds and their skilful deployment. What all this says is that Maze – surely under the influence of Stevie Wonder – were willing to embrace all kinds of music-making equipment and state-of-the-art technology as a means to an end, so they could translate ideas into sound as effectively as possible. There is a very clear continuity between 'Twilight' and 'Pastime Paradise', the highlight of *The Secret Life Of Plants*, the concept album Wonder recorded in 1976.

Lyrically, that set may be opaque but sonically it is an explosion of colour, ideas and astute manipulations of those ideas. It sends out a vital message about the fervour with which soul music in the 1970s would incorporate anything and everything novel into its audio landscape – something a musician like Bernie Worrell was already doing in his work with George Clinton's P-Funk agglomeration.

Soul in the 1980s, the decade in which Maze's 'Twilight' was recorded, splits opinion. It is fair to say that the music suffers by comparison with the '70s, a time when the genre hit several creative heights. Yet it would be wrong to dismiss '80s soul too rashly. Perhaps fewer quality albums were recorded but there was a plethora of interesting twelve-inch releases, many of them the result of one-off studio projects, that found favour on dance floors and in which electronics took an increasingly prominent role.

One of the problems is that we still haven't collated all the relevant information to provide an accurate overview of the period. But even though an item like Charades' 'Goin' Out Dancing' may be obscure, it is not simply a train spotter's trump card. It is a piece of highly creative music that was only issued in limited quantities, a 45-rpm song that, with no long player to follow, disappeared after its initial burst of club popularity in New York. Yet it is a valuable footnote. The names of its producers, Tunde Ra and Taharqa Aleem, are also worth remembering.

There are more songs like this waiting to be excavated and reassessed. The problem is, though, that there is little commercial motivation to do so, as the market for this music has shrunk considerably. Yet these tracks are essential to any real understanding of modern black pop.

The story of 1980s soul is as much about singles as albums.

Home cookin'

A fascination with the ever-evolving world of keyboards, synthesizers, sequencers and drum machines made its presence felt in no uncertain terms throughout the 1980s and '90s. Anyone from Jam & Lewis in the USA to broken-beat progenitor I.G. Culture in Britain showed a voracious appetite for new sounds and for new ways of constructing and layering fresh polyrhythms – or rather old polyrhythms in astute new permutations.

I.G. took the idea of percussion as a pervasive, incendiary, energizing force, something that can be traced back to Earth, Wind & Fire, to another level.

Crucially, the work of both did not entirely obviate the need for musicians or instruments, but rather entered into a tantalising relationship with them. Although the advent of both acid jazz and neo soul signalled to a large extent the reaction of musicians against electronics and studio producers, the tension and interaction between these two constituencies has always been an integral part of the fabric of soul music, as exemplified by artists such as Stevie Wonder, Maze and I.G. Culture.

Speaking in the late 1990s, I.G. adopted an attitude to the creative act that was full of both gung-ho bravado and a quasi-scientific discipline based on respect for his forebears. 'Basically, you put it all in the blender; you see what happens … and then you really work on getting everything as tight as possible. That's what a man like Quincy Jones used to do. If I wanna be anything, it's the son of Quincy Jones.'[3]

Ultimately, the value of soul music lies in that very paternity. Broken beat, disco, house and hip hop all have, to varying degrees, a historical relationship with soul and rhythm and blues. But music industry partitioning has largely obscured this connection, making soul appear a creatively static genre, when in fact it has continued to evolve by way of its offshoots. Soul has new as well as old figureheads.

It may be much easier to say that Quincy Jones belongs to 'old soul', to the undersoil of tradition, and I.G. Culture to 'new dance music', to the topsoil of modernity – and that one is not relevant to the other. But I see, or rather hear, the two figures as sound adventurers who are inextricably linked. The modernity has flowered from the tradition.

Ten years have now elapsed since I.G. recorded pieces like 'My History', yet this music has not acquired the mildew of something faddish or inconsequential. The rhythmic and textural finesse, the artful extension of an Afro-Latin groove heritage, still impress. How the music will measure up in the next decade is hard to tell, but at this point in time it sounds very much like a worthy addition to the soul-funk canon.

The same prognosis could be made for *EclecticIsM*, the 2009 album by M. Nahadr, which is one of the best debuts I've heard in any genre in years. To a large degree, it acts as a brilliant summary of the infinite flexibility and modernity of the basic verse-chorus song structure, and of blues chords that have been at the core of black popular music for almost a century. It is a new sound deeply rooted in old ways.

Some of the bass lines that have been bumping around in funk for decades are still present and correct. Yet they are invigorated by novel arrangements using two bass guitars, heavily distorted trumpet and all manner of keys and electronics, none of which diminishes the work's strong melodic base. There are great songs. But there is more: 'I suppose that I have a real affection for sound', said Nahadr tellingly.[4]

She is not alone. Contemporary soul music counts artists of a similar ilk, who are dedicated to exploring form as well as content in the art of songwriting and arranging, and who are restless in their search for newness. Me'Shell NdegéOcello, Bilal Oliver, Peven Everett, Jhelisa Anderson, I.G. Culture, Omar Lye-Fook and Erykah Badu are arguably the cutting edge along with Nahadr, but there are several others who have struggled to achieve the same profile as these artists. Like Marvin Gaye, Stevie Wonder and Donny Hathaway, they all have marked jazz sensibilities. Me'Shell and her contemporaries challenge listeners.

None of which gives artists with this kind of talent much hope of attracting the substantial major-label investment that enabled soul greats such as Earth, Wind & Fire to fulfil their musical vision. Perhaps what is needed more than anything by their descendants is simply more resources. Electronics have been deployed with considerable creativity by the likes of Nahadr, but there is an argument that someone of her talent might well produce a work of epoch-defining beauty if she were given the budget for a full horn section, several backing singers and a string orchestra – something that countless artists yearn for.

A key strand of soul music, lest we forget, has been orchestral. It is essential that this rich element in the genre's vocabulary is not lost.

If *What's Going On* is unthinkable without Marvin Gaye's voice and lyrics, then hearing it without strings is an equally grim prospect.

It could be said that the relative commercial failure of recent soul works – above all, Bilal Oliver's quite magnificent 2001 debut *First Born Second* – sends out an SOS on the lowly ranking of soul in a pressurised record industry. Yet recordings such as this and *EclecticIsM* reveal the music's enduring ability to land a surprise punch seemingly from out of nowhere.

Then again, Nahadr did come from *somewhere*. And that place was history; more specifically, the history of the New York jazz scene. Her time spent under the aegis of veteran clarinettist Sabir Mateen was a vital factor in shaping the uniqueness of her musical vision. Hence the borders between generations and genres are crossed in one fell swoop – which can be worthwhile, since it increases the exchange of information that might take an artist out of his or her comfort zone.

Whether or not soul music can continue to fashion an artistically fruitful relationship with other genres remains to be seen. One of the great ironies of the Internet age, where information is more or less limitless, is how unwilling some new artists are to see the full picture of an art form's evolution. What it means is that Stevie Wonder is cited as an influence by all and sundry these days, whereas few hail or, more to the point, reflect in their work what enabled Stevie to *become* a Wonder – namely, intense study of Duke Ellington and John Coltrane as well as Ray Charles. This is possibly because the 'noodling' jazz of Ellington and Coltrane is widely stigmatised in pop. That can't mask an essential truth though: if you want to write the next 'Too High', clear 'Giant Steps' first.

Soul is still perceived first and foremost as the domain of singers. The idea that the soul musician, the player, has made a significant contribution to the canon remains an argument that needs to be won. Yet we do a great disservice to both vocalists and instrumentalists by not recognising that it is precisely the combination of their efforts that makes the soul songbook so rich.

Some of the most treasured moments in the genre are really about this union: how a singer, pianist or horn player creates a sonic symbiosis that can have a deep effect on the listener, and how removing one or other element from the equation leaves the music sadly bereft. When the first few bars of Marvin Gaye's 'Let's Get It On' ache into life, it is not just the heated, hazy sensuality of the singer's voice that catches the ear, but the way it is paralleled and enhanced by the caressing purr, the immodest sigh of Wah Wah Watson's guitar.

This book has been a humble attempt to reveal some of the artistry in the soul-music canon and to point out that it has stemmed from a desire to push the envelope instrumentally as a jazz musician would – and that communication between the two genres has been widespread. King Curtis's 'Memphis Soul Stew' was designated as the backbone of the text: the 'one', the downbeat that I return to again and again because it pools the virtues of soul and jazz and formalises an appreciation of instruments in its spoken intro.

'Memphis Soul Stew' is also a tribute to that invaluable commodity in black popular music, the band. It is vital that this vehicle, this motor, keeps on running.

Consider Curtis's group: the family of musicians that, with its rhythm and horn sections, held a residue of the orchestras that were so important in the genesis of rhythm and blues. The players. The backroom-boy pistons in the engine of soul, all creating sonic brilliance to enhance that of Aretha, Otis, Marvin *et al*. The sheer groovacious verve of their performance is to this day astounding. Curtis's saxophone is magnificent, as is the rhythm section that 'cooks' when he instructs: 'Place on the burner and bring to the boil, now beat … well!'

Since 1967, when that song was recorded, soul music has bubbled away in a number of different forms, the chefs found in Europe as well as America, the barriers of race crossed as the genre has become increasingly multicultural, particularly in places like London. Then again, it was never a monoracial genre, despite the equation of soul with blackness.

Listening to 'Memphis Soul Stew', there is little doubt that Curtis is 'talking black'. And one might say that, for its extreme funkiness, the rhythm section is 'playing black'. Granted. But they were not the people who were 'darker than blue'. Some were actually sidemen to Elvis Presley and in Bill Black's Combo. One of the most soulful units in rhythm and blues comprised a righteous black man with a horn and a bunch of funky white boys with guitars. You couldn't make it up.

Actually, you could. From The Daps and Booker T. & The MGs in the 1960s to The Brand New Heavies and Young Disciples in the '90s, the history of soul music has been marked by many fine white and multiracial groups. The incontrovertible truth is that great black pop has consistently crossed the colour line. It doesn't really matter whether the white boys come from a Birmingham with a southern US drawl or a Birmingham with a Brummie burr, as long as they know how to make it hot when the leader tells them to bring the groove to the boil, then beat well.

'Play That Funky Music, White Boy' may be a thought-provoking summons,[5] but it is not as meaningful as 'Play That Funky Music Right'.

21 A Memphis aftertaste

One more time … one more time … early in the morning.
(King Curtis, lead vocal/tenor saxophone)

Big in Smalls

King Curtis died in 1971, just four years after the recording of 'Memphis Soul Stew'. In circumstances that were never fully explained, he was tragically stabbed outside his apartment in New York. Curtis was thirty-six years old. The *Herald Tribune* granted him a four-paragraph obituary.

At the peak of his powers in the late 1960s, Curtis was whizzing through up to sixteen sessions a week for anybody and everybody at the cutting edge of soul, playing solos, arranging and producing. Examples of his consummate skill can be found on many records but his association with Aretha Franklin was something of a high watermark. Their combined forces on 'Respect' – the superb blend of the charge from her voice and the voltage from his tenor sax – is a treasured pop moment.

While ever moving forward, Curtis's engagement with the deep history of black music was unstinting. Just three months before his death, he played a quite unforgettable set at the Montreux Jazz Festival with pianist and vocalist 'Champion' Jack Dupree, one of the founding fathers of New Orleans blues, who began his recording career in 1940.

What stands out from that gig is both the raucous electricity the blues can generate and Dupree's capacity for lateral thinking, be it desultory surges in volume or, as was the pianist's wont, a puckish decision to put not four but three bar tags onto the end of a solo.

Playing mostly in the shuffle groove of one of his role models, Louis Jordan, King Curtis Ousley was on superb form that night. His improvising was rich in quasi-gymnastic grace, his tone displayed great vigour. The combined effect was to make some of the saxophone phrases sound as though they were gravel somehow skipping like pebbles on the pulse of a song.

There was a strong communicative side to Curtis's artistic character that stood in equilibrium with his desire to push himself creatively and technically. He was as much a jazz artist as a blues man.

More to the point, Curtis was a blues *singer*. Other concerts revealed that. For example, a decade before the Montreux gig Curtis played Smalls Paradise, New York. He was on stage with a combo of relatively little-known musicians that included a brilliant guitarist, Al Casey, former sideman to 1930s jazz legend Fats Waller, and a tidy drummer, Belton Evans. Completing the line-up were a very good pianist, Paul Griffin, and a bassist, Jimmy Lewis, who was unfortunately so badly miked that he is reduced to little more than a barely audible muffle.

The set largely features Curtis blowing with as much sass and invention as he would at the Montreux gig several years later. But one of the highlights of the Smalls Paradise set is a reprise of Ray Charles's 'What'd I Say', on which the saxophonist sings in a hugely commanding baritone. His high-pitched scream on the coda goes: 'One more time … one more time … early in the morning'. He's an absolute revelation.

That Curtis was a blues singer, albeit a largely closeted one, as well as a player strikes me as significant. If a virtuoso musician not only sings but does so in front of an audience, there is every chance he may become a more rounded artist, since his communicative powers are manifold. The musician's first-hand, 'lived' experience of voicing words may make him less inhibited when it comes to the world of wordless notes.

If Lester Young, one of jazz's great soloists, playing tenor sax is a thing of beauty, then Lester Young singing also has considerable charm.

Audiences count too. Some are more receptive to wordless expression than others. Soul may have hit a peak creatively at various points in its history because listeners not only accepted but welcomed an artist's desire to alternate between vocal and instrumental work – a group such as Earth, Wind & Fire being a very obvious case in point.

In the final part of the Smalls set, Curtis switches from R&B to bebop as easily as if he were unbuttoning his mohair suit. He proceeds to rip through that standard of standards, 'How High The Moon', bringing his tenor-sax solo to a potent climax by quoting the theme of Charlie Parker's 'Ornithology'. People just lose it. During the long and winding statement, executed at speed, the rhythm section throbs behind Curtis, the crowd noise rises to a feverish buzz, the detonation of yelps and whoops suggests the patrons either know the piece or are simply excited by a luscious lick handled with such style and, dare one say it, such a huge amount of soul. It is as if the audience is hearing words of some kind in a tune with no lyrics. You can imagine everybody having something of a righteous feeling. You can imagine everybody grooving together. You can imagine everybody in the house having a funky good time.

Notes

2. What is this thing called soul?

1. Common, *Like Water For Chocolate* (Universal, 2000).
2. Interview with the author, London (2005).
3. Eulogies to the South and 'country' life are numerous in black music, no more so than in Allen Toussaint's 'Southern Nights' (Reprise, 1975). I saw him perform this piece at London's Jazz Café in 2009, where Toussaint launched into a lengthy reminiscence of visits to relatives in the country when he was a boy. He became almost misty-eyed during this very engaging spoken-word interlude. One should also remember that the protagonist of Gladys Knight & The Pips' 'Midnight Train To Georgia' makes the journey to the comfort zone of the South because the West Coast – "L.A. was too much for the man" – represented alienation.

   Having said that, the South is also a byword for terror and oppression in the black mindset, something vividly captured in the chant 'I'll never go back to Georgia' featured on Dizzy Gillespie's 'Manteca'.

   The hell–heaven duality of the South is a reflection of the complexity of the African-American experience.
4. See tenor saxophonist Sonny Stitt's *Soul People* (Prestige, 1965).
5. Freddie Roach, *My People (Soul People)* (Prestige, 1967).
6. Stokely Carmichael, Black Power Address, Berkeley, CA (October 1966).
7. James Brown, 'Soul Power', on *Soul Classics* (Polydor, 1972).
8. James Brown, 'Get on the Good Foot', on *Get On The Good Foot* (Polydor, 1972).
9. See Brother Jack McDuff, *The Natural Thing* (Cadet, 1968). Here, a very attractive black couple both sport natural hair – sharply cut Afros – as well as dashikis.
10. Funkadelic, 'What is Soul?', on *Funkadelic* (Westbound, 1970).
11. See Nelson George, *The Death of Rhythm & Blues* (Harmondsworth: Penguin, 1988) and Greg Tate, *Flyboy In The Buttermilk* (London: Simon & Schuster, 1992).
12. As quoted in Michael Lydon, *Ray Charles: Man and Music* (London: Canongate, 1997), 270.
13. As quoted in W. E. B. Du Bois, *The Souls of Black Folk* (New York: Dover, [1903] 1994), v.
14. It's interesting that two black footballers, one Trinidadian, the other a Briton of Jamaican descent – Dwight Yorke and Andy Cole – were dubbed the 'soul brothers' by fans when they were playing for Manchester United in the mid-1990s. On the other hand, another black footballer, Arsenal's Ashley Cole, referred to the alienation he felt from the 'French clique' led by Thierry Henry, a black Frenchman whom the coach of

the Spanish national team, Luis Aragones, called 'a black shit'. Maybe Cole felt brotherly then.

15. De La Soul, 'Patti Dooke', on *Buhloone Mindstate* (Tommy Boy, 1993).
16. *Ibid.*
17. *Ibid.*
18. Jazz pianist and author Ben Sidran wrote an influential book about black music called *Black Talk* (Payback Press, 1995).
19. All the flyers were lying next to each other in a Caribbean takeaway in Dalston, east London.
20. As featured on the programme 'Jazz In The Open Air' (BBC Radio 4, July 2010), produced by John Goudie, presented by Kevin Le Gendre.

3. Aged in soul

1. Green did not smile as he said this. He appeared deadly serious.
2. See Berendt's paradox, quoted in Alyn Shipton, *A New History Of Jazz* (London: Continuum, 2007), 418.
3. It's interesting that the difference between electric and acoustic music is a hotly debated issue in both jazz and folk, going as far as biblical references to betrayal, but has never been a big problem in soul. Yet 'plugging in' significantly changed the music. Having said that, the greater use of electronics in the 1980s did turn some listeners off.
4. Prior to his solo career, Jeffrey Osborne was the drummer-vocalist in an excellent soul band called LTD, who were active between the early and late 1970s.
5. As quoted on the sleeve of *Sounds of Blackness, Evolution of Gospel* (Perspective, 1991).
6. *Ibid.*
7. See Mica Paris, D'Angelo, Maxwell, Lynden David Hall *et al.*, *Nu Classic Soul* (Cooltempo/EMI, 1997).

4. The soul jazz continuum

1. It's interesting to note that when 'Who's That Lady' was re-versioned in 1973 (T-Neck/Epic), The Isley Brothers devoted a large chunk of it to a lengthy guitar improvisation. The full-length cut is more of an instrumental than a vocal piece.
2. 'Little' Stevie was dubbed 'the twelve-year-old genius' at the start of his career to emphasize his inordinately precocious nature.
3. Telephone interview, London (2006).
4. See Louis Jordan, *Jivin' With Jordan* (Charly, 1985).
5. As featured on Clinton, 'Atomic Dog' (Capitol/EMI, 1982).
6. As featured on Clinton, 'Do Fries Go With That Shake?' (Capitol/EMI, 1986).
7. Certainly a piece such as 'Full Nelson', with Marcus Miller's eruptive bass, is as much funk as it is jazz.
8. A Tribe Called Quest, 'Vibes and Stuff'', on *The Low End Theory* (Jive/RCA Records, 1991).
9. A Tribe Called Quest, 'Jazz (We've Got)', on *The Low End Theory*.
10. ?uestlove took part in *The Philadelphia Experiment* (Ropeadope, 2001) with two much lauded jazzers, pianist Uri Caine and bassist Christian McBride.

5. The soul–funk continuum

1. Lester Young, *With The Oscar Peterson Trio* (Verve, 1952).

2. James Brown: "I like Ahmad Jamal, [Dave] Brubeck. But then if I want to hear a cat drive I like Horace Silver, Jimmy Smith, [Brother] Jack McDuff, Jimmy McGriff, I like them because they're real soulful" (interview with Ira Gitler, *Downbeat* [1968], quoted by Alan Leeds in his sleeve notes for James Brown, *Jazz* [Verve, 2007]).
3. Bill Doggett's 'Hold It' and 'Honky Tonk' were staple cover songs for both British and American R&B artists in the late 1950s and early '60s.
4. Funkadelic, *Free Your Mind And Your Ass Will Follow* (Westbound, 1970).
5. As featured in Prince, 'Alphabet Street' (Paisley Park/Warners, 1988). The album the piece came from, *Lovesexy*, carries on the left-hand side of the inner sleeve the word 'Yes', and on the right-hand side the words 'New Power Soul'.
6. Anita Baker, *Rapture* (Elektra, WEA, 1986).
7. See Gladys Knight & The Pips's version of Sly & The Family Stone's 'Thank You' (Motown, 1973).
8. As featured on The Roots, 'Mellow My Man' (Geffen, 1994). The piece also has a great line from Black Thought: 'I'm cooler than ice bricks/I got soul like those Afro picks/with the black fist'.
9. Me'Shell NdegéOcello, *Plantation Lullabies* (Maverick/Warner, 1993); Maxwell, *Urban Hang Suite* (Columbia, 1996); D'Angelo, *Brown Sugar* (Cooltempo/EMI,1995); Erykah Badu, *Baduizm* (Universal, 1997).

6. The soul–rock continuum

1. Charlie Gillett, *The Sound Of The City* (London: Souvenir Press, 1996), 34–5.
2. Bobby Womack, *Midnight Mover* (London: John Blake, 2006), 61 .
3. See the symbolically titled Bar-Kays album *Black Rock* (Polydor, 1971).
4. As featured on Pointer Sisters, 'Fire' (Planet, 1978).
5. See Living Colour, *Vivid* (Epic, 1988).
6. See Chocolate Genius, *Black Music* (V2, 1998). Interestingly, Marc Anthony Thompson was hired as a guitarist by none other than Mr 'Fire' himself, Bruce Springsteen.
7. Email interview with the author, 2011.
8. From an interview I conducted with the artist in London in 1999. It's tempting to say that Vernon Reid is a hugely important figure in black music, but he's really an important figure in music period. He stars in Living Colour, guest stars with The Roots and produced one of Salif Keita's best albums (*Papa*). Need one say more? Yes, he's one of the most intelligent artists I've ever had the pleasure of interviewing.
9. The advert also quotes the song title 'Voodoo Child' from Jimi Hendrix, *Electric Ladyland* (Reprise, 1968). Shame they didn't use 'Voodoo Chile', which is a resonant use of the African American and Caribbean vernacular. Maybe the British government felt safer with the standard English.

7. A recipe From Memphis

1. Think of the iconic sleeve of Ray Charles, *Live At Newport* (Atlantic, 1956). Charles is holding an alto saxophone, standing next to tenor saxophonist David 'Fathead' Newman.
2. Ivory Joe Hunter, *Ivory Joe Hunter Sings* [compilation] (King, 1988).
3. Joining Curtis and Hathaway on the session were bassist Chuck Rainey and guitarist Cornell Dupree, two session gods for Atlantic Records during the 1960s and '70s.
4. Curtis's version of Led Zeppelin's 'Whole Lotta Love' is featured on *Live At Filmore West* (Atlantic, 1971). Other covers include Buddy Miles's 'Them Changes' and Stevie Wonder's 'Signed, Sealed, Delivered, I'm Yours'. 'Soul Serenade' and 'Memphis Soul

Stew' are the Curtis originals on the set list.

5. See Cannonball Adderley, *Country Preacher* (Capitol, 1969). This is a live recording of a concert performed by the alto saxophonist in support of the civil rights initiative, Operation Breadbasket, and it features compelling speeches by Adderley and the Reverend Jesse Jackson.

6. As featured on King Curtis, 'Memphis Soul Stew' (Atlantic, 1967).

7. As featured on Sly & The Family Stone, 'Dance To The Music' (Epic/CBS, 1968).

8. As featured on Wingy Manone, 'The Music Goes 'Round And Around', on *Wingy Sings, Manone Plays* (Jasmine, 2000).

9. *Ibid.*

10. See Beginning Of The End, *Funky Nassau* (Atlantic, 1971).

11. Things came full circle in 2007. When Maceo Parker introduced one of his players, the excellent British trombonist Dennis Rollins, at the Cheltenham jazz festival, he said: 'Here's a man so funky he has his own band!'

12. As featured on Brand New Heavies/Large Professor, 'Bonafield Funk', on *Heavy Rhyme Experience, Vol. 1* (Delicious Vinyl, 1992).

13. As featured on King Curtis, 'Memphis Soul Stew' (Atlantic, 1967).

14. Ultramagnetic MCs, 'Raise It Up', on *The Four Horsemen* (Wild Pitch, 1993).

15. See The Roots, *The Tipping Point* (Geffen, 2004).

8. A half a teacup of bass

1. Rainey's solo discography is relatively slim but it's worth seeking out *Coalition* (Skye, 1972). It has very good writing as well as playing, and features a crack cast that includes organist Richard Tee, drummer Bernard Purdie and guitarist Cornell Dupree. Although Rainey was a key member of the Atlantic Records house band in the 1960s and '70s, he also freelanced with a number of jazz musicians, such as guitarist Grant Green and vibraphonist Cal Tjader.

2. As featured on James Brown, 'I Got Ants In My Pants' (Polydor, 1972).

3. The Daps were an all-white band from Cincinnati, Ohio who auditioned for James Brown in the late 1960s but lost out to another local ensemble feature, Bootsy Collins and his brother Catfish.

4. Collins's ability as a bassist is possibly overshadowed by his larger-than-life persona, his general jocularity ... and those glasses. Apparently James Brown's bassist 'Sweet' Charles Sherell was something of an influence on Collins. In fact, according to author Cliff White, Bootsy 'would hang around the studio studying Sweet's style' (sleeve notes for *For Sweet People From Sweet Charles* [Polydor, 1988]). As well as recording with Brown, Sherell worked with Aretha Franklin in 1967. A fine soul tune cut by Sherell in 1974, 'Yes It's You' – written by none other than the legendary Atlantic Records producer Ahmet Ertegun – became much loved during the mid-1980s 'rare groove' revival.

5. Interview with the author, in *Echoes* (2011).

6. Henderson's solo work lacks the kudos of his Miles Davis association, but some of the songwriting, arranging and playing on his mid-1970s releases for the Buddah label are very good.

7. On Miller's performances with Luther Vandross and Aretha Franklin (above all, *Jump To It* [Arista, 1982]) he hammers the bass with considerable force. The combination of his and Franklin's aggression is striking, to say the least.

8. See Change, *Change of Heart* (WEA, 1984), produced by Jam & Lewis. The slapped bass as a form of punctuation against the dredging bass synthesizer is highly effective here.

9. Tidd, an outstanding player, was part of the London ensemble Quite Sane (alongside pianist Robert Mitchell) but moved to America and worked with The Roots, Steve

Coleman and Me'Shell NdegéOcello. A few other notable British bassists straddling jazz and funk are Neville Malcolm, Julian Crampton and Dean Mark.

9. A pound of fatback drums

1. Idris Muhammad's beat is inspired on Lou Donaldson's version of The Isley Brothers, 'It's Your Thing' (Blue Note, 1969). It substantiates the claim that the funkiest funk is often slow, relaxed and leisurely.
2. David Weiss, "The Complexities of Simplicity", *Drum!* 16(9) (October 2007).
3. This has been stated by countless bass players over the years. Victor Bailey is just one who springs to mind.
4. Bailey is a highly respected player on the British calypso and soul scene, having worked with Billy Ocean and Incognito among others.
5. Interview with the author, London (2008).
6. Cuban percussionist Candido Camera worked with many prominent jazz musicians in America between the 1950s and '70s, including Billy Taylor, Sonny Rollins and Errol Garner. Candido's 1979 hit *Jingo* (Salsoul) and is a dance-floor classic written by Nigerian percussionist Babatunde Olatunji and hitherto covered by Latin-rocker Santana.
7. Interview with the author, St. Lucia jazz festival, 2011.
8. Numerous Fatback tunes have a Caribbean flavour. The most obvious is 'Spanish Hustle' (Event, 1976), which leans very much towards calypso-soca.
9. Ralph McDonald, 'Calypso Breakdown' (Marlin, 1976) is a significant piece of jazzy, soulful calypso in which the percussion – particularly the sound of the 'cowbill' bottle – takes centre stage, and thus loosely parallels arrangements in go-go music from Washington, DC.
10. Vocalist-organist Timmy Thomas, who had a hit with the 1972 anti-war anthem 'Why Can't We Live Together' (TK, 1972), also made creative use of the Rhythm Ace, particularly on the track 'Funky Me'.
11. For a good overview of broken beat, see the compilations *People Make The World Go Round Parts 1–3* (People, 2000–2001), which feature New Sector Movements, Quango and Restless Soul among others.

10. Four tablespoons of boiling Memphis guitars

1. Some of Bo Diddley's guitar playing is riotous to say the least. On 'Who Do You Love?' (Chess, 1956) he and Jody Williams scythe away like men possessed to the effect that there's a long, relentless grinding and grating of sound under his voice.
2. Listen to Womack on *The Womack Live* (Liberty, 1970). On the reprise of the Mamas & Papas' 'California Dreamin'', he calls out the other guitarist in the band for a jazz-style 'cutting contest'. Womack teases his bandmate yet his tone of voice suggests that when he takes a solo, the time for joking is over.
3. Herbie Hancock and producer David Rubinson go as far as saying that *Manchild* (CBS, 1975) would not have been possible without Wah Wah Watson: celebrity endorsement indeed.
4. See The Temptations, 'Papa Was A Rolling Stone' (Motown, 1972).
5. A great two-CD Zapp anthology, *We Can Make You Dance* (Rhino, 2002), features classics like 'More Bounce To The Ounce' and 'Dancefloor' as well as precious archive photos of Roger Troutman – the best of which depicts him as a boy holding a guitar about three times bigger than he is.
6. Tashan, 'Chasin' A Dream' (Island Def Jam, 1986) can justifiably be called a piece of hip

hop funk-rock. It's definitely part of the soul–rock continuum, in any case, and it's not inconceivable that Jimi Hendrix would have made music similar to this, had he lived to hear turntable scratches.

7. Telephone interview with the author, 2005. You can hear a very similar thing happening when Bobby Womack takes on another guitarist on *The Womack Live* (Liberty, 1970). Womack essentially slays his rival with a string of pulsating rhythmic figures that whip the crowd into a frenzy.

8. Jef Lee Johnson's 1997 CD *Blue* is a very underrated album released on the small Coconut Grove/Black Label imprint. It has wonderful modern blues songs, embellished by Johnson's excellent guitar work and his sharp, at times quite sardonic lyrics.

11. Just a little pinch of organ

1. Quoted in the sleeve notes to *A Change Is Gonna Come* (Atlantic, 1966).

2. Smith was formidable at the Jazz Café gig. On the encore, he took a solo that turned into a full-on riot of sounds, some of them generated by Smith's palms, elbows and, with considerable theatricality, his rump. Maybe he was making a subliminal reference to Jimmy Smith, *Sit On It* (Mercury, 1977).

3. See Greg Phillinganes, *Significant Gains* (Planet/Elektra, 1981).

4. See Ramsey Lewis, *Don't It Feel Good* (CBS, 1976). It is produced by Charles Stepney and is one of the great, overlooked jazzy soul records of the decade. It's also mighty funky.

5. Kevin Le Gendre, "Face is the Place", *Echoes* 28(3) (March 2004).

6. *Ibid.*

7. See Loose Ends, *Hanging On A String* (Virgin, 1985), which Nick Martinelli produced. See One Way, *Cutie Pie* (MCA, 1982); Cameo, *Attack Me With Your Love* (Ace/Polygram, 1986); Kleeer, *Intimate Connection* (Atlantic, 1984); Aurra, *Such A Feeling* (Salsoul, 1983); Fatback, *The Girl Is Fine (So Fine)* (Spring/Polydor, 1983); and Gap Band, *Disrespect* (Total Experience, 1984).

8. James Ingram of the Ingram family – they recorded as a band, making jazz-tinged albums such as *That's All*, *Would You Like To Fly* and *Nightstalkers* – is not to be confused with James Ingram, the vocalist best known for his 1983 hit 'Yah Mo B There' (Qwest Records), a fine duet with Michael McDonald, singer with pop-soul group The Doobie Brothers.

9. David Frank and Omar was a match made in heaven. Their collaboration on *For Pleasure* (BMG, 1994) was outstanding. One might argue that Frank's work with another British singer, Phil Collins, has less credibility but I would contend that his synth programming on 'Sussudio', a hit single from the album *No Jacket Required* (Virgin, 1985), is funkier than thou. Shame no instrumental version is available.

10. Mark de Clive-Lowe's Freesoul sessions were a very exciting monthly jam that took place at London's Jazz Café around 2005. They featured many guests from soul, jazz and hip hop augmenting the core band, which was essentially Richard Spaven on drums and de Clive-Lowe on keyboards and samplers. Some of the moog bass lines that de Clive-Lowe played and looped on the spot, before adding layers of chords, were impressive. One particularly good session featured jazz musician Jason Yarde on sax.

11. DJ Premier, best known as the producer of the duo Gangstarr, has been one of the most significant 'sound sculptors' in hip hop since the early 1990s. His work for Bahamadia, Nas and Notorious B.I.G. provides an example of his ability to use creatively drifting, hazy long tones, often stretching them out so that they become teasing vapour trails around the voice of the rapper.

12. Telephone interview with the author (2009).

13. *Ibid.*

12. A half a pint of horn

1. Lavern Baker, 'Jim Dandy' (Atlantic, 1956).
2. Justly lauded as a great sophisticate in jazz, Duke Ellington nonetheless made a lot of blues-based music that was really 'rockin' in rhythm', as he himself would put it.
3. Vernard Johnson is a little-known player but an interesting one with, dare one say it, raucous, avant-garde leanings. See Vernard Johnson, *Soul Metamorphosis*: *Rare & Unreleased Gospel Funk, 1968-78*, (Funky Delicacies/Tuff City, 2003).
4. Imagine the horn section on 'Get Up Offa That Thing' as clarinets and you can hear an echo of both Ellington and New Orleans swing.
5. The way the horns burst out of the electric piano led-intro on Brass Construction's 'Movin'' makes for one of the great dramatic openings in 1970s soul. It's like a royal fanfare by trumpeters who are about to slay their own monarch. It's a rebel army on the march.
6. Acid jazz was largely about a return to bands and live playing. But in some cases, its exponents built a bridge with hip hop and electronics – none more so than Young Disciples, who used sampling very astutely on *Road To Free*dom (Talkin' Loud, 1991).
7. David Sanborn, *Voyeur* (Warner, 1981) and Grover Washington Jnr, *Winelight* (Elektra, 1980) are often derided as smooth jazz, but I really hear them as accomplished instrumental soul.
8. See Kenny Garrett, 'G.T.D.S.' (Warner, 1999), which features Marcus Miller on bass. It's really a super-funky updating of Maceo Parker and James Brown, conveyed by the meaning of the acronym: Give The Drummer Some.
9. Kevin Le Gendre, "Spontaneous Reaction", *Jazzwise* 124 (October 2008).

13. We gonna tell you right now

1. Lou Rawls's spoken intro on 'Dead End Street' (Capitol, 1967) is extremely poignant, detailing the hardship endured by a poor black family in Chicago, where the wind, 'the almighty hawk', made for testing winters. Rawls voices a determination to escape the hopelessness of his situation, to make something of himself and return in triumph.
2. Gary Byrd is best known for his collaboration with Stevie Wonder, on whose 1976 opus *Songs in the Key Of Life* (Motown) he contributed lyrics. Wonder returned the favour by writing and performing the music for Byrd's black-and-proud rap 'The Crown' (Motown, 1983). Even more interesting is Byrd's spoken-word album based on his radio show on WWRL-AM, *Presenting The Gary Byrd Experience* (RCA, 1972). The album includes various soliloquies set to arrangements by Latin-jazz bandleader Chico O'Farrill.
3. Maceo Parker, 'The Soul Of A Black Man', on *US* (People, 1974).
4. Sonny Terry and Brownie McGhee, introduction to 'Mama Blues', on *Get On Board* (Not Now, 2009).
5. Isaac Hayes, 'Use Me', on *Live At Sahara Tahoe* (Stax, 1973).
6. Millie Jackson's spoken-word pieces are very funny and often X-rated. See *Live And Uncensored* (Towerbell, 1985).
7. Bill Withers's storytelling on *Live At Carnegie Hall* (CBS, 1973) is an integral part of the whole performance. His introductions to pieces such as 'Grandma's Hands' and 'I Can't Write Left Handed' are masterful and remind me a lot of the way Richie Havens charms an audience.
8. See Ursula Rucker, *Supa Sista* (!K7, 2001).
9. Jill Scott, *Who Is Jill Scott? Words And Sounds Vol. 1* (Hidden Beach, 2000).

14. One final ingredient

1. I'm thinking of The Four Tops's 'Standing In The Shadows Of Love' (Motown, 1966). In the breakdown, the sound of Levi Stubbs's voice against the congas is supremely rugged and primal. The entrance of the orchestra and strings marks a very effective contrast, as the textures are much smoother.
2. Wilson Pickett, *Don't Knock My Love* (Atlantic, 1971) is a very interesting album, not just for Wade Marcus's arrangements but for the combination of Atlantic and Motown personnel such as guitarist Dennis Coffey, drummer Roger Hawkins and percussionists Jack Ashford and Eddie 'Bongo' Brown. Collectively, they were known as The Pickers.
3. Kevin Le Gendre, "The Funk is Elemental", *Echoes* 28(5) (May 2004).
4. David Axelrod is a very gifted composer and arranger whose work has exerted an enormous influence on the hip hop producers who have extensively sampled his moody, epic arrangements. Recommended albums are the two William Blake-inspired sets, *Songs Of Innocence and Songs Of Experience* and *Earth Rot* (Capitol 1968-70).
5. MFSB, which stands for Mother Father Sister Brother, was the Philly International Records house band. It supplied music for the label's commercial heavy hitters, such as The O'Jays and Billy Paul. The bulk of MFSB's string scores were done by Don Renaldo.
6. There are many pictures of Barry White holding the baton and surrounded by a large string orchestra of white players – which is ironic, considering he was a former L.A. gang member who couldn't read music. The existence of a black string group such as The Reggae Philharmonic Orchestra therefore broke cultural stereotypes.
7. Charles Stepney's influence on 1990s soul and dance music has been considerable, and can be heard in Incognito and Zero 7 as well as 4hero.
8. I.G. Culture actually described Wayne Shorter, *The All Seeing Eye* (Blue Note, 1965) as good music 'to make love to', which is interesting because abstract, highly complex jazz is not usually associated with eroticism. It just goes to show that purveyors of black music do not refer solely to Barry White for their romantic soundtracks.

15. A recipe not from Memphis

1. Interview with the author (1999).
2. Incognito are often derided as jazz-lite or jazz-funk, a term with negative connotations, especially in 'straight-ahead' jazz circles. But I hear them as a hugely important keeper of Earth, Wind & Fire's flame.
3. See Roy Hargrove/RH Factor, *The Hard Groove* (Universal, 2003) featuring D'Angelo, Erykah Badu, Q-Tip, Common, Me'Shell NdegéOcello, Steve Coleman and Cornell Dupree – a veritable neo-soul jazz-rap fest.
4. See Bloodstone, *Natural High* (Decca, 1972).
5. 'Rush Over' (featuring Me'Shell NdegéOcello) is on both Marcus Miller, *Tales* (Dreyfuss, 1995) and the soundtrack to the romantic comedy *Love Jones* (Sony, 1997), which also has excellent soul and jazz by Dionne Farris, Cassandra Wilson, Refugee Camp All-Stars featuring Lauryn Hill, Brand New Heavies, Duke Ellington and John Coltrane. Playing the bass clarinet on Omar, 'Syleste' (Oyster/Naïve, 2000) is Ben Castle, son of the late British comedian/trumpeter Roy Castle.
6. Telephone interview with the author (2009).

16. Universoul sounds I

1. Telephone interview with the author (2009).
2. Sandra Nkaké is a very impressive Cameroon-born, Paris-based singer who can sing

jazz and soul to a high standard. She is also in a band called Push Up. In addition, Nkaké has forged links with artists in London and worked with members of the broken beat scene, namely Mark de Clive-Lowe and Phil Asher.

3. Telephone interview with the author (2009).
4. Kevin Le Gendre, "Nouveau Classic Soul", *Echoes* (39 October 1999).
5. Amp Fiddler/Sly & Robbie Serious featured on album *Inspiration Information* (Strut, 2008).
6. Geno Washington inspired the song 'Geno' (Fame/EMI, 1980) by pop outfit Dexy's Midnight Runners, who wrote the piece in a 1960s Stax vein.
7. As part of *Promised Heights: The Story of Cymande*, BBC London, broadcast 30 December 2000. Presented by Kevin Le Gendre. Produced by Ollie Chase and Ray Paul.
8. Late-1970s Brit funk ensemble Hi-Tension gave saxophonist Courtney Pine, who would become a major name in jazz during the 1980s, one of his first gigs.
9. 'Lovely Day' was released as a twelve-inch single (Mercury, 1983) and also featured on the album, *Choice* (Mercury, 1984).
10. Apart from producing Gil Scott-Heron, British jazz musician Malcolm Cecil played double bass on Stevie Wonder, 'Visions' (Motown, 1973), while Cecil and Robert Margouleff also programmed all of the ARPs and Moogs played by Wonder on that album. Further details of Cecil's work in EmCee Five can be found in Alyn Shipton's biography of Ian Carr, *Out Of The Long Dark* (London: Equinox, 2006).
11. Jhelisa Anderson is an excellent singer from Atlanta who settled in London in the mid-1990s. Bridging soul and jazz, Anderson worked with saxophonists Steve Williamson and Courtney Pine, and recorded three very good solo albums, *Galactica Rush* (Dorado, 1994) and *Language Electric* (Dorado, 1997) as well as *A Primitive Guide To Being There* (Infracom, 2006).

17. Universoul sounds II

1. Highly respected Atlantic Records session drummer Roger Hawkins played on The Staple Singers, 'I'll Take You There' (Stax, 1972). He said the Jamaican feel of the track came from his exposure to reggae and ska in London, when he was there as a member of British rockers Traffic's touring band. 'We applied the reggae formula to the song and it worked,' Hawkins tells Jim Payne in *Give The Drummers Some* (Miami, FL: Warner Brothers Publications, 1996).
2. See Amp Fiddler/Sly & Robbie, *Inspiration Information* (Strut, 2008).
3. Interview with the author, London (2008).
4. See Alyn Shipton, *Hi-De-Ho: The Life Of Cab Calloway* (Oxford: Oxford University Press, 2010).
5. Earth, Wind & Fire greatly enriched their work with Latin rhythms. Their love of Afro-Brazilian music is signalled by the group's reprise of Milton Nascimento's 'Ponta De Areia' (retitled 'Brazilian Rhyme') on the classic *All 'N All* (CBS, 1977).
6. Liner notes, from Joe Bataan, *Salsoul* (Salsoul, 1976).
7. You can spot Paulinho Da Costa playing congas in the video for Madonna's 'La Isla Bonita'. Whether Madonna fans knew it was THE Paulinho Da Costa is another matter. Latin-Jazz fans recognised his very distinctive, beaming smile and rotor-blade hands.
8. Gwen Ansell, *Soweto Blues: Jazz, Popular Music & Politics In South Africa* (London: Continuum, 2004), 138.
9. Interview with the author, London (2008).

18. Soulful house, techno soul, hip hop soul

1. In the Trinidadian vernacular, this is one of the most common expressions for the act of dancing – sensually.
2. Ray Charles, 'What'd I Say' (Atlantic, 1959).
3. Kevin Le Gendre, "He's Got the Power", *Echoes* 32(2) (February 2007).
4. See Barbara Tucker, 'Beautiful People' (Strictly Rhythm, 1994).
5. See Larry Heard, *Genesis* (Mecca, 1999).
6. Sleeve notes from Stacey Pullen, *Today Is The Tomorrow You Were Promised Yesterday* (Virgin, 2001).
7. *Ibid.*
8. Ray Charles, 'I Got A Woman' (Atlantic, 1962).
9. Interview with Jean-Paul 'Bluey' Maunick of Incognito, London (1999).
10. Kris Kristofferson's 'For The Good Times' is covered by Al Green on *I'm Still In Love With You* (Hi, 1972) and by Isaac Hayes on *Black Moses* (Enterprise/Stax, 1973).
11. I find R. Kelly immensely frustrating. He produces R&B dross like 'She's Got That Vibe' and brilliant soul music like 'Bad Man', featured on the soundtrack to the remake of the film *Shaft* (LaFace, 2000). The problem is that there is much more of the former than the latter.
12. See 'Thank You Father' for more inspired gospel-soul-hop from Tashan Rashad, on *Chasin' A Dream* (Def Jam/Columbia, 1986).
13. Harry Dixon Loes, 'This Little Light of Mine' (Circa, 1920).
14. Erykah Badu performed a brilliant gig at the Brixton Academy in London in July 2010, confirming her status as a major figure in black popular music.
15. See Cee-Lo Green, ... *Is The Soul Machine* (Arista, 2004).
16. Dred Scott's records featured the logo 'Yes, I do my own beats'. Adrianna Evans, the soul singer he collaborated with, told me in a 1997 interview that Scott had done that after a television company sampled his tracks without seeking legal clearance, since they assumed he had sampled other artists in the first place. They were wrong. Scott took them to court to tell them as much.

19. Divorcing neo to marry soul

1. For a good overview of Tashan Rashad's music, see *A Retrospective* (1986–1993) (Expansion, 2002).
2. Badu's press conferences are entertaining affairs. In Barbados in 2008, she said that 'being humble was so 2007'. In London in 2010, after turning up an hour and a half late, she apologised and then said the first thing she wanted to know about the baying journos was 'how long these people have been kept away from their cell phones'.
3. Sleeve notes from Erykah Badu, *Worldwide Underground* (Universal, 2003).
4. Interview with the author, London (2008).
5. The first time I saw Bilal Oliver was at the Jazz Café in the late 1990s, when he made a guest appearance with Common. He looked like a madman on stage. The second time was a few years later, again at the Jazz Café, with Oliver leading his own band. He looked even madder. He had what looked like a bottle of whisky on the piano. The third time I saw him was at Fabric in 2010. He toted a large bottle of red wine on the encore.
6. D'Angelo's meagre output since his mid-1990s breakthrough, 'Brown Sugar', is, like that of his peer Lauryn Hill, enough to make a grown man cry. Were he to make another album, it would have to be a real game changer, simply because he's made us wait so long for it. Imagine the pressure. It's enough to make a grown man's tears cry.
7. Telephone interview with the author (2009).
8. Compare the two versions of his song 'All Matter' that Bilal Oliver has recorded thus

far. The first, featured on pianist Robert Glasper's 2009 set *Double Booked*, is slinky and jazzy while the second, on Bilal's own 2010 set *Airtight's Revenge*, is rugged, rocky and funky. The change of emphasis in the pulse and harmonies is marked, but underneath it all in both cases is a majestic folk blues that would sound great if the vocal were backed only by an acoustic guitar – or a flute.

9. It's a great piece of television. The two men look as if they are from different planets. But as Living Colour guitarist Vernon Reid points out, that was the first time he had seen a person of colour 'like Hendrix' – in other words, so flamboyantly individual – on the small screen. That is a cultural highlight not to be taken lightly.

10. The O'Jays, 'I Love Music' (PIR, 1975).

11. Jill Scott, 'Let It Be', from *The Real Thing: Words and Sounds Vol. 3* (Hidden Beach, 2007). Jill Scott has also pursued an acting career, appearing as Precious Ramotswe in the television adaptation of Alexander McCall Smith's novel *The No.1 Ladies' Detective Agency*.

20. Soul is stranger than fiction

1. *Interpretations: Celebrating The Music Of Earth, Wind & Fire* (Stax, 2007) is an Earth, Wind & Fire tribute album that features the Randy Watson Experience with Bilal Oliver, Chaka Khan, Angie Stone, Mint Condition and Me'Shell NdegéOcello among others.

2. Maze's 'Twilight' is on the B-side of the twelve-inch single of 'Too Many Games' (Capitol, 1985).

3. Interview with the author, London (2001).

4. Telephone interview with the author (2009).

5. These lyrics are from Wild Cherry's 'Play That Funky Music' (Epic, 1975). I'm still waiting for the answer record, 'Play That Rocky Music, Black Boy'.

Bibliography and select discography

Bibliography

Du Bois, W. E. B. [1903] 1994. *The Souls of Black Folk*. New York: Dover.
George, N. 1988. *The Death of Rhythm & Blues*. Harmondsworth: Penguin.
Gillett, C. 1996. *The Sound Of The City: The Rise of Rock and Roll*. London: Souvenir Press.
Lydon, M. 1997. *Ray Charles: Man and Music*. London: Canongate.
Shipton, A. 2006. *Out of the Long Dark*. London: Equinox.
Shipton, A. 2007. *A New History Of Jazz*. London: Continuum.
Shipton, A. 2010. *Hi-De-Ho: The Life Of Cab Calloway*. Oxford: Oxford University Press.
Tate, G. 1992. *Flyboy In The Buttermilk*. London: Simon & Schuster.
Womack, B. 2006. *Midnight Mover*. London: John Blake.

Select discography

Adrianna Evans, *Adrianna Evans* (BMG/Loud, 1997).
Amp Fiddler, *Waltz Of The Ghetto Fly* (PIAS, 2004).
Amp Fiddler/Sly & Robbie, *Inspiration Information* (Strut, 2008).
Art Blakey's Jazz Messengers, 'Moanin'' (Blue Note, 1958).
A Tribe Called Quest, *The Low End Theory* (Jive/RCA Records, 1991).
Al Green, *I'm Still In Love With You* (Hi, 1972).
Anita Baker, *Rapture* (Elektra, WEA, 1986).
Aretha Franklin, 'Respect' (Atlantic, 1967).
Aretha Franklin, *Jump To It* (Arista, 1982).
Barbara Tucker, 'Beautiful People' (Strictly Rhythm, 1994).
Bar-Kays, *Black Rock* (Polydor, 1971).
Beatnuts, *Classics Vol.1* (Epic/Loud, 2002).
Bilal Oliver, *First Born Second* (Interscope/Universal, 2001).
Bilal Oliver, *Airtight's Revenge* (Plug Research, 2010).
Bill Withers, *Live At Carnegie Hall* (Sussex, 1973).
Blaze, *25 Years Later* (Motown, 1990).
Bloodstone, *Natural High* (Decca, 1972).
Bo Diddley, 'Who Do You Love?' (Chess, 1956).
Bobby Byrd, 'I Know You Got Soul' (King, 1971).

Bobby Womack, *The Womack Live* (Liberty, 1970).
Brother Jack McDuff & David Newman, *Double Barreled Soul* (Atlantic, 1968).
Bruce Springsteen, *Greetings From Asbury Park, N.J.* (Columbia, 1973).
Brass Construction, *1* (United Artists, 1975).
James Brown, *Soul Classics* (Polydor, 1972).
Cameo, *Single Life* (Polygram, 1985).
Cee-Lo Green... *Is The Soul Machine* (Arista, 2004).
Central Line, 'Lovely Day' (Mercury, 1983).
Change, *Change of Heart* (WEA, 1984).
Charades, 'Goin' Out Dancing' (Blue Parrot, 1984).
Charles Mingus, 'Better Git It In Your Soul' (Columbia, 1959).
Charlie Parker, 'Now's The Time' (Savoy, 1945).
Charlie Parker, 'Ornithology' (Dial, 1946).
Chic, *C'est Chic* (Atlantic, 1978).
Chocolate Genius, *Black Music* (V2, 1998).
Chuck Rainey, *Coalition* (Skye, 1972).
Common, *Like Water For Chocolate* (Universal, 2000).
Cymande, *The Message* (Compilation) (Sequel, 1999).
D'Angelo, *Brown Sugar* (Cooltempo/EMI, 1995).
David Sanborn, *Voyeur* (Warner, 1981).
De La Soul, *Buhloone Mindstate* (Tommy Boy, 1993).
De La Soul, *Three Feet High And Rising* (Tommy Boy, 1989).
Dred Scott, *Breakin' Combs* (Tuff Break, 1994).
D-Train, 'You're The One For Me' (Prelude, 1981).
Duke Ellington, *Happy Go Lucky Local* (Musicraft, 1992).
Earth, Wind & Fire, *All 'N All* (CBS, 1977).
Earth, Wind & Fire, *The Need Of Love* (Warner, 1972).
Earth, Wind & Fire, *Head To The Sky* (CBS, 1973).
Earth, Wind & Fire, *Last Days And Time* (CBS, 1972).
Earth, Wind & Fire, *That's The Way Of The World* (CBS, 1975).
Eddie Harris, 'Listen Here' (Atlantic, 1967).
Eddie Harris, *The Reason Why I'm Talking S- - t* (Atlantic, 1976).
Eric B & Rakim, *Let The Rhythm Hit 'Em* (MCA, 1990).
Erykah Badu, *Baduizm* (Universal, 1997).
Erykah Badu, *Mama's Gun* (Universal/Motown, 2000).
Erykah Badu, *Worldwide Underground* (Universal/Motown, 2003).
Fatback, 'Spanish Hustle' (Event, 1976).
Fatback, 'The Girl Is Fine (So Fine)' (Spring/Polydor, 1983).
4-Hero, *Two Pages* (Talkin' Loud, 1998).
Freddie Roach, *My People* (*Soul People*) (Prestige, 1967).
Funkadelic, *Free Your Mind And Your Ass Will Follow* (Westbound, 1970).
Funkadelic, 'What Is Soul?' (Westbound, 1970).
Galliano, 'Golden Flower' (Talkin' Loud, 1992).
George Duke, *Don't Let Go* (Epic, 1978).
George Duke, *Reach For It* (Epic, 1977).
Gladys Knight & The Pips, 'Thank You' (Motown, 1973).
Greg Phillinganes, *Significant Gains* (Planet/Elektra, 1981).
Gretchen Parlato, *The Lost And Found* (Obliqsound, 2011).
Grover Washington Jnr, *Winelight* (Elektra, 1980).
Hall & Oates, 'Sara Smile' (Atlantic, 1976).
Herbie Hancock, *Manchild* (CBS, 1975).
Horace Silver, 'Opus De Funk' (Blue Note, 1953).
Howlin' Wolf, 'Spoonful' (Chess, 1960).

Hugh Masekela, 'Don't Go Lose It Baby' (Jive Afrika, 1984).
Incognito, *No Time Like The Future* (Talkin' Loud, 1999).
India.Arie, *Acoustic Soul* (Universal/Motown, 2001).
Ingram, *Would You Like To Fly?* (Streetwave, 1983).
Isaac Hayes, *Black Moses* (Enterprise/Stax, 1973).
Isaac Hayes, *In The Beginning* (Atlantic, 1972).
Isaac Hayes, *Live At The Sahara Tahoe* (Stax, 1973).
Isley Brothers, 'Who's That Lady' (Liberty/Capitol, 1964).
Isley Brothers, 'That Lady' (T-Neck, 1973).
Isley Brothers, 'It's Your Thing' (T-Neck, 1969).
Ivory Joe Hunter, *Ivory Joe Hunter Sings* [Compilation] (King, 1988).
Izzi Dunn, *The Big Picture* (FireWorX, 2003).
Jackie Wilson, 'Your Love Keeps Lifting Me Higher' (Brunswick, 1967).
Janet Kay, 'Silly Games' (Arawak, 1979).
Jef Lee Johnson, *Blue* (Coconut Grove/Black Label, 1997).
Jeffrey Osborne, 'Don't You Get So Mad About It' (A&M, 1983).
Jelly Roll Morton, *I Thought I Heard Buddy Bolden Say* (RCA,Victor, 1968).
Jhelisa Anderson, *Galactica Rush* (Dorado 1994).
Jill Scott, *Who Is Jill Scott? Words And Sounds Vol. 1* (Hidden Beach, 2000).
Jimi Hendrix, *Electric Ladyland* (Reprise, 1968).
Jimi Hendrix, *First Rays Of The New Rising Sun* (Sony, 2010).
Junior Walker, '(I'm a) Roadrunner' (Motown, 1966).
Kaidi Tatham, 'Betcha' Did' (Bitasweet, 2001).
Kenny Garrett, 'G.T.D.S.' (Warner, 1999).
King Curtis, 'Memphis Soul Stew' (Atlantic, 1967).
King Curtis, 'Willow Weep For Me' (Prestige, 1970).
King Curtis, *Live At Filmore West* (Atlantic, 1971).
King Oliver, *Dippermouth Blues* (ASV, Living Era, 1997).
Kleeer, *Intimate Connection* (Atlantic, 1984).
KRS-One, 'The Sound Of Da Police' (Jive, 1993).
Kurtis Blow, *Party Time* (Mercury, 1983).
Lou Donaldson, 'It's Your Thing' (Blue Note, 1969).
L.T.D., 'Love Ballad' (A&M, 1976).
Larry Heard, *Genesis* (Mecca, 1999).
Lauryn Hill, *The Miseducation Of Lauryn Hill* (Columbia, 1998).
Lavern Baker, 'Jim Dandy' (Atlantic, 1956).
Leadbelly, *The Definitive Leadbelly* (Not Now, 2008).
Lester Young, *With The Oscar Peterson Trio* (Verve, 1952).
Living Colour, *Vivid* (Epic, 1988).
Loose Ends, 'Hanging On A String' (Virgin, 1985).
Lou Rawls, 'Dead End Street' (Capitol, 1967).
Louis Jordan, *Jivin' With Jordan* (Charly, 1985).
Love Unlimited Orchestra, *My Sweet Summer Suite* (King, 1976).
Luther Vandross, *The Night I Fell In Love* (Epic, 1985).
Lynden David Hall, *Medicine 4 My Pain* (Cooltempo/EMI, 1997).
M. Nahadr, *EclecticIsM* (LiveWired, 2009).
Maceo Parker, *US* (People, 1974).
Manu Dibango, *Soul Makossa* (Atlantic, 1972).
Marc Evans, *The Way You Love Me* (Defected, 2008).
Marcus Miller, *Tales* (Dreyfuss, 1995).
Marvin Gaye, *What's Going On* (Motown, 1971).
Maxwell, *Urban Hang Suite* (Columbia, 1996).
Maze, 'Too Many Games'/'Twilight' (Capitol, 1985).

Me'Shell NdegéOcello, *Plantation Lullabies* (Maverick/Warner, 1993).

Me'Shell NdegéOcello, *Cookie: The Anthropological Mixtape* (Maverick, 2002).

Me'Shell NdegéOcello, *The World Has Made Me The Man Of My Dreams.* (Bismillah, 2007).

Mica Paris, D'Angelo, Maxwell, Lynden David Hall et al., Nu Classic Soul (Cooltempo/EMI, 1997).

Miles Davis, *Tutu* (Warner, 1986).

Millie Jackson, *Live And Uncensored* (Towerbell, 1985).

Minnie Riperton, *Les Fleurs: The Minnie Riperton Anthology* (EMI, 2001).

Mint Condition, *Livin' The Luxury Brown* (Caged Bird, 2005).

Mr Fingers, 'Can You Feel It?' (Trax, 1986).

Muddy Waters, 'Mannish Boy' (Chess, 1955).

Odyssey, 'Use It Up And Wear It Out' (RCA, 1980).

Omar, 'Syleste' (Oyster/Naïve, 2000).

Omar, *For Pleasure* (BMG, 1994).

One Way, 'Cutie Pie' (MCA, 1982).

Oscar Brown Jnr, *Sin & Soul* (Columbia, 1960).

Patrice Rushen, 'The Hump'/'Roll With The Punches' (Prestige, 1980).

People Make The World Go Round Parts 1–3 (People, 2000–2001).

Peven Everett, *Power Soul* (Soul Heaven, 2006).

Pigmeat Markham, 'Here Comes The Judge' (Chess, 1968).

Pointer Sisters, *Energy* (Planet, 1978).

Pointer Sisters, *Steppin'* (ABC/Blue Thumb, 1975).

Prince, 'Alphabet Street' (Paisley Park/Warners, 1988).

Professor Longhair, *Mardi Gras In New Orleans* (1949–57) (Nighthawk, 1981).

Q-Tip, *Kamaal/The Abstract* (Battery, 2009).

Quincy Jones, *You've Got It Bad Girl* (A&M, 1973).

Ralph McDonald, 'Calypso Breakdown' (Marlin, 1976).

Ramsey Lewis, 'Eternal Journey' (Chess, 1968).

Ramsey Lewis, *Don't It Feel Good* (CBS, 1976).

Ray Barretto, 'El Watusi' (Tico, 1963).

Ray Charles, *Genius + Soul = Jazz* (Impulse!, 1961).

Ray Charles, *Hallelujah! I Love Her So* (Atlantic, 1962).

Ray Charles, 'I Got A Woman And Some Blues' (Atlantic, 1959).

Ray Charles, *Live At Newport* (Atlantic, 1956).

Robert Glasper, *Double Booked* (Blue Note, 2009).

Sister Rosetta Tharpe, *The Original Soul Sister* (Proper, 2002).

Rotary Connection, *Black Gold: The Very Best Of* (Chess, 2006).

Roy Brown, *Good Rockin' Tonight: Best Of* (Rhino, 1994).

Roy Hargrove/RH Factor, *The Hard Groove* (Universal, 2003).

Rufus Thomas, 'Soul Food' (Stax, 1970).

SOS Band, 'Just Be Good To Me' (Tabu, 1983).

Sam & Dave, 'Hold On I'm Comin'' (Stax, 1967).

Sam Cooke, 'A Change Is Gonna Come' (RCA, 1964).

Sam Cooke, 'Willow Weep For Me' (RCA, 1963).

Sandra Nkaké, *Mansaadi* (Phantom Sound & Vision, 2008).

Sarah Winton, *You Can't Keep A Good Woman Down* (Sound Of Money, 1993).

Slave, *Just A Touch Of Love* (Cotillion, 1979).

Sly & The Family Stone, *There's A Riot Goin' On* (Epic, 1971).

Sly & The Family Stone, *Dance To The Music* (Epic, 1968).

Solomon Burke, 'Just Out Of Reach (Of My Two Open Arms)' (Atlantic, 1961).

Solomon Burke, 'Everybody Needs Somebody To Love' (Atlantic, 1964).

Sonny Stitt, *Soul People* (Prestige, 1965).

Sonny Terry and Brownie McGhee, *Get On Board* (Not Now, 2009).

Soul II Soul, *Club Classics. Vol.1* (10 records, 1989).

Soweto Kinch, *A Life in the Day of B19: Tales Of The Tower Block* (Dune, 2006).

Sounds of Blackness, *The Evolution Of Gospel*, (Perspective, 1991).

Stacey Pullen, *Today Is The Tomorrow You Were Promised Yesterday* (Virgin, 2001).

Stanley Turrentine, *Sugar* (CTI, 1971).

Staple Singers, 'I'll Take You There' (Stax, 1972).

Stevie Wonder, 'Fingertips' (Motown, 1963).

Stevie Wonder, *Songs In The Key Of Life* (Motown, 1976).

Stevie Wonder, *Innervsions* (Motown, 1973).

Sylvester, 'You Make Me Feel Mighty Real' (Fantasy, 1978).

Tashan Rashad, *Chasin' A Dream* (Island Def Jam, 1986).

Tashan Rashad, *A Retrospective (1986–1993)* (Expansion, 2002).

Ten City, 'That's The Way Love Is' (Atlantic, 1989).

The Coasters, Yakety Yak' (Atlantic, 1958).

The Crusaders, *Street Life* (MCA, 1979).

The Four Tops, 'Standing In The Shadows Of Love' (Motown, 1966).

The Last Poets, *This Is Madness* (Douglas, 1971).

The O'Jays, 'I Love Music' (PIR, 1975).

The Roots, *Do You Want More?!!!??!* (DGC/Geffen, 1995).

The Roots, *The Tipping Point* (Geffen, 2004).

The System, 'You Are In My System' (Polydor, 1982).

The Temptations, *Masterpiece* (Motown, 1973).

The Temptations, 'Papa Was A Rolling Stone' (Motown, 1972).

The Undisputed Truth, *Face To Face With The Truth* (Gordy, 1971).

Thelma Houston, 'You Used To Hold Me So Tight' (MCA, 1984).

Thelonious Monk, 'Straight, No Chaser' (Columbia, 1966).

Washington Philips, *Denomination Blues* (Agram, 1980).

Wayne Shorter, *The All Seeing Eye* (Blue Note, 1965).

Wilson Pickett, *Don't Knock My Love* (Atlantic, 1971).

Wu-Tang Clan, *Enter The Wu-Tang (36 Chambers)* (Loud, 1993).

Young Disciples, *Road To Freedom* (Talkin' Loud, 1991).

Index